VISUAL BASIC 2005
BY PRACTICE

VISUAL BASIC 2005
BY PRACTICE

MIKE MOSTAFAVI

CHARLES RIVER MEDIA
Boston, Massachusetts

Cover Design: Tyler Creative
Cover Image: Sara Mostafavi

CHARLES RIVER MEDIA
25 Thomson Place
Boston, Massachusetts 02210
617-757-7900
617-757-7969 (FAX)
crminfo@thomson.com
www.charlesriver.com

This book is printed on acid-free paper.

Mike Mostafavi. *Visual Basic 2005 by Practice.*
ISBN: 1-58450-441-2

All brand names and product names mentioned in this book are trademarks or service marks of their respective companies. Any omission or misuse (of any kind) of service marks or trademarks should not be regarded as intent to infringe on the property of others. The publisher recognizes and respects all marks used by companies, manufacturers, and developers as a means to distinguish their products.

Library of Congress Cataloging-in-Publication Data
Mostafavi, Mike.
 Visual Basic 2005 by practice / Mike Mostafavi.
    p. cm.
 Includes index.
 ISBN 1-58450-441-2 (alk. paper)
 1. Microsoft Visual BASIC. 2. BASIC (Computer program language) I. Title.
 QA76.73.B3M6724 2006
 005.2'768--dc22
                      2006007733

06 7 6 5 4 3 2 First Edition

CHARLES RIVER MEDIA titles are available for site license or bulk purchase by institutions, user groups, corporations, etc. For additional information, please contact the Special Sales Department at 800-347-7707.

Requests for replacement of a defective CD-ROM must be accompanied by the original disc, your mailing address, telephone number, date of purchase and purchase price. Please state the nature of the problem, and send the information to CHARLES RIVER MEDIA, 25 Thomson Place, Boston, Massachusetts 02210. CRM's sole obligation to the purchaser is to replace the disc, based on defective materials or faulty workmanship, but not on the operation or functionality of the product.

This book is dedicated to Haydeh,
my beautiful wife, college classmate, and best friend,
and my two gorgeous daughters, Beata and Sara,
who have supported me for the past 15 months.

Contents

8 Reptition Structures   **303**

Preface

You can teach programming the way it has always been taught, but that doesn't mean it will work. Take it from this author, who has been teaching complex programming languages of the computer world for 25 years.

This book offers a different approach to teaching Visual Basic that has worked for both traditional and nontraditional settings and for a diverse population of students for years.

Most teachers will tell you they don't always teach according to the sequence of the chapters in their class textbooks but in an order best suited to their needs. Many go through a trial-and-error phase before finding the best method.

The sequence of units suggested by *Visual Basic 2005 by Practice* displaces the traditional order often used to teach Visual Basic. Concepts are dispersed through chapters in a practical way appropriate for a classroom structure, making it much easier for students to relate themes and understand theories. Rather than introducing all of Visual Basic's controls in one chapter, for example, the author has placed them into the chapters where they fit best and in the context that will make the most sense to students.

This approach is based on evidence that too much information at once tends to overwhelm nonadvanced programmers and get in the way of learning the language. In this book, students will observe some concepts and build on them as they go.

The author also strives to use a simple approach and provide plenty of opportunities to practice concepts to make the text user-friendly, for beginners especially. This book's unique sequence, ample examples and simple approach make it a very efficient tool for learning Visual Basic.

Visual Basic is quickly becoming a programming giant of the real world. Few colleges opt not to offer courses on the subject, and a growing number of students take Visual Basic as more employers require knowledge of the language. It has undoubtedly become one of the most popular and important programming languages to learn today. Unfortunately, it is also one of the most challenging to teach, especially in the realm of online classes. Everything in this book is based on the author's years of experience teaching programming in both traditional and nontraditional schools and what has proven to work best for different types of learners time and time again.

One caveat: this book should be used as a springboard to expanding knowledge. It is catered toward entry-level and intermediate Visual Basic programmers. Practicing concepts regularly, keeping abreast of program updates, and using multiple resources are all vital steps to becoming an advanced programmer. To get the most out of this book, users are advised to use companion resources.

The Dot Net Framework—Visual Basic's development environment—is explained as thoroughly as the author thought would be adequate to learn programming, but students are encouraged to do further research.

The Microsoft Development Network (MSDN) is like the encyclopedia for programming and has been used as a primary source for some of the writing of this book. It is the best reference for additional guidance, such as samples, programming tips, and definitions. MSDN is a strongly recommended companion resource for anyone using this book.

For updated and additional information from the author, visit the publisher's Web site, where there will be a page dedicated to this book. You may also email the author at *mike.mostafavi@beasa.com*. He appreciates your feedback on the book.

One final note: you may find minor differences between the sample codes printed in the book and those included on the CD-ROM in the wording, comments, and variable names. However, the programs function the same way.

VISUAL BASIC 2005 AS A COMPONENT OF VISUAL STUDIO 2005

Visual Studio 2005 is an integrated development environment that contains several programming languages such as Visual Basic, C#, C++, and J# and other products such as SQL Server 2005™ and Visual Web Developer 2005™.

WHY VISUAL BASIC?

According to students who have been exposed to several programming languages, Visual Basic provides tools that allow nonprogrammers to develop professional Windows and Web programs. The GUI allows the users to drag and drop objects into a Form and create a user interface. Since Visual Basic 2005 is designed for Windows operating systems, users feel comfortable with the environment, and the tools are known to them. Visual Basic 2005 also fully supports object-oriented programming and Web development techniques.

THE COMPANION CD-ROM

The companion CD-ROM contains the source codes and related files for all projects discussed in this book. They are located in the Solution folder under the specific chapter titles. You will be asked to view specific samples within related chapters, and you need to copy and paste the solution folders into your hard drive before you can execute them. These programs are written in Visual Basic.NET 2005 and will not run on the older version of Visual Basic.

ON THE CD

The companion CD-ROM also includes the full color images that are used in the book. In addition, you are provided with a multimedia file that demonstrates the Integrated Development Environment in audio and video.

WHO SHOULD USE THIS BOOK?

This book is written under three assumptions:

1. You are not a programmer but are familiar with computers and their components, such as hardware, software, and utilities.
2. You have programmed in other programming languages, such as C++, Java, and BASIC, but now you are interested in learning Visual Basic.NET 2005.
3. You have programmed in older versions of Visual Basic and would like to sharpen your skills using new features in Visual Basic.NET 2005.

This book is not meant to teach you what you already know, which is why some of the history of computers is skipped. This book will also not cover the installation steps. You need to refer to your software manual for specific installation steps, the list of preferred and required operating systems, and hardware and software that suits your system.

Acknowledgments

Over the past fifteen months, many people have helped me directly or indirectly as I worked on this book. Now that it is finished, I have more respect for all authors. Writing a textbook requires constant research and accuracy that I was not fully aware of.

I am thankful to my two beautiful daughters, Beata and Sara, who have helped me on the editorials and graphic designs of the book all along. I thank my wife Haydeh who has allowed me to hide in the basement where I spent more time with my computer some days than with her.

I also thank my colleague and friend Ernest Bonat who occasionally has helped me research the new features of Visual Basic 2005.

I would like to extend my thanks to the University of Phoenix, Oregon campus, the Academic Affair department and the students for their excellent support and encouragement.

I should also thank my colleagues at the CIS department at Portland Community College, Sylvania campus, for their commitment to providing the latest technology to students.

I thank the editors and publishers at Charles River Media/Thomson Learning for their patience and support.

1 Introduction to Programming in Visual Basic

In This Chapter

- Introduction
- A Few Words about Computers
- In-House and Canned Programs
- Programming Languages
- Mainstream Support for the Visual Basic 6.0 Family
- Other Areas of Programming
- Structured Programming Techniques
- Procedural vs. Nonprocedural
- Object-Oriented Programming
- Why Object Oriented?
- Object-Oriented Programming Languages
- The Visual Studio 2005 Product Line

INTRODUCTION

"We wish there was a magic potion that would make us learn programming. We read the materials and understand everything, but we cannot write programs." Programming instructors often hear such comments from students. No one is aware of any potion that will make you a programmer. Learning a programming language, however, is not that much different from learning a foreign language, such as French, Arabic, Persian, or Spanish.

Many programmers believe programming is an art and that there are many ways to write codes. Perhaps that is why every programmer uses his own style to develop a program, but you may know by now, programs are a series of instructions telling the computer what to do. Once you become a programmer, you will be giving these instructions to the computer. Consider the following example:

Say you want to learn chess. You can get a chess coach and read books to learn the rules and terms that are used in the game, but to play well, you need to practice and play with other chess players. Although everyone must follow the same rules, each individual applies them differently. That could be why players develop their own styles and savvy tactics. The same logic can be applied to programming.

Learning a new programming language does not require studying the whole programming concept again. You can review examples, study screenshots, and, of course, practice, practice, and practice in order to learn the new programming language. In this book, you will be provided with a great deal of examples and syntax, so that not only can you study the concept but you can also review the codes and working programs.

Many programming languages can be used to communicate with the computer. Some people prefer Visual Basic for a variety of reasons. This group thinks the visual interface of Visual Basic makes programming much easier and more fun to work with. The new changes in the Visual Basic programming language and the advancement of Dot NET technology have made this programming language one of a kind.

A FEW WORDS ABOUT COMPUTERS

We do not know when man decided to use numbers for calculations. There is no real proof of what man was using to add and deduct numbers. However, history remembers the abacus as the first known tool that man used to calculate numbers. The abacus is a manual calculator that allows the users to add, subtract, divide, and multiply, similar to the pocket calculator many of us use today. With some practice you can operate the abacus as fast as you operate a calculator. Computer history credits Charles Babbage as fathering the concept behind modern computers. Computers are designed to process raw input and generate meaningful information by calculating, organizing, formatting, and generating reports. Most computers consist of the following components:

- Hardware
- Software

Hardware

Hardware is the physical components of the computer such as input devices (keyboard, mouse, microphone, camera, etc.), output devices (printer, monitor, speaker, etc.), storage devices (hard drive, memory, floppy disks, CDs, etc.), and the central processing unit (CPU). The CPU is known as the brain of the computer. All processes are done by CPU.

Software

Software is collections of computer instructions or programs. Programs are written by programmers and instruct the computer what to do and how to do it. We can divide software into two major categories:

- System Software
- Application software

System Software

System software is designed to manage computer resources. Consider system software a host that serves all invited guests. System software interacts with the users and the computer. System software includes operating systems, such as Windows®, which most people are familiar with. In addition to operating systems, there are utility programs that go under the system software umbrella as well. Utility programs may or may not be included with the operating systems, but they are there to assist you with your day-to-day tasks. An example of a utility program would be a backup program that allows you to copy and save your files for later use.

Application Software

The other category that plays an important role for computer users is the application programs, also known as end user software. These are designed to do specific tasks.

IN-HOUSE AND CANNED PROGRAMS

Application software can also be divided into canned programs and in-house programs. Canned, or out-of-box, programs are software packages such as *word processing*, *database*, *spreadsheet*, and *presentation packages* that can be purchased from software stores. These programs are mass produced and made available to everyone. No matter where you buy them, all of those programs function in the same way. As a user, you need to adopt their options. In-house programs are designed by in-house programmers to meet a company's specific needs. Application programs can be written for business and scientific needs (see Figure 1.1).

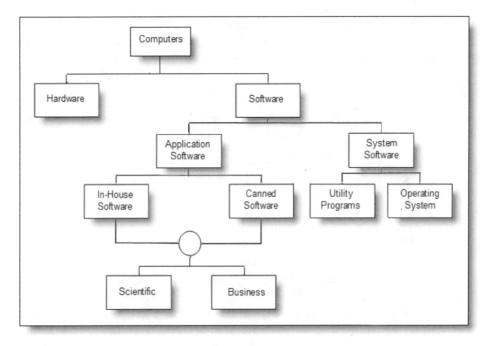

FIGURE 1.1 Hardware and software organization.

PROGRAMMING LANGUAGES

In order to communicate with computers, we need to speak a language that computers can understand. Like verbal languages, programming languages have their own grammar, punctuation, and vocabulary. Programming languages have gone through many changes and evolved to be more understandable to humans. Let's look at the history of programming languages.

Low-Level Programming Language

Machine language is the only language computers can understand. The instruction is given to computers in binary digits, or a combination of 0s and 1s. *Bi* in Latin means two, referring to two states of ON and OFF that 0 and 1 represent. Machine language is the lowest-level language and is understood by machines only. It would be very hard for a human to program in binary codes, if not impossible. The smallest units of data is called *bits*, which stands for *binary digits*. Machine language is hardware specific, and each processor needs its own machine language. The code also contains the instructions to load, store, move, halt, and other functions needed to perform arithmetic operations.

The lack of standards among machine languages used by different computer manufactures prevented computers from exchanging information. Later, in the 1960s, *ASCII* codes were developed to standardize machine language codes to allow computers designed by different manufactures to communicate with each other and exchange data. ASCII, which stands for *American Standard Code for Information Interchange*, was the product of this effort. The ASCII character set represents 128 characters that are found on most standard keyboards. These 128 characters consist of numbers, letters, and special characters, such as commas, parentheses, and dollar signs. This character set ranges from 0 to 127. This is known as a 7-bit character set that can represent the first 128 characters. Since most computers have additional special character sets beyond the first 128 characters, the 8-bit or byte ASCII character set known as *Extended ASCII* was developed later on. Although ASCII codes provided some standards for the exchange of information between computers, the codes remained semistandard. Table 1.1 shows the ASCII and binary codes for a few characters:

TABLE 1.1   ASCII and Binary Codes

ASCII	Binary	Character
065	01000001	A
066	01000010	B
067	01000011	C
068	01000100	D
069	01000101	E
070	01000110	F
071	01000111	G
072	01001000	H
073	01001001	I
074	01001010	J

As you can see, the ASCII code for the capital character A is 65. You can find most of the ASCII codes and characters in Appendix A. If we want to see how the word "hi" is represented in binary and ASCII, it will be as shown in Table 2.1.

TABLE 1.2   Examples of ASCII and Binary

	H	I
ASCII	72	73
Binary	01001000	01001001

We can use ASCII codes in our Visual Basic Programs to validate the input. You will learn how to do it in later chapters.

Second Generation of Low-Level Programming Language

As stated above, machine language is designed for a machine and is not readable by humans, but humans are the ones who must write instructions for the computers. To make it possible for humans to read and write computer instructions, *assembly language* was developed. Assembly language uses a translator called an *assembler* to translate programmers' instructions to machine language. The structure of assembly language is very similar to machine language. However, programmers can use symbols instead of the raw numbers, which makes programming easier. Assembly language is also known as a low-level programming language because like machine language, it is designed to be used by machines. Like machine language, assembly language is hardware specific and it varies from CPU to CPU. There is no machine language that can be used on all processors.

A simple example of an assembly language instruction would be:

```
LOAD R5 #20
ADD  R2 R3 #10
```

In the first instruction, you load the value 20 into register number 5. In the second instruction, you add 10 to the value that is stored in register number 3 and store the result in register number 2. Each instruction will be abbreviated into a three-letter name known as its mnemonic. For instance, JMP would represent the JUMP instruction.

High-Level Programming Languages

Although assembly language is easier to use than machine language, it is still hard to learn. As we learned, computers can understand only machine language, and we know humans cannot use machine language directly to comfortably instruct the computer to perform tasks. As a result, the *high-level* programming languages were developed. The grammar (syntax) of some of the high-level programming languages is close to English, so programmers can learn and use them faster and more easily.

Under the category of high-level programming languages, you will find many programming languages that were developed to solve specific problems. Unlike machine language and assembly language, high-level programming languages are designed to interact with humans, not machines. The high-level programming languages need to be translated into machine language in order to be understood by computers, which can be accomplished by using *compilers* and *interpreters*.

Compilers and Interpreters

A *compiler* is a computer program that translates the entire program into *object codes*. You can execute this object code without the need to compile it again. Most executable programs that you receive and execute are object codes, and you do not need the source code to run these applications. Once they are compiled, they will run as many times as you need. If you need to modify the program, you can go back to your *source codes*, make the changes, recompile it, and generate a new object code (executable program). Since the program is already compiled, running the executable program is much faster than compiling and running the program simultaneously. During compilation, *syntax errors* will be identified, and the program will not compile if errors are found. The compiler will break down your errors into unrecoverable errors and warnings. Some programs can still execute with less serious warnings. Consider a compiler as your English teacher. When you submit your essay, your teacher reviews it for spelling, punctuation, and grammar. At the end your teacher will count the number of errors and assign a grade to you. This is very similar to what a compiler does.

An *interpreter* translates one instruction at a time, rather than translating the whole program. Object codes will not be generated when interpreters are used. As a result, every time you execute this program, it will go through the translation process again. This will cause it to be slower than programs that use compilers. Because interpreters translate one instruction at a time, some errors can be identified once the user hits the enter key. This interaction will help beginners find their errors without waiting until the entire program is translated. Interpreters are not as efficient as compilers and are slower. Many versions of BASIC use compilers as well.

Let's look at some of the high-level programming languages:

- FORTRAN
- BASIC
- COBOL
- C
- Pascal
- C++
- Visual C++
- JAVA

- Visual J++
- VISUAL BASIC
- Visual C#

FORTRAN

FORTRAN, which is an acronym for *formula trans*lator, is the oldest third-generation programming language. It was developed in the 1950s as a scientific programming language designed to solve mathematical problems. FORTRAN uses a compiler to translate English, high-level third-generation source codes into a language the computer can understand. The programmer needs to follow the syntax of the language and not worry about the way the instructions are read by the machine. The compiler will also give hints for possible errors in the program and will not compile the source code (your program) if it contains errors. FORTRAN is still around, and new versions of it are available. Let's look at one simple code:

```
print*,'Enter a number'
read*,num1
print*,'The number you entered was ',num1
```

In the above statement, the user's input will be stored in the num1 variable and will be displayed back to the user.

COBOL

COBOL is an acronym for *Common Business Oriented Language* and was designed to solve business problems. COBOL was developed in the 1960s and was intended to be an easy-to-understand programming language, and most application programs designed in COBOL are still in use. Inventory, payroll, and accounting applications are among programs that COBOL is good at. COBOL is a wordy language, and you need to spell out many statements to make the program work. This makes COBOL more readable. COBOL can process a large number of input files, which is a convenient feature for business applications. Like FORTRAN, COBOL has its own compiler. COBOL has gone through many changes, and newer versions are designed for PCs.

COBOL has four specific divisions that need to be ordered in sequence, and this hierarchical structure has made the program a very dominant programming language (see Figure 1.2).

As you can see in Figure 1.2, each COBOL program consists of up to four divisions. Two of them, the identification division and the procedure division, are required to execute the program. Each division may have several sections, and each section may be composed of one or more paragraphs. Each paragraph may have one or more sentences, and so on. These divisions must appear in the following order:

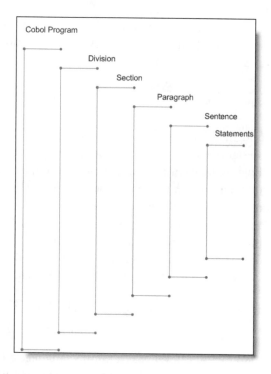

FIGURE 1.2 COBOL hierarchy structure.

- Identification division
- Environment division
- Data division
- Procedure division

The identification division is designed to collect information about the program:

```
PROGRAM-ID.      MY-FIRST-PROGRAM.
AUTHOR.          Mike-Mostafavi.
DATE-WRITTEN.    September-2005.
DATA-COMPILED.   October-2005.
SECURITY.        None.
INSTALLATION.    Testing.
```

Not all of the items within the divisions are required, but most programmers supply all the information for documentation purposes. For instance, within the identification division, only Program-ID is required. COBOL statements are not case sensitive.

The environment division is designed to collect information about the source of input/output and other external devises to centralize all resources in one area. Here is an example of that:

```
CONFIGURATION SECTION.
SOURCE-COMPUTER. mine.
OBJECT-COMPUTER. yours.
INPUT-OUTPUT-SECTION.
FILE-CONTROL.
```

The data division contains information about data items that will be processed within the program. It may have sections such as file section, working-storage section, linkage section, and report section.

The procedure division is designed to hold codes to process data that will be used within the program. It supplies the necessary codes to produce the required information and reports. As stated before, COBOL has English-type statements that can be understood by nonprogrammers as well. Here is an example:

```
multiply pay-rate by hours-worked giving gross-pay
```

BASIC

BASIC is another high-level programming language developed in the 1960s. BASIC is an acronym for *Beginner's All-purpose Symbolic Instruction Code*. BASIC is a general-purpose programming language but has been widely used in the business world. BASIC was developed at Dartmouth College to teach students the concept of programming. Compared to some other programming languages, BASIC is the easiest to learn. Newer versions of BASIC languages, such as Visual Basic, share syntax with the old version. Here is an example for a BASIC program:

```
PRINT "Enter Your Name";
INPUT N$
PRINT "Enter your password"
INPUT P$
IF P$ <>"BASIC" THEN
PRINT "Wrong Password"
```

BASIC was using an interpreter instead of a compiler, which have several differences.

PASCAL

Pascal is another scientific high-level programming language that was designed in the 1970s. Pascal was named after the French mathematician Blaise Pascal. Pascal was very popular before programmers became familiar with C language. It is capable of doing scientific applications and is still used by some programmers. Pascal was famous for being a very structured programming language, and some educators use it to teach structured programming techniques. Here is a portion of a Pascal code:

```
Writeln(Make Your Choice);
    writeln;
    writeln("English");
    writeln("Spanish');
    writeln('"Persian');
    writeln;
Readln(menuchoice);
```

C

C is another high-level programming language, which was developed in the 1970s in the Bell Laboratory. C is the third try after two other similar programming languages, BCPL (Basic Combined Programming Language) and B, did not meet expectations. C was used to write the UNIX Operating System and works well within that operating system. C, which is easier than assembly language but harder than other third-generation programming languages, is still widely used by a large number of programmers.

```
{
/* The following will display a message to the user */
printf("Display My Message\n");
return 0;
}
```

Visual Basic, Early Versions

Although Visual Basic was not the first programming language designed to develop a Windows application, it is perhaps the first Visual programming environment that has been introduced to programmers. Since Visual Basic syntax is based on the early version of BASIC, we need to expand our discussion of it and explore its background a little deeper.

As we know, the first generation of BASIC programming language used an interpreter. BASIC used an interpreter and ran on Mainframe computers, and students could use it at their campus computer labs. The same method was used when the DOS Operating System was developed for personal computers. BASIC-A was a version that was developed for IBM™ PCs. Later on, Microsoft developed GW-BASIC, which was bundled with MS-DOS Operating System for IBM compatible machines. GW-BASIC was named after Greg Whitten, a former Microsoft employee.

GW-BASIC was replaced by QBASIC (stands for Quick Beginner's All-purpose Symbolic Instruction Codes). QBASIC accompanied the Windows 95 Operating System package. QBASIC is different from QuickBASIC, which was sold separately from the bundled versions of BASIC. QuickBASIC was a commercial package that had more programming capabilities and used a compiler rather than an interpreter.

Along with the development of Windows 3.0 in 1991, the first official version of Visual Basic was developed. Visual Basic's drag and drop features that ran under the Windows operating systems created an easier development environment.

Visual Basic 2.0 was released in 1992 and introduced new features and better performance. Version 3.0 hit the market in 1993, with new features including a database engine to connect to databases. It was also offered in both professional and standard versions. Version 4.0 was released in 1995, and one of its top new features was the ability to create custom-made controls and classes. In 1997, Visual Basic 5.0 was introduced, offering much faster performance and ActiveX controls.

Visual Basic 6.0 was released in 1998 and offered new features, including Web-based applications. This version was offered as a studio package that included other applications, such as Visual C++, Visual FoxPro, Visual Interdev, and Visual J++.

Although Visual Basic 6.0 became a very popular programming language, it was often criticized for not being a fully object-oriented language. Many people considered Visual Basic 6.0 an event-driven programming language, not an object-oriented programming language. The .NET version of this programming language has corrected all of the object-oriented shortcomings found in previous versions of Visual Basic.

MAINSTREAM SUPPORT FOR THE VISUAL BASIC 6.0 FAMILY

Visual Basic 6.0 is still used around the word, but Microsoft has stopped its mainstream support for this product family. The Visual Basic 6.0 family of products includes the standard, professional, and enterprise editions of Visual Basic 6.0. According to Microsoft, the mainstream support was in effect for six years after the software was available to the general public. Since Visual Basic 6.0 was released in 1999, mainstream support ended March 31, 2005.

OTHER AREAS OF PROGRAMMING

You should look into other high-level programming languages in order to be familiar with their nature. ADA and PL/1 are among many others that need recognition.

The Internet

With the evolution of the Internet, the need for other programming languages became unavoidable. The traditional stand-alone programming paradigms couldn't meet the demands of this new communication media. As a result, a new language was developed to facilitate communications among users. The developers of this new language intended to keep it simple and easy to learn. HTML, which stands for *Hyper Text Markup Language*, was developed in the 1990s. This language uses tags for specific instructions, which are translated into meaningful Web pages by special software called browsers. Here is a short sample of HTML code:

```html
<html>
<head>
<title>Visual Basic 2005</title>
</head>
<body>
<h2>Visual Basic 2005</h2>
<h3>In this book we learn how to program</h3>
<p>Here are topics we will cover:</p>
<ul>
    <li>History of programming languages</li>
    <li>Visual Basic</li>
    <li>other topics</li>
</ul>
</body>
</html>
```

Is HTML a programming language? This has been the center of many debates. According to a lot of experts, HTML is a markup language but not a programming language. Whether HTML is a markup language or a programming language is not important. HTML is the backbone of the Web pages we visit every day.

JavaScript

Since we talked about JAVA and HTML, we should talk about another language that most Web developers use in their day-to-day design. Although JAVA and JavaScript share a lot of similarities in both name and structures, they are two different programming languages. JAVA is a stand-alone programming language that can run on any platform. JavaScript, on the other hand, is a scripting language that must be included within HTML codes and be processed by browsers. JavaScript was developed by Netscape® in the 1990s to allow Web developers to add more interactive features to their Web sites. Here is a short sample code for JavaScript:

```html
<HTML>
<HEAD>
    <TITLE>My JavaScript page</TITLE>
    <SCRIPT LANGUAGE="JAVASCRIPT" TYPE="TEXT/JAVASCRIPT">
        alert("Welcome to my JavaScript page!")
    </SCRIPT>
</HEAD>
</BODY>
</HTML>
```

Most of the newer browsers support JavaScript. Programmers use JavaScript to enhance their Web pages. Password protection and animations are among the features JavaScript offers that appeals to programmers.

VBScript

VBScript is a Microsoft Scripting language that is based on the Visual Basic programming language and shares some similarities. Like JavaScript, VBScript was designed to help Web developers add more interactive functions to their Web pages. VBScripts can be viewed by the Internet Explorer browser, but Netscape doesn't support it. Due to such limitations, VBScript is not as commonly used as JavaScript. Here is a short sample of VBScript that is included within HTML codes:

```
<html>
<head>
<TITLE>This is a sample</TITLE>
<SCRIPT LANGUAGE="VBScript">
    MsgBox "This is Visual Basic 2005 Textbook"
</SCRIPT>
</head>
<body>
<h2> Table of Content :</h2>
</body>
</html>
```

STRUCTURED PROGRAMMING TECHNIQUES

You should also be familiar with another common term that is used in the programming environment: *structured programming techniques.* You may hear structured programming techniques and top-down design used interchangeably. With this technique, you start writing the most general part of your program first and test it. Then you write codes for the most specific part of your program. With this hierarchical programming technique, modules are used to break down the program into smaller sections. These modules normally have single entry and single exit points. The control is normally passed downward. An example would be creating a main menu for your program that gives the options of Add, Delete, Update, and Undo to your users. You create the menu by using the *stub testing* technique and make sure that it branches out to the routine that you want. At this time, you haven't written the codes for the Add, Delete, Update, and Undo sections of your program, but you know that the control is passed to that section. Stub testing refers to an empty section that returns feedback to the programmer. For example, you can have a message box within the Add section of your program read "Add routine was accessed." After this test, you start writing codes for these tested empty routines.

The opposite of top down is the *bottom up* technique, which requires you to start with the most specific part of your program and then go to the most general parts. For example, you could write codes for the Add, Delete, Update, and Undo sections first and then create a menu to connect these sections together. The structured programming techniques can be applied to procedural programming languages such as ADA, Pascal, FORTRAN, COBOL, and C but are not as applicable to object-oriented programming techniques these days.

PROCEDURAL VS. NONPROCEDURAL

If you do a Web search or review programming textbooks, you will notice that some Web sites and authors divide programming languages into five generations: first generation (machine language), second generation (assembly language), third generation (FORTRAN, BASIC, COBOL, etc.), fourth generation (Focus, Fourth, etc.), and fifth generation (Prolog). You will also notice that some of them list *object-oriented* programming languages as fourth-generation programming languages. We cannot find solid and unified definitions for the generations of programming languages but we can see some agreement about topics mentioned in this section.

Further research will show you other interesting topics in the area of programming languages:

- Procedural programming languages
- Nonprocedural programming languages

Older high-level programming languages are *procedural languages*. Under this category, programmers need to follow specific orders to write their codes. The program consists of at least one main routine and may have several subroutines. Under this category, you need to tell the computer what to do and how to do it. Examples of programming languages that are listed under procedural are:

- FORTRAN
- COBOL
- PASCAL
- BASIC
- C

Nonprocedural programming languages, however, do not follow a specific sequence. Object-oriented programming languages such as Visual Basic.NET, which are *nonprocedural* in nature, provide an environment that puts the user in control. The user, in turn, can choose the sequence in which the program should be executed.

Object-oriented programming languages that fall under the nonprocedural category continue to get more attention. The efficiency, reusability, and performance of object-oriented programming has convinced many programmers to move to that direction.

OBJECT-ORIENTED PROGRAMMING

If you have taken programming classes recently, you have most likely heard the phrase *object-oriented programming* from your teachers or textbooks. Since Visual Basic 2005™ supports object-oriented programming, let's get familiar with some of the terms that are associated with this concept.

Object

Object-oriented programming refers to a program that uses *objects*, such as TextBoxes, Buttons, and Labels. In real life, consider an object such as your cell phone. Your cell phone, as a device, can be represented to the computer by an object. The model, color, size, price, frequency, and other features will be used to represent your cell phone. We use tools or controls to create these objects.

Attributes or Properties

We use attributes or properties to identify objects. Each object must have a name, color, size, and other characteristics. Each object has several attributes or properties. In our cell phone example, model, color, size, price, frequency, and other characteristics that are used to describe a cell phone are attributes or properties of the cell phone. We use properties to define objects. A TextBox, for example, has properties such as Name, BackColor, Size, Font, BorderStyle, and Text. We can use these properties to create TextBoxes according to our needs.

Methods

Each object is designed to perform specific operations or actions. These actions are called *methods*. For our cell phone example, End, Send, and Clear are considered methods. Objects have standard methods that can be used by the programmers to do specific tasks. For example, an object such as a button can have methods such as Refresh, Hide, Show, Focus, and so on. In Visual Basic, the programmer can reference the object's methods by using the object's name and the name of the method separated by a dot: Object.Method.

Let's say the object is a button and we have renamed this object processButton. This can be demonstrated by the following examples:

- `processButton.Hide`
- `processButton.Show`
- `processButton.Focus`
- `processButton.Refresh`

Events

Objects can react to the user's input according to the *event* that the developer has programmed for. For example, `Click` is one of `Button`'s many events that can be used by the user to perform a task. Let's say you see a button that reads Exit Program. Once you push this button, the program will be terminated. The programmer has placed a set of codes within the event subprocedure of the `Exit` button to fulfill your request. Other events for the `Button` and other objects will be discussed later on.

Classes and Instances

One of the important elements of object-oriented programming is *class*. Think of a class as a rubber stamp you have made for your name, address, and zip code. Any time you use this rubber stamp, an identical instance of the information will be printed on paper. The class is like a rubber stamp or template that maintains the properties and methods needed for each object. In our cell phone example, `Folding Phones` could be defined as a class that represents similar cell phones. A `Button` class maintains all properties and methods needed to create a button. Every time you use a tool, such as a `Button` class to create an object, you make an instance of that class. An instance is like a photocopy of the original that can be reproduced x number of times.

Encapsulation

The objects communicate with the users through the interface that is designed by the programmer. The user shouldn't know what properties of the object have been used or what kind of processing takes place behind the object. *Encapsulation* is used to hide the properties and methods of the object. Based on the service that the encapsulation provides, the user will communicate with the objects only through the interface. This allows the programmers to change the data source with no effects on the users.

Inheritance

Inheritance is another term you should be familiar with. Consider the cell phone example again. All cell phones of a particular make, model, and year will inherit the same characteristics. Now, we will apply this term to programming. Let's say you have created a `Form` with specific parameters, such as specific background color, size, and so on. You would like to make some changes to this Form but you want to keep the original intact. In this case, you create another class from the Form class you created before, and the new class inherits all properties and methods of the original. This will enable you to reuse an existing class. The terms *parent class* and *child class* refer to the original and duplicated classes.

Polymorphism

There is one more term to understand before moving on: *polymorphism*. *Poly* in Greek means "many," and *morph* means "forms." This means different objects that have methods and properties with the same name react to them differently. For example, two different objects could have similar methods. Although the methods' names are the same, they function differently when you execute the program. Here's an example. Say you plan to wake up at 6:00 a.m. every day. You have three ways to accomplish this task: an alarm clock, a clock radio, or having your spouse wake you up. The alarm clock will ring, the clock radio will sing, and your spouse will kick. As you can see, each will respond differently to your request.

It is also possible that one method within a class has different names and behaves differently. The classic programming example used by many teachers is the drawing method that is available for the Shape class. By using the drawing method you can draw different shapes such as triangles, squares, and so on.

Reading these concepts without hands-on practice is like reading a driving manual without a car. Just be patient, and most of these terms will make sense to you as we proceed.

WHY OBJECT-ORIENTED?

As stated before, the industry is moving toward object-oriented design. Although the move was slow in the beginning, it has received positive acceptance in recent years. We are not going to get into a debate to prove which of these, procedural or object oriented, is better. There are valid arguments from both sides. However, with the popularity of object-oriented programming languages such as JAVA, C++, C#.NET, and Visual Basic.NET, object-oriented programming languages prove to be faster to learn and easier to maintain. In addition, object-oriented programming languages provide a way to break large and sometimes difficult-to-manage programming projects into smaller modules that can be managed easily. Encapsulation hides technical and complex details from the users and allows the programmers to make changes to the data and code without affecting the users. The author is a firm believer of object-oriented design and uses it professionally for programming projects.

OBJECT-ORIENTED PROGRAMMING LANGUAGES

Now that you are familiar with object-oriented terms, we will introduce you to some object-oriented programming languages.

C++

C++, which is an extension of the C programming language, was also developed at the Bell laboratory. C++ was introduced in the 1980s and became a popular object-oriented programming language. The distinct features of the C++ language are class- and object-oriented features that were added to it. C++ was also designed for the UNIX operating system. It is used by many developers and is taught at many schools. Here is a portion of the C++ source code:

```
#include<myfile.h>
int main() {
int A;
cout << "Enter a Number ";
cin >> A;
cout << "The number you entered was:" << A;
return 0;
}
```

In the above code, `#Include` is a header statement that is equivalent to `Import` in other programming languages. It is used to import functions from other files.

Visual C++

After the introduction of C++ programming, Microsoft introduced a new version of C++ that ran on Windows operating systems. This new version of C++ is called Visual C++. Visual C++ is added to the Integrated Development Environment (IDE) of the Visual Studio family and supports a 32-bit Windows application and has its own library. This library, which is designed to help programmers, is called Microsoft Foundation Classes (MFC). The new Visual Studio.NET 2003 and Visual Studio.NET 2005 include Visual C++ as Visual C++.NET.

JAVA

JAVA, which is another object-oriented high-level language, was introduced in the 1990s. Unlike other programming languages, JAVA is not dependant on any specific platform and can run on any operating system and platform. JAVA was developed by Sun Microsystems, but Microsoft has a different version of it included in Visual Studio packages. Sun Microsystems' JAVA became popular for the new features it offered for the Web. It can run as a stand-alone program or use a browser to execute JAVA Applets. Here is a small portion of JAVA code:

```
System.out.print ("Enter Your Name");
System.out.flush();
Username=system.in.read();
System.out.println("Your Name was: " + username);
```

Visual J++

Visual J++ is the Microsoft version of JAVA. This graphical user interface (GUI) development tool helps users develop JAVA programs using the graphical editor and debugger. Microsoft's Visual Studio series, which is a collection of several integrated languages, includes Visual J++ as well. Visual J++ allows developers to enhance their development skills by using a GUI.

Visual C#.NET

C# (pronounced C Sharp) is the newest object-oriented programming language added to the Visual Studio.NET IDE family. Visual C# has incorporated the ease of the GUI that Visual Basic offers and the capabilities of other programming languages such as C and JAVA. Most JAVA programmers are attracted to C# for these two futures. Here is a sample code for it:

```
public class HelloWorld {
    public static void Main() {
        System.Console.WriteLine("Hello World!");
    }
}
```

Visual J#.NET

This is the replacement for J++ offered by a previous version of Visual Studio. Visual C#.NET was designed by Microsoft to facilitate JAVA programmers' transition into the Visual Studio.NET integrated environment. Although Visual J# (pronounced J Sharp) is not fully compatible with Sun™'s JAVA, it has attracted a lot of attention. The syntax of Visual C#.NET resembles Visual J# .NET.

Visual Studio.NET

In 2001, Visual Basic.NET, which was included in the new Visual Studio.NET suite, came with new features that were not offered by any of its predecessors. Unlike other versions of Visual Basic, the .NET version provided a complete object-oriented environment. Visual Basic.NET, Visual C++.NET, Visual C#.NET, and Visual J#.NET were all part of the same IDE. This new version also simplified the development of Web-based applications by providing support for ASP.NET. However, Visual Studio.NET is not backward compatible, so projects that were developed using the previous versions of Visual Studio cannot run on the new version.

Visual Studio.NET 2003 was released in 2003 and included wireless support for the first time. The performance of VS.NET has improved in many areas.

THE VISUAL STUDIO 2005™ PRODUCT LINE

Visual Studio 2005 products are offered at several levels: *Team Systems, Professional, Standard,* and *Express Edition*.

Express Edition

Microsoft has released six Express product lines that consist of Visual Basic 2005, Visual C++ 2005, Visual C# 2005, Visual Web Developer 2005, Visual J# 2005, and SQL Server 2005. This edition, which is relatively light and inexpensive, is designed for beginners, hobbyists, students, and novices who want to learn Windows and Web programming.

Standard Edition

Visual Studio Standard edition is a development tool with the simplicity of the Express edition but it is designed to be used by small businesses. This edition includes tools to design Web applications.

Professional Edition

Professional developers will have two options: Visual Studio 2005 Professional edition, and Visual Studio 2005 Tools for the Microsoft Office System. Each edition has comprehensive tools that help professionals develop Windows or Web applications.

Team Edition

This edition is designed to foster a productive and professional team environment, improve communication among the team members who work on business projects, and reduce the complexity of the solutions.

SUMMARY

In this chapter, we covered the background of programming languages and provided you with simple codes in each programming language. We also discussed the differences between procedural and nonprocedural programming languages and structured techniques, explained the concept of object-oriented design and provided you with all terms used in object-oriented programming.

Next

In Chapter Two, we will discuss Visual Basic 2005's IDE and cover some of its new features. You will learn about the Properties window, the Solution Explorer, Document window, Toolbox, tool bar and Menu bar. You will also become familiar with the IntelliSense feature, Code Snippets, and many other terms.

DISCUSSION QUESTIONS

1. What are the differences between procedural and nonprocedural programming languages?
2. Why do we call machine language a low-level programming language? Please explain.
3. What was the role of BASIC programming language in the development of Visual Basic?
4. Explain class and method in the context of object-oriented programming and provide examples.
5. Is Visual Basic an event-oriented programming language? Why?

Exercise

Visit the publisher's Web site and right-click on any page. Select the View Source option and review the codes. Try to locate HTML tags and JavaScript codes. List your findings and briefly explain them.

Key Terms

- Class, Parent class, and Child class
- Encapsulation
- Events
- Event subprocedure
- Inheritance
- Instance
- Methods
- Objects
- Object-oriented programming
- Polymorphism
- Properties

2 Getting to Know Visual Studio 2005™

In This Chapter

- Exploring Visual Studio 2005 with .NET Framework 2.0 Support
- Some of the Changes in .NET Framework 2.0
- Getting Familiar with Some Terms
- Installing the Software
- Launching Visual Studio 2005
- Understanding the IDE
- Adding Controls to the Form using the Snap Line
- Docking
- Auto Hide
- Resetting the Layout
- Saving the Project
- Multimedia Demonstration
- Getting Help
- Code Snippets

EXPLORING VISUAL STUDIO 2005 WITH .NET FRAMEWORK 2.0 SUPPORT

Whether you are new to Visual Basic programming or not you need to know that Visual Studio.NET 2005 comes with many new and enhanced features that affect you as a programmer or project leader. Most programmers remember the .NET Framework 1.00 innovations when the earliest version of Visual Studio.NET was released. Visual Studio 2005, like the earliest .NET version, is based on the .NET Framework. The .NET Framework 2.0 comes with new, improved, and enhanced features. Sharing objects among different programming languages, providing easier environments, and providing more support for the .NET products are among the many reasons for releasing the new version. Among new, improved, and enhanced features are the support for 64-bit platforms, significant enhancements to

ASP.NET, new features of ADO.NET, FTP support, data protection, application program interface (API), and many more.

Visual Basic 2005 is among the four programming languages that target .NET Framework 2.0. The new release of this software promises more simplicity and more productivity. Changes to the Visual Studio 2005 version take place in many areas.

SOME OF THE CHANGES IN .NET FRAMEWORK 2.0

We will highlight some of those changes that affect you as a Visual Basic programmer in the following areas: development environment, code editing, building, testing, debugging and deployment, help for Visual Studio, and language enhancements.

Visual Studio has gone through many changes to become a powerful integrated suite. In addition to the new language tunings, the new improvements are geared toward the improvement of *common language specifications* (CLS), which provides an object-oriented environment that allows all of the languages to communicate with each other. The new Visual Studio is committed to providing more features with less coding. We will briefly discuss some of these features:

New presetting features: These allow users to customize their work environment. The settings are Saved, Imported, and Exported for future use.

Task List: This includes Text Display, Column Sorting and Multiple Column Sorting, Show Column, Move Column, and Show Files. Text Display can now display multiple lines of texts, including the full description. Column Sorting and Multiple Column Sorting can be used to sort one or more columns. A sort triangle is added to the column heading to sort the columns in ascending or descending order. Show Column can be used to show desired columns. This version also includes a Move Columns feature that allows users to move the desired columns by using the drag and drop method. The Show Files feature provides options such as Hide File Path.

Error List: This allows users to list all of the errors and warnings as they compile the codes.

Just My Code: This is a debugging option that allows you to see the codes you have written, not the one the system has added to the project.

IntelliSense and Code Snippets: You will see more improvements using these two features. *IntelliSense* provides syntax tips and as you type the codes, it can show you all of the valid options and complete the code for you. *Code Snippets* help you find many prewritten codes and ready-to-use codes that can be inserted into your program. Code Snippet Manager allows you to create your own Code Snippets or modify existing ones. Right-clicking on the active documents causes a list of Code Snippets to be displayed.

Design Time Expression Evaluation: This discontinued Visual Basic 6 feature returns to the 2005 version. It allows you to type in your expressions in the Immediate window and test them. It is a great tool to use to test methods for their functionality at design time.

Snap Lines: This is used to align controls during drag and drop. It is useful for aligning controls with the other existing controls on the Form.

Window Docking: As you drag a window, such as the Properties window, within the integrated development environment (IDE) framework, you will notice a diamond-shaped guide with four arrows. If you are allowed to drop the window in the selected location, then the center of the guide becomes darker. This is very helpful in finding a location where you can dock the active window. You can move any window within the IDE. However, you can only dock it in specific locations.

Start Page: This new IDE design allows users to open Existing Files, New Files, News, or Headlines. This is entirely different from the previous version.

Community Menu: This new menu item allows users to send feedback to Microsoft or ask for help from an MSDN newsgroup. You can access many more resources. Please explore it yourself for more information.

My Namespace: This allows you to access hard-to-find classes in a short time and access the My classes, which include Application, Computer, Forms, Resources, Settings, and User. Each class comes with many useful members for programmers.

Edit and Continue: This is another Visual Basic 6 discontinued feature that is back. Edit and Continue allows users to edit most of their codes during debugging and execute them immediately. You can revise your codes or fix errors during break mode and execute them immediately. You do not have to be in the design mode to make changes.

AutoCorrect: This allows you to fix your typing errors by displaying similar valid options.

Exception Assistant: This provides a help window for correcting unhandled runtime errors. It refers you to a specific location of the errors and gives you hints on how to handle them.

OneClick Installation: This can facilitate simple deployment and easy installation of your project on other machines. Any updates to your project can be done through the Web.

Language Innovation: Visual Basic 2005 comes with many new changes to the language. These changes include the addition of Using Block, IsNot keyword, partial classes, and many more.

You can explore the other changes in 2.0 Framework at the following URL: *http://msdn2.microsoft.com/en-us/library/t357fb32.aspx.*

GETTING FAMILIAR WITH SOME TERMS

Before we launch Microsoft Visual Studio 2005™, we need to be familiar with a few terms:

- Solution
- Project
- File

Let's consider a simple analogy to understand these three terms better. Say you are taking several classes and you need to organize your disk in a way that lets you find course materials more easily. We assume that you have a floppy disk or a USB flash drive and you want to use it to store your course materials. Let's say you have taken five classes and you have lecture notes, presentation slides, and homework assignments that need to be organized. You will create five folders and name them after the name of the classes. You will store lecture materials, slide presentations, and homework assignments in each related folder.

If we want to relate this scenario to the three terms mentioned above, your USB flash drive would be like a *solution*. The folders you created for each course is like a *project*. The lecture materials, slides, and homework assignments you saved within each folder is like a *file*.

A solution is a container that can store one or more projects. Projects, in turn, are folders that files are saved in. Visual Basic 2005 uses a folder-based model to create solutions. Solution Explorer allows us to view the solution's structure in a tree view format.

INSTALLING THE SOFTWARE

You need to install the software according to Microsoft instructions. The installation may vary from one system to another. Please follow the installation instructions as recommended in the Microsoft documents. It is important that you review the system requirements before you install the software and install the software according to the suggested instructions.

LAUNCHING VISUAL STUDIO 2005

Let's launch Microsoft Visual Studio 2005 and explore the development environment. Follow the steps below to start the application. We are assuming that you have installed the software already. The screenshots are from the professional edition of Visual Studio 2005, not the Beta edition. We also installed the software on the XP Professional Operating System. It is possible that you will find a few of these screenshots differ from yours. In Windows XP®

1. Click on the Start button.
2. Point to All Programs and point to the Microsoft Visual Studio 2005 folder.
3. Open the Microsoft Visual Studio 2005 file (see Figure 2.1).

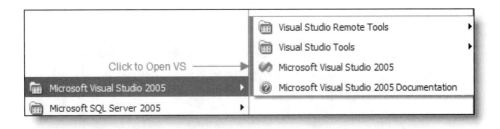

FIGURE 2.1   Microsoft Visual Studio 2005 startup files.

Setting the Default Environment

If this is the first time you are executing your Visual Studio 2005, you need to select a default environment. You should see a Default Environment Setting dialog box (Figure 2.2) with a list of options. Select the Visual Basic Development Setting and click on Start Visual Studio. Once you select your default environment, you should not see this dialog box any longer.

After you click on Start Visual Studio, the Configuration Progress box will appear (see Figure 2.3).

FIGURE 2.2   Default Environment Setting dialog box.

FIGURE 2.3   Configuration Progress box.

After this step, you will see the Visual Studio integrated development environment (IDE). You should see the screenshot shown in Figure 2.4.

Recent and New Project Boxes

In the Recent Projects box, you will see the names of your recent files. Obviously, the first time that you fire up Visual Studio, that section will be blank. You can also create new projects or open existing projects (see Figure 2.5).

Click on Create Project to see the New Project dialog box. There are many options for project type and templates. We want to use Windows Application

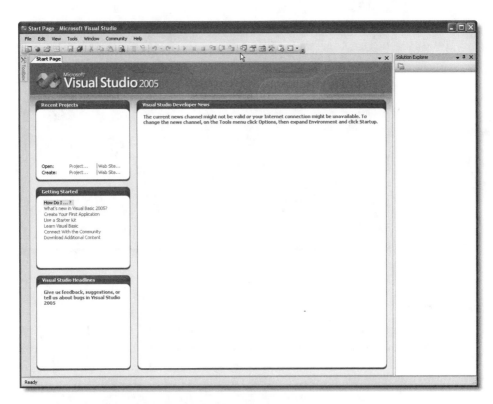

FIGURE 2.4   Microsoft IDE initial dialog box.

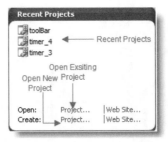

FIGURE 2.5   Recent Projects box.

templates for this project and many other future projects, so select Windows as Project Type and Windows Application as Template (see Figure 2.6).

FIGURE 2.6 New Project Dialog box.

In the Name dialog box, type "myFirstProgram" and click on the OK button. Once you do this, you should see the Visual Studio 2005 IDE (see Figure 2.7).

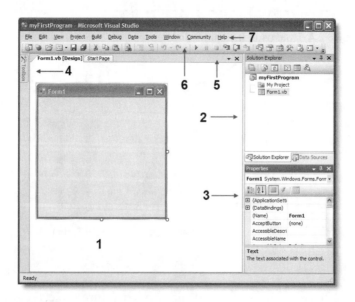

FIGURE 2.7 Visual Studio 2005 IDE.

We have moved the IDE's windows closer to each other to save space. Within the IDE, you will notice the following:

- Form Designer window
- Solution Explorer window
- Properties window
- Toolbox
- Document window
- Toolbar
- Menu bar

We will discuss these windows in further detail in the next section.

Once this phase is complete, Visual Studio will create a new project with one form file within it.

UNDERSTANDING THE IDE

Think of the IDE as the control panel for your application program. Within this environment, you can design, develop, edit, test, debug, and execute your programs. This interactive environment allows you to drag and drop controls into your forms and can be customized according to your style.

Once you fire up your Visual Studio and choose Visual Basic's Windows Application template, you enter the design mode of the IDE, which acts as an editor that allows you to add controls and codes to your Form. During the design phase, you have a chance to view your program and make the desired changes. The layout, format, fonts, and images can be selected within this phase.

The IDE has several parts that need our attention. As shown in Figure 2.7, these parts are numbered, so we can explain each part according to its number.

1. Designer Window

The Form is located inside the Designer window. The Form object is like a tray that can hold other objects that we add to it. We can resize the Form by using the size handles included in it. Users will use the Form to interact with your program. The Form's default name is Form1, which can be changed. The default text property of Form1 is also Form1, which appears on the title bar of the Form (see Figure 2.8).

2. Solution Explorer and Its Toolbar

On the right-hand corner of the screenshot, you should find the Solution Explorer (see Figure 2.9).

FIGURE 2.8   Windows Form.

FIGURE 2.9   Solution Explorer.

The Solution Explorer allows users to access all projects and files within the solution. This shows all of the projects that are included in the solution and the items each solution owns. As shown in Figure 2.9, each solution can have one or more projects. Each project can have one or more files. Under the solution name that we created, you will see the project name and Form1 name. We will discuss these files in more detail later on. In our case, you see the project folder (My Project) and Form file (Form1). You will also notice two tabs called Solution Explorer and Data Source. There is also a Context menu that can be activated by right-clicking on the Solution Explorer title bar or by clicking on the Windows Position smart tag.

On the top of the Solution Explorer window, is a toolbar. Once you move the mouse over each tab, a pop-up tool tip will display the name of each icon (see Figure 2.10).

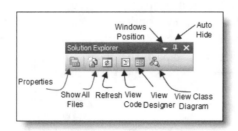

FIGURE 2.10   *Solution Explorer* toolbar.

We will now explain the nature of these icons.

- *Properties* shows the properties of the selected item. For example, if you have selected the Form object, then the Properties icon will show you all properties for the Form in the Properties window. You will use the Properties window for most of your projects.

■ *Show All Files* displays a list of all files included in the solution. You may want to hide or unhide all files by clicking on this icon. If all files are open, then you will see something resembling Figure 2.11.

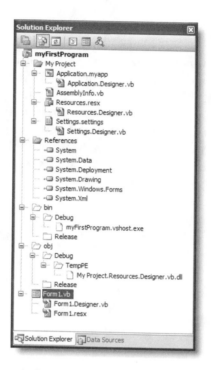

FIGURE 2.11   Show All Files.

■ *View Code* will take you to the code environment. This will open the code editor and allow you to enter new codes or revise the existing ones. A code block is shown in Figure 2.12.

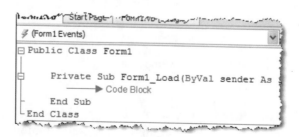

FIGURE 2.12   Code block within Code Editor.

- *View Designer* returns you to the design mode. Occasionally there is a need to switch between View Code and View Designer mode.
- *Refresh* refreshes the active window.
- *View Class Diagram* allows you to view the class.

3. Properties Window

The Properties window shows all of the properties for the selected objects. As we discussed in Chapter 1, you could think of a Properties window as a car's factory specifications, such as model, color, make, engine power, and so on. You can set the properties for the objects by selecting them from this window. Using this window allows you to set the properties for the objects more efficiently. However, we can set the properties through codes as well, which we will discuss later. Now we will take a look at the Properties window. While the Form is selected, look at the Properties window (see Figure 2.13).

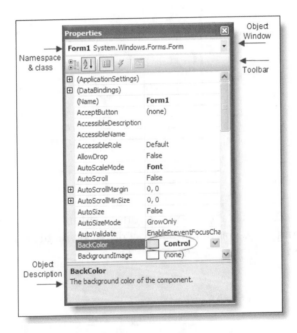

FIGURE 2.13   Properties window.

In the Properties window is a table that contains rows and columns. In the left column are the property names, and in the right column the property values are listed. Look at the circled property value of the BackColor property. Currently it shows the Control color, which is the default color given to it by Visual Basic. We will change the `BackColor` of our `Form` by clicking on the right column of the `BackColor` property while the `Form` object is selected. A drop-down arrow will appear next to the color rectangle shape (see Figure 2.14).

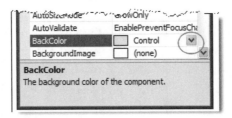

FIGURE 2.14 `BackColor` **property setting.**

Click on the down arrow to see the color palette shown in Figure 2.15. The figure shows the *Custom Palette* but the default is *System*. To switch between different color sets, just click on their tabs. On the Custom Palette, select the white color box from the pop-up palette. As soon as you click on your `Form`, you should notice that the `BackColor` of your `Form` changes to white.

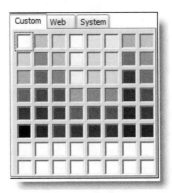

FIGURE 2.15 Color Palette set to custom colors. (Color version on companion CD-ROM)

Now, the `Form`'s `BackColor` is white and the property for it has changed to `White` as well (see Figure 2.16).

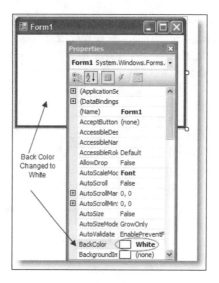

FIGURE 2.16 The Form's BackColor is white.

You will you notice a toolbar on the top of the Properties window (see Figure 2.17).

FIGURE 2.17 Properties window toolbar.

If you move your mouse over each icon, you should see a pop-up tool tip. Figure 2.17 shows those items.

- The *Categorized* icon *sorts* the properties based on their category.
- The *Alphabetic* icon *sorts* the properties alphabetically.
- The *Properties* icon *sorts* all of the properties based on the names of the properties.
- The *Event* icon *sorts* the properties according to their event names.
- The *Property Pages* is disabled and is used for *Custom properties*.
- There is no OK or Cancel button for the Properties window. Once you make your changes, you can see the result of your change immediately or after you click on the Form.

4. Toolbox

The *Toolbox* is a sliding control that is included within the IDE. The Toolbox has an auto hide feature, like the Solution Explorer window, and it is set to hide it by default but will appear once you move your mouse over it. The Toolbox is the rubber stamp example that we discussed in Chapter 1. You can drag and drop objects such as TextBoxes, Labels, and Buttons into your Form from the Toolbox, and you will be more productive and develop your project more quickly. The segments within the Toolbox are called tabs, and by clicking on the plus (+) sign next to the segments, you can expand them to access their items. The tabs will be collapsed once you click on the minus (–) sign of the tab. The Toolbox, which is not visible while you are working on your codes, can only be used in the design mode. It also displays icons that represent the object you want to use. The Toolbox is customizable and can be rearranged or include additional tabs (see Figure 2.18).

FIGURE 2.18 Toolbox tabs and items.

5. Document Window

The IDE consists of two types of windows:

- *Document* windows
- *Tool* windows

As explained before, tool windows, such as the Properties window and Solution Explorer, are available to design the document, which in our case is the Form. In addition to these windows, we can reference other windows, such as document windows, that are opened dynamically. You can access these opened documents by clicking on their tabs (see Figure 2.19).

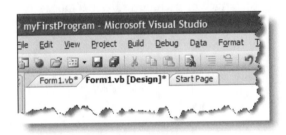

FIGURE 2.19   Document windows tabs.

It is also possible to view these documents as a *Multiple-Document Interface* (MDI). This option allows you to have all of your documents opened at once and move from one document to another by just clicking on them. You can change the default setting from Tabbed Documents to Multiple Document by following the following steps:

1. Click on the Tools menu item, and select Options from the drop-down list.
2. Click on the General page under the Environment folder.
3. Check the Multiple Document radio button under the Window Layout section to switch to MDI format (see Figure 2.20).

6. Toolbar

The *Toolbar* acts as a shortcut for the tasks that are performed more frequently. Rather than selecting these tasks from the menu, you can click on the corresponding icons on the toolbar and accomplish the same task. Figure 2.21 shows what you will see when you move your mouse over the toolbar.

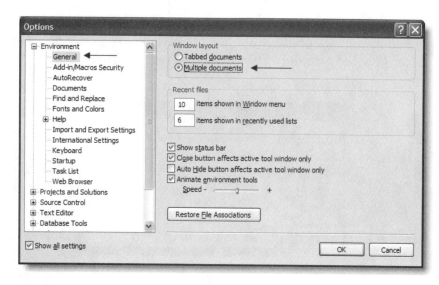

FIGURE 2.20   Changing the document layout.

FIGURE 2.21   Toolbar.

The toolbar shown in Figure 2.21 is the Standard toolbar. You can add more buttons by clicking on Toolbar Options.

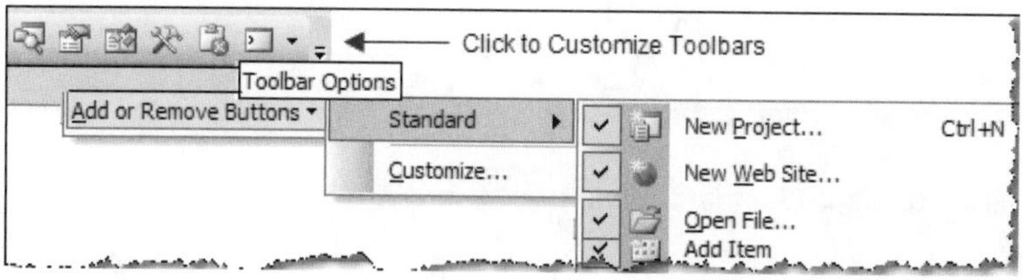

FIGURE 2.22   Adding more buttons to the Standard toolbar.

You can add more toolbars to your menu area by selecting the Customize button from Add or Remove buttons shown in Figure 2.22. Many different toolbars can be added to the menu bar to facilitate your tasks (see Figure 2.23).

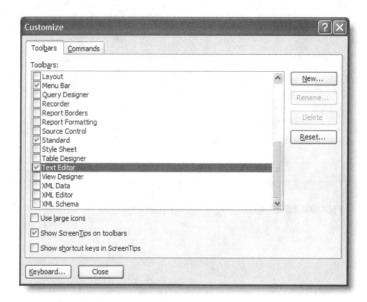

FIGURE 2.23 Customizing toolbars.

7. Menu Bar

If you have been working with Windows or Web applications, you must have seen menu bars, which are located beneath the Form's title bar. Menu bars contain menu items, such as File, Edit, View, and other related items. Menu bars can have shortcuts to minimize the need for using the mouse so often. Visual Basic 2005 comes with a menu bar to make programming tasks easier than before (see Figure 2.24).

FIGURE 2.24 Standard menu bar.

Restoring Windows

Occasionally, you might lose these windows by mistake. You can easily get them back by going to the View menu item and clicking on the window that has disappeared from your IDE (see Figure 2.25).

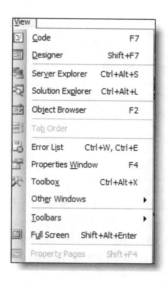

FIGURE 2.25   *View* menu item used to restore windows.

You can accomplish the same task by using the Windows function key or shortcut. For example, if you have lost the Properties window, hit F4 to get it back.

ADDING CONTROLS TO THE FORM USING THE SNAP LINE

You will learn how to use the Toolbox in other chapters. However, we want to be familiar with one control, which is called Button. You will be using this control in the next chapter and we will cover all of its characteristics later on. To add a Button in design mode, just move your mouse over the Toolbox, expand the *Common Controls* tab if it is not expanded already, click on the Button item and drag it to your form. You can also do this by double-clicking on the desired control, but the control will not be placed in the desired location. The Button was added to your Form. You can see the resize handles all around the Button (see Figure 2.26).

These handles allow you to resize the control from every side and angle. Now we will add another Button to the Form. While you are dragging the button into your

Form, the aligning snap line helps you align the new control with the existing ones (see Figure 2.27).

FIGURE 2.26 Resize handles around *Button* control.

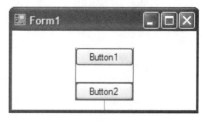

FIGURE 2.27 Aligning snap lines.

DOCKING

Occasionally programmers want to move the Tools window to a location in the IDE that is more convenient. Depending on your preference, you may want to move the Tools window to any location in IDE that adds to your productivity. Visual Studio 2005 comes with great docking features that guide you through docking these windows and snapping them in appropriate locations. The window that you want to dock must be *dockable*. To prepare a window for docking, right-click on the Tools window's title bar or just click on the Windows Position arrow and select Dockable from the list of options (see Figure 2.28).

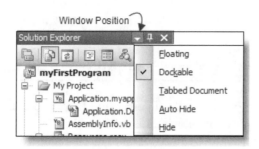

FIGURE 2.28 Selecting Dockable.

Once this is done, you can drag the Tools window toward the center of your IDE. A guide diamond appears in the middle of the IDE along with four other arrows that point toward each edge of the IDE (see Figure 2.29).

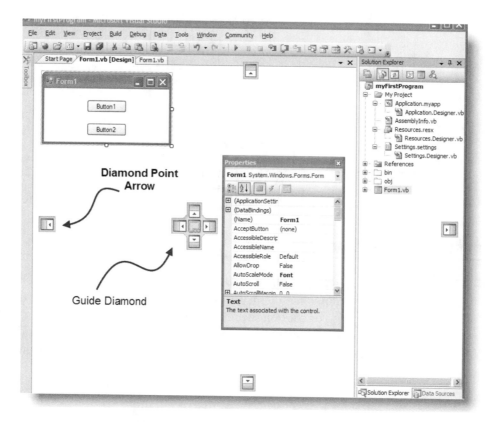

FIGURE 2.29 Docking guides.

When you find a position where the Tools window should land, move your mouse over the arrow that points toward the desired direction. At this time, a blue panel covers the docking location. Once you release the mouse, the Tools window will be snapped into its new place.

If you just want to move the Tools window to a new location without docking, hold the Ctrl key while you are dragging the window.

AUTO HIDE

Another useful feature of the Tools window is its *Auto Hide* capability. When the window is Auto Hide enabled, it slides into its tab and hides there until you move the mouse over it again. This will give you more room within your IDE for development (see Figure 2.30).

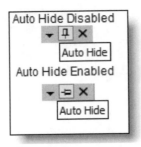

FIGURE 2.30 Setting the Auto Hide feature.

RESETTING THE LAYOUT

If you are not happy with the new layout, you can reset it to the default setting. Click on the Window menu item and select *Reset Window Layout* from the dropdown menu options or click on the related toolbar icon (see Figure 2.31). Once you click on this option, you will see a warning letting you know that your windows will be reset to the default setting. Click YES to proceed with this task (see Figure 2.32).

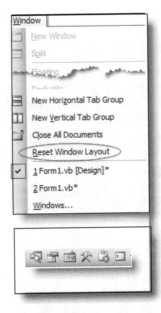

FIGURE 2.31 Resetting a window's layout through menu and toolbar.

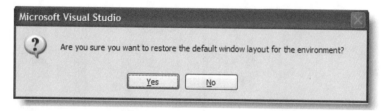

FIGURE 2.32 Warning message for resetting the windows.

SAVING THE PROJECT

There is nothing more frustrating than working on your project for hours only to lose it for some unknown reason. Visual Basic 2005 allows you to save your work automatically and allows you to restore your work after any unwanted interruptions. You can set your *autosave* and *recovery* features according to your needs. Click on Tools and pick Options from the drop-down list. Under the Environment, click on General and then click on the AutoRecover option. Check the AutoRecover checkbox and enter the values you desire (see Figure 2.33). To save your program, click on File. Then select the Save All option or click on the Save icon on the toolbar (see Figure 2.34). If this is the first time you are saving the solution, you will see the dialog box shown in Figure 2.35. You can also save your file by holding Ctrl-Shift-S.

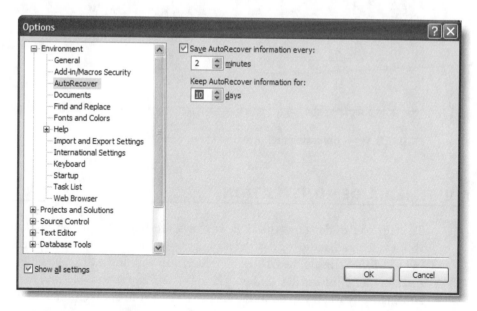

FIGURE 2.33 Setting AutoRecover page.

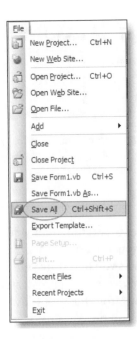

FIGURE 2.34 Save All from the File menu.

FIGURE 2.35 Confirming the location of saving the file.

MULTIMEDIA DEMONSTRATION

To help you understand the IDE windows, we have prepared a multimedia file (both video and audio) and saved it under the Chapter 2 folder in the accompanying CD-ROM. Inside the Chapter 2 folder, you will find a file called ide-explorer-final in the Multimedia folder. This is a self-extracting file and will execute automatically when you double-click it. Turn on your speaker to take advantage of the audio portion of it as well.

GETTING HELP

One of the most important resources available to you is the MSDN resources. This includes the online sources and files that are installed by Visual Studio 2005 on your hard drive. By using this valuable resource, you can find the syntax tips, sample codes, and other materials you need. You can search by Index or by Phrase (see Figure 2.36).

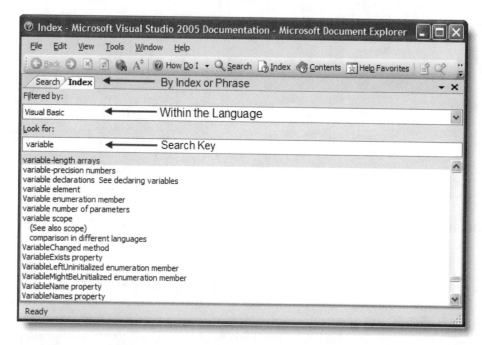

FIGURE 2.36 Getting Help by using the Help tab within IDE.

CODE SNIPPETS

To improve the programmers productivity, Visual Studio 2005 comes with another new feature called Code Snippet. Programmers can insert many ready-to-use codes into their programs by using the IntelliSense and Code Snippet features and add their own codes to the existing codes by using the *Code Snippets Manager*. This feature is very helpful to minimize the amount of typing you have to do. It allows you to select the most common type of statements from the list of existing codes and insert them into your codes and revise the inserted code to fit your program. We will briefly show you how to apply the existing codes to your program.

Right-click anywhere within your code editor and select the Insert Snippet drop-down menu (see Figure 2.37). As soon as you click on the Insert Snippet option, you will see a list of folders. Visual Basic Language is one of them (see Figure 2.38).

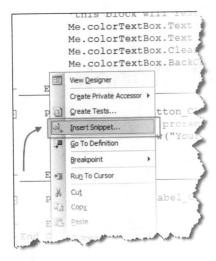

FIGURE 2.37 Using Insert Snippet.

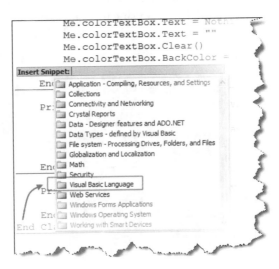

FIGURE 2.38 Finding the Visual Basic Language folder.

Now double-click on the Visual Basic Language folder to open it. You will see the list of many ready-to-use codes. You can select any of them as a test and click on the Tab key to insert it into your program (see Figure 2.39). Once the code is inserted, you can click on the Edit menu item and click on Undo to remove the insertion.

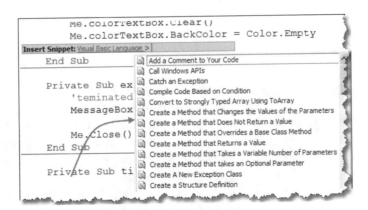

FIGURE 2.39 Inserting Visual Basic Language Snippet.

You can also add your own IntelliSense Code Snippet to the existing codes. Just to see how it is done, click on Tools and select Code Snippets Manager (see Figure 2.40). The next screen shows you how to add or remove codes from the Code Snippets folders (see Figure 2.41).

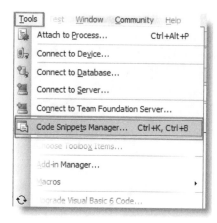

FIGURE 2.40   Getting into Code Snippets Manager.

FIGURE 2.41   Using Code Snippets Manager.

SUMMARY

In this chapter, we focused on the Integrated Development Environment and showed you how to open and save your programs. We also talked about the Properties window, Solution Explorer, and other tools you need to develop programs. By using the Toolbox, you can easily drag and drop controls to your Form and manipulate them for business or personal uses.

Next

In Chapter 3, we will discuss the programming concepts, problem-solving techniques, Naming Conventions, and tools such as TextBoxes, Labels, Buttons, Picture-Box, and many more. We will also cover Design, Compile, and Execution modes.

DISCUSSION QUESTIONS

1. Is it possible to develop Visual Basic programs without using the toolbox? Search the MSDN resources to find the answer to this question.
2. Start a new project and explore the Properties window for the form. What is the function of BackColor?
3. What is the hierarchy of solution files? Please explain.
   Is the Form an object? Justify your response.
   What does Save As do in Visual Basic? Please explain. Search the MSDN resources and note your findings.

Exercise

Use the View tab and try to hide and unhide the following IDE components:

1. Solution Explorer
2. Properties widow
3. Start page
4. Toolbox

Key Terms

- Alphabetic
- Categorized
- Forms
- IDE
- Solution Explorer contents
- Toolbox items
- Windows application
- Windows template

3 | Writing Programs

PROBLEM-SOLVING TECHNIQUES

The first two chapters introduced various terms and tools that you need to write programs. You probably think you are ready to start coding. Well, not quite. Before you write any codes, you should get familiar with problem-solving techniques. You need to identify inputs, processes, and outputs that the program will deal with, and you must be able to define the problem that your program will solve. By breaking down your large problems into smaller segments, you can solve them more easily. You also need to develop decision-making skills to be able to write sound codes. The *problem definition* is probably the most important step any programmer needs to take before he can write a program. Let us use an analogy to explore this concept. You are a manager of a hotel. You receive complaints about the quality of your hotel's restaurant services. Before you can solve this problem, you need to identify factors that could be causing the complaints, such as:

- Your cooks prepare food that is not desirable to the majority of your customers.
- Your customers are not truthful about their claims.
- Your competition's food is better than yours.
- Your menu does not include international food.
- The menu prices are high, and that raises your customers' expectations.
- Not all menu items are available at all times.
- Your room service is not timely enough.
- The dessert menu does not have much variety.
- The menu does not offer low-fat food.
- Customers cannot find vegetarian items.
- Restaurant hours are not accommodating your customers' needs.
- Menu items include more red meats than white meats.
- There are too many deep fried items.
- Your hostess is not familiar with the ingredients of the menu items.
- There are no nutrition facts available.
- Most ingredients are frozen.
- The food is served too late and often it is too cold.
- Substitution of items is not allowed.
- Discounts are not available for large groups.
- No coupons are offered for special occasions.

As you can see, there are many factors that could be the source of your customers' unhappiness. Which one, or what combination of factors, has caused the problems? Which one is the real problem? How would you define the problem? Before you can define the problem, you need to do research, starting with narrowing down the customers' complaints as much as possible. You can create questionnaires, interview the unhappy customers, or talk to your staff or hire food experts to analyze the problem. These tools enable you to be more accurate in your problem definition. Problem definition is the most important step of the problem-solving phase and cannot be skipped. There is nothing worse than spending time and money to solve the wrong problem. During the analysis phase, you would differentiate between the real problem and the symptoms of the problem. For example, sneezing is a symptom of a cold or allergy. Smoke is a symptom of fire, and low sales volume could be the result of poor marketing. However, you need to focus on the problem, not its symptoms. The symptoms lead you to the actual problems. Many managers try to solve the symptoms rather than the actual problems.

Once you identify the problem, you need to come up with the *statement of the problem*. When you prepare the statement of the problem, you need to consider these questions:

- How did you learn about the problem?
- Why is it important to the management to know about it? How would this problem affect the business in the short term and long term?
- How much do you know about the problem? Is your research done or still in progress?
- Did you make any assumptions, or does all data that you gathered represent facts?
- How objective are you in your assessment? Is it based on your personal experience, or do you have other facts to back it up?

The language you use in your problem definition should be simple and clear. Let's look at one example for the restaurant case that we discussed: In the past two years, management has received complaints about the quality of service at our restaurant located on the first floor of our hotel. The sales volume in the past two years has decreased by 28%. The survey indicates the following:

- 15% of customers said the food was served cold at lunch time.
- 30% of customers said the room service was very slow and there were a great deal of mix-ups in the orders.
- 20% of customers said prices were 40 to 50% higher than food sold elsewhere.
- 10% of customers said they had to wait a long time before the food was served. There were no statistics on how long they had to wait.
- 5% of customers said the menu items are vague and they do not show the ingredients.
- 5% of customers said they didn't care about the quality of restaurant service and they were happy about it.
- 5% of customers declined to respond.
- 10% of customers were not happy with the lack of vegetarian items.

A flowchart could present this information better. We will show you a programming problem statement, flowchart, and other tools later on.

DATA AND INFORMATION

In computer terms, data is raw or unorganized facts. Data could be characters A–Z; numbers 0–9; all special characters such as $, #, and @; or a combination of all of these. The data may or may not be meaningful to all people. For example, weather-forecasting data that is collected by a satellite does not tell ordinary people any-thing. However, if this data is processed by an expert or computer and translated into a language that people can understand, then it is called *information*. Organiz-ing, classifying, reformatting, sorting, and calculating are processes that can convert data as an unorganized or raw fact into organized and meaningful output or infor-mation. We use programs to transform data into information.

WHAT IS A PROGRAM?

Programs are instructions that we give the computer to perform specific tasks. These tasks are the combination of sequenced and nonsequenced tasks. Let's say you ask a babysitter to watch your kids while you are at a concert. You have a list of things you want your babysitter do:

1. Arrive at 7 p.m. Do not ring the doorbell. Knock on the door.
2. At 7:30, warm up the food in the refrigerator for 45 seconds and wait 2 minutes before you serve it to my child. He has been sick for the last 3 days, so please give him his medicine before you feed him. His medicine is in a pink container and is located on the top shelf above the refrigerator. You should only give him one spoon of medicine. If he resists taking it, do not force him. It is OK to skip a dose at night.
3. After dinner, let him watch a movie. The movie is already in the VCR. If he wants to watch another movie instead, let him pick one from the small library above the TV.
4. He likes to play computer games. If you know how to play it, please play with him until he gets tired of it.
5. If he gets sleepy, please put him in bed. He likes to hear stories before he sleeps. There are some storybooks on the bottom shelf of his bookcase. Please read books until he goes to sleep.
6. We should be home before 10 p.m. We have left our cell phone number on the fridge. Call us if you have any questions.
7. Feel free to fix a meal for yourself.

THE NATURE OF THE INSTRUCTIONS

In the example above, you will notice the following:

■ Some instructions were *sequenced*. In sequenced instructions, steps will be taken after each other in specific orders. For example, the babysitter needed to arrive before she could knock on the door.

■ You can also see that the babysitter needed to make some decisions. For example, if the child wanted to play a game, she would play it with him. This is called *selection*. Under selection structure, steps do not need to be in sequence and will depend on the condition. The babysitter would not play the game if the child did not ask for it.

■ You will also notice some repetition. For example, the babysitter should play games as long as the child is not tired of it. This is called *loop* or *repetition*. Under this type of structure, the actions will be repeated as long as a condition exists.

Now that you are more familiar with these terms, let's apply them to a real computer program. We will design a program that introduces three colors to children:

■ Yellow
■ Green
■ Red

Problem Statement, Input, Process, and Output

Here is the problem statement in this project: Design an interactive program that introduces three colors to kindergarten kids. This program will have five Buttons, one Label, and one TextBox. The text color (ForeColor) of the TextBox will change as the user clicks on different color Buttons.

The input would come from the user. The user will click on different Buttons to perform different tasks. These Buttons are Yellow, Green, Red, Clear, and Exit.

Processes would be displaying text, changing the back color of the TextBox, clearing the TextBox, and exiting the program. The outputs would be the colored TextBox and texts. Let's look at what we want to create in Figure 3.1.

FIGURE 3.1 Finished design.

Naming Conventions

There are different ways that you can use to name your objects and identifiers. This is known as naming conventions. Before we go further, we need to learn about standards for naming your controls. The new naming convention that Microsoft recommends is different from what we have used in the past.

Pascal Casing

Under this naming convention, you capitalize the first letter of the identifier and each subsequent name. Here are some examples:

- `TextAlign`
- `ForeColor`

Camel Casing

The difference between this method and the Pascal casing method is that the first letter of the identifier is lowercase:

- `textAlign`
- `foreColor`

Uppercase

With this method, all letters in the identifier are capitalized:

- `BACKCOLOR`

In Visual Basic 2005, use the following guidelines:

- Do not use underscore in the names you use.
- Use Pascal casing for all public members, types, and namespace. Example: `ForeColor`
- Use Camel casing for all parameters names. Example: `totalPriceDouble`
- Capitalize two-character acronyms Example: IO

Table 3.1 shows some of the object naming conventions and examples. Refer to the MSDN resources for other tips on naming rules: *http://msdn2.microsoft.com/en-us/library/ms229043.aspx.*

TABLE 3.1 Naming Conventions

Control Names	Example
CheckBox 7	loadPictureCheckBox
ComboBox	englishComboBox
Button	openButton
ColorDialog	customDialogBox
DataGridView	titleDataGridView
Form	telephoneSurveyForm
GroupBox	statesGroupBox
ImageList	photoAlbumImageList
Label	firstNameLabel
ListBox	paymentListBox
MenuStrip	editMenuStrip
RadioButton	choicesRadioButton
PictureBox	myPicturePictureBox
TextBox	lastNameTextBox
Timer	animationTimer

How to Name Objects

It is very important that we name our objects according to the current standards. Object names must be meaningful and appropriate. Here are a few rules you should consider when you name your objects:

- The name of the object should start with a letter. However, you can use an underscore as the first character, as well.
- The name can consist of an underscore, letters, and digits.
- The name cannot be a reserved word by itself, but a reserved word may be used as a part of the object name. For example, *exit* is a reserved word and cannot be used as a solid name for an object. However, exitButton is an acceptable object name.
- No other special character, such as $ or a space, can be used in object names.
- As a good practice, always start your control names by using a lowercase character. Other words can be added to the object name to make it more meaningful. Start the additional words with uppercase characters. For example, as

shown in Table 3.1, `telephoneSurveyForm` is a descriptive name that can represent the nature of the `Form`.

Avoid abbreviations as much as possible. Occasionally we may use abbreviations in examples to expedite the process, but in the real world we shouldn't do that. Always spell words out.

Knowing the Nature of Our Tools

Before we use Visual Basic tools, let us review their basic functions.

Forms

A `Form` is a class that is used as a primary user's interface. We place other controls or objects on the `Form` so the user can access them. By using the `Form`'s standard features, we can minimize or maximize it, and we can resize or close it. To resize a `Form`, simply use the size handle and drag it until you reach the desired size. Once we put other controls on the `Form`, they become a part of the `Form`'s collection, which we will talk about in more detail in other chapters.

TextBoxes

A `TextBox`'s primary function is to receive the user's input, which can be stored in temporary storage for future use. However, you can use them to display output as well by assigning values to the `TextBoxes`. The following will assign a value to a `TextBox` and display "Mike" on the screen:

```
Textbox1.Text="Mike"
```

Labels

`Labels` are used to display data or deliver messages to the users. The user will not be able to alter the content of a `label`. Consider a `Label` as a tool that is used to display outputs. We can assign values to the `Labels`. The following will display the word Mike:

```
Label1.Text="Mike"
```

GroupBoxes

`GroupBoxes` are containers that can hold other controls. There are many features for this control, but in this project, we use it to organize our `Form`. (We will expand our discussions on the `GroupBox` in later chapters.) Once you put controls inside a

GroupBox, Visual Basic will treat them as a single control. If you move the GroupBox to a different location of the Form, the controls inside it will be moved as well. If you change properties, such as BackColor, ForeColor, or text size, the change will affect the GroupBox and controls within it. If the GroupBox is deleted, all of the controls that you placed inside it will be gone. The GroupBox has a text property that can be used to place a Label for the GroupBox.

PictureBoxes

A PictureBox is a tool that can be used to display images. This control has many useful properties, including BorderStyle and SizeMode, which will be discussed later. Once you place the PictureBox on your Form, you can import images into it. Many image files including .gif, .bmp, and .jpg can be imported into a PictureBox by placing the images into a Resource file list, which includes all of the resources that are attached to your project.

ToolTips

ToolTips are pop-up messages that are displayed when the user moves the mouse over an object. This component can be added to a Form and be available to all other objects within the Form. ToolTips allow the programmer to provide more descriptive help tips for each object.

Properties

As explained in Chapters 1 and 2, properties are attributes that are used to identify an object. For example, Name is one of an object's properties. We use the Name property to refer to an object in our codes. Let's briefly talk about some common properties that we use in programming and utilize them in the examples in this chapter. You do not need to remember the names of these properties. The Properties window and IntelliSense feature of Visual Basic will help you remember them during the design and coding of your projects. You assign values to these properties, so they behave differently from their default settings.

Name: The Name property is the most important property that each object can carry. We talked about the naming rules above, but you also need to know that names must be unique within each namespace. Therefore, in each Form, each object must carry a unique name. If you choose a name for an object and accidentally use the same name for another object, Visual Basic will not accept it and will issue you a warning.

Text: The Text property is another common property that is used to display a text within that object. For example, when you set the Text property of a Label to "Please Type in Your Name," the Label will display this message for the users.

Multiline, ForeColor, and **BackColor:**   The MultiLine property needs to be set to True to allow the TextBox to display multiple lines of text. ForeColor and Back-Color carry the text color and background color of the object. This can be done at design time or through codes.

PasswordChar: The PasswordChar property is a TextBox property that forces the typed characters to be displayed in a specific format. For example, if you set the value of this property to "&" all characters the user inputs will be converted to the & character. The common character that is used for this property is asterisk (*) so the user password is not readable.

StartPosition: The StartPosition property is used for the Form that tells Visual Basic where on the screen the Form should be displayed.

BorderStyle: The BorderStyle property allows you to choose the desired border style for an object. If the object carries a border property, then you can chose from FixedSingle, Fixed3D, or None.

TextAlign: The TextAlign property will position the text in the specified location of the control. For example, if it is set to MiddleCenter, the text will appear in the center of the object.

AutoSize: The AutoSize property can have the values of True or False. If it is set to True, the size will be adjusted automatically depending on the size of input. The Locked property can carry a True or False value as well. Once you set it to True, you will not be able to edit it.

SizeMode: The SizeMode property allows you to set values such as AutoSize, Normal, Zoom, StretchImage, and CenterImage. These SizeMode properties of PictureBoxes will be explained in detail later. Other properties will be introduced through examples.

Visible: Setting this property to False forces the control to be invisible at run time. Occasionally there is a need to use this property under specific conditions. Most of the time programmers use this property to hide objects and make them visible when a special condition is met.

IntelliSense

IntelliSense is a feature of Visual Basic Editor that helps you complete your codes without the need to remember all properties or methods. You can write the codes and get help from IntelliSense while you are in the code editor environment. You can type the name of the class or structure and a period (.) after it to activate Intel-liSense, which will list all valid members of that class so you can scroll through them and select the one that fits your purpose. Once you find the item you are looking for, you can press Tab to insert the item into your code.

In our project, you will see that as soon as you place a period after colorTextBox, the IntelliSense drop-down list appears and shows all valid properties for the TextBox phrase. You can make it more accurate by typing a few characters of the item you want to find (see Figure 3.2).

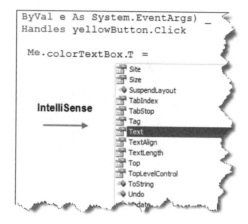

FIGURE 3.2 IntelliSense in action.

Namespace

The .NET technology uses a new term called *namespace*. We use namespace to or-ganize object names as we do in organization charts. It follows a hierarchy to ad-dress classes and keeps track of them. Consider this analogy: Your friend has two kids. He bought two identical toys for them to prevent problems. However, he bought these two toys from two different stores. Both stores had a return policy. One would accept the toy up to three weeks after the date it was purchased and the other one would accept it up to four weeks after it was purchased. The original packaging was saved in a safe place. However, to make sure these two identical toys were not mistaken, the father asked his kids to put their initials on the toys. The toy with the initial R belonged to Robert and the toy with the initial M belonged to Mike. Your friend documented this transaction in his notebook as follows:

■ Store_1_Downtown_Portland_Robert_Train_Toy
■ Store_2_Downtown_Beaverton_Mike_Train_Toy

The initials on these two items have no effect on the toys' functions. They just help the kids recognize them. Let us apply this simple idea to Visual Basic programming. As you saw before, once you placed a control such as `TextBox` on your `Form`, it became part of the `Form's` collection item. Visual Basic uses a hierarchy to access the `TextBox` class:

```
System.Windows.Forms.TextBox
```

The phrase `System.Windows.Forms` is known as the namespace and includes the `TextBox` class. If we place a `TextBox` on a Web `Form`, we will see the following:

```
System.Web.UI.WebControls.TextBox
```

The namespace for this `TextBox` placed on the Web `Form` is `System.Web.UI.Web-Controls`. This is similar to what your friend did to distinguish his kids' toys. Both `TextBoxes` have the same function, but they are used by two different namespaces. As stated, this hierarchy has internal usage. You do not have to type the namespace phrase for using a class.

Assembly

Some people use the terms *assembly* and namespace interchangeably. As explained above, namespace is a logical way to organize names to prevent system collision. Namespace is used to group the codes logically. Assembly, on the other hand, takes care of the physical grouping of the codes. The assembly and namespace are there to complement each other. Assembly contains the resources and types a unit needs to perform. Without the assembly, the common language runtime cannot function. The assembly and namespace can have the same name but they function differently.

Reserved Words

Like human languages, Visual Basic has its own rules, grammar, punctuation, and vocabulary. The vocabulary that Visual Basic uses is known as *reserved words* that cannot be used as programmers' supplied identifiers. There are many reserved words in Visual Basic that you should be familiar with. Words such as `next`, `exit`, `friend`, `global`, `static`, `if`, `when`, and `return`, are reserved for Visual Basic and cannot be used by themselves for naming variables or objects. For example, the following statement is illegal in Visual Basic: `Next = 20`. However, the following is an acceptable statement if it is declared prior to use: `nextInteger = 20`. As you can see, you can use reserved words along with other names. Here is another acceptable name: `exitButton`.

EXAMPLE 1

Based on the steps we covered in Chapter 2 and the screenshot shown in Figure 3.1, create a new project and name it `myfirst_visualBasic_project1`.

Now, select the `Form` by clicking on the `Form` title bar and change the `Name` property from `Form1` to `myFirstForm`. Scroll down and change the `form`'s `Text` property from `Form1` to `My First Try!`

Now, click on the `Form` again and you will notice that the title bar wording has changed to the new title. When we name our controls, we should follow the naming conventions explained above.

ADDING CONTROLS TO THE FORM

Adding Labels

In Chapter 1, we briefly showed you how to add controls to your `Form`. Now we need to expand our discussion and provide you with more detail. A `Form` is an interface that the user sees as a communication tool to interact with your program. In the first step, we will add a `Label` to our `Form` to be seen by the user. Move the mouse over the Toolbox to unhide it and then navigate through the tools. Look for the Common Controls category and click on the plus sign next to it to expand the list. If you see a minus sign instead, it means the list is already expanded. Once you find the `Label` control, either double-click on it or just drag it and drop it into your `Form` (see Figure 3.3). We suggest that you drag the objects to have control over where they land.

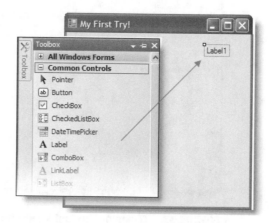

FIGURE 3.3 Adding `Label` controls to your `Form`.

Highlight the Label, and move your mouse over the Properties window. Find the Name property and change it from Label1 to titleLabel. Now find the Text property in the Properties window and change it from Label1 to My First Program! To add text to the Text container, you need to click on the drop-down arrow (see Figure 3.4). While the Label is still selected, click on the Font property and change the Font to 16 points (see Figure 3.5).

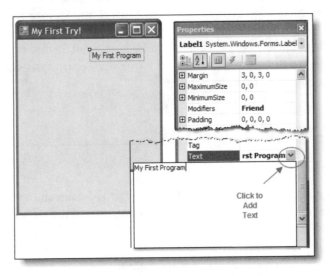

FIGURE 3.4   Changing the Text property of the label.

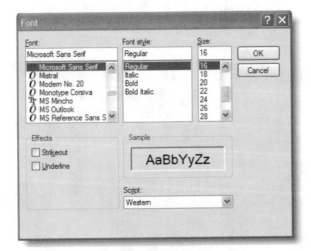

FIGURE 3.5   Changing the font size of the Label control.

Now click on the ForeColor property of the Label and pick the Custom tab from the dialog box. From the color pallette, select red. On the right corner of the Label is a small square indicating that the Label is set to AutoSize. This means you cannot resize your Label control; it will be adjusted automatically. If you need to change the size of it manually, you must set the AutoSize property to False.

Adding Buttons

Now we will add a Button to our Form. Use the same method as the one used to add the Label. As you are placing the Button into your Form, an aligning blue snap line will appear on the edge of the control, as you saw in previous chapters. This snap line will appear any time you want to add new controls to the existing ones. Highlight the Button you just added to your Form and move your mouse to the Properties window. Change the name of the control from Button1 to yellowButton (see Figure 3.6).

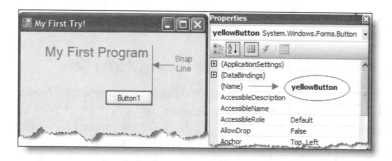

FIGURE 3.6   Changing the Name property.

Now scroll down and change the Text property from Button1 to &Yellow (see Figure 3.7). You will notice an ampersand (&) before the Y character. This is a shortcut, and we will discuss its function soon. You may also notice the size handles around the Button that you added to your Form. These handles allow you to resize the Button in vertical and horizontal directions.

Adding Shortcuts

Some users use their keyboards more than their mices, and making the program convenient for the majority of users should be the programmer's main objective. Most Windows programs are written in a way that responds to both mouse and keyboard actions. We can easily add shortcuts to our Visual Basic program. Shortcuts are also known as hot keys or access keys. Once the hot key is added, the user can use Alt+ the character that has been defined as a hot key to activate that Button.

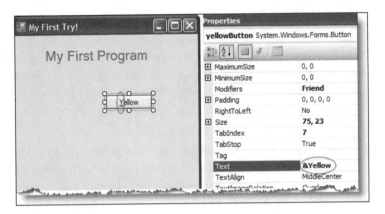

FIGURE 3.7   Changing the `Text` property value.

As shown in Figure 3.7, the designated hot key is underlined, so the user knows which character should be hit with the Alt key.

Setting Up a Windows Environment for Showing Access Keys

It is important that we set up our Windows environment to recognize the hot keys. Right-click anywhere on your desktop and select Properties from the Context menu options (see Figure 3.8). On the desktop Display Properties dialog box, click on the Appearance tab (see Figure 3.9). While you are in the Display Properties page, click on the Effects button to bring up the Effects page and make sure the checkbox with the text "*Hide underlined letters for keyboard navigation until I press the Alt key*" is unchecked (see Figure 3.10). Please note that the screenshot in Figure 3.10 is from the Windows XP Pro Operating System. You may see some differences between this screenshot and your own operating system.

FIGURE 3.8   Selecting the desktop properties.

FIGURE 3.9 Setting the appearance of Windows.

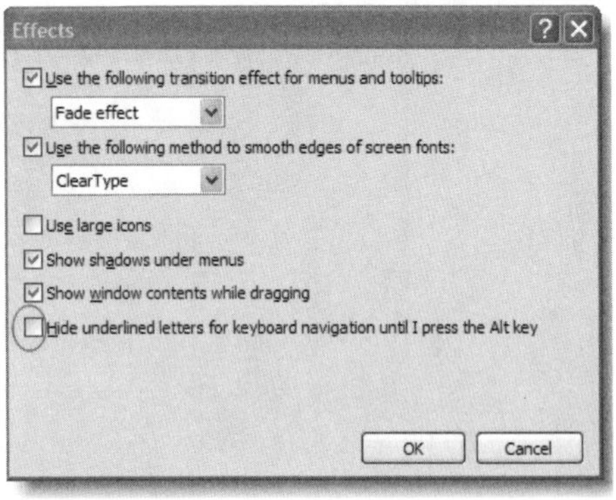

FIGURE 3.10 The Effects page.

Adding More Buttons

You just need to add four more Buttons. Let us change the Name property of the next Button to greenButton and the Text property of the same Button to &Green. Add another Button and change its Name property to redButton and its Text property to &Red. Add one more Button and name it clearButton and change its Text property to &Clear.

Add the last Button and call it exitButton and change its Text property to E&xit. Now we need to add a TextBox to our Form. Once you add the TextBox, change its Name property to colorTextBox. While the TextBox is selected, you will be able to see the size handles on the left and right sides of it, which allow you to resize the control horizontally but not vertically. As default, TextBox is set to display a single line of text. To allow multiple lines of texts within one TextBox you need to set the Multi-line property to True. You can also click on the *Smart Task* arrow or *Smart Tag*, which is located in the upper-right corner of the TextBox, and check the Multiline checkbox in the dialog box. Once you set the Multiline property to True, you can drag the TextBox size handle toward the bottom of the Form and make it longer (see Figure 3.11). We have added some of the controls that we needed and changed their names according to the naming conventions.

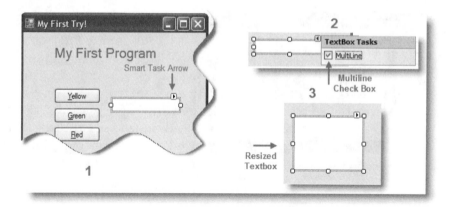

FIGURE 3.11   Resizing the `TextBox` by using the `Multiline` Smart Task arrow.

Rearranging Controls

Let's look at some other possibilities. In some cases, we need to rearrange the control's location or change its size. For this `Form`, we want to increase the size of the `Buttons`. Select the first `Button` on the `Form`, which we named `yellowButton`, and drag the center handle toward the right to make it bigger. Now, unselect this `Button` and select the last `Button` on the `Form`, which we named `exitButton`. Hold down the Shift key and select all other `Buttons` on the `Form` (see Figure 3.12).

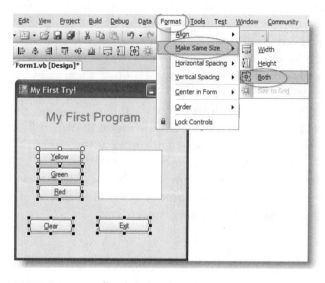

FIGURE 3.12   Adjusting the size of `Buttons`.

Adding ToolTip

It is time to add another useful component to your project: ToolTip. Once you add this component to any control, the user will see a pop-up message when he moves the mouse over this control. The ToolTip component is added to the Component Tray, which becomes accessible to all other controls. A component is a reusable class that can interact with the other controls, so once you add it, all other objects in your Form have access to it and can use new instances of it. After adding this control, select it and change a few things in its Properties window. Click on the ToolTip icon drop-down arrow and pick one of the options, such as Info (see Figure 3.13).

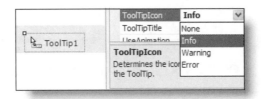

FIGURE 3.13   Selecting a global icon for the ToolTip component.

Add text, such as "Please Note," to the ToolTipTitle property of the ToolTip component. The text you added is global as well and is available to all controls within the Form, but you can customize the individual controls' ToolTip messages. Change the Name property of this component from ToolTip1 to colorToolTip. Select the YellowButton control and add the following text to its colorToolTip property: "This Button Will Change the Backcolor of the TextBox to Yellow" (see Figure 3.14). Now, hit F5 and move your mouse over the *Yellow* Button. A small MessageBox will pop up and stay on the screen for a few seconds (see Figure 3.15). Do the same for all the other Buttons.

It is a good habit to rename your control names *before* you run the program. If you change their names after you have added codes to the controls' subprocedure, the new names will not appear in the heading of the subprocedure.

Would your program work even if you did not change the control names? The answer is yes. It still runs, but it becomes hard to keep track of the codes as the program grows.

You are now done with the design part of your program. Click on File and select Save All to save your program. You will see the Save Project dialog box. Either click on the Save button or change the location and then save your project. Now, hit F5 to execute the program and click on all Buttons. Other than the ToolTips, nothing shows up.

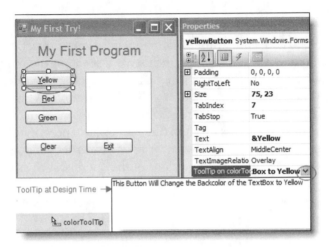

FIGURE 3.14 ToolTip component in design mode.

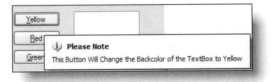

FIGURE 3.15 ToolTip component at Run Time.

Coding

In the previous step, when you executed the program by hitting F5 and clicked on the Buttons, nothing happened because we did not instruct the program to do anything. Now it is time to give life to the program we designed and instruct each Button to perform a specific task. In this program, we provide instructions for each Button to react to the user's actions. Double-click on the Yellowbutton control and get into the code editor. We are going to place a code under each Button, so when the user clicks them, they will react.

Events, Procedures, and Event Handlers

Each object has many *events* that can be used by programmers. When the user interacts with the Form by clicking on a Button, moving the mouse over a control, or double-clicking on an object, a signal is sent to the Form that something just happened. The signal tells the Form that the user needs attention. The Form in return decides on how to handle the user's request. Each event has its own *event handler procedure*. For example, Click is different from Double Click, and the program will handle them differently. The instructions you provide for handling each event will be placed inside a block called *subprocedure*. Let's double-click on the *Yellow* Button and look at it closely (see Figure 3.16).

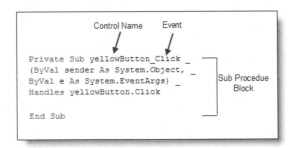

FIGURE 3.16   Event handler subprocedure.

Visual Basic program codes will be written inside a block called a subprocedure. The class-level variables and constants are declared outside procedures. We will be talking about these in later chapters. Many procedures can be created and used within a Form. The yellowButton subprocedure starts with the keyword Sub and ends with the keyword End Sub. The subprocedure also includes the name and the event the object is using. For our example, it shows Private Sub yellowButton_Click. Once you double-click on an object, the default subprocedure for that object will be opened to handle the event. Notice that the block is created and named automatically and all you need to do is to put your own codes inside the Sub and End Sub block.

```
Private Sub yellowButton_Click _
(ByVal sender As System.Object, _
ByVal e As System.EventArgs) _
Handles yellowButton.Click


End Sub
```

In this book, we will list the entire subprocedures, not just the programmer-supplied codes. The programmer-supplied code appears in *italics*. This way you know where the codes should be inserted. You should use only the programmer-supplied codes and ignore the codes that are supplied by Visual Basic Editor. In the design mode, any time you double-click on a Button, the Click subprocedure will be opened by default.

Assignment Statement

The assignment statement is used to assign a value, which is on the right side of the equation, to the property of the object, or a variable, which is on the left side of the operator. Here are some examples:

```
A=20
```

As you can see, the value of A is 20 now. Let's look at the following:

```
Me.colorTextbox.Text="20"
```

In the above statement, we are assigning "20" to the Text property of the TextBox called colorTextbox. From this point on, the value of colorTextBox.Text is 20.

Now, apply what you learned here to our project. As you may remember from our problem statement, the *Yellow* Button will change the background color of the Text to yellow and will display the word "Yellow" inside the TextBox. To accomplish this task, we need to use the assignment statement. As stated above, we assign values to the property of an object or variables. We will talk about variables later. Here is another example of an assignment statement:

```
Me.colorTextBox.Text = "Yellow"
```

Type this statement in the yellowButton subprocedure. Remember that you need to double-click on the Button to add this code:

```
Private Sub yellowButton_Click _
(ByVal sender As System.Object, _
ByVal e As System.EventArgs) _
Handles yellowButton.Click

Me.colorTextBox.Text = "Yellow"

End Sub
```

This causes Visual Basic to display the text "Yellow" inside the TextBox. Notice that the programmer's supplied code appears in italic. In this book, every time you see codes in italic, it means those codes are generated by us not Visual Basic.

Me Keyword and Collection

Notice that we added Me before our one-line statement. Me is the current instance of the object you are using, which is the Form. Me can be used to address the controls you have placed on the Form. For example, you could address a TextBox that you put on your Form like this:

```
Me.colorTextBox.Text = Nothing
```

As long as you consider yourself a beginner, try to use Me even though it is not required in most cases, and your program will work without any problem. By using the Me keyword, you will be referencing valid control names that are currently placed on the Form and the chance of misspelling will be minimized. As you put a period (.) after the Me keyword, notice that Visual Basic Editor will show you the names of all controls and methods that you placed on the Form (see Figure 3.17). This is done through the IntelliSense feature that we discussed before. Once you have placed the controls on your Form, you have added them to the Form's collection. A *collection* is a group of items that are gathered within one unit and will function as intended. These items include properties, methods, functions, and so on. You will become more familiar with collections later on.

Now that you know what Me means, let us use it in our program.

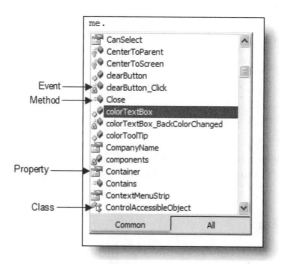

FIGURE 3.17   Using the Me keyword.

Methods

As explained in Chapter 1, each object can perform specific tasks according to the method we choose for it. A method is an action that is taken by the control. Many predefined methods are associated with the object and can be called within the program. You can also write your own methods. When you type the name of the object followed by a period (.), the IntelliSense feature of the code editor will show you the list of classes, methods, properties, and so on. Figure 3.17 shows some of the items identified by their icons. Methods also require parentheses, which are supplied by the editor.

MouseMove **and** MouseLeave **Events**

We can explain methods and events by using the MouseMove and MouseLeave events as examples. MouseMove is an event that uses an Event Handler method. Once the Mouse-Move event occurs, the Event Handler method is called to take care of it. The code that we place under each MouseMove Event Handler is executed once the mouse moves over an object. When the user moves the mouse away from the object, the Mouse-Leave Event Handler method will be executed. These methods are placed under a related event subprocedure for that control. Almost everything the user does on a computer can be detected. For example, when he clicks, we can call the Click Event Handler subprocedure to take action. Some events are irrelevant and we do not want to handle them. This concept will be explained in detail later on.

Double-click on the *Exit* Button and add the following method inside the exit-Button subprocedure:

```
Private Sub exitButton_Click _
    (ByVal sender As System.Object, _
    ByVal e As System.EventArgs) _
    Handles exitButton.Click

    Me.Close()

End Sub
```

By doing this, you will instruct the program to terminate the current active Form by closing it. Once the user clicks on the Exit Button, the application will be terminated.

Adding More Codes

By placing the assignment statement inside the Button_Click Event subprocedure, we gave the following instructions to the Visual Basic program: If the user clicks on YellowButton, then display the word *Yellow* inside the TextBox. Now we need to change the background color of the TextBox to yellow as well. We will use another assignment statement to accomplish this task. Type the following assignment statement inside the yellowButton subprocedure:

```
Private Sub yellowButton_Click _
(ByVal sender As System.Object, _
ByVal e As System.EventArgs) _
Handles yellowButton.Click

    Me.colorTextBox.Text = "Yellow"
    Me.colorTextBox.BackColor = Color.Yellow

End Sub
```

Notice that a drop-down list appears. This happens after you place a period after the control name, and you picked BackColor property instead of Text property, which you picked for the last statement. Here is what we asked our little Visual Basic program do: If the user clicks on YellowButton, then change the BackColor of the TextBox to yellow.

So far, we have instructed our Visual Basic program to perform two tasks according to the order in which they appear. First, Visual Basic displays "Yellow" inside the TextBox and then changes the background color to yellow.

Remarks or Comments

Let's develop a good programming habit and document our small program. Documentation is an important part of any programming task. This tells you and other programmers, who will review your programs, what you have done. The program is very small now and you remember what it does, but you will not remember the function of your program years later. In-program documentation requires the minimum amount of information about the program and its functions. This kind of documentation is known as *remarks* or *comments*. We would like to make a short note about what we did.

Just above the two statements that you have written, put a single quote and add the following: "This segment will display the word yellow in the textbox and changes the background color of the textbox to Yellow."

```
Private Sub yellowButton_Click _
(ByVal sender As System.Object, _
ByVal e As System.EventArgs) _
Handles yellowButton.Click
    'This segment will display the word yellow in
'the textbox and changes the background color of the
    'textbox to Yellow
    Me.colorTextBox.BackColor = Color.Yellow
End Sub
```

Notice that the color of the comment you typed changes to green. This means that this statement will not be evaluated by Visual Basic, and it is treated as a note to the programmer. In most programming shops, you are required to provide comments for your codes. Comments do not have to be very long. They need to be concise and clear.

There are many other tools in Visual Basic that we are not going to cover in this chapter. However, we need to talk about a few of them so you can use them in your project. We saw how to add comments to our program, but sometimes we need to hide some of the codes from the compiler to find a bug within our program by the process of elimination. Since we are not sure which section of the program is causing the problem, we do not want to remove the codes yet. We just want to hide them from the compiler temporarily. Visual Basic has two valuable tools on its toolbar. One of them is *Comment out the Selected Lines* and the other one is *Uncomment the Selected Lines*. These two tools are visible only when you work with the code editor (see Figure 3.18). This is a useful tool because you can use it to comment on a large number of code lines in a second, test the program, and then put the codes back into the program by clicking on Uncomment the Selected Lines.

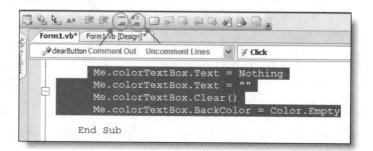

FIGURE 3.18   Comment and Uncomment tool.

Now run the program by hitting F5 and click the YellowButton. What do you see? If everything follows the instructions, you should see a yellow box with the word *Yellow* in it. Right? You do not see the comments you added at all. Congratulations!

Fine-Tuning the Program

We need to do the same thing for the other two color Buttons that you placed on your Form. We want to copy and paste our last code and make some changes to it. Here is what you need to put in the greenButton subprocedure:

```
Private Sub greenButton_Click _
(ByVal sender As System.Object, _
ByVal e As System.EventArgs) _
Handles greenButton.Click
    'This segment will display the word green
    'in the textbox and changes the background
    'color of the textbox to green

    Me.colorTextBox.Text = "Green"
    Me.colorTextBox.BackColor = Color.GreenYellow
End Sub
```

The black font color on top of the green is hard to read, but you will learn how to adjust it later on. Let us do the same thing for the redButton subprocedure as well. Here is what we put there:

```
Private Sub redButton_Click _
(ByVal sender As System.Object, _
ByVal e As System.EventArgs) Handles redButton.Click
    ''This segment will display the word red
    'in the textbox and changes the background
    'color of the textbox to red
    Me.colorTextBox.Text = "Red"
    Me.colorTextBox.BackColor = Color.Red
End Sub
```

Let's run the program and test these three Buttons by clicking on each Button. Now we want to test it using the keyboard. Test the program by holding the Alt key and pressing the underlined character within the Buttons. For example, while you are holding Alt, press Y for yellow, G for green, and R for red. The program works by using the keyboard or the mouse. Now let's take care of the other two Buttons we have placed on the Form.

We will be using an assignment statement for this one as well. We need to clear the text that is displayed inside the TextBox and reset the color to the default color. There are many ways that we can accomplish this task. Here are five different ways that you can clear the TextBox (pick only one of them and insert it into the clearButton subprocedure):

```
Me.colorTextBox.Text = Nothing
Me.colorTextBox.Text = ""
Me.colorTextBox.Clear()
Me.colorTextBox.Text = String.Empty
Me.colorTextBox.ResetText()
```

Two of these statements are methods and the rest of them are assignment statements. It is up to you which one you use. Now we need to add another statement to reset the TextBox background color to the default color:

```
Me.colorTextBox.BackColor = Color.Empty
```

Since you know that the background color of the TextBox was white, you could write your code this way as well:

```
Me.colorTextBox.BackColor = Color.White
```

Let's double-click on the clearButton and add the following statements:

```
Private Sub clearButton_Click _
(ByVal sender As System.Object, _
ByVal e As System.EventArgs) _
Handles clearButton.Click
    'this block will reset the Text
    'and Backcolor properties to default
    Me.colorTextBox.Clear()
    Me.colorTextBox.BackColor = Color.Empty
End Sub
```

DESIGN, COMPILE/BREAK, AND RUNTIME

Design Mode

We are almost done with our project. As you know by now, we can add controls to our Form in the design mode. The design mode of Visual Basic is a friendly environment that works like Microsoft Publisher™. Even nonprogrammers can use the design environment to create something that makes sense to others.

If while typing the codes, you misspell these reserved words, ignore grammar and punctuation rules, or try to use undefined names, Visual Basic Editor is going to warn you. These errors are known as *syntax errors*, and Visual Basic Editor can catch and correct most of them for you as you type them in. For example, Visual Basic Editor will format your lines as you type them. If you see a blue squiggly line under any of your typed words, it means the Visual Basic Editor has found an error in that word (see Figure 3.19).

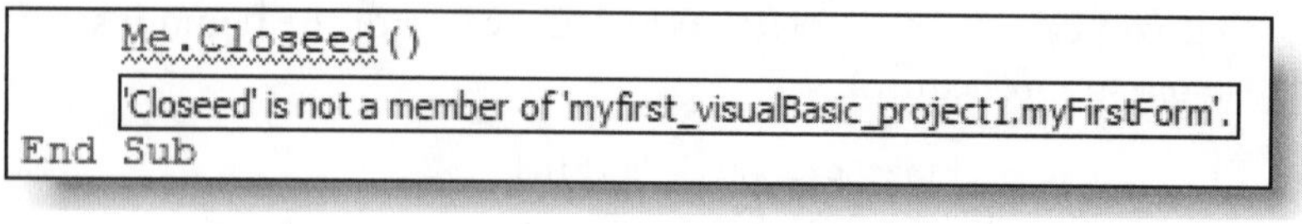

```
    Me.Closeed()
    'Closeed' is not a member of 'myfirst_visualBasic_project1.myFirstForm'.
End Sub
```

FIGURE 3.19   Syntax error.

AutoCorrect

Visual Basic also comes with a great autocorrect feature that is helpful to correct your errors. It gives you the description of the error, the option to correct it for you, and the nature of error. When you see a red mark under the last character of your statement, move your mouse over it and the little red mark will turn into a small red circle with an arrow inside it. When you click on the arrow or Shift-Alt-F10, you will see the list of options (see Figure 3.20).

Compile

Now you need to compile your program and execute it. On the toolbar, click on Start and wait until the Form pops up or hit F5. Clicking the Start button or F5 will do the same thing. You will most likely not have any syntax, compile, or runtime errors.

When you are done with your codes, you need to compile the program. As discussed in Chapter 1, compiling is the process of translating your program into a machine language. Compile errors are different from syntax errors. If there is a data error, the compiler will catch it. These errors are violations that are more serious.

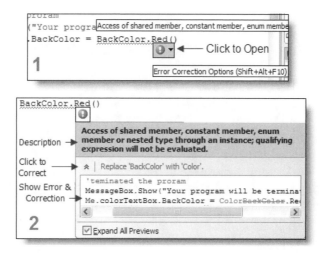

FIGURE 3.20 Autocorrect example.

The compiler will stop the process to issue you an error message. The error shown in Figure 3.21 was not in our program. We just changed a line to cause this error.

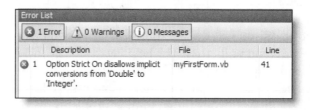

FIGURE 3.21 Compiler error.

Runtime, Logic Errors, Test, and Debug

This is not all. If you pass this phase, there is still a chance that another Visual Basic guard will stop you. Your program could be terminated during the execution time. This is known as a *runtime error* and can be caused by illegal mathematical operations (see Figure 3.22). You should also be aware of another checkpoint. Your program could pass all of these tests but still produce unwanted outputs. The editor and compiler cannot catch *logic errors*. You need to debug your program to remove all of these errors. The term *debug* describes the process of finding and correcting errors. Many programming teachers believe that your debugging time will be reduced greatly if you spend more time on planning and designing your program.

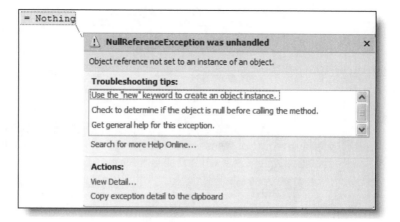

FIGURE 3.22   Run time error.

After hearing about these road hazards, are you ready for coding? Most programmers have made that decision and avoided these roadblocks. You can do it too. You may wonder if you have to memorize all reserved words, rules, grammar, and punctuation. What if you forget? Obviously, you need to know the concepts, but you do not need to memorize everything. A proficient programmer learns how to use references, resources, and examples. He learns how to find answers to his questions. As you will see later on, Visual Basic will help you remember many of these words and properties. The help files available in Visual Studio become your best friends. If you use them efficiently, you can learn a great deal. In addition to the MSDM help files and resources, you have access to many newsgroups and Web sites to find solutions to your programming problems. By doing a quick Web search, you can locate many of them, which offer samples that you can look at.

Dot Notation

You learned that we could change the property settings for objects through the Properties window. You also saw that we could access and set these properties within our codes by placing a dot after the object name. This is known as dot notation. Dot notation is used to reference the objects' members such as properties and methods. Here is an example:

```
Me.colorTextBox.BackColor
```

In this case, Me is the name of the Form class, ColorTextBox is a class that belongs to the Form Collection, and BackColor is a property of ColorTextBox. They are divided by dots and ordered according to their hierarchy. If you are using a control name and the drop-down list does not appear after the period, it means the control name is not valid.

Introducing the `MessageBox`

Most of you have seen pop-up messages on Web sites or Windows applications. Popups usually indicate that you have entered invalid or incomplete data, such as your user name, password, or credit card number. They are also used to confirm input or display an output. This is an effective way to get the user's attention. Once the `MessageBox` is displayed, it will prevent the user from performing any other task until he clicks on it. `MessageBox` in the Visual Basic environment is a class in the `System.Windows.Forms`. It allows programmers to display text massage, buttons, and icons (symbols). You can call it up anywhere within your program, and it performs its task. `MessageBox` has its own class and can display text, buttons, and icons in pop-up messages. `MessageBox` has several members, one of which is a method called `Show`. The `Show` method causes the message box to pop up. The general format for the `MessageBox` is

```
MessageBox.Show ("Main Message," "Title bar Message")
System.Windows.Forms.MessageBox.Show("You waited too long","Warning")
```

The main message is what you are trying to tell your users, such as "Your program will be terminated." The Title bar message is what appears on the title bar of the `MessageBox`, such as "Warning!" (see Figure 3.23). Although `MessageBox` is a class, it is not possible to have new instances of it, and you need to use the `static` `show` method to display it.

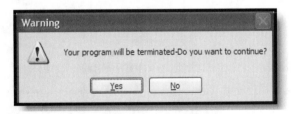

FIGURE 3.23 `MessageBox`.

Now that you know about `Messagebox`, you can use it to enhance your color program. It is a great idea to let users know when the program is going to be terminated even if the user has made that decision. Double-click on the `exitButton` if needed to get to the code editor and add the following statement in the `exitButton` subprocedure, just above the `Me.Close` statement:

```
MessageBox.Show("Your program will be terminated", "Warning")
```

We will show you other features of MessageBox later on, but for now, let us get familiar with its basic features.

Now hit F5 to run the program and then click on Exit. At this point, we are not giving the user any chance to change his mind, and the program will be terminated after the user clicks on the OK button. However, later on you will learn how to stop this process and resume normal operation. Now save your project.

ON THE CD

You can view this solution under the Chapter 3 folder on the companion CD-ROM. The project is saved under the name myfirst_visualBasic_project1. Just copy the project folder to your hard drive, and double-click on the .sln file.

SELECTING MULTIPLE CONTROLS

You have learned how to select a group of controls by holding down the Shift key. You can also select a group of controls by dragging the mouse around them to draw a selection line. Once you release the mouse, the controls inside the selected area are selected and you can apply changes to all of them at once or move them to other locations (see Figure 3.24).

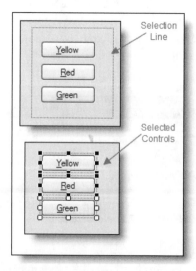

FIGURE 3.24   Selecting a group of controls.

KNOWING THE SOLUTION FILES

As soon as you create and run the Visual Basic project, several associated files and folders will be created. Here are some of the file names and their nature:

FileName.sln: The solution file is used to keep information about the solution and the projects within it. You need to double-click this file to open the project.

FileName.suo: The solution user options file stores the options you selected and the customizations you have made to your workspace.

form.rexs: The resource file keeps track of the resources your project uses, including graphics.

FileName.vbproj: The project file maintains information about the project and all related files within it.

FileName.vb: This file holds information about the project Form and all the controls and procedures within it.

FileName.vbpro.user: This is a user option file. As the name indicates, this file stores the user's option settings. It allows the user to save the changes made to the Integrated Development Environment (IDE) default setting.

Other files such as the app.config file are used by Web applications.

In addition to these files, Visual Basic creates several folders. Among these folders, the *bin* folder is Visual Basic's home directory, and the project's *exe* file is located within its subfolders. If you double-click the Bin folder, you will notice the *Debug* and *Release* folders. We need to explain these two folders in more detail. Visual Studio uses different configurations for these two folders. Once your program is compiled, it will be placed in the Debug folder. The compiled version of your program is not optimized and holds symbolic debugging information. The Release program is fully optimized and doesn't hold any debugging information. Store your images and data files within the debug folder to avoid using paths. When the program is debugged and ready to be released, you can select *Build* from the menu bar and choose "Build (name of the project)."

SETTING LINE CONTINUATION

The statements you typed were sometimes very long, which makes them difficult to read. We can use the Line Continuation feature to overcome this problem by adding a space before the breaking point, adding the Line Continuation symbol, which is an underscore, adding a space after it, and hitting enter to go to the next line. Here is an example:

```
Me.magicButton _
        .Visible = True
```

`Me.magicButton` was separated from the rest of the code.

PRACTICING WITH EVENTS

As we discussed before, each control has many different events that can respond to the user's requests. Events can be a change of mouse position or a press of a keyboard key. All controls that we place on our `Form` have several events. For example, when we click on a `Button`, the `Click` event is detected and is handled by the `Click Event Handler` method. We need to put instructions under the `Event Handler` method to react to this click. To find an event different from the default, we need to search the Method window. Just double-click on the `Form` and from the left-side window, select the `Button`'s name. Now, click on the right-side window to expand the drop-down `ComboBox`. The left-side window is known as Class Name and the right-side window is known as Method Name (see Figure 3.25).

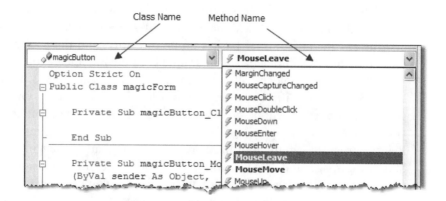

FIGURE 3.25 Class and Method windows.

When you pick a new method such as `MouseMove`, a new event subprocedure will be created in the body of the `Form`:

```
Private Sub magicButton_MouseMove _
    (ByVal sender As Object, _
    ByVal e As System.Windows.Forms.MouseEventArgs) _
```

```
        Handles magicButton.MouseMove

    End Sub
```

EXAMPLE 2

In Example 1, we used the `Click` event of the `Button` to respond to the user's input. Now we want to explore another event. Let us create a new program and name it `invisible`. Place a `Button` on the `Form` and set its properties as follows (see Figure 3.26):

▪ **Form1**
  Name: magicForm
  Text: Magic
▪ **Button1**
  Name: magicButton
  Text: &Click Me!

FIGURE 3.26 The `invisible` program interface.

Double-click on the `Form` and from the Class Name window, pick `magicButton`. From the Method Name drop-down window, find `MouseMove` and click on it. Notice that a new subprocedure is created for the `MouseMove`.

Let's play a little game with the user. Type the following code inside this new subprocedure. This code will be executed when the user moves the mouse over the button:

```
Private Sub magicButton_MouseMove _
(ByVal sender As Object, _
ByVal e As System.Windows.Forms.MouseEventArgs) _
Handles magicButton.MouseMove
    'The following code will hide the button
    Me.magicButton.Visible = False
End Sub
```

Repeat this process and this time click on `MouseLeave` method. In the `MouseLeave` event subprocedure, type the following statement:

```
Private Sub magicButton_MouseLeave _
(ByVal sender As Object, _
ByVal e As System.EventArgs) _
Handles magicButton.MouseLeave
    'The following code will unhide the button
    'The line Continuation is used below as well
    Me.magicButton _
    .Visible = True
    End Sub
```

This code will be executed when the user moves the mouse away from the But-ton. As soon as the user moves the mouse over the Button, it disappears. When the mouse is moved away, the Button appears again. By setting the Visible property of the Button to True or False, you can unhide or hide the Button.

ON THE CD
You can view this solution under the Chapter 3 folder on the companion CD-ROM. The project is saved under the name invisible. Just copy the project folder to your hard drive and double-click on the .sln file.

SETTING TAB ORDER

Sometimes we have to rearrange the location of the controls we place on the Form. This rearrangement will change the user's tab order. Most users navigate through the Form by clicking on the tab key, and now the cursor will jump to the wrong con-trols. To fix this problem, highlight the first control, and by using the Properties window change the Tab Index property. The first tab stop is 0.

SETTING THE OPTIONS

Not all users are happy with the default settings of the Visual Basic environment. For example, some users would like to have larger fonts when they type their codes or change the default color of Visual Basic. To accomplish this task, on the menu bar, click on Tools and select Options (see Figure 3.27). Check the Show All Options checkbox to see all available options. Click on the Fonts and Colors menu item to open up all available options within that category. If you wish, change the font size to see the effect of it on your code editor environment.

Printing Codes

If you need to print your codes, you can click on File and select Print from the menu. This will print the codes for you.

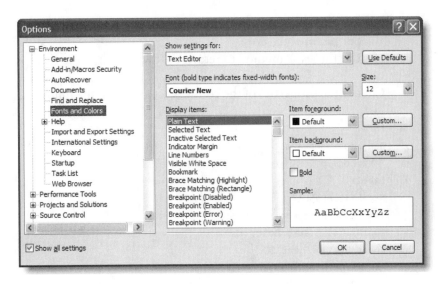

FIGURE 3.27   Option settings.

EXAMPLE 3: USING PasswordChar, StartPostion, Size, Location, Lock, BorderStyle, TextAlign, **AND** SizeMode **PROPERTIES AND** Focus **METHOD**

Practice is vital to learning a programming language. Each project can teach you new tricks, and that is what we will do in this book. Let us set up another project. Save the project that you were working on and we will do the following:

1. Start a new project and name it passwordSet.
2. Select the Form and find StartPosition in the Properties window.
3. Click on the drop-down arrow and change the StartPosition property from WindowsDefaultPosition to CenterScreen. This will force the Form to be displayed in the center of the screen at runtime.
4. Set the PasswordChar property to an asterisk (*) so the password the user types will not be readable. You can place any other character instead of an asterisk, but most users are accustomed to seeing asterisks in the password field.
5. Assign a specific value to the Location property of a control to move it to the place we desire.
6. Set the Size property to force the control to have specific size.
7. Change the Lock property to prevent the control from moving.
8. Utilize the BorderStyle property to change the control style to a 3D style.
9. Change the TextAlign property to force the text to appear in the middle of the control.

10. Use the `PictureBox`'s `SizeMode` property to resize the picture according to our picture box size.
11. Use the `Focus` method to return the focus back to the `TextBox`.

Change the properties of the controls according to the following:

- **Form1**
  Name: passwordForm
  Text: Log In
- **Label1**
  Name: titleLabel
  Text: Log in Screen
  Font: Arial Black, Bold, 12
  BorderStyle: Fixed 3D
  TextAlign: MiddleCenter
  Size: 304, 40
  Location: 58, 9
  Locked: True
- **Label2**
  Name: nameLabel
  Text: Enter User Name
  TextAlign: MiddleCenter (see Figure 3.28)
- **Label2**
  Name: passwordLabel
  Text: Enter Password
- **TextBox1**
  Name: nameTextBox
  Text: Blank (nothing is placed in this property)
- **TextBox2**
  Name: passwordTextBox
  Text: Blank
  PasswordChar: *
- **Button1**
  Name: displayButton
  Text: &Display
- **Button2**
  Name: clearButton
  Text: &Clear
- **Button3**
  Name: exitButton
  Text: E&xit

■ **PictureBox1**
 Name: keyPictureBox
 SizeMode: StretchImage

Your Form should look like Figure 3.29.

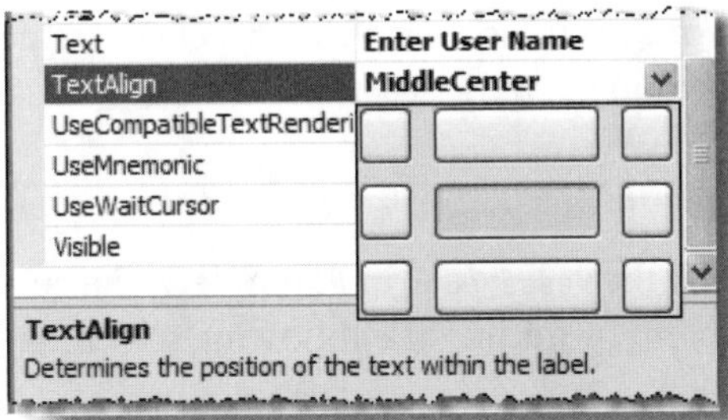

FIGURE 3.28   TextAlign setting.

FIGURE 3.29   Example 3 screen design.

Double-click on the displayButton and add the following code in the display-Button subprocedure:

```
Private Sub displayButton_Click _
(ByVal sender As System.Object, _
ByVal e As System.EventArgs) _
Handles displayButton.Click

    'the following will display the content
    'of the textbox in a messagebox
    MessageBox.Show _
```

```
(passwordTextBox.Text, "Password Display")
Me.passwordTextBox.Text = Nothing

    End Sub
```

The subprocedure heading and ending are already there so you only need to type the main code. Also notice that the lines are broken into smaller lines using the Line Continuation character. Now hit F5 and enter your name in the first TextBox. Enter a password in the second field and click on the displayButton. The password now is displayed in the MessageBox.

Using the Focus Method

After displaying the MessageBox in Example 3, the cursor disappears. We need to fix the Focus problem by adding the following statement:

```
Me.passwordTextBox.Focus()
```

This statement turns the focus back to the Password TextBox field and allows the users to find the input field more easily. Focus is a method that can be used to set the focus on specific controls.

Double-click on the clearButton and add the following codes to the clearButton subprocedure:

```
Private Sub clearButton_Click _
(ByVal sender As System.Object, _
ByVal e As System.EventArgs) _
Handles clearButton.Click

    'The following statements will clear the textboxes
    'and return the focus back to the first textbox
    Me.nameTextBox.Text = Nothing
    Me.passwordTextBox.Text = Nothing

    Me.nameTextBox.Focus()

End Sub
```

Both fields are cleared, and the Focus goes back to the first field. Now double-click on the exitButton and type the following statement in the subprocedure:

```
Private Sub exitButton_Click _
(ByVal sender As System.Object, _
ByVal e As System.EventArgs) _
Handles exitButton.Click

    'a warning message will be displayed before
    'the program is terminated
```

```
MessageBox.Show("You decided to quit", "Warning")
Me.Close()

End Sub
```

Adding `PictureBoxes` and Resources

We can enhance our new program a little more by adding a `PictureBox` to the `Form`. A `PictureBox` is a container that can hold a picture. As shown in the project specification, using the Toolbox, add a `PictureBox` to your `Form` and name it `keyPictureBox`. Before we change the `PictureBox`'s other properties, let's look at `PictureBox` controls a little closer. Now that you learned about the Smart Task arrow (Smart Tag) and Task Pane in the `TextBox` control, you need to know that the same pop-up menu is available for `PictureBox` (see Figure 3.30).

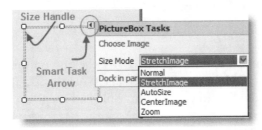

FIGURE 3.30   `PictureBox` *Smart Task* Arrow and *Task Pane.*

In the `PictureBox`'s Task Pane, find the `SizeMode` property and select `StretchImage` from the drop-down menu (shown in Figure 3.30). This allows you to resize the image according to your needs. Now, select the `Image` property and click on the File Open dialog icon. You will see the Select Resource dialog box. Within the Resource Context `GroupBox`, check the `RadioButton` for Local Resource if it is not already checked. Click on the Import button, change the directory to the following location, and select the Keys.ico file from the list of icons: C:\Program Files\Microsoft Visual Studio 8\Common7\VS2005ImageLibrary\VS2005ImageLibrary\icons\WinXP.

The icons and other useful graphics that you need to use for your projects can be found in the vs2005ImageLibrary folder. Make sure you choose the *All Files* (*.*) option from the Files Type dialog box to view all files within that folder. Once you find the image, you can click on the Open button. This action will bring you back to the Select Resource dialog box. Notice that the selected image appears inside the preview panel. As soon as you click on *OK*, the image will be displayed inside the `PictureBox`. You can adjust the size now if you wish (see Figure 3.31).

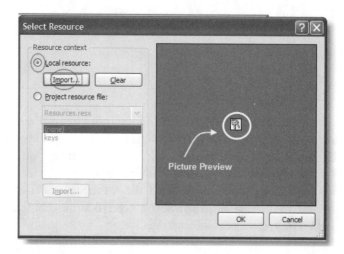

FIGURE 3.31   *Select Resource* dialog box.

You can also remove the image by clicking on the Remove button. Another checkbox is called Project Resource File. You can add resources such as icons, images, and audio files to your resource file and use them in the project.

Accept and Cancel Buttons

Are you ready for more enhancements? Just a few more and you will be done with this exercise. Occasionally you may want to create default buttons. *Default buttons* are buttons that will be activated by hitting the Enter or Esc key. These buttons make it very convenient for users to perform specific tasks by hitting the keyboard keys rather than clicking on the interface's buttons.

Let's see how this works. First, stop your program if it is still running. Then pick two of these buttons as default buttons. The *Display* button is a good candidate for the Enter key, and the exitButton would be a good choice for the Esc key. Select your Form by clicking on the Form's title bar and find the AcceptButton property in the drop-down list. Pick displayButton (see Figure 3.32). Now find CancelButton and click on exitButton from the drop-down list. If you run your program and hit the Enter key, you should see the MessageBox for displaying the password, and the Esc key will terminate the program.

ON THE CD
You can view this solution under the Chapter 3 folder on the companion CD-ROM. The project is saved under its name, passwordSet. Just copy the project folder to your hard drive and double-click on the .sln file.

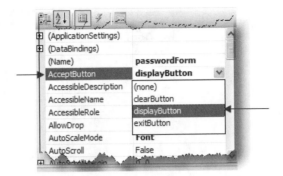

FIGURE 3.32   The Form's AcceptButton property.

What is GroupBox?

Visual Basic has a tool called GroupBox that allows you to organize your Form and make it easier to navigate. GroupBox is like a tray that can hold other controls that are placed inside it. GroupBox is also used to increase the functionality of RadioButtons, but for this example, we will just use it as an organizer. We will expand our discussion on this tool in later chapters.

Concatenation Operators

In this project, we would like to join multiple strings into a single string by using a *concatenation operator*. This task can be accomplished by placing an ampersand (&) between two strings. Here are some examples:

```
Messagebox.show("Mike" & " "& "Mostafavi"&" " &"Portland")
```

The result will be:

```
Mike Mostafavi Portland
```

This concatenation is designed just for strings and should not be used for numeric values.

EXAMPLE 4

This example is an application of what we have discussed so far. Figure 3.33 shows what we want to create. We will be creating a user interface with eleven Buttons, five

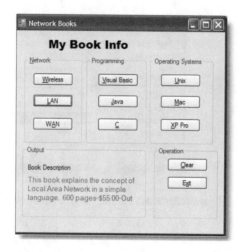

FIGURE 3.33   Example 4: the user interface.

GroupBoxes, two Labels, and one ToolTip. Here are the specifications for the property settings of those controls:

- **Form1**
  Name: networkBookForm
  Text: My Book Info
- **GroupBox1**
  Name: networkGroupBox
  Text: Networking
- **GroupBox2**
  Name: programmingGroupBox
  Text: Programming
- **GroupBox3**
  Name: osGroupBox
  Text: Operating System
- **GroupBox4**
  Name: outputGroupBox
  Text: Output
- **GroupBox5**
  Name: operationGroupBox
  Text: Operation

- **Button1**

  Name: visualBasicButton

  Text: &Visual Basic

  ToolTip: Information about Visual Basic books

- **Button2**

  Name: javaButton

  Text: &Java

  ToolTip: See information about Java Books

- **Button3**

  Name: cButton

  Text: &C

  ToolTip: See Information about C Programming books

- **Button4**

  Name: unixButton

  Text: &Unix

  ToolTip: See Information about Unix OS Books

- **Button5**

  Name: xpButton

  Text: &XP Pro

  ToolTip: See Information about XP OS Books

- **Button6**

  Name: macButton

  Text: &Mac

  ToolTip: See Information about MAC OS Books

- **Button7**

  Name: wirelessButton

  Text: &Wireless

  ToolTip: See information about Wireless Network Books

- **Button8**

  Name: lanButton

  Text: &LAN

  ToolTip: See Information about Local Area Network Book

- **Button9**

  Name: wanButton

  Text: W&AN

  ToolTip: See Information about Wide Area Network Books

- **Button10**

  Name: clearButton

  Text: &Clear

  ToolTip: Will Clear the Text Area

- **Button11**
  Name: exitButton
  Text: E&xit
  ToolTip: Will terminate the program
- **Label1**
  Name: titleLabel
  Text: My Book Info
  AutoSize: False
- **Label2**
  Name: descriptionLabel
  Text: Book Description
  AutoSize: False
- **Label3**
  Name: displayLabel
  Text: Blank
  AutoSize: False
  Forecolor: Red (find it under Custom tab)

We set the AutoSize property of the Label to False to have more control over the appearance of the text.

The purpose of this project is to create a program that will help users find short descriptions of the books available in our bookstore. We have used GroupBox to organize our Form and divided it into three areas: programming, networking, and operating systems. In each GroupBox, we have placed three related textbook titles. To see the description for any of these books, the user needs to click on its Button. Double-click on the wirelessButton and add the following code into the wirelessButton subprocedure:

```
Private Sub wirelessButton_Click _
(ByVal sender As System.Object, _
ByVal e As System.EventArgs) _
Handles wirelessButton.Click
    'Dispay text in the Description label
    displayLabel.Text = _
    "Information about Wireless Network. 500 pages-$60.00"

End Sub
```

Hit F5 to run the project and click on the wirelessButton. Under Output Group-Box the following statement will appear in red: "This book provides information about Wireless Network. 500 pages-$60.00."

Now, let's add more codes. Double-click on the lanButton and add the following statement into the lanButton subprocedure:

```
Private Sub lanButton_Click _
(ByVal sender As System.Object, _
ByVal e As System.EventArgs) _
Handles lanButton.Click
    'display text about C and C++
    displayLabel.Text = _
"This book explains the concept" _
& " of Local Area Network in a simple language. " _
& " 600 pages-$55.00-Out of Print Now"

End Sub
```

Now change all other subprocedures according to the following codes:

```
Private Sub wirelessButton_Click _
(ByVal sender As System.Object, _
ByVal e As System.EventArgs) _
Handles wirelessButton.Click
    'Dispay text in the Description label
    displayLabel.Text = _
"Infornation about Wireless Network. 500 pages-$60.00"

End Sub

Private Sub lanButton_Click _
(ByVal sender As System.Object, _
ByVal e As System.EventArgs) _
Handles lanButton.Click
    'display text about C and C++
    displayLabel.Text = _
"This book explains the concept" _
& " of Local Area Network in a simple language. " _
& " 600 pages-$55.00-Out of Print Now"

End Sub

Private Sub wanButton_Click _
(ByVal sender As System.Object, _
ByVal e As System.EventArgs) _
Handles wanButton.Click
    'display text about WAN
    displayLabel.Text = _
"This book is written to show all features of Wide Area Network" _
& " 5th Edition-300 Pages-$60.00"

End Sub

Private Sub unixButton_Click _
(ByVal sender As System.Object, _
ByVal e As System.EventArgs) _
Handles unixButton.Click
    'display text about Unix
    displayLabel.Text = _
```

```vb
                    " We have 30 titles about Unix Operating systems-" _
                    & "Prices Range from $35.00-$80.00"

        End Sub

        Private Sub visualBasicButton_Click _
        (ByVal sender As System.Object, _
        ByVal e As System.EventArgs) _
        Handles VisualBasicButton.Click
            'display text about Visual Basic
            displayLabel.Text = _
            "Complete Source for Visual Basic. Intoductory-450" _
            & "Pages-$58.00"

        End Sub

        Private Sub macButton_Click _
        (ByVal sender As System.Object, _
        ByVal e As System.EventArgs) Handles macButton.Click
            'display text about MAC
            displayLabel.Text = _
            "We carry 35 Titles about MAC Operating Systems- " _
                & "Prices Range from $40.00-$90.00"

        End Sub

        Private Sub javaButton_Click _
        (ByVal sender As System.Object, _
        ByVal e As System.EventArgs) _
        Handles javaButton.Click
            'display text about Java
            displayLabel.Text = _
            "The best reference book for Java programming " _
             & "language-600 Pages-$70.00"

        End Sub

        Private Sub cButton_Click _
        (ByVal sender As System.Object, _
        ByVal e As System.EventArgs) Handles cButton.Click
            'display text about C and C++
            displayLabel.Text = _
            "The only textbook that covers both C and C++ " _
            & "languages-460 Pages-$50.00"

        End Sub

        Private Sub xpButton_Click _
        (ByVal sender As System.Object, _
        ByVal e As System.EventArgs) Handles xpButton.Click
            'display text about XP
            displayLabel.Text = _
    "An excellent book about XP Operating Systems-560 Pages-$70.00"
```

```
            End Sub

            Private Sub clearButton_Click _
            (ByVal sender As System.Object, _
            ByVal e As System.EventArgs) Handles clearButton.Click
                'clear the label
                displayLabel.Text = Nothing

            End Sub

            Private Sub exitButton_Click _
            (ByVal sender As System.Object, _
            ByVal e As System.EventArgs) Handles exitButton.Click
                'Close the program
                MessageBox.Show("This will terminate your program", "Warning")
                Me.Close()

            End Sub
```

In the above code, we use an ampersand (&) to concatenate two strings. Remember that you will be typing programmer's supplied codes that appear in italic.

Form_load and FormClosing Events

Now, let's talk about two other events before we end this chapter. The first event is Form_Load. You can see this event in your code editor. The Form_Load event has special value for programmers. Since this event will be executed before the Form is displayed, it gives programmers the opportunity to set properties or place other needed codes in this procedure. Please note that we are using the Form keyword as a generic name. You will notice that in the following example, Form_Load phrases have changed to netWorkBookForm_Load.

To test this event, place the following statement inside the Form_Load subprocedure from Example 4:

```
            Private Sub netWorkBookForm_Load _
            (ByVal sender As System.Object, _
            ByVal e As System.EventArgs) _
            Handles MyBase.Load
                'this section will be executed before the form is loaded
                MessageBox.Show("Welcome to my bookstore. Click to continue", _
                "Welcome!")

            End Sub
```

Hit F5 to run the project. You will see the MessageBox before your main program is displayed. We will discuss other applications of the Form_Load event later on.

The other event we want to look at is FormClosing. This event will be activated when the user closes the Form by clicking on the X button located at the upper-right corner of the Form. This is helpful for detecting the user's actions. While the Form is selected, under the Event Browser drop-down list, find FormClosing method and add a MessageBox to its subprocedure:

```
Private Sub netWorkBookForm_FormClosing _
(ByVal sender As Object, _
ByVal e As System.Windows.Forms.FormClosingEventArgs) _
Handles Me.FormClosing
    'will be activated when the X button is hit
    MessageBox.Show("Are you leaving? Make sure your data is saved", _
    "Warning")

End Sub
```

ON THE CD

Now, hit F5 to run your project and then click on the *X* button. Save your project. You can view this solution under the Chapter 3 folder on the companion CD-ROM. The project is saved under its name, groupBox_example. Just copy the project folder to your hard drive and double-click on the .sln file.

Introducing the My Namespace

To facilitate users' productivity, Microsoft has added another new feature to Visual Basic 2005. This feature is known as My. By using My, you become more efficient in programming and write fewer codes for your applications. Programmers can use My to access many classes included in the .NET framework to expedite their work. My includes several new classes that can be utilized by programmers:

- My.Application
- My.Computer
- My.Forms
- My.Resources
- My.Settings
- My.User
- My.WebServices

Consider the My namespace as an elevator that is used instead of stairs for climbing a tall tower. An example of using the My namespace is:

```
My.Computer.Audio.Play("FileName.wav")
```

Efficiency and Effectiveness

Every day, programmers and teachers get into arguments with coworkers or students about these two concepts. Some students think that if their program does what it is supposed to and meets the requirements, they should receive full points. They are only half right. In addition to effectiveness, the program should be efficient as well. Here is an exaggerated example to consider. Let's say your spouse has asked you to buy a gallon of milk. You need to take it home in an hour. If you rent a helicopter and get the milk, you can still consider yourself very effective because you met all the requirements and did what you were asked to do. However, this probably was not very efficient. To apply this example to programming, you can compare two programs written by two programmers. Both programs meet the requirements and both behave exactly the same. However, one programmer used 5000 lines of code while the other wrote it in less than 500 lines. Obviously, one of them was more efficient than the other one. The program with fewer codes, which uses fewer resources, takes less space and is easier to follow.

PROGRAMMING TIPS

Some programmers still remember the old days when they could write code in any way they liked. There was not anyone to check their work and force them to follow rules. Programmers had lifetime job security, so they wrote their programs in a way that made sense to only them. The phrase *spaghetti coding* was coined during that time. Well, those good old days are gone. Programmers are now expected to maintain reasonable standards. One of the factors developers and teachers consider is a programmer's consistency. *Consistency* is the programmer's style. Each programmer develops or follows a programming style or technique. For example, one programmer spends a lot of time developing a short logic. He uses different background colors for different error messages. He believes that if error messages were color coded, it would be easier for the users to remember them. However, at the time of programming and debugging, most people will not remember the color of the message. Worse than this, some programmers randomly display error messages in different locations and randomly move them around. This is wrong as well. Users want to find error messages in one part of the screen.

Figure 3.34 shows a sample of bad programming habits designed for this book. As you can see, the settings for the TextBoxes are not consistent. The programmer has used different font sizes and colors for this Visual Basic program. The background colors of the different TextBoxes are chosen randomly and do not serve any purpose. The programmer has used a gray back color for one of the TextBoxes. The gray color represents protected, read-only, or disabled fields, when in fact, this is not the case. Inconsistent programs also include inconsistent naming and documentation.

In addition to consistency, we can speak about *functionality* as well. If the program does not do what it promises, then it is not functional.

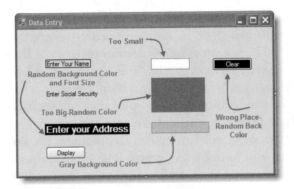

FIGURE 3.34 Sample of bad design.

When you write a Visual Basic program, you need to take advantage of the graphical user interface (GUI) environment. There is no other programming language that can compete with Visual Basic in GUI features. However, this does not mean that we must make our Forms colorful and add animations to our programs. Programs must be *user friendly*, and GUI tools can facilitate this objective.

After ensuring user-friendliness, portability should be considered. *Portability* means projects run on machines other than the one the programmer has used to generate it.

The last item on our list is *maintainability*. Programs must be maintained and upgraded regularly. This should be a routine task for every programmer.

HOUSEKEEPING HINTS

Another area that requires attention is the View menu items. Sometimes when students work on the features of Visual Basic, they lose major components of the IDE. For example, in the middle of their work, suddenly the Properties window disappears. This is not done intentionally. Luckily, it is very easy to recover. (This was briefly explained in Chapter 2 but is worth mentioning again.) Just click on the View menu tab and restore your loss. If you are not happy with the changes you have made with your IDE, you can easily discard your changes. On the menu bar, click on Window and select Reset Window Layout.

FLOWCHART

Flowchart is a graphic tool that is used to represent the sequence of logic we have used in our program. It is similar to the organization chart you may have seen at work. Programmers used to employ this tool to visualize their programming logic. Most managers drew flowcharts to explain the type of processes and outputs they had in mind. Flowchart would be used as a blue print for computer programs. Programmers use standard symbols to communicate with others. The flowchart would show logical paths to other segments of the program. This was a visual method used to map out what they had in mind and a standard tool to communicate with others. We still see some programmers or project managers who insist on using flowcharts. Most word processors such as Microsoft Word or drawing programs like Visio™ provide flowcharting templates. There are standard symbols for input, process, output, decision, and other functions. Since Visual Basic has a visual programming environment, most programmers do not use flowcharts for Visual Basic projects as often as they used to. In addition, it is hard to show all events by using flowcharts. Does this mean we should no longer use flowcharts in object-oriented programming projects? Not really. Flowcharts still can be used for data modeling and other tasks in Visual Basic. Since this project is simple and does not present new features, Flowchart can be used to show the logic (see Figure 3.35).

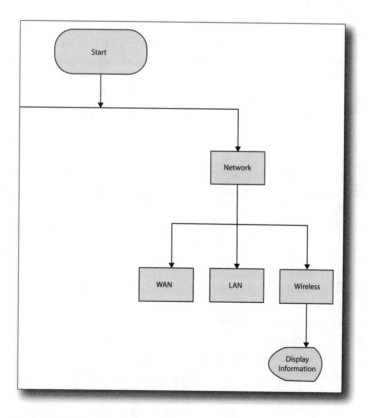

FIGURE 3.35 Flowchart example.

SUMMARY

In this chapter we discussed the basics of program structure, data and information, problem definition, efficiency vs. effectiveness, and other related topics. We focused on all necessary steps you need to take before you can program. The programming tips highlighted important areas you need to focus on. Topics such as `GroupBoxes`, `Buttons`, `TextBoxes`, `Labels`, `MessageBoxes`, tab order, line continuation, and events were discussed as well.

Next

In Chapter 4 we will introduce new controls such as `RadioButtons`, `CheckBoxes`, `MaskedTextBoxes`, `LinkLabels`, `Panel`, and more. We will also expand our discussion on the `MessageBox` and provide you with more of its features.

DISCUSSION QUESTIONS

1. We explained the way data can be converted to information. This is called data processing. Explain information processing and provide examples.
2. Are all short programs automatically efficient? Justify your response.
3. What are the components of the solution folder?
4. What is the difference between an event and a method?
5. Can we still use flowcharts in event-driven programs?

Exercise

Draw a flowchart and write an algorithm to apply for a home loan. Make sure you provide all required decisions, input, output, and processing related to it.

Key Terms

- Access keys
- Dot notation
- Error Types
- Flowchart
- `GroupBox` and `MessageBox`
- Line connection
- `MouseMove` and `FormClosing`
- Visible
- `My` namespace
- `Me` keyword
- Events and methods

4 More Controls

In This Chapter

- More about GroupBox
- What are RadioButtons
- CheckBoxes
- Introducing the MaskedTextBox
- What is a LinkLabel?
- System.diagnostic.Process.Start Method
- More about MessageBoxes
- Enabled Properties and MouseEnter Methods
- Loading Images at Runtime Using the FromFile Method
- Debugging the Project
- Simple Debugging Practice
- More Programming Tips

MORE ABOUT GROUPBOX

In Chapter 3, we briefly talked about GroupBox and gave you an example in which GroupBox was used to organize the Form and break it into several functional areas, such as input, process, output, and operations. However, GroupBoxes have other advantages that we need to get familiar with. The role of GroupBoxes becomes very important when we add a group of RadioButtons to our form. In the following discussions, we will explain the functions of the RadioButtons and then demonstrate the potential problems associated with the group of them. We will be using the Group-Boxes to resolve these problems.

WHAT ARE RADIOBUTTONS

RadioButtons are push-button controls that are very similar to the Buttons you used in Chapter 3. RadioButtons are used to give the users a choice to pick one option from many options. RadioButtons are normally used in forms to collect information from the users. They can decrease the users' typing time by eliminating the need to ask them to type in information. They also help minimize typing errors and the need for validation. As you will see in our first example, RadioButtons can be presented in groups to collect related inputs.

RadioButtons present two statuses: True or False. If the user selects the RadioButton, then its status will be True. Otherwise, the status will be False.

You can display text and images in the RadioButton and it can act like a Button if you wish. If a group of RadioButtons is placed on the Form, when one is clicked, all of the others will be cleared automatically. To overcome this problem, we need to place them inside containers, such as panels or GroupBoxes, which will be demonstrated in the next example.

CHECKBOXES

Unlike RadioButtons, which allow users to pick one option from many choices, the CheckBox allows users to select several options. CheckBoxes, which appear as little square boxes, are used in many Windows and Web Forms. They are easy tools to use to collect information from users. Like RadioButtons, CheckBoxes represent a True or False status and can be a great tool for collecting data from users.

INTRODUCING THE MASKEDTEXTBOX

In previous chapters, you became familiar with the features of TextBox and you were provided with examples of how to set different properties for TextBoxes. Now we are going to introduce you to a different class called MaskedTextBox. This class forces users to enter data in a proper format. For example, you may want users to enter phone numbers in a specific format, such as (xxx)xxx-xxxx, so the user will have no choice but to enter the data in the format you specified. The format is the Mask property of this control. The Smart Tag of this control allows you to pick one format from many mask formats that are available. The Text property of this control can be used to display the user's input. This class is used in Example 7.

WHAT IS A LINKLABEL?

This control is similar to the Label class we discussed in Chapter 3, but LinkLabel can accept URLs and use your default browser to access the Internet. LinkLabel has many properties, some of which we will highlight for you below. There are other useful properties that you can look up if you wish.

- The ActiveLinkColor property allows you to select the color of active link.
- The Text property allows you to type the text that the user will click on.
- The LinkColor property is used to set the color of your link. The default color is Blue.
- The VisitedLinkColor property will let you choose the color of the Label text once it has been clicked.
- The LinkBehavior property is used to change the look of the label. You can set it to be underlined or not. We will be using this control in our Example 7.

SYSTEM.DIAGNOSTIC.PROCESS.START METHOD

So far, you have been using methods such as Close and Focus to instruct Visual Basic to perform tasks for you. We now want to introduce a new method called Start. The Start method belongs to the System.Diagnostic.Process class that can be used to access and control other processes within the system. The Process class has many other members, but for now, we want to focus on the Start method which we will be utilizing in Example 7.

EXAMPLE 1

Let's say you want to create a survey form to collect personal information from the users. To facilitate the data entry process, we want to use RadioButtons. Start a new project and call it incomeAge_RadioButton.

In this survey, you want to collect information about the user's age group and income range. The information will help the management see the correlation between age and income.

The age groups are divided into the following ranges:

- Group 1: 20–29
- Group 2: 30–39
- Group 3: 40–49
- Group 4: 50–59

The income level is broken into the following ranges:

- Group 1: $10,000–$20,000
- Group 2: $20,001–$30,000
- Group 3: $30,001–$40,000
- Group 4: $40,001–$50,000

Now follow the steps below to put together a form with the design shown in Figure 4.1.

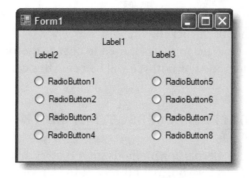

FIGURE 4.1   Survey Form design.

1. Click on the Toolbox to find the Label control and drag it to your form. Follow the same process and add two more Labels to your form.
2. Drag eight RadioButtons and place them on the Form as you see in the screenshot.
3. Now change the control names according to the following:

- **Form1**
  Name: ageForm
  Text: Age and Income
- **Label1**
  Name: titleLabel
  Text: Age and Income
- **Label2**
  Name: ageLabel
  Text: Age

- **Label3**
  Name: incomeLabel
  Text: Income
- **RadioButton1**
  Name: ageFirstRadioButton
  Text: 20-29
- **RadioButton2**
  Name: ageSecondRadioButton
  Text: 30-39
- **RadioButton3**
  Name: ageThirdRadioButton
  Text: 40-49
- **RadioButton4**
  Name: ageFourthRadioButton
  Text: 50-59
- **RadioButton5**
  Name: incomeFirstRadioButton
  Text: $10,000-$20,000
- **RadioButton6**
  Name: incomeSecondRadioButton
  Text: $20,001-$30,000
- **RadioButton7**
  Name: incomeThirdRadioButton
  Text: $30,001-$40,000
- **RadioButton8**
  Name: incomeFourthRadioButton
  Text: $40,001-$50,000

Figure 4.2 shows what the Form should look like.

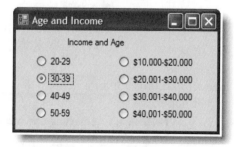

FIGURE 4.2 Property changes for the survey Form.

Now save your program and then hit F5. Try to select one option from the age group and one option from the income group. You can only select one RadioButton in your Form. As soon as you select one of the RadioButtons, the other ones become unselected. Now save your project.

EXAMPLE 2

To resolve this issue, we need to move our RadioButtons into GoupBoxes. Drag two GroupBoxes into your form and rename them as follows:

- **GroupBox1**
  Name: ageGroupBox
  Text: Age Group
- **GroupBox2**
  Name: incomeGroupBox
  Text: Income Group

Note that there is no need for ageLabel and incomeLabel because the GroupBoxes provide their own text property.

By dragging your mouse around the ageRadioButtons, you can select all four of them. While they are selected, drag them by the drag handle located on the top-left corner of the selection line and move them into the ageGroupBox (see Figure 4.3).

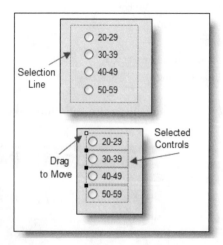

FIGURE 4.3   Selecting and moving a group of RadioButtons.

Now that you have moved the selected `RadioRuttons` into the first `GroupBox`, select the `incomeRadioButtons` and move them to the `incomeGroupBox`. When this task is complete, hit F5 to run the program and select one option from the age group and one option from the income group. This time you can select one option from each group (see Figure 4.4). Save your project now.

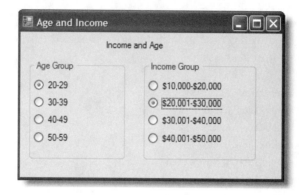

FIGURE 4.4 `GroupBox` effect.

 You can view this solution under the Chapter 4 folder on the companion CD-ROM. The project is saved under its name, `incomeAge_RadioButton`. Just copy the project folder to your hard drive, and double-click on the .sln file.

MORE ABOUT MESSAGEBOXES

In previous chapters, we briefly discussed `MessageBox`. Let us explore `MessageBox` options a little further. As we introduce you to more topics, we will get back to this subject and provide you with more details.

As you may have seen in other programs, `MessageBoxes` can display different `Buttons`, texts, and icons. The following are the `Buttons` that can be added to the `MessageBoxes`:

- `MessageBoxButtonButtons.AbortRetryIgnore`
- `MessageBoxButtonButtons.OK`
- `MessageBoxButtonButtons.OKCancel`
- `MessageBoxButtonButtons.RetryCancel`
- `MessageBoxButtonButtons.YesNo`
- `MessageBoxButtonButtons.YesNoCancel`

You can add these Buttons to your MessageBox by placing a comma (,) after the MessageBox title. Here is the format:

```
MessageBox.Show("Do you really want to exit?", "Warning",
MessageBoxButtons.YesNo)
```

During this process, a pop-up listing of Buttons allows you to select from a list of options (see Figure 4.5).

In addition to buttons, you can add icons to your MessageBoxes. Icons are visual warnings that will get the user's attention. Here is the list of possible icons that you can add to your MessageBox:

- MessageBoxIcon.Asterisk
- MessageBoxIcon.Error
- MessageBoxIcon.Exclamation
- MessageBoxIcon.Hand
- MessageBoxIcon.Information
- MessageBoxIcon.None
- MessageBoxIcon.Question
- MessageBoxIcon.Stop
- MessageBoxIcon.Warning

Similar to the Button's pop up, an icon pop up will be displayed once you place a comma (,) after the code you added for the Buttons (see Figure 4.6).

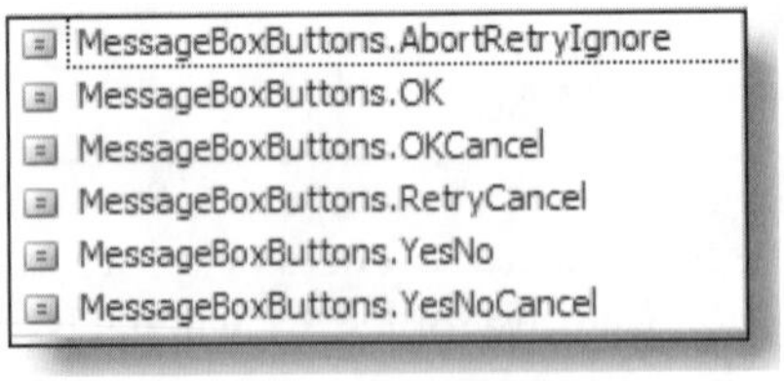

FIGURE 4.5   MessageBox Buttons.

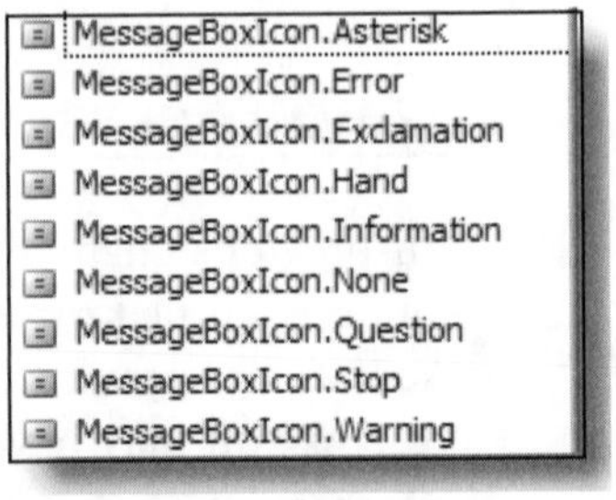

FIGURE 4.6   MessageBox icons.

EXAMPLE 3

Look at a sample code:

```
Private Sub testButton_Click _
(ByVal sender As System.Object, _
ByVal e
As System.EventArgs) Handles btnButtonTest.Click
```

```
'a messagebox with buttons and icons

    MessageBox.Show("Wrong Input - Do you want to retry?", _
    "Warning",MessageBoxButtons.YesNoCancel, _
    MessageBoxIcon.Information)

End Sub
```

Once you click on the testButton, you should see a MessageBox with the Buttons and icons shown in Figure 4.7.

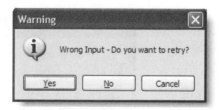

FIGURE 4.7 MessageBox displayed with Buttons and icons.

Multiline MessageBox using ControlChars.CrLf

Occasionally we need to break up the MessageBox or other text messages into multiple lines. Visual Basic provides many classes with a few constants that can be used to accomplish this task. Let's review some of these constants and apply them to our project.

The ControlChars module has many constants that can be used in order to control the output. Once you use it, a new instance of Microsoft.VisualBasic.ControlChars will be initialized. Here are some of the members of this class:

ControlChars.CrLf: Carriage control and linefeed

ControlChars.Cr: Carriage return

ControlChars.Lf: Linefeed

ControlChars.NewLine: New line

ControlChars.Back: Backspace

EXAMPLE 4
Here is how we can use the above constants:

```
MessageBoxIcon.Information)
MessageBox.Show("You have unsaved data" & _
Microsoft.VisualBasic.ControlChars.Back & "Quit Now?", _
"Save Data", MessageBoxButtons.YesNo, _
MessageBoxIcon.Information)
```

ControlChars.CrLf will force "Quit Now?" to be displayed in the second line (see Figure 4.8). ControlChars.CrLf also works with other controls, such as TextBox. We can have a multiline TextBox and display a message in two or more lines even if they can be displayed in one line. Example 5 shows TextBox's Multiline feature.

FIGURE 4.8 A Multiline MessageBox.

EXAMPLE 5

Create a new project and name it multilineTest. We need the following:

- **Form1**
  Name: multiLineForm
  Text: Multiline
- **Label1**
  Name: titleLabel
  Text: Multiline Text
- **TextBox1**
  Name: multilineTextBox
- **GoupBox1**
  Name: textFormatGroupBox
  Text: Text Formatting
- **RadioButton1**
  Name: singleLineTextRadioButton
  Text: Single Line
- **RadioButton2**
  Name: multiLineTextRadioButton
  Text: Multi Line Text

- **RadioButton3**

  Name: tabControlTextRadioButton

  Text: Text Tab Control

- **RadioButton4**

  Name: mutilineMessageBox

  Text: Multiline Messagebox

- **RadioButton5**

  Name: multiLineTextRadioButton

  Text: Multi Line Text

- **RadioButton6**

  Name: backSpaceRadioButton

  Text: Back Space

- **CheckBox1**

  Name: resetCheckBox

  Text: Reset

In this project, we will be showing several new features we have learned. Double-click on the SingleLineTextRadioButton and add the following under the event subprocedure:

```
Private Sub singleLineTextRadioButton_CheckedChanged _
(ByVal sender As System.Object, _
ByVal e As System.EventArgs) _
Handles singleLineTextRadioButton.CheckedChanged
    'Displaying single line
    Me.multilineTextBox.Multiline = False
    Me.multilineTextBox.Text = "First Line"
    End Sub
```

We first set the Multiline property of the TextBox to False so it will display a single line. This is for the time that other controls set this property to True. Now double-click on the multilineTextRadioButton and type the following:

```
Private Sub multilineTextRadioButton_CheckedChanged _
    (ByVal sender As System.Object, _
    ByVal e As System.EventArgs) _
    Handles multilineTextRadioButton.CheckedChanged
        'displaying multiline textbox
        Me.multilineTextBox.Multiline = True
        Me.multilineTextBox.Height = 100
        Me.multilineTextBox.Width = 190
        Me.multilineTextBox.Text = "First Line" & _
        Me.ControlChars.CrLf & "Second Line" & _
        Me.ControlChars.CrLf & "Third Line"
    End Sub
```

In this block, we will set the `Multiline` property of the `TextBox` to `True` and assign values for the `height` and `width` of the `TextBox` so it appears at our desired measurements. The code forces each line to be displayed in a separate line.

Now add the following under the Text Tab control:

```
Private Sub tabControlRadioButton_CheckedChanged _
    (ByVal sender As System.Object, _
    ByVal e As System.EventArgs) _
    Handles tabControlRadioButton.CheckedChanged
        'tab control
        Me.multilineTextBox.Multiline = False
        Me.multilineTextBox.Text = "First Word" _
        & ControlChars.Tab & "Second Word"
    End Sub
```

Now find the `Click` event of the `multilineMessageBox` and add the following statements under it:

```
Private Sub multilineMessageBox_Click _
    (ByVal sender As Object, _
    ByVal e As System.EventArgs) _
    Handles multilineMessageBox.Click
        'displaying multiline messagebox
        MessageBox.Show("You have unsaved data" & _
Microsoft.VisualBasic.ControlChars.CrLf & _
        Microsoft.VisualBasic.ControlChars.CrLf & _
        "Quit Now?", _
        "Save Data", MessageBoxButtons.YesNo, _
        MessageBoxIcon.Information)
    End Sub
```

The preceding code will display a `Multiline` `MessageBox`.
Now find the `Click` event of the `BackSpaceRadioButton` and type the following:

```
Private Sub backSpaceRadioButton_Click _
    (ByVal sender As Object, _
    ByVal e As System.EventArgs) _
    Handles backSpaceRadioButton.Click
        'displaying single line
        Me.multilineTextBox.Multiline = False
        Me.multilineTextBox.Text = "First Word" _
        & ControlChars.Back & ControlChars.Back & "Second Word"
    End Sub
```

Now type the following under the `resetCheckBox`.

```
Private Sub resetCheckBox_CheckedChanged _
    (ByVal sender As System.Object, _
    ByVal e As System.EventArgs) _
    Handles resetCheckBox.CheckedChanged
        'reset all controls
```

```
            Me.singlelineTextRadioButton.Checked = False
            Me.multilineTextRadioButton.Checked = False
            Me.tabControlRadioButton.Checked = False
            Me.backSpaceRadioButton.Checked = False
            Me.multilineTextBox.Clear()
            Me.multilineTextBox.Multiline = False
            Me.resetCheckBox.Checked = False
        End Sub
```

The above code resets all controls to the default setting. Now save your program, hit F5 and click on different controls (see Figure 4.9).

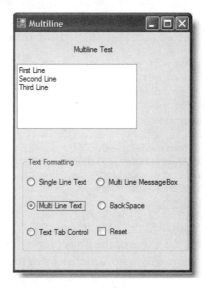

FIGURE 4.9 Multiline TextBox and ControlChars class.

You can view this solution under the Chapter 4 folder on the companion CD-ROM. The project is saved under its name, multilineTest. Just copy the project folder to your hard drive and double-click on the .sln file.

Introducing the Panel

Panel is a container very similar to GroupBox and can contain other controls, such as RadioButtons. Unlike a GroupBox, a Panel cannot have a caption. Instead, it has a scrollbar that can be used by developers. Like GroupBox, Panel has a global environment that can be applied to all of the controls within in it. For example, if the Panel's Visible property is set to False, all controls within it will be invisible.

By default, Panel does not display any border, but you can set it to FixedSingle or Fixed3D. There are several kinds of Panels, but for now, we will discuss only one of them. Panels have a Smart Tag that can be used to set the docking.

With Block

You may have noticed that any time you want to reference a property or method of an object, you have to type the name of the object as well. In some cases, you want to manipulate several methods or properties of the same object and you do not want to type them for every statement. Visual Basic has a block called With block or With statement. Your statements must appear within a With and End With block. You need to reference the name of the object once and reference all of its methods and properties followed by a period (.). Here is the syntax:

```
With NameOfObject
.Properties or Methods
End With
```

Here is an example:

```
With Me.optionsPanel
    .BackColor = Color.Beige
    .BorderStyle = BorderStyle.Fixed3D
    .ForeColor = Color.Red

End With
```

As you can see, the name of the object is referenced only once. This is very useful when you are setting many properties from the same object.

ENABLED PROPERTY AND MOUSEENTER EVENT

Each object comes with many properties and methods. We will be able to use some of them in this book. However, if you look at the Objects Properties window, you will notice many more properties that can be employed by programmers.

You have used the Visible property to show and hide controls. You used the MouseMove and MouseLeave events and used methods to handle these events in Chapter 3, and now it is time to introduce you to a few more properties and methods. An Enabled property will give you the option of making the control enabled or disabled. Once the control is disabled, the user cannot use it. We normally use this property when the user needs to provide preliminary information before he can move to the next phase. For example, the user needs to fill out a survey before he can click on the Submit Button. As long as the survey is incomplete, the Submit Button will remain disabled.

The MouseEnter event is very similar to the MouseMove event that we discussed before. The codes will be executed once the mouse enters the control boundary.

EXAMPLE 6: USING BorderStyle **AND** Enabled
Start a new project and call it panel. Add the following controls to it:

- One Panel
- One Button
- Two RadioButtons

Figure 4.10 shows a screenshot of Example 6. Here is what we need:

FIGURE 4.10   Example 6 screenshot.

- **Form1**
  Name: panelWithForm
  Text: Panel
- **Panel1**
  Name: optionsPanel
  BorderStyle: FixedSingle
- **RadioButton1**
  Name: backgroundRadioButton
  Text: Back Color Change
- **RadioButton2**
  Name: backColorRadioButton
  Text: Back Color Change
- **Button1**
  Name: exitButton
  Text: E&xit

In this project, we utilize the With block and Panel. In addition, we use several events so that once the user moves the mouse over the controls, their backgrounds change.

Double-click on the exitButton and type the following code in the subprocedure:

```
Private Sub exitButton_Click _
    (ByVal sender As System.Object, _
    ByVal e As System.EventArgs) _
    Handles exitButton.Click
    'close the program
    Me.Close()
End Sub
```

Now double-click on the Form and type the following in the Form_Load subprocedure:

```
Private Sub panelGroupForm_Load _
    (ByVal sender As System.Object, _
    ByVal e As System.EventArgs) _
    Handles MyBase.Load
    'make the exit button disabled
    Me.exitButton.Enabled = False

End Sub
```

In the above statement, we made the exitButton disabled. It will remain disabled until the user moves the mouse over it.

Now find the Panel's MouseEnter event and type the following statements under its subprocedure:

```
Private Sub optionsPanel_MouseEnter _
    (ByVal sender As Object, _
    ByVal e As System.EventArgs) _
    Handles optionsPanel.MouseEnter
    'when mouse moves over the panel,
    'the exit button enabled set to true
    Me.exitButton.Enabled = True
    'changing the properties of panel
    With Me.optionsPanel
        .BackColor = Color.Beige
        .BorderStyle = BorderStyle.Fixed3D
        .ForeColor = Color.Red

    End With
```

As soon as the user moves the mouse into the Panel, the exitButton becomes available. At the same time, the BackColor of the Panel changes to beige, the BorderStyle changes to Fixed3D, and the ForeColor of the text changes to red.

Now we find the Panel's MouseLeave method and type the following statements under its subprocedure:

```
Private Sub optionsPanel_MouseLeave _
    (ByVal sender As Object, _
    ByVal e As System.EventArgs) Handles optionsPanel.MouseLeave

    'changing back the properties of panel
    With Me.optionsPanel
        .BackColor = Color.Empty
        .BorderStyle = BorderStyle.FixedSingle
        .ForeColor = Color.Black

    End With
End Sub
```

The above statements will change everything back to default.
Here are the rest of the codes. Type them under their appropriate subprocedures:

```
Private Sub backgroundRadioButton_MouseLeave _
    (ByVal sender As Object, _
    ByVal e As System.EventArgs) _
    Handles backgroundRadioButton.MouseLeave
        'changing the background of RadioButton under
        'Mouseleave
        Me.backgroundRadioButton.BackColor = Color.Empty
    End Sub

Private Sub backgroundRadioButton_MouseMove _
    (ByVal sender As Object, _
    ByVal e As System.Windows.Forms.MouseEventArgs) _
    Handles backgroundRadioButton.MouseMove
        'changing the background of RadioButton under
        'Mouse Move
        Me.backgroundRadioButton.BackColor = Color.Ivory
    End Sub


Private Sub BackcolorRadioButton_MouseLeave _
    (ByVal sender As Object, _
    ByVal e As System.EventArgs) _
    Handles backcolorRadioButton.MouseLeave
        'changing the background of RadioButton under
        'Mouse leave
        Me.backcolorRadioButton.BackColor = Color.Empty
    End Sub

Private Sub backColorRadioButton_MouseMove _
    (ByVal sender As Object, _
    ByVal e As System.Windows.Forms.MouseEventArgs) _
    Handles backColorRadioButton.MouseMove
        'changing the background of RadioButton under
        'Mouse Move
        Me.backcolorRadioButton.BackColor = Color.Ivory
    End Sub
```

Now save your program and hit F5 to run your project. Move your mouse over the `Panel` and test its features.

You can view this solution under the Chapter 4 folder on the companion CD-ROM. The project is saved under its name, `panelWith`. Just copy the project folder to your hard drive and double-click on the .sln file.

LOADING IMAGES AT RUNTIME AND USING THE FROMFILE METHOD

In Chapter 3, you learned how to display an image in a `PictureBox`. You hand-picked those images and stored them in a Resource file to be used by the `Picture-Box` control. What do we need to do when the user wants to load images directly from image files? In this case, we use the `FromFile` method. This method is used to create an image from the referenced file. Here is the general syntax:

```
Me.PictureBox1.Image =
System.Drawing.Bitmap.FromFile(My.Application.Info.DirectoryPath &
"\Filename.extension")
    An example for the shorter version would be:
Me.PictureBox1.Image = image.FromFile("mike.jpg")
```

EXAMPLE 7

In this project, we will be using the following: `Panel`, `GroupBox`, `RadioButton`, `Label`, `PictureBox`, `MaskedTextBox`, `Button`, `LinkLabel`, `CheckBox`, and `Process.Start`.

Start a new project and name it: `imageload`. Add the following controls to the new form:

- Two `Labels`
- One `PictureBox`
- One `Panel`
- Two `GroupBoxes`
- Three `Buttons`
- Three `RadioButtons` to the `Panel` you just added
- One `CheckBox`
- One `MaskedTextBox`

Here is what we need:

- **Form1**
  Name: bookForm
  Text: Book Selection

- **Panel1**
  Name: optionsPanel
  BorderStyle: FixedSingle
- **Label1**
  Name: titleLabel
  Text: Book Selection
  ForeColor: Red
  Font: Microsoft Sans Serif, 8.25pt
- **Label2**
  Name: priceLabel
  Text: Price
- **PictureBox1**
  Name: bookPictureBox
  SizeMode: StretchImage
  BorderStyle: Fixed3D
- **RadioButton1**
  Name: basicRadioButton
  Text: Visual Basic
- **RadioButton2**
  Name: cobolRadioButton
  Text: COBOL
- **RadioButton3**
  Name: fortranRadioButton
  Text: FORTRAN
- **Button1**
  Name: clearButton
  Text: &Clear
- **Button2**
  Name: exitButton
  Text: E&xit
- **Button3**
  Name: submitButton
  Text: &Submit
- **CheckBox1**
  Name: addressCheckBox
  Text: Call Me
- **MaskedTextBox**
  Name: phoneMaskedTextBox
- **GroupBox1**
  Name: contactGroupBox
  Text: Contact Author

■ **GroupBox2**
  Name: contactMeGroupBox
  Text: Contact Me
■ **LinkLabel1**
  Name: emailLinkLabel
  Text: Author's Email
  LinkColor: Blue
  ActiveLinkColor: Red
  VisitedLinkColor: Fuchsia
  TextAlign: MiddleCenter
  LinkBehavior: HoverUnderline
■ **LinkLabel2**
  Name: webSiteLinkLabel
  Text: Author's Website
  LinkColor: Blue
  ActiveLinkColor: Red
  VisitedLinkColor: Fuchsia
  TextAlign: MiddleCenter
  LinkBehavior: HoverUnderline

Before we move on, we need to have three images. You can find three images of your own or use those we have placed in the solution folder of this project, in the bin\Debug folder. The names of these images are:

- basic.tif
- cobol.tif
- fortran.tif

Copy and paste these images into the following folder in the `imageload` project you just created: \imageload\imageload\Bin\Debug. This folder will be generated when you run the program, so first hit F5, stop the program, and then paste the images in the referenced directory. We will use these images in this project.

Double-click on the `Form` and type the following in the `Form_Load` event subprocedure:

```
Private Sub bookForm_Load _
    (ByVal sender As System.Object, _
    ByVal e As System.EventArgs) _
    Handles MyBase.Load
        'make the contactMeGroupBox small
        Me.contactMeGroupBox.Width = 119
        Me.contactMeGroupBox.Height = 43
        'making the contactGroupBox invisible
        Me.contactGroupBox.Visible = False
    End Sub
```

We make the size of the contactMeGroupBox smaller so the MaskedTextBox and submitButton will not be seen. Once the user checks the callMeCheckBox, we can set the size of the GroupBox bigger so the other controls are visible. We are also making the contactGroupBox invisible. The GroupBox will be visible under the Visual Basic RadioButton. What we put under the Form_Load subprocedure will be executed before the form is loaded.

Double-click on the Visual Basic RadioButton and select the Click method. Remember that the default event subprocedure would be CheckedChanged, so you need to select the Click method from the Method Name window. Now type the following lines of code in the RadioButton_Click subprocedure:

```
Private Sub basicRadioButton_Click _
    (ByVal sender As Object, _
    ByVal e As System.EventArgs) _
    Handles basicRadioButton.Click
        'display BASIC book image and price
        Me.bookPictureBox.Image = _
        Image.FromFile("basic.tif")
        Me.priceLabel.Text = "Visual Basic book price:$49.99"
        'make the Contact GroupBox visible
        Me.contactGroupBox.Visible = True
    End Sub
```

This will accomplish a few tasks:

- It displays the basic.tif image in the bookPictureBox.
- It displays the price of the book in the priceLabel.
- It makes the contactGroupBox visible. This GroupBox is displayed only when the user clicks the Visual Basic RadioButton. Other authors have not provided Web sites and email addresses.

Now put the following statements under the fortranRadioButton click subprocedure:

```
Private Sub fortranRadioButton_Click _
    (ByVal sender As Object, _
    ByVal e As System.EventArgs) _
    Handles fortranRadioButton.Click
        'Make the contactgroupbox invisible
        Me.contactGroupBox.Visible = False
        'display Fortran book image and price
        Me.bookPictureBox.Image = _
        Image.FromFile("fortran.tif")
        Me.priceLabel.Text = "FORTRAN book price:$50.00"
    End Sub
```

Now do the same thing for the cobolRadioButton:

```
Private Sub cobolRadioButton_Click _
    (ByVal sender As Object, _
    ByVal e As System.EventArgs) Handles cobolRadioButton.Click
        'Make the contactgroupbox invisible
        Me.contactGroupBox.Visible = False
        'display COBOL book image and price
        Me.bookPictureBox.Image = _
        Image.FromFile("cobol.tif")
        Me.priceLabel.Text = "COBOL book price:$47.00"
    End Sub
```

Now the `contactGroupBox` that appeared under the Visual Basic `RadioButton` is invisible because there is no contact information for this author.

Let us go back to the design mode and highlight the `phoneMaskTextBox` control you placed on the form. Notice the Smart Tag on the top of the control. Click on it. In the `MaskedTextBox` Task Pane, see the Set Mask link. When you click on it, it takes you to the Input Mask dialog box. Select the Phone Number Mask format from the list of options (see Figure 4.11).

FIGURE 4.11   `MaskedTextBox` mask option.

Now find the `addressCheckBox` `Click` event subprocedure and type the following:

```
Private Sub addressCheckBox_Click _
    (ByVal sender As Object, _
    ByVal e As System.EventArgs) _
    Handles addressCheckBox.Click
        'make the size of the contactMeGroupBox smaller
```

```
        Me.contactMeGroupBox.Width = 119
        Me.contactMeGroupBox.Height = 100
    End Sub
```

We need to add codes to the *Submit* Button as well:

```
Private Sub submitButton_Click _
    (ByVal sender As System.Object, _
    ByVal e As System.EventArgs) _
    Handles submitButton.Click
        'confirms the submission
        MessageBox.Show("Your Phone " & phoneMaskedTextBox.Text, _
        "Thanks We will Contact ", _
        MessageBoxButtons.OK, MessageBoxIcon.Information)
        'clears the maskedtextbox
        Me.phoneMaskedTextBox.Text = Nothing
        'clears the checkbox
        Me.addressCheckBox.Checked = False
        'reset the contactMeGroupBox
        Me.contactMeGroupBox.Width = 119
        Me.contactMeGroupBox.Height = 43
    End Sub
```

It is time to add codes to the emailLinkLabel. Double-click on the label and place the following code under the label's Click event subprocedure. This is the default subprocedure for LinkLabel and you do not need to pick it from the Method Name window:

```
Private Sub emailLinkLabel_LinkClicked _
    (ByVal sender As System.Object, _
    ByVal e As System.Windows.Forms. _
    LinkLabelLinkClickedEventArgs) _
    Handles emailLabel.LinkClicked
        'call for the default email
        System.Diagnostics.Process.Start _
        ("mailto:Mike.Mostafavi@beasa.com")
    End Sub
```

As stated before, the Process.Start method starts the requested processes and lets you access them. In this case, the program runs your default email program. Now do the same thing for the webSiteLinkLabel:

```
Private Sub webSiteLabel_LinkClicked _
    (ByVal sender As System.Object, _
    ByVal e As System.Windows.Forms. _
    LinkLabelLinkClickedEventArgs) _
    Handles webSiteLabel.LinkClicked
        'call for the default browser
        System.Diagnostics.Process.Start _
        ("http://vbnet.beasa.com")
    End Sub
```

Now double-click on the Clear button and add the following:

```
Private Sub clearButton_Click _
    (ByVal sender As System.Object, _
    ByVal e As System.EventArgs) _
    Handles clearButton.Click
        'Clear all controls
        Me.basicRadioButton.Checked = False
        Me.cobolRadioButton.Checked = False
        Me.fortranRadioButton.Checked = False
        Me.bookPictureBox.Image = Nothing
        Me.addressCheckBox.Checked = False
        Me.phoneMaskedTextBox.Text = Nothing
        Me.contactGroupBox.Visible = False
        Me.priceLabel.Text = Nothing
        Me.contactMeGroupBox.Width = 119
        Me.contactMeGroupBox.Height = 43
    End Sub
```

Here is the code for `exitRadioButton`:

```
Private Sub exitRadioButton_Click _
    (ByVal sender As System.Object, _
    ByVal e As System.EventArgs) _
    Handles exitButton.Click
        'ending your program
        MessageBox.Show("This will end your project", _
        "Warning", MessageBoxButtons.OK, _
        MessageBoxIcon.Information)
        Me.Close()
    End Sub
```

Figure 4.12 shows a screenshot of the running project.

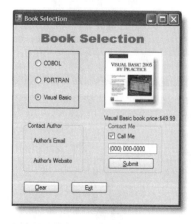

FIGURE 4.12 Screenshot of book selection project.

Panels are very useful when dividing the Form into several distinct areas. This allows us to treat each section of the form differently.

ON THE CD

You can view this solution under the Chapter 4 folder on the companion CD-ROM. The project is saved under its name, imageload. Just copy the project folder to your hard drive and double-click on the .sln file.

DEBUGGING THE PROJECT

Writing a bug-free program is every programmer's dream. However, this does not happen too often. Every programmer will find a bug in his program eventually. Fortunately, Visual Basic 2005 has many tools that can be utilized to find errors. Even if the program runs fine, you still want to see how your program accesses the values and whether the right sequence is followed or not. All programmers eventually get into more complicated projects, so they learn how to debug their programs. Visual Basic 2005 provides powerful tools to monitor your program and see where the problems are.

Debugging controls are placed on the standard toolbar and have different functions (see Figure 4.13). You can also access the debugging tools through the toolbar or the Debug tab, which is also located on the menu bar. This toolbar consists of the following:

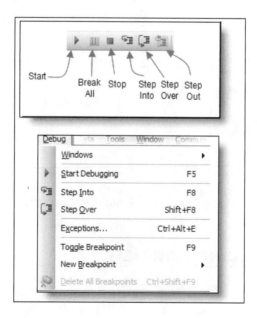

FIGURE 4.13 Debugging toolbar and drop down.

Starting or Continuing Execution is used to start debugging or continue it if it is paused.

Breaking Execution occurs when the execution reaches a breakpoint or an exception.

Stopping Execution means terminating the debugging session. This is different from breaking execution.

Stepping Through the Application involves three steps: Step Into, Step Over, and Step Out. These steps allow the execution of codes line by line.

Running to Specified Location allows you to run the program to a specific location of your program.

Setting the Execution Point can be used to move the execution point from one place to another place and skip codes that do not need to be debugged.

Debugging at Design Time

It is possible to execute a portion of your project in a separate window, even if your program is in design mode. This is known as debugging at design time. During the debugging process, several windows will be opened to help you display, edit, and evaluate your codes. Each window has three columns to show name, value, and type. You can find the names of your variables under the Name column and the corresponding values and types under the other two columns (see Figure 4.14).

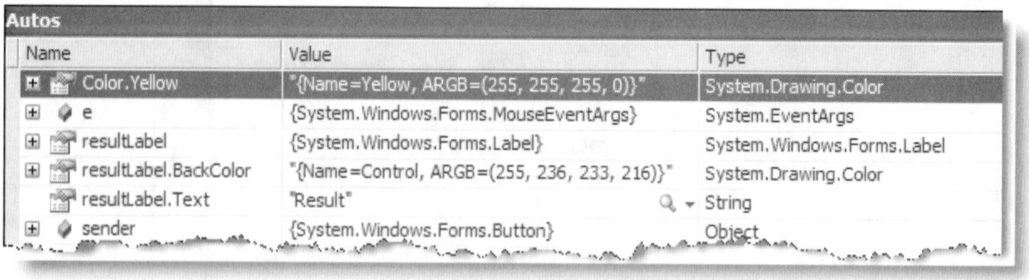

Autos		
Name	Value	Type
Color.Yellow	"{Name=Yellow, ARGB=(255, 255, 255, 0)}"	System.Drawing.Color
e	{System.Windows.Forms.MouseEventArgs}	System.EventArgs
resultLabel	{System.Windows.Forms.Label}	System.Windows.Forms.Label
resultLabel.BackColor	"{Name=Control, ARGB=(255, 236, 233, 216)}"	System.Drawing.Color
resultLabel.Text	"Result"	String
sender	{System.Windows.Forms.Button}	Object

FIGURE 4.14 Debugging windows and their columns.

SIMPLE DEBUGGING PRACTICE

Start Visual Studio 2005 and place a Button on the form. Resize the Button to a larger scale so the text will fit into it. Double-click on the Button and type the following statements:

```
Me.Button1.Text = "I was pushed"
    Me.Button1.Text = "Pushed again"
```

Breakpoint, Start Debugging, Step Into, Continue, Step Over, Step Out, and Stop Debugging

Think of the breakpoint as a stop sign that has appeared in front of the compiler. The compiler will break the execution of your application once it sees the breakpoint. Your application will be in break mode from this point and wait for your action. As a programmer, you need to decide where the breakpoint should go.

Now we want to add a breakpoint to this program. Move the cursor over the left margin of the first line of the code you added and click on it. As soon as you do this, you will notice a red highlighted line of code, which was the first statement you typed. There will also be a red ballpoint on the margin of that statement (see Figure 4.15). This task can also be accomplished by right-clicking on the first statement, pointing to the Breakpoint Context menu item and selecting the Insert Breakpoint option from the list (see Figure 4.16).

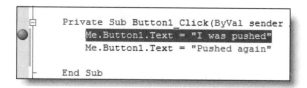

FIGURE 4.15   Breakpoint on the source code.

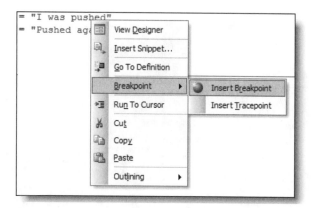

FIGURE 4.16   Inserting a breakpoint from the *Context* menu.

Start debugging by hitting F5, clicking on the Start icon on the toolbar, or choosing Start Debugging from the Debug menu (see Figure 4.17). Once you do this, the program will run as it normally does.

FIGURE 4.17   Starting debugging from menu and toolbar.

Do not click on the button yet. Instead, click on the Debug menu, select Windows and move your mouse over the Watch menu item. Once you move the mouse over the Watch menu item, another submenu will be displayed. Click on the Watch1 submenu item (see Figure 4.18).

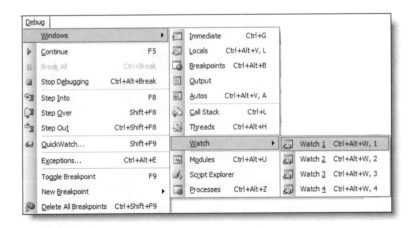

FIGURE 4.18   Opening the *Watch* window.

By now, the Form is most likely inactive. Click on the Form button located in the bottom taskbar of your screen to activate the Form. Click on the Button1 you placed on the Form. The program breaks and the highlighting color of the breakpoint statement changes from red to yellow. A yellow arrow is placed inside the red dot representing the breakpoint (see Figure 4.19).

```
Private Sub Button1_Click(ByVal sender
    Me.Button1.Text = "I was pushed"
    Me.Button1.Text = "Pushed again"

End Sub
```

FIGURE 4.19 Program stopped at breakpoint.

The program now is in break mode and is ready for debugging. One of the reasons for debugging is so you can watch the flow of the program to monitor the value of the variables and properties. A Watch window is added to the bottom of your form. Move your mouse over the Watch1 window and click on a blank spot under the Name column. Now type the following phrase and hit the Enter key.

```
Me.Button1.Text
```

As soon as you hit Enter, Visual Basic shows you the value and type of the Button's text property in the Value and Type columns (see Figure 4.20). The value of the Button1.Text is Button1 and the value type is String. Now choose Step Into from the Debug menu or the Debug toolbar and click on it. You can also use F8 to execute this command. Step Into tells the compiler to move to the next statement and execute it. Once this is done, the second line of the code will be highlighted in yellow and an arrow will have appeared in its margin. Now the first statement is highlighted in red again and the value of the Button1.Text in the Watch1 window has changed to I was pushed (see Figure 4.21).

Watch 1		
Name	Value	Type
me.Button1.Text	"Button1"	String

FIGURE 4.20 Using the *Watch* window.

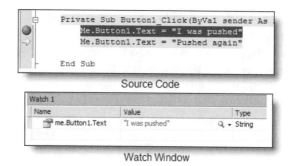

Source Code

Watch Window

FIGURE 4.21 Using *Step Into.*

As you can see, Step Into allows us to execute the program line by line. Let's continue debugging by pressing the Continue button in the Debug menu or pressing F5. This resumes the execution of the program. The Form pops up again and you can click on its Button. Once you click the Button, the program goes to break mode again and highlights the first line of your code in yellow. The value of Button1.Text is Pushed again! and is displayed in the Watch1 window (see Figure 4.22).

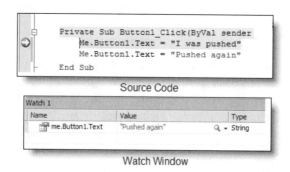

Source Code

Watch Window

FIGURE 4.22 Next line value.

Another command is called Step Over. This command is very similar to the Step Into command. The major difference is that Step Over executes the entire function, while Step Into executes the statement that calls for a function and breaks the program once the first line of the function is seen. For more information, refer to the Code Stepping Overview of MSDN resources at *http://msdn2.microsoft.com/en-us/library/ek13f001.aspx*.

Now choose Step Out from the toolbar to make the program go back to the statement that called for that function and break at the first line of the function. The Form pops up again, and after you push Button1, it breaks on the first line of the code (see Figure 4.23).

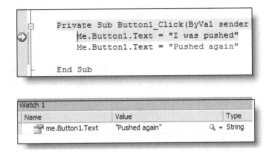

FIGURE 4.23 *Step Out* command.

You can stop debugging by clicking on the Stop Debugging icon on the toolbar. The breakpoint is still on your code source. You can right-click on the highlighted line and either delete the breakpoint or disable it (see Figure 4.24).

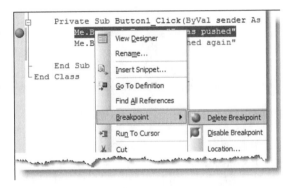

FIGURE 4.24 Deleting or disabling the breakpoint.

Edit and Continue

This feature was included in Visual Basic 6 but was discontinued in Visual Basic.NET. Visual Studio 2005 has brought back this popular feature, and it is available to C#, C++, and Visual Basic programmers now. This feature allows programmers to make changes or make corrections to their codes while the program is in break mode. Using this feature, you can get into the break mode and correct the error. After you make changes to your code, you can continue the execution of your program without recompiling it. Although this feature has some limitations, it works great for most programming projects. To activate this feature do the following:

1. From the Tool menu, choose Option.
2. Look in the Options and expand the Debugging folder by clicking on the plus sign next to it.
3. Click on the Edit and Continue option and check the Enable Edit and Continue checkbox. You can uncheck the checkbox if you want to stop this feature (see Figure 4.25).

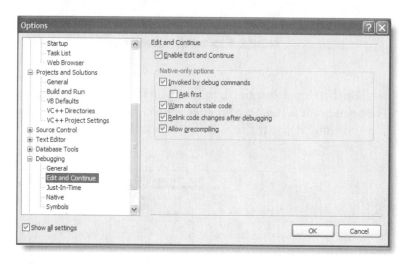

FIGURE 4.25   Edit and Continue setting.

Now if there is an error in your program and the program stops because of it, you can correct the error and click on the Continue button or hit F5 to continue. As explained, there are cases in which you have to stop the program after you make the change and run it again. An example of this would be when you change the type of a variable.

MORE PROGRAMMING TIPS

As we discussed in previous chapters, although the visual features of Visual Basic make it very easy to develop the users' interface, there are rules that we need to follow. Designers need to look at the Forms from users' perspectives, not just their own. Designing a user-friendly Form that collects the user's information is an art. Dragging and dropping controls into the Forms without planning will cause problems in the future. Designing your Form based on a calculated plan will minimize the need for modification and adjustment. Here are a few additional tips related to Form design:

■ While you need to take maximum advantage of the Form space that is available to you, you do not want to overcrowd your Form. There should be enough blank space to allow the user to find things quickly. If the Form is too crowded, it affects the user's speed and efficiency.

■ Take advantage of visual effects. The user should not be confused about the controls, so make them stand out and be visible to the user. If the control is a push button, use the 3D option to make sure the user knows what it is.

■ Color plays an important role in visual programming. Although it is beneficial to users to have different colors on a Form, color can be a source of confusion if it is not used appropriately. Obviously, with the advancement of technology, we can use many colors in our input and output design. We do not pick colors just for beauty. The safe rule of thumb is usually to stay away from strong colors and pick neutral colors as much as possible. This is, of course, a general rule and can be overridden in specific situations or different targets. Some programmers are more conservative and avoid using colors that may play a key role in their program. This method will allow more users with different types of monitors to view pages.

■ Keep your Forms simple. Some programmers think the interface must be fancy and flashy to attract users, but that is not correct. Simple Forms will get better reviews. Our job is to develop programs that are easy to follow, not to impress the users with flashy features.

■ Use images and icons appropriately. Relevant icons, menus, and images will enhance your interface.

■ Try to group the controls logically and position them appropriately. For example, all of the controls related to receiving input from the user can be placed in the same GroupBox, and *Submit* Buttons can be placed at the bottom of the form. Users look for the *Submit* Button in that area.

■ Pick the right tool. Many similar tools are offered by Visual Basic. It is the programmer's responsibility to find the best tool that serves the purpose.

■ Utilize proper fonts. Decide when to use bold, italic, or larger fonts, according to the application.

As a programmer, based on your audience and the norm of the company, you will develop your own standards. As noted before, programmers should always strive for consistency when developing forms.

SUMMARY

In this chapter, we introduced you to new tools, such as Panel and LinkLabel. We also expanded our discussion of MessageBox and provided you with several examples that showed you how Buttons and icons can be added to the MessageBox. This chapter also provided you with a method used to load images dynamically and gave you a chance to experiment with tools such as RadioButtons and CheckBoxes.

Next

In Chapter 5 we will cover Calculations, Data Types, Constants, Variables, and Conditional Statements. You will also learn how to convert data types, set the scope of your variables, format your output, and use Option Explicit and Option Strict to have a strong type program.

DISCUSSION QUESTIONS

1. What are the major differences between GroupBoxes and Panels?
2. What are the differences between CheckBoxes and RadioButtons?
3. Can a Panel control be used in place of a GroupBox? Briefly justify your response.
4. What icons can be added to a MessageBox? List them.
5. List all possible buttons that can be added to a MessageBox and briefly describe their nature.

Exercises

1. Write an interactive program to collect information from users. Use TextBox to gather information and display it back to the user using a MessageBox.
2. Make sure you use GroupBox, Label, Button, TextBox, and MessageBox.
3. Try to debug your program by following the steps we listed in the chapter.

Key Terms

- CheckBox
- RadioButton
- GroupBox
- Panel
- MaskedTextBox
- LinkLabel

5 Calculations, Constants, Variables, Conditions, and Data Types

In This Chapter

ARITHMETIC OPERATIONS

In previous chapters, you witnessed the capabilities of several controls. You learned how to add these controls to your Form, how to add codes, and how to terminate your program. However, we did not mention one of the most important features of programming. This feature is available in all programming languages, but each programming language deals with it differently. This feature is the *calculation* capability of any programming language. We will now turn our attention to this feature.

Arithmetic Expressions

Before we write a program to calculate numbers, we need to be familiar with arithmetic expressions. These are very similar to the arithmetic operations that we do by hand or calculator. When you use a calculator, you punch specific keys such as a minus sign or plus sign to deduct or add numbers. Computers need to know these operators as well.

Arithmetic Operators

Like your calculator, computers need to know what type of arithmetic operations you would like to perform. You communicate your needs through symbols that a computer can understand. These symbols are called *arithmetic operators*. Table 5.1 shows the operators that are used to perform arithmetic operations.

TABLE 5.1 Arithmetic Operators

Operator	Symbol	Function
Exponentiation operator	^	Raises a number to the power of an exponent
Multiplication operator	*	Multiplies two numbers
Division operator	/	Divides two numbers and returns a result
Integer division operator	\	Divides two numbers and returns an integer result
Mod operator	mod	Divides two numbers and returns the remainder
Addition operator	+	Sums two numbers
Subtraction operator	–	Finds the difference between two numbers

In addition to these, as you remember from previous chapters, the ampersand (&) is a *concatenation operator*.

Precedence of Operations

We need to become familiar with the term *precedence*, or *order of operations*, for these operators. Precedence is the hierarchy or the priority that Visual Basic gives to these operators. Simply put, Visual Basic uses a guideline to perform arithmetic operations. This becomes important when more than one kind of arithmetic operator appears within one expression. Under the normal order of operation, these operators are treated as follows:

1. Exponentiation
2. Multiplication or division, depending on the order of their appearance from left to right
3. Integer division
4. Mod
5. Addition or subtraction, depending on the order of their appearance from left to right

This list tells Visual Basic to perform the exponentiation calculation first. An example will help us understand this concept better:

$$3+2*5$$

The result is 13, not 25. How did that happen? If we follow the rules given above, the first operation will be 2*5, which returns 10. The second operation will be 3+10, which returns 13. Let us look at some more examples.

$$2*10^2+2$$

The result is 202. Here is how: the first operation is 10^2 because exponentiation has the highest priority of the operators in this arithmetic operation. The result of the first operation, which is 10^2, is 100. The second operation is 2*100 because multiplication has a higher priority than addition. The result of the second operation is 200. Now the third operation will take place, which is 200+2, because the addition has the lowest priority in this expression. Therefore, the result is 202. Occasionally we want to force a specific order of operation. Considering our first example, 3+2*5, let us say we really want 3+2 to be calculated first and then be multiplied by 5. Then we need to change the order of operation. In this case, the parentheses are used to give higher priority to an operation:

$$(3+2)*5$$

The result is 25. Therefore, the operation in parentheses always has the highest priority in any arithmetic operation.

Here is an example of a mod operator.

$$10 \ mod \ 8$$

The result is 2. Mod divides 10 by 8 and reports the reminder of the calculation.

DATA TYPES

Every day, people receive a large volume of data and process it. Humans can differentiate between various types of data without confusing them. For instance, humans can look at a series of data and categorize dates, numbers, payments, and so on with minimal effort. However, computers need specific instructions to be able to process data. For example, if you just type 123, you cannot assume that the computer knows you entered numbers. You have to tell the computer about the type of data that is entered. Understanding *data type* can be a little confusing and requires some more explanation.

To illustrate data type, consider the following scenario: You have invited some of your friends over for a chess game, so you get the chessboard and all of the pieces prepared. The board has 64 black and white squares and you need to place each piece on a specific square. Each piece has its own movement rules and authorities. You cannot place the king piece in the queen's square or use white pieces in place of black ones. You need to place each piece in its own square. Data type is very similar to this. Each piece of data will be stored in a different storage area and will be processed differently. Identifying data type is very important to computers. The computer reserves special storage for each data type and keeps track of them internally. You may enter an address that includes numbers as well as alphabet characters. Although the address has numbers in it, by setting the data type as string, you can treat it as alphabetical data. Table 5.2 shows most of the data types that Visual Basic can recognize:

TABLE 5.2 Data Types in Visual Basic 2005

Data Type	Function
Boolean	Holds True or false values
Byte	Values ranging from 0 to 255 unsigned
Char	Unsigned characters 0–65535
Date	0:00:00 (Midnight); 1/1/00001; 11:59:59; 12/12/9999
Decimal	Holds signed 128-bit values such as numbers and fractions
Double	Holds signed IEEE Institute of Electrical and Electronic Engineers 64-bit double precision floating-point numbers
Single	Holds signed IEEE 32-bit single precision floating-point numbers
Short	Holds signed 16-bit integers –32,768 through 32,767

→

Data Type	Function
Integer	Holds signed 32-bit integer values –2,147,483,648 through 2,147,483,647
Long	Holds signed integer values from –9,223,372,036,854,775,808 through 9,223,372,036,854,775,807
String	All characters including alphanumeric and digits
Object	Holds 32-bits (4 bytes) of any type

The most common data types we use are integer, string, and decimal. The following sections give descriptions and examples of some of the data types in Visual Basic 2005.

Boolean

The values that can be stored in boolean data can only be True or False. We use this data type if we expect two possible states: yes/no or true/false. The default value of boolean data is False. We will give you an example later on when we introduce you to conditional statements.

Integer

Integer data can contain signed whole numbers ranging from –2,147,483,648 through 2,147,483,647. The default value for integer type data is 0. If you assign a value that is outside this range, you will get an error message. If you would like to store the result of the calculation, then do not use integer. Integer will not show the fractions. Here are some examples of integer data:

- 21
- 3
- 25000
- –11
- 6543218I

Long

Long is another integer data type that should be used for signed whole numbers that are larger than the integer range. The range for long data is –9,223,372,036,854,775,808 through 9,223,372,036,854,775,807 (9.2...E+18). The default value for long data is 0. Here are some examples of long integer data:

- 1234567890998
- −123456789099
- −77898588098L

Short

The short data type is used to hold signed integer values ranging from −32,768 through 32,767. We use this for values that do not require the whole range of the integer type. The default value for short data is 0. Here are some examples:

- −32764
- 22769
- 32764S

Decimal

The decimal type of data can hold numbers in a fixed-point format and allows fractions and decimal points. Here are some examples:

- 6.05
- 550.500
- −300
- 200D

Byte

This data type can contain integers ranging in value from 0 through 255. We use this data type to store binary data. Remember that the byte data type cannot contain the negative sign for the values, so if the negative sign plays a significant role in your data, other data types should be considered. The default value for byte data is 0.

Double

Double data can store double-precision floating-point numbers ranging in value from −1.79769313486231570E+308 through −4.94065645841246544E-324 for negative values and from 4.94065645841246544E-324 through 1.79769313486231570E+308 for positive values. The default value for double data is 0. Here are some examples:

- 6575.3
- 5189.2R
- −5467.3

Object

Object data is used to hold any type of data and was introduced in the Visual Basic.NET version. The default value for object data is `Nothing`.

String

String data may contain letters such as A–Z or a–z, numbers 0–9, and all special characters such as %, $, and #. The numbers you use as string type cannot be used in calculations unless they are converted. The default value for string is `Nothing`. Here are some examples for string type data:

- "Mike"
- "2005"
- "$100.00"
- "Visual Basic 2005"

Char

The char data type should be used when you plan to store one unsigned character. If only one character should be stored, using the char type instead of the string type will prevent unneeded overhead. Unicode characters refer to the 128 characters (0–127) that are found on standard U.S. keyboards. It can hold values from 0 through 65535.

EXAMPLE 1

Let us look at a simple calculation. Start a new project and call it `Calculation`. Drag and drop five `Buttons` and a `Label` on the `Form`. Name these controls according to the following:

- **Form1**
  Name: calculationForm
  Text: Simple Calculation
- **Button1**
  Name: addButton
  Text: &Add
- **Button2**
  Name: subtractButton
  Text: &Subtract
- **Button3**
  Name: divideButton
  Text: &Divide

- **Button4**
  Name: multiplyButton
  Text: &Multiply
- **Button5**
  Name: exitButton
  Text: E&xit
- **Label1**
  Name: resultLabel
  Text: Result
  Font: Arial Black, 12pt

Each Button will perform a different arithmetic operation. In addition to this task, each Button will change the background color of the Result label box.

Let us add the code. Double-click on the addButton and add the following code. You will see the entire subprocedure here but you only need to type the codes that are in italic.

```
Private Sub addButton_Click _
(ByVal sender As System.Object, _
ByVal e As System.EventArgs) _
Handles addButton.Click
    'Changes the background color to yellow
    Me.resultLabel.BackColor = Color.Yellow
    'displays a message and the result of claculation
    Me.resultLabel.Text = "The result of 20 + 25 is " & 20 + 25
End Sub
```

This is an assignment statement, which was covered in Chapter 3. The result of the calculation will be stored in the text property of resultLabel and will be displayed on the screen (see Figure 5.1).

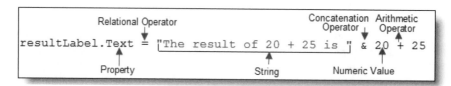

FIGURE 5.1 Assignment statement.

Visual Basic will display the following first:

```
The result of 20 + 25 is:
```

It is not important what we place inside the quotation marks because Visual Basic will ignore the content of it completely. It will display the content of whatever you placed inside the quotation marks without any code evaluation. That is how Visual Basic treats strings. However, the piece next to this line will be evaluated by Visual Basic, and the arithmetic operation will be performed on it. Visual Basic differentiates between the two 20 + 25s that appear inside and outside the quotation marks and treats them differently.

Now double-click on Subtract and type the following code:

```
Private Sub subtractButton_Click( _
ByVal sender As System.Object, _
ByVal e As System.EventArgs) _
Handles subtractButton.Click
    'Changes the background color to Sandybrown
    Me.resultLabel.BackColor = Color.SandyBrown
    'displays a message and the result of claculation
    Me.resultLabel.Text = "The result of 25 - 20 is " & 25 - 20
End Sub
```

This statement is very similar to the last statement. The only difference is that it changes the label's background to a different color and subtracts the second number from the first one. Let's add the following codes as well. Under the divideButton type:

```
Private Sub divideButton_Click _
(ByVal sender As System.Object, _
ByVal e As System.EventArgs) _
Handles divideButton.Click
    'displays a message and the result of Aqua
    Me.resultLabel.BackColor = Color.Aqua
    'displays a message and the result of claculation
    Me.resultLabel.Text = "The result of 40 /10 is " & 40 / 10
End Sub
```

Under the multiplyButton type:

```
Private Sub multiplyButton_Click _
(ByVal sender As System.Object, _
ByVal e As System.EventArgs) _
Handles multiplyButton.Click
    'displays a message and the result of CornflowerVlue
    Me.resultLabel.BackColor = Color.CornflowerBlue
    'displays a message and the result of claculation
    Me.resultLabel.Text = "The result of 20 * 25 is " & 20 * 25
End Sub
```

You have learned how to code the exitButton, so code it yourself now. Figure 5.2 shows what your Form should look like when you run your project.

ON THE CD

You can view this solution under the Chapter 5 folder on the companion CD-ROM. The project is saved under its name, `Calculations`. Just copy the project folder to your hard drive and double-click on the .sln file.

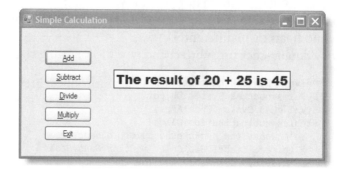

FIGURE 5.2   Completed `Form`.

CONSTANTS AND VARIABLES

In Example 1, we stored the result of the calculation in the `text` property of a `Label`. However, this is not a practical style. Instead of storing the data in the `text` property of a control, we can store it in a temporary space and use it throughout the project. This is a routine task for programmers. They reserve special temporary spaces within their programs and store values in them.

Variables

A *variable* is a temporary storage space that can hold different values. However, variables can hold only one value at any given time. You can assign values to variables anywhere in the program. Once you assign a new value to a variable, the old value will be replaced by the new one. That is why they call variables a temporary storage.

Visual Basic needs to know what type of data will be stored in each variable. Although most known programming languages require declaring data types, not all of them deal with it the same way. Some programming languages are loose with their data types, and some are very restricted. It is highly recommended that you declare your variables with their data type to conserve memory resources.

We need to assign a name to each variable that we use within our program and identify the types of data these variables can hold. This action in programming is known as *declaration*. We declare our variable names and their types by using the

Dim keyword. DIM stands for dimension and identifies the name of the variables. Here is the general format for variable declaration:

```
Dim variableName As DataType
```

The (As) clause is used to define the data type of the variable and is a reserved word. To declare a variable we can do the following:

```
Dim messageString As String
```

When you type the above statement, you will notice that all valid data types will be shown by the IntelliSense feature after you type the (As) clause.

We can define several variables by using only one DIM statement:

```
Dim A, B, C As String
Dim M, N As String, J, K As Integer
Dim valueInteger As Integer = 10
```

As you can see in the first statement, A, B, and C are variables and their data type is string. In the second statement, M and N are declared as string, and J and K are defined as integer. In the third statement, we have already assigned a value to the variable. If you reference the valueInteger within your program, its value would be 10.

We assign values to the variables by using the assignment statement. Review the following statements:

```
Dim nameString as String
nameString="Mike"
nameString="My School"
```

As you can see, we declared a variable as the String type. Then we assigned two values to it: Mike and My School. What would be the value of this variable now? The value is My School because the variable holds the last value that is assigned to it.

Constants

In contrast to variables, *constants* are locations that hold values that remain unchanged during the execution of the applications. For example, you as a student may take many classes with different names and titles, but your name will remain the same during the process. Unlike for variables, assigning a value to a constant is not optional. You may have noticed that we could declare a variable with or without initial values. Assigning a value to a constant is not optional. You must assign a value to a constant when you declare it.

We can declare a constant by using the Const keyword. We can declare constants anywhere in the program:

```
Const socialSecurityString As String = "xxx-xx-xxxx"
```

Constants have one more difference from variables. They cannot be the target of an assignment statement. Therefore, the following statement is incorrect:

```
socialSecurityString="5555-xx-xxxx"
```

As shown in Table 5.2, each data type has its own parameters and characteristics. You can set your variables or constants to hold any of these data types.

Naming Conventions for Variables and Constants

In Chapter 3, we used standard guidelines to identify control names. Variable and constant names have their own naming rules as well:

- Variable and constant names must begin with an alphabetic character or an underscore (_).
- If the variable or constant name begins with an underscore, then it must contain at least one decimal digit or alphabetic character.
- It must contain only alphabetic characters, decimal digits, and underscores.
- Variable and constant names, which are called identifiers, should not be too short or too long. During coding, you may not remember long variable names, and short variable names may not be descriptive enough. Try to spell out the whole names rather than using abbreviations.
- Identifier names should describe what they represent. This will be very helpful when you modify the program a few years later. By looking at the identifiers' names, you can guess what they do. This will also be very helpful to others who may need to work with your codes. You also should include the type of data a variable or constant carries.
- Variable and constant names cannot be the same as the Visual Basic reserved words. For example, you cannot call your variable Integer. This will conflict with the existing names within Visual Basic.
- Variable and constant names are not case sensitive, so you should not use upper- and lower-case as a distinguishing factor. Therefore, the following statements are identical to Visual Basic, and you will receive an error message for the second statement:

```
Dim intCIS_570 As Integer = 100
Dim intcis_570 As Integer = 100
```

Here are some examples of valid variable and constant names:

- `Dim phoneNumbersString as String`
- `Const ADDRESSString as String= "Portland, Oregon"`
- `Dim commisionRateDecimal as Decimal`
- `Const COURSECreditNumberInteger as Integer = 4`

In general, the constant names should be in uppercase. You can also use an underscore to break up the words to make them more readable.

IDENTIFIER TYPE CHARACTERS

You have learned how to declare indenters and specify their types by using declaration statements. However, Visual Basic provides a series of characters that can be used to force the data types on the identifiers (see Table 5.3).

TABLE 5.3 Type Characters

Type Character	Data Type	Examples
%	Integer	`Dim accountCode%`
@	Decimal	`Const payRate@ = 7.50`
$	String	`Dim password$ = "hiSSS!"`
&	Long	`Dim accountNumber&`
!	Single	`Dim quantity!`
#	Double	`Dim commissionRate#`

The type character must be placed immediately after the identifier's name. There should not be any intervening characters between the identifier name and the type character. The type character is not available for all of the existing data types. You can reference the identifier without the type character:

```
Dim hourWorked%
    hourWorked = 10
```

The above statement is equal to the following:

```
Dim hourWorked As Integer
    hourWorked = 10
```

OTHER TYPES OF CONSTANTS

In addition to user-defined constants, you will be working with system-defined constants. Visual Basic has many predefined constants that can be used by developers (see Table 5.4).

TABLE 5.4 Some Predefined Constants

Constant	Description
cvCrLf	Carriage return/linefeed
vbCr	Carriage return
vbLf	Linefeed
vbTab	Tab character
vbBack	Backspace character

Default Literal Types

A *literal* is text that can represent the value of a specific data type. Here is an example:

```
TextBox1.Text = "School"
```

The quotation marks represent the string value. The following represents the value of the double data type:

```
payRate = 5.75
```

Forced Literal Types

In Visual Basic, you can append literal characters (shown in Table 5.5) to the end of literals to force them to carry a type other than the default data type. There are no type characters for the boolean, byte, date, object, Sbyte, or string data types. Here is an example:

```
resultLabel.Text = ("A")
```

In the above statement, the default type for the "A" character is string.

```
resultLabel.Text = ("A"c)
```

By adding the "c" literal type character, we forced the "A" to change its type from string to char. Here is another example:

```
Dim m As Double
    m = 100S
```

In the above statements, we declare m as double type. However, by appending an s to the literal, we changed its type to short.

TABLE 5.5 Literal Type Characters

Character	Data Type	Example
S	Short	Result=100S
I	Integer	Result=989I
L	Long	Result=654L
D	Decimal	Result=876D
F	Single	Result=320.0F
R	Double	Result=689.0R
C	Char	Result="M"C

Here are some examples:

```
Forcing the literal to type single:    Dim m As Double
      m = 100.0F
```

Forcing the literal to type long:

```
Dim p As Single
      p = 15L
```

ADDING UP STRINGS

In previous chapters, we added string values and displayed the result on the screen. We can accomplish this task by using a concatenation operator. These operators can join multiple strings into a single string.

```
TextBox1.Text = "This is" & " " & "my message"
```

When you run this program, you should see the following output:

```
This is my message
```

This is equal to the following statement:

```
Textbox1.Text = "This is" + " " + "my message"
```

Once the data is placed inside the quotations, it automatically receives string type. Here is an example:

```
resultLabel.Text = "20" + "30"
```

The value of `resultLabel.Text` is 2030.

We will now experiment with a small test. Create a new program and call it `addString`. Add two `TextBoxes`, one `Label`, and one `Button` to the `Form`. Do not worry about changing the names of controls. Change the text properties of these controls according to the screenshot shown in Figure 5.3.

FIGURE 5.3 `addString` program screenshot.

Now, double-click on the `addButton` and type the following codes into it:

```
Private Sub Button1_Click _
(ByVal sender As System.Object, _
ByVal e As System.EventArgs) _
Handles Button1.Click
    Me.Label1.Text = Me.TextBox1.Text + Me.TextBox2.Text
End Sub
```

Now run the program. Type "10" in `TextBox1` and "50" in `TextBox2` and click on the `addButton`. What is displayed in the label? It should be 1050. This is similar to the example we showed you before:

```
Label1.Text = "10" + "50"
```

This shows that the default type for the data that is entered into a `TextBox`, is string. It is apparent that Visual Basic concatenated the two strings and joined them into a single value.

ON THE CD
You can view this solution under the Chapter 5 folder on the companion CD-ROM. The project is saved under its name, addString. Just copy the project folder to your hard drive and double-click on the .sln file.

OTHER OPERATORS

In addition to the operators discussed above, here are some other operators that can be used in programming:

& Operator

As you saw before, this string operator concatenates two expressions:

```
Label1.Text = "Hello " & "VB"
```

&= Operator

This string operator is used to concatenate two variables and assign the result to the variable on the left side of the operation.

```
Dim a As String = "Learn "
Dim b As String = "Visual Basic"
a &= b
Label1.Text = a
```

The value of the a variable now is Learn Visual Basic.

+= Operator

This numeric operator is used to combine the value of a numeric expression to the value of a numeric variable or property.

```
Dim k As Integer = 10
Dim m As Integer = 20
k += m
```

The value of the k variable is 30.

− = Operator

This numeric operator is the opposite of the += operator and subtracts the value that appears on the right side of the equation from the expression on the left side.

```
Dim k As Integer = 30
Dim m As Integer = 10
k -= m
```

The value of the k variable is 20.

/ = Operator

This numeric operator divides the value that appears on the right side of the equation by the expression on the left side and assigns a floating-point value to the first variable.

```
Dim k As Integer = 35
Dim m As Integer = 10
k /= m
```

The value of k is 4.

* = Operator

This numeric operator multiplies the value that appears on the right side of equation by the value of the expression on the left side and assigns the result to the first variable.

```
Dim k As Integer = 20
Dim m As Integer = 10
k *= m
```

The value of k is 200.

\ = Operator

This numeric operator divides the value that appears on the right side of the equation by the expression on the left side and assigns an integer value to the first variable.

```
Dim k As Integer = 35
Dim m As Integer = 10
k \= m
```

The value of k is 3

^ = Operator

This numeric operator is similar to the others. It will raise the value of the first variable to the power of the value of the second variable and return the resulting value back to the first variable.

```
Dim k As Integer = 2
Dim m As Integer = 4
k ^= m
```

The value of k is 16.

DATA TYPE CONVERSIONS

You may have noticed that the numeric value we typed in a TextBox turned into a string value. This means we need to convert the data types into similar types before we can apply arithmetic operations to them.

Implicit Conversion

In this type of conversion, some data types are automatically allowed to be converted to other data types. We do not need to use any conversion keywords to convert these data types. The implicit conversion can be broken into two categories:

- Widening
- Narrowing

Implicit Widening Conversion

Widening conversion is performed when the receiving type is equal to or larger than the input type. This is like parking a car in a parking space equal in size or bigger than the car. Table 5.6 shows types that can be converted under widening rules.

TABLE 5.6 Valid Widening Types

Type	Can Be Converted To
Byte	UInt16, Int16, UInt32, Int32, UInt64, Int64, single, double, decimal
SByte	Int16, Int32, Int64, single, double, decimal
Int16	Int32, Int64, single, double, decimal
UInt16	Int32, Int32, UInt64, Int64, single, double, decimal
Char	UInt16, UInt32, Int32, UInt64, Int64, single, double, decimal
Int32	Int64, double, decimal
UInt32	Int64, double, decimal
Int64	decimal
UInt64	decimal
Single	double

Here is a valid conversion:

```
Dim k As Single
Dim m As Double
m = k
```

Here is another valid conversion:

```
Dim T As Byte
Dim J As Single
J = T
```

Here is an example of a disallowed conversion:

```
Dim T As Double
Dim J As Decimal
J = T
```

Some these conversions may cause data loss problems. Refer to the details in MSDN library: *http://msdn2.microsoft.com/en-us/library/08h86h00.aspx*

Implicit Narrowing Conversion

It is unlikely that we will lose data when we apply the widening conversion rules on them. However, data loss is almost unavoidable when we convert data types under the implicit narrowing conversion. Logically it is not possible to fit a big box into a smaller one. If Visual Basic strong types rules are enforced, this type of conversion is not allowed in programming. However, if one decides to ignore these rules, it is possible to convert a given type into disallowed types under the implicit narrowing conversion. Although Visual Basic allows us to convert one data type to another type, this does not mean that the identity of the data is preserved after the conversion. This requires careful consideration and planning. Here is an example of a disallowed conversion.

```
Dim T As Double
Dim J As Decimal
J = T
```

There is a chance of data loss when this operation is performed.

Explicit Conversion and Casting

Some programming languages require the explicit conversion in order to allow changing a data type to another. This is known as *casting*. Casting means using the data conversion prefixes to convert one data type to another.

System.Convert Class

To perform explicit conversion we can use methods that are provided by the `System.Convert` class. This class is used to convert one base data type to another. Here is the general format: `Expression=System.Convert.Method(expression)`. Here are some examples:

```
Dim T As Double
Dim V As Integer
Dim N As Decimal
Dim P As Single
Dim J As Decimal
N = System.Convert.ToDecimal(T)
V = System.Convert.ToInt32(T)
P = System.Convert.ToSingle(J)
```

Type Conversion Keywords

Explicit conversion is also possible by applying the type conversion keywords (see Table 5.7) known as *conversion functions*. By using these keywords, you can perform explicit type conversion.

TABLE 5.7 Type Conversion Keywords Types

Keyword	Function
CBool	Converts the input to a boolean type; can hold only True or False values
CByte	Used to convert the input into the byte type; can hold unsigned integers from 0 through 255
CChar	Used to convert any valid char or string values; the value can be from 0 through 65535
CDate	Used to convert any valid date and time expressions
CDbl	Converts expressions to the double type
CDec	Converts input to decimal type
CInt	Converts expressions to the integer type; the result will be rounded
CLng	Converts expressions to the long type; the result will be rounded
CObj	Convents to object type
CSByte	Converts to SByte and rounds the fractions

$\rightarrow$

Keyword	Function
CShort	Converts expressions to the short type; the result will be rounded
CSng	Converts input to single type
CStr	Converts input to a string; if the value is a date, this will contain the short date format
CUInt	Converts input to an unsigned integer
Val	Returns numbers that are included in String

To see the complete list of type conversion keywords, see the MSDN library at *http://msdn2.microsoft.com/en-us/library/s2dy91zy.aspx.* Here are some examples:

```
Dim myNameString As String = "Mike"
Dim myFirstCharacter _
As Char = CChar(myNameString)
Label1.Text = myFirstCharacter
```

As you can see, type string is converted to char type. The value of the Text property for the Label would be M. The following statements convert the double type. In order to display the decimal type value in the string type, we will be using the CStr function.

```
Dim myPayRateDouble As Double = 50.99
Dim myPayRateDecimal _
As Decimal = CDec(myPayRateDouble)
Label1.Text = CStr(myPayRateDecimal)
```

The following example converts the input to integer. The result of the operation will be converted into string.

```
Label1.Text = CStr(CInt(TextBox1.Text) _
+ CInt(TextBox2.Text))
```

CType Function

This is another explicit conversion function and is a little different from those explained above. This useful function can be used to convert any given type to any other type. This conversion is also known as direct cast. Here is the format: CurrentType=CType(FormerType, Type).

```
Dim myInputDouble As Double = 100.77
Dim myOutputDecimal As Decimal
myOutputDecimal = _
```

```
CType(myInputDouble, Decimal)
Label1.Text = CStr(myOutputDecimal)
```

Conversion Methods

In addition to the functions we discussed above, two useful methods are used widley to convert data from one type to another. We will explain them below:

ToString Method

This method can be used to get the string representation of the object. We can revise our last statement to the following:

```
Dim myInputDouble As Double = 100.77
Dim myOutputDecimal As Decimal
myOutputDecimal = _
CType(myInputDouble, Decimal)
Label1.Text = (myOutputDecimal.ToString)
```

Parse Method

This method is used to get the numeric representation of the string value. Here is an example:

```
Dim acceptedInteger As Integer
acceptedInteger = Integer.Parse(TextBox1.Text) _
+ Integer.Parse(TextBox2.Text)
Label1.Text = acceptedInteger.ToString
```

Conversion Errors

Occasionally when we try to convert one data type to another, we receive error messages. If we try to perform invalid conversions, the compiler will give us exception errors. We will cover exception handling in Chapter 6 and you will learn how to handle errors that are caused by invalid conversions.

Round Method

Some of the functions round the decimal output based on their own behavior. However, we may want to round the output to the nearest integer values. This can be done by using the methods that are provided in Visual Basic:

```
Decimal.Round(decimal) Method
```

This method, which is new to the .NET Framework 2.0, is used to round a given decimal to the nearest integer value. Here is the general format for this method:

```
Decimal.Round(decimal,decimalpositions)
```

Here are a few examples:

```
Label1.Text = Decimal.Round(33.49)
```

The result of the above rounding is 33.

```
Label1.Text = Decimal.Round(33.51)
```

The result of the above rounding is 34.

It is also possible to indicate the number of decimal fractions that should be returned after rounding:

```
Dim valueDecimal As Decimal = 33.666
Label1.Text = Decimal.Round(valueDecimal, 1)
```

The result of the above rounding is 33.7.

EXAMPLE 2

We want to have an interactive version of our last program. Therefore, instead of having static numbers, we want to give the user the ability to provide data for calculations.

Start a new project and call it variableTest. Drag and drop the following controls into your Form:

- Five Labels
- Two TextBoxes
- Six Buttons

Here is the naming you should use for this project:

- **Form1**
  Name: variableForm
  Text: Using Variables
- **Label1**
  Name: titleLabel
  Text: Calculations
  Font: Arial Black, 24pt, style=Bold
- **Label2**
  Name: num1Label
  Text: Enter a Number
- **Label3**
  Name: num2Label
  Text: Enter a Number

- **Label4**

    Name: resultMessageLabel

    Text: Result of Calculation:
- **Label5**

    Name: resultLabel

    Font: Arial Black, 12pt

    Backcolor: Yellow

    Forecolor: Red
- **TextBox1**

    Name: num1TextBox
- **Textbox2**

    Name: num2TextBox
- **Button1**

    Name: multiplayButton

    Text: &Multiply
- **Button2**

    Name: subtractButton

    Text: &Subtract
- **Button3**

    Name: addButton

    Text: &Add
- **Button4**

    Name: divideButton

    Text: &Divide
- **Button5**

    Name: clearButton

    Text: &Clear
- **Button6**

    Name: exitButton

    Text: E&xit

As stated, the objective is to receive the inputs from the user, perform the arithmetic operations on them, store the result of calculations in a numeric variable, and display the result back to the screen.

Double-click on the multiplyButton and type the following codes:

```
Private Sub multiplyButton_Click _
(ByVal sender As System.Object, _
ByVal e As System.EventArgs) Handles multiplayButton.Click
    'Declare resultDecimal as a numeric variable
    Dim resultDecimal As Decimal
    'Multiply the first number by
    'the second one and store the result in resultDecimal variable
```

```
resultDecimal = _
Decimal.Parse(Me.num1TextBox.Text) _
* Decimal.Parse(Me.num2TextBox.Text)
'assign the value of result to
'the text property of label
Me.resultLabel.Text = resultDecimal.ToString

    End Sub
```

We used the Parse method to perform the operation.

As you probably noticed, we defined our resultDecimal as a decimal type variable to hold the result of the calculation. When you want to store the results of calculations in a variable, it is recommended that you declare them as a decimal to hold the fractions. You also probably noticed that we assigned the value of the resultDecimal variable to the text property of the resultLabel.Text to display it on the screen.

Hit F5 and run the project. Enter numbers in the blank text boxes and click on Multiply. The result should be displayed in the result field (see Figure 5.4).

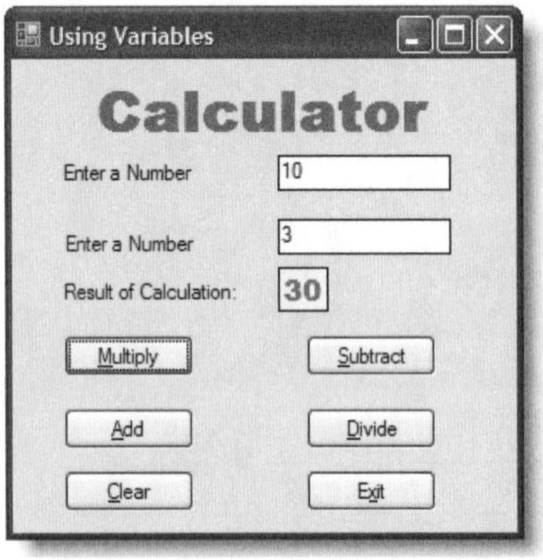

FIGURE 5.4   Result of multiplication.

We need to do something similar to the other controls, with the exception of changing the operator. Under the subtractButton type

```
Private Sub subtractButton_Click _
(ByVal sender As System.Object, _
ByVal e As System.EventArgs) _
Handles subtractButton.Click
    'Declare resultDecimal as a numeric variable
    Dim resultDecimal As Decimal
```

```
        'subtract the second number from
        'the first one and store
        'the result in resultDecimal variable
        resultDecimal = System.Convert.ToDecimal _
        (Me.num1TextBox.Text) - _
        System.Convert.ToDecimal(Me.num2TextBox.Text)
        Me.resultLabel.Text = resultDecimal.ToString
    End Sub
```

We haved used the Convert method to calculate the input. Now double-click on the addButton and add the following codes.

```
    Private Sub addButton_Click _
    (ByVal sender As System.Object, _
    ByVal e As System.EventArgs) _
    Handles addButton.Click
        'Declare resultDecimal as a numeric variable
        Dim resultDecimal As Decimal

        'Add the first number to the
        'second one and store the result in
        'resultDecimal(variable)
        'Assign the value of
        'result to the text property of label
        resultDecimal = CType(Me.num1TextBox.Text, Decimal) _
        + CType(Me.num2TextBox.Text, Decimal)
        Me.resultLabel.Text = CStr(resultDecimal)
    End Sub
```

To show you different ways to handle the calculations, we used the CType method in the above calculations. We can use any of these methods and functions, as explained above.

Under the divideButton type

```
    Private Sub divideButton_Click _
    (ByVal sender As System.Object, _
    ByVal e As System.EventArgs) _
    Handles divideButton.Click
        'Declare resultDecimal as a numeric variable
        Dim resultDecimal As Decimal

        'Divides the first number by
        'the second one and stores the
        'result in resultDecimal variable
        resultDecimal = Decimal.Parse _
        (Me.num1TextBox.Text) / Decimal.Parse _
        (Me.num2TextBox.Text)
        'assign the value of _
        'result to the text property of label
        Me.resultLabel.Text = resultDecimal.ToString
    End Sub
```

Now, under the `clearButton` type

```
Private Sub clearButton_Click _
(ByVal sender As System.Object, _
ByVal e As System.EventArgs) _
Handles clearButton.Click
    'this section resets all affected controls
    Me.num1TextBox.Text = Nothing
    Me.num2TextBox.Text = Nothing
    Me.resultLabel.Text = "Result"
End Sub
```

Code the `exitButton` and hit F5 to run the project. We will get back to this `But-ton` later.

ON THE CD

You can view this solution under the Chapter 5 folder on the companion CD-ROM. The project is saved under its name, `variableTest`. Just copy the project folder to your hard drive and double-click on the .sln file.

THE SCOPES AND LIFETIMES OF VARIABLES AND CONSTANTS

In Example 2, we used a variable that needed to be declared in every subprocedure. That was an example of a procedure-level scope. The variable scope is set by the programmer and tells the Visual Basic program where the variable can be accessed. The lifetime of a variable or constant shows how long it remains accessible to the authorized codes.

Block-Level Variables and Constant Scopes

Block-level variables and constants are accessible to the codes, which are in the block within which the variable or constant is declared. A block is a set of statements that have initiating and terminating points. An example of a block-level variable would be the `If-Then-Else` block that will be covered shortly. You can only use DIM statements to declare the variables within the block. When the procedure is ended, the lifetime of the block is over as well.

Procedure-Level Variables and Constant Scopes

When a variable is declared within a subprocedure, it cannot be accessed from the other procedures. These variables, also known as local variables, can only be used by the codes within the subprocedure in which the variable is declared. The scope of procedure-level variables or constants is the entire subprocedure. All of the statements within the procedure have access to these variables and constants. Their lifetime ends as soon as the procedure is ended.

Module- and Class-Level Variables and Constant Scopes

It is possible to declare the variable or constant that can be accessed from modules, classes, and structures. This can be accomplished by declaring the variables outside the subprocedures. This declaration must be done within the module, class, or structure. We will talk about modules in Chapter 7 and you will learn how to declare variables within them. The lifetime of the module-level variables ends when the project ends. The lifetime of the class-level variables ends when the garbage collector cleans up the class.

You can develop several declarations for your project. We are going to discuss three of them here:

- Private
- Friend
- Public

When you declare the variables as *private* within a class or module, they are available to every procedure in that module and class. However, codes in other modules and classes cannot access them. These variables must be declared within the `Class … End Class` or `Module …End Module` statements.

If the variables are declared as *friend*, all of the codes can be accessed within the same project or assembly.

Public variables can be accessed anywhere inside or outside the project.

Namespace or Project-Level Variable Scopes

If variables or constants are declared as public at a module level, they are accessible by all of the codes and procedures within the entire project. The term *namespace scope* in most cases means the project scope. Here is an example of a namespace declaration:

```
Module intDeclare
'Delaring a public namespace variable
Public intDelaration As Integer
End Module
```

The lifetimes of these variables end when the project is terminated. You will see an example of this in Chapter 7.

CONDITIONAL STATEMENTS

So far, we have used all of the programming features that do not require any comparisons or validations. Conditional statements will be covered further in later chapters. In this section, we will briefly talk about the IF statement and its applications. As discussed in Chapter 3, we have three different structures: sequence, selection, and iteration. The IF-THEN-ELSE statement can help us process the statements based on specific conditions. Here is the structure:

```
IF Condition is true THEN
Process Statement 1
Process Statement 2
Process Other Statements
END IF
```

Here is an example:

```
IF Graduate Student THEN
You Pay Higher Tuition
End IF
```

As you can see, if you are not a graduate student, then the condition is false, and you will not pay higher tuition. Under this structure, we will test the condition for true/false. If the condition is true, one set of statements will be executed, and if the condition is false, another set of statements will be executed. We will leave the Else part of conditional statements for the next chapter.

Based on this structure, we can make decisions and process different things depending on the outcome of our decision (see Figure 5.5).

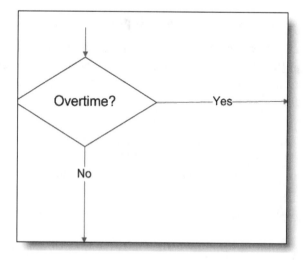

FIGURE 5.5   Conditional structure flowchart.

EXAMPLE 3: ADDING MORE CODES TO EXAMPLE 2

Let's apply this structure to Example 2. Recall that we asked you to code the exit-Button. In previous examples, when the user wanted to exit the program, we would have displayed a warning and terminated the program. In this project, under the exitButton, we want to give the user the choice to exit or resume the program. We need to do the following:

1. Create a variable in which to store the user's response to the dialog box.
2. Evaluate the user's input and make a decision depending on the condition.
3. Create constants and use them in the MessageBox.

To make our job easier, we will display a MessageBox with two Buttons on it. These Buttons are Yes and No. Visual Basic can detect the Button that is clicked by the user and allows us to react to it. The user's input will be saved in the DialogResult, and we can detect it directly. However, for this project, we want to do it through the variables and constants. Double-click on the exitButton and type the following:

```
Private Sub exitButton_Click _
(ByVal sender As System.Object, _
ByVal e As System.EventArgs) _
Handles exitButton.Click
    'set the outgoing message as a constant
    Const messageString As String = _
    "Do You Really Want to Quit?"
    'set the message title as constant
    Const warningString As String = "Warning"
    'set a variable to store the user's input
    Dim myDialogResult As DialogResult
    'Display the messagebox with, title,
    ' two buttons, one icon and a message
    myDialogResult = MessageBox.Show _
    (messageString, warningString, _
    MessageBoxButtons.YesNo, _
    MessageBoxIcon.Exclamation)
    'check to see if the user wants to quit
    If myDialogResult = _
    System.Windows.Forms.DialogResult.Yes Then
        'if the user has clicked on yes _
        'button, then terminate the program

        Me.Close()
        'end of conditional statement
    End If
End Sub
```

In this code, we have declared two constants and one variable. The two constants, warningString and messageString, will hold the two strings: "Warning!" and "Do

You Really Want to Quit?" The variable `myDialogResult` will hold the user's input. If the user clicks on the *Yes* button, the statement `If myDialogResult = DialogResult.Yes` becomes true, so the following statement will be executed: `me.close()`. If the user clicks on the *No* button, the condition would be false, and the user can resume the program without interruptions.

Now run the program and click on the Exit button. You should see a `Message-Box` with two `Buttons` (see Figure 5.6).

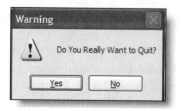

FIGURE 5.6   The two-`Button` `MessageBox`.

EXAMPLE 4

Let's create a new program. Call it `blockLevel` and add the following controls to it:

- One `Label`
- One `TextBox`
- Two `Buttons`

Change the control names according to the following:

- **Form1**
  Name: passwordForm
  Text: Login Screen
- **Label1**
  Name: passwordLabel
  Text: Enter Your Password
- **TextBox1**
  Name: paswordTextBox
  PasswordChar: *
- **Button1**
  Name: validateButton
  Text: &Log In

■ **Button2**

Name: exitButton

Text: E&xit

Your Form should look like Figure 5.7. Double-click on the loginButton and type in the following:

```
Private Sub validateButton_Click _
(ByVal sender As System.Object, _
ByVal e As System.EventArgs) _
Handles validateButton.Click
    'Setting a procedure level variable to capture user's password
    Dim passwordString As String _
    = Me.passwordTextBox.Text
    'checking the password
    If passwordString = "Mike" Then
        'setting a block level variable
        Dim outMessageString As String _
        = "Successful Log In!"
        Dim warningString As String = "Thank You!"

        'displaying a message box using
        '(outMessageString)variables
        MessageBox.Show(outMessageString _
        , warningString, MessageBoxButtons.OK, _
        MessageBoxIcon.Information)

    End If
End Sub
```

FIGURE 5.7   Example 4 screenshot.

In this code, two variables are declared within the If Then block and are not accessible from outside the If Then block. You can access them only from within this block. To test this, type the following code after the End If statement:

```
outMessageString = "Not Successful Log In"
```

Notice that Visual Basic underlined the variable name as an undeclared variable (see Figure 5.8).

```
~~MessageBoxIcon~Information)~~

      End If
      outMessageString = "Not Successful Log In"
End   Name 'outMessageString' is not declared.
```

FIGURE 5.8 Undeclared variable outside block.

ON THE CD

Make sure you complete the exitButton yourself. You can view this solution under the Chapter 5 folder on the companion CD-ROM. The project is saved under its name, blockLevel. Just copy the project folder to your hard drive and double-click on the .sln file.

EXAMPLE 5

In Example 2, we declared the resultDecimal variable as a procedure-level variable and repeated the same declarations within each subprocedure. However, we could declare our variable as a class- or form-level variable and access it from within each subprocedure. In this example, we are using public and private class-level variables that are declared within the form class.

- **Form1**
  Name: classLevelForm
  Text: Class Level
- **Button1**
  Name: privateButton
  Text: &Display Private Variable
- **Button2**
  Name: publicButton
  Text: &Show Public Variable
- **Button3**
  Name: exitButton
  Text: E&xit

In this project, we would like to declare our variables within the Form's declaration section (see Figure 5.9). Type the following codes in the Form's declaration area on the top of your Form right under Public Class ClasslevelForm.

```
Option Strict On
Public Class classLevelForm
    'Declare class Level Variables
    Private valueInteger As Integer = 100
    Public valueString As String = "Mike"
```

FIGURE 5.9   Example 5 screenshot.

Double-click on the Display the Private Variable button and type the following:

```
Private Sub privateButton_Click _
(ByVal sender As System.Object, _
ByVal e As System.EventArgs) _
Handles privateButton.Click
    'Accessing Private variable from sub procedure
    MessageBox.Show(valueInteger.ToString, _
    "Private Class Level Variable")
End Sub
```

Now double-click on the Show Public Variable button and type the following:

```
Private Sub publicButton_Click _
(ByVal sender As System.Object, _
ByVal e As System.EventArgs) _
Handles publicButton.Click
    'accessing public variable from sub procedure
    MessageBox.Show(valueString, _
    "Public Class Level Variable")
End Sub
```

Complete the exitButton. Now run the project and click on each Button to see how the subprocedure can access the private and public class-level variables.

The module code sections are very similar to the classes you saw above. However, public variables that are declared within modules are shared across the entire project rather than within the module only. We will see more examples of modules in Chapter 7.

You can view this solution under the Chapter 5 folder on the companion CD-ROM. The project is saved under its name, `classLevelVariables`. Just copy the project folder to your hard drive and double-click on the .sln file.

EXAMPLE 6

Start a new project and call it `dataConversionPractice`. Add the following controls:

- Three `Labels`
- Six `Buttons`

Rename the controls according to the following:

- **Form1**
  Name: `dataConversionForm`
  Text: `Data Conversion`
- **Label1**
  Name: `titleLabel`
  Text: `Data Conversion`
  Font: `Arial Black, 21.75pt, style=Bold`
  Forecolor: `Red`
- **Label2**
  Name: `messageLabel`
  Text: `Converted Data`
- **Label3**
  Name: `dataLabel`
  Text: `Data Here`
- **Button1**
  Name: `cintButton`
  Text: `&Integer`
- **Button2**
  Name: `cdecButton`
  Text: `&Decimal`
- **Button3**
  Name: `cstrButton`
  Text: `&String`
- **Button4**
  Name: `dateButton`
  Text: `D&ate`
- **Button5**
  Name: `clearButton`
  Text: `&Clear`

■ **Button6**

Name: exitButton

Text: E&xit

Now, let's apply the concept we learned. Double-click on the integerButton and add the following codes:

```
Private Sub cintButton_Click _
(ByVal sender As System.Object, _
ByVal e As System.EventArgs) _
Handles cintButton.Click
    'Declare the Integer and String Data type
    Dim dataString As String = "$50,000.45"
    Dim dataInteger As Decimal

    'Convert String to Integer type
    dataInteger = CInt(dataString)
    'Display the converted data to the screen
    Me.dataLabel.Text = _
    " $50,000.45 was converted to: " & dataInteger

End Sub
```

Under the decimalButton type

```
Private Sub cdecButton_Click _
(ByVal sender As System.Object, _
ByVal e As System.EventArgs) _
Handles cdecButton.Click
    'Declare String and Decimal type
    Dim dataString As String = "$1,000.30"
    Dim decDecimal As Decimal

    'Convert String to Decimal Type
    decDecimal = CDec(dataString)
    'Display converted data to the screen
    Me.dataLabel.Text = _
    " $1,000.30 was converted to: " & decDecimal

End Sub
```

Under the stringButton type

```
Private Sub cstrButton_Click _
(ByVal sender As System.Object, _
ByVal e As System.EventArgs) _
Handles cstrButton.Click
    'declare string and decimal data type
    Dim dataDecimal As Decimal = _
    Decimal.Parse("1666.77")
    Dim dataString As String
```

```
'convert decimal data to String data type
dataString = CStr(dataDecimal)
'Display the converted data to the screen
Me.dataLabel.Text = _
" 1666.77 was converted to: " & dataString

End Sub
```

Under the `dateButton` type

```
Private Sub dateButton_Click _
(ByVal sender As System.Object, _
ByVal e As System.EventArgs) _
Handles dateButton.Click
    'declare String and Date type variables
    Dim strDate As String = "September,20, 2005"
    Dim aDate As Date
    'Converting String to Date type
    aDate = CDate(strDate)
    'Displaying the converted data to the screen
    Me.dataLabel.Text = _
    "September,20, 2005 was converted to " & aDate

End Sub
```

Complete the Clear and Exit buttons yourself. Run the project and click on each button to see the type conversion (see Figure 5.10).

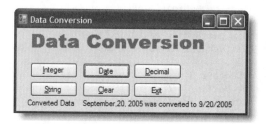

FIGURE 5.10 Example 6 screenshot.

You can view this solution under the Chapter 5 folder on the companion CD-ROM. The project is saved under its name, `dataConversionPractice`. Just copy the project folder to your hard drive and double-click on the .sln file.

STATIC **VARIABLES**

As discussed above, once the subprocedure or element that contains the variable expires, the variable's lifetime ends. However, it is possible to make the lifetime of a variable longer. You can add the keyword static in the DIM declaration statement:

```
Static variableString As String
```

The lifetime of the static variable will be as long as the application is running.

READ-ONLY **VARIABLES**

We explained that the values of variables can change as we assign new values to them, but there is an exception to this. If you want the value of a variable to remain unchanged after the first time value is assigned to it, you can declare your variable as a ReadOnly variable. This is different from the constant discussed above. The Read-Only variables can accept a value only once and the value cannot change during the execution of the program. We can declare these variables in two different ways:

```
ReadOnly nameString As String
ReadOnly mikeNameString As String = "Mike"
```

In the first statement, we declared the variable as string type but did not assign any value to it. This variable can accept a value only once. In the second statement, we have assigned a value to the variable, and the value cannot change during the execution of the program. Occasionally you may want to declare a ReadOnly variable instead of the constants. Type the following URL in the search window of your browser to read an article about this. This is an MSDN resource: *http://msdn2. microsoft.com/en-us/library(d=robot)/w4bxy2s7.aspx.*

OPTION EXPLICIT

In Visual Basic, this option is used to force all variable declarations before they are used. Option Explicit must appear at the top of your program before any other source codes. Option Explicit gives you two possible options: ON and OFF. Here is where it should appear:

```
Option Explicit On
Public Class frmDataConversion
```

If you turn it on, all variables must be declared before you can use them. If you turn it off, you can use variables without declaring them first. This is similar to the old days when BASIC language did not require the variable declaration. You do not need to change this setting. The default is Option Explicit On.

OPTION STRICT

Like Option Explicit, Option Strict must appear at the top of your program before any other source codes. As you saw in this chapter, Visual Basic allows type conversion. The result of this conversion could be data loss. Option Strict will ensure that the user is notified of the possible data loss at compilation time. Option Strict also enforces the strong type rules we discussed before.

It is highly recommended that you set the Option Strict to On through the options. This will help you design stronger codes. Follow these instructions:

1. Click on Tools and choose Options.
2. From the Options expand the Project and Solution folder.
3. Click on the VB Default link. On the right side of the screen, set the Option Explicit and Option Strict to On (see Figure 5.11).

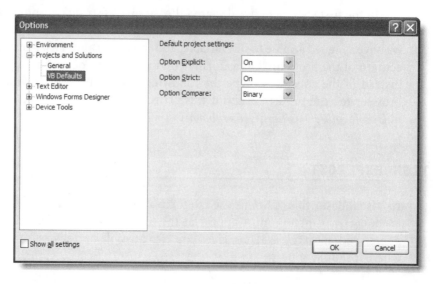

FIGURE 5.11 Option Strict on.

All of the samples for this book have been tested with Option Strict on.

FORMATTING THE OUTPUT

Visual Basic provides many formatting features for numeric and string data. We are going to look at a few of these formatting features that are widely used in programming (see Table 5.8):

- Format currency
- Format numbers
- Format date and time

The syntax for them is

```
outputFeild = (inputFeild.ToString("Formatting Character"))
```

TABLE 5.8   Some of the Formatting Codes

Format Code	Name	Description
C or c	Currency	The number will be converted to String and currency; format will be applied on it.
D or d	Decimal	Used for integer data types; numbers will be converted to decimal with decimal points.
F or f	Fixed-Point	Numbers are converted to string with the "-d.ddd…E+ddd"; each "d" represents a digit (0–9).
N or n	Numbers	Numbers are converted with the form "-d,ddd,ddd.ddd."
D or d	Long and short date	Used to format date.

There are many formatting features, and we recommend that you look them up in the MSDN library at: *http://msdn2..microsoft.com/en-us/library/dwhawy9k.aspx.*

EXAMPLE 7

Let's start a new project and call it `format`. Add the following controls to your form:

- Two Labels
- Four Buttons

Rename the controls according to the following:

- **Form1**
  Name: formatForm
  Text: Formatting the Output
- **Label1**
  Name: formatLabel
  Text: Formatted Output
- **Label2**
  Name: formattedLabel
  Text: Formatted
- **Button1**
  Name: currencyButton
  Text: &Currency
- **Button2**
  Name: numberButton
  Text: &Number
- **Button3**
  Name: dateButton
  Text: &Date
- **Button4**
  Name: exitButton
  Text: E&xit

Now double-click on the currencyButton and type the following codes:

```
Private Sub currencyButton_Click _
(ByVal sender As System.Object, _
ByVal e As System.EventArgs) _
Handles currencyButton.Click
    'Declaring an integer variable

    Dim currencyInteger As Integer = 1000055
    'Formatting the output
    Me.formattedLabel.Text = (currencyInteger.ToString("C"))

End Sub
```

Double-click on the `numberButton` and type the following codes:

```
Private Sub numberButton_Click _
(ByVal sender As System.Object, _
ByVal e As System.EventArgs) _
Handles numberButton.Click
    'Declaring Integer variables
    Dim numberInteger As Integer = 46587

    'Formatting the output
    Me.formattedLabel.Text = (numberInteger.ToString("N"))
End Sub
```

Now double-click on the `dateButton` and add the following codes:

```
Private Sub dateButton_Click _
(ByVal sender As System.Object, _
ByVal e As System.EventArgs) _
Handles dateButton.Click
    'formats the date in Long format
    Me.formattedLabel.Text = ((Now.ToString("D")))
End Sub
```

Code the Exit section. Now run the project and see it in action (see Figure 5.12).

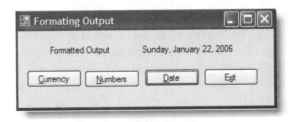

FIGURE 5.12 Example 7 screenshot.

ON THE CD You can view this solution under the Chapter 5 folder on the companion CD-ROM. The project is saved under its name, `format`. Just copy the project folder to your hard drive and double-click on the .sln file.

CLICKONCE DEPLOYMENT

Visual Studio 2005 has made the deployment of your projects easier than the previous versions. ClickOnce deployment allows you to distribute your work to other users and provide tools to access updates for your software. You can publish your work in a folder on your own hard drive and send the folders to your clients. Like many Windows applications there will be a Setup.exe file that can be used by the users to install your application on their computers. To publish your application, follow these steps:

1. Right-click on the solution name in the Solution Explorer and select Properties to see all options available.
2. From the available tabs, click on Publish.
3. Choose the publish location and review all other options.
4. Click on Publish Wizard and follow the instructions.

PROGRAMMING TIPS

- Always declare your variables and data types. If data types are not declared, they will be assumed to be an object data type. This will cause slower execution. Declaring variable data types allows you to see properties and other related information about the data type. It allows you to catch errors as the compiler starts type checking and will make your program run faster. Option Strict will minimize type errors and forces you to declare your variables and their types before you use them.
- If the result of the calculation contains fractions, you need to decide on the desired data type to prevent possible loss of data.
- Use local variables as much as possible. Name conflicts will not occur if identical variable names are used inside the subprocedures. You can declare the same variables in two subprocedures. Local variables use memory only when the subprocedure is executing. On the other hand, module-level variables reserve the memory as soon as the program starts.

SUMMARY

In this chapter, you were introduced to variables, constants, data types, and arithmetic operations. You learned how to declare block-, procedure-, class-, and project-level variables. The topic of operator priorities was covered, and you had hands-on experience with it. The conditional statements and functions were briefly covered as well.

Next

In Chapter 6 we will focus on conditional statements and provide you with many examples. We will also cover exception handling and validations. You will be introduced to many new concepts including case statement and logical operators.

DISCUSSION QUESTIONS

1. How can we change the order of arithmetic operators? Briefly explain.
2. Can you declare a variable without declaring its type? What would happen if the type of data was not declared?
3. What is the difference between `Option Explicit` and `Option Strict`?
4. What is a variable lifetime? How can you change it? Please explain.
5. What are the scopes of variables and constants? Please explain and provide examples.

Exercise 1

Create a project with the following specifications: the program will accept a pay rate and hours worked from the user, calculate the gross pay, and display the formatted output to the screen. You need to use the following features:

1. A simple `IF THEN` statement must be used.
2. Local- and form-level variables and constants must be used.
3. A message box with buttons and icons should be included.
4. Document your document.

Exercise 2

Let's say you want to develop a form to collect customer information. The form will allow users to order one type of pizza with several toppings, soup or salad, cold or hot drink, and a choice of dessert (see Figure 5.13).

FIGURE 5.13 Exercise 2 screenshot.

We can design a form using radio buttons and check boxes to accommodate the users. Follow the following steps to design the form:

1. Start the Visual Studio program. Select Visual Basic and name your program `checkboxRadiobutton`.
2. Add a `Label` to your form and drag five `GroupBoxes`. Drop them on the new form you created. Change the `text` property of your form from `Form1` to `Order Form`. This action will change the title bar's text to Order Form.
3. Add `RadioButtons`, `CheckBoxes`, and `Buttons` into these `GroupBoxes` as shown in the screenshot.

In this project, you will accept the users' input and react to it. For Pizza Type, you will display images of related pizzas. The same technique will be used to display images for Hot Drink, Cold Drink, and Desserts. Just use your creativity. We have supplied the images under the bin\Debug folder. You can run the project to be familiar with its features if you like. We have provided some basic codes to get you started. Enhance the project by using variables, constants, and conditional statements. Add a label to calculate the order.

ON THE CD

You can view this solution under the Chapter 5 folder on the companion CD-ROM. The project is saved under its name, `checkboxRadiobutton`. Just copy the project folder to your hard drive and double-click on the .sln file.

Key Terms

- Static variables
- Constants and variables
- `GroupBox`
- Data types
- Type conversion
- Module- and procedure-level variables

6 Selection Structures

CONDITIONAL STATEMENTS

In Chapter 5, we briefly discussed a simple selection structure with the IF-THEN statement but did not discuss the ELSE part of this conditional statement. Programming requires us to make a number of decisions every day, and the if-then-else structure is one of the many ways we can use to accomplish this task. Here is the syntax of IF-THEN-ELSE statements:

```
If Condition is True Then
    One or Many Statements
ElseIf Another condition is True then
    One or Many Statements
Else
    Statements
End If
```

If the condition is True, a set of statements will be executed. If the expression returns a False result, the computer will branch out to execute a different set of statements. We must have at least one condition and one Then statement to build a conditional statement. It is possible to use the If-Then statement in one line:

```
Dim a As Integer
    If a <> 1 Then MessageBox.Show("Wrong Input")
```

In this case, there is no need for an End If clause. This works only in single statements. It is best to use multiline If-Then-Else statements for readability purposes.

In most decision-making processes, we need to be able to compare values and decide what we want to do. The If-Then-Else conditional block appears between the If and End If blocks. As soon as you type in the IF statement, Visual Basic will automatically add the End for you. The Else clause is usually optional.

Let us look at relational, or comparison, operators that are used in conditional statements.

RELATIONAL OPERATORS

As you can see from Table 6.1, these operators are used to compare values, which is an important function of the decision-making process.

TABLE 6.1   Relational Operators

Symbol	Meaning	Example
<	Less than	If Income < Expenses THEN see financial counselor
>	Greater than	If age > 55 THEN qualified for senior discount
=	Equal to	If Income = Expenses THEN you are breakeven
<>	Not equal	If password <> "Mike" THEN cannot log in
<=	Less than or equal to	If no of accidents<= 2 THEN lower insurance rate applies
>=	Greater than or equal	IF age >= to 65 then qualified for retirement

COMPARING VALUES

By using the relational operators, we will be able to compare the values of numeric and string variables and constants. Comparing numbers is not the same as comparing strings. When numbers are compared, the sign of the values plays an important role in the comparison process. Negative numbers are smaller than positive numbers, and computers can compare them by their sign. However, computers use a different technique to compare string values that are enclosed in quotation marks. As you remember from Chapter 1, we referred to ANSI codes that are used to store characters in the computer memory. Computers use these codes to compare string values from left to right, one character at a time. A complete list of ANSI codes is in the appendix of this book, but we are going to list some of them here so you can see how computers compare them (see Figure 6.1).

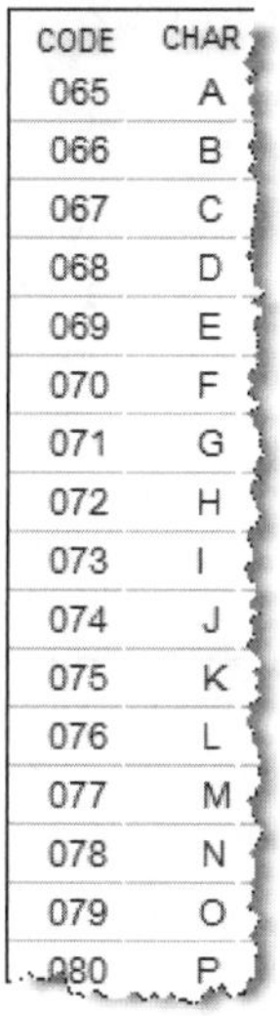

CODE	CHAR
065	A
066	B
067	C
068	D
069	E
070	F
071	G
072	H
073	I
074	J
075	K
076	L
077	M
078	N
079	O
080	P

FIGURE 6.1 Some of the ANSI codes.

Here is an example:

```
If (Me.TextBox1.Text) = "A" Then
    MessageBox.Show _
    ("Excellent", "Grade Entry", _
    MessageBoxButtons.OK, MessageBoxIcon.Exclamation)
End If
```

Here is another example using an `Else` clause:

```
If (Me.TextBox1.Text) = "W" Then
     MessageBox.Show("Did you drop it?", _
     "Grade Entry", MessageBoxButtons.OK, _
     MessageBoxIcon.Exclamation)
     'checking for invalid input
     Else
          MessageBox.Show("Not valid", "Grade Entry",
MessageBoxButtons.OK, MessageBoxIcon.Information)

     End If
```

ToUpper and ToLower **Methods**

As shown in Figure 6.2, each character has a specific value that can be used as comparison criteria. "A" and "a" do not have the same value. Visual Basic uses a table of additional characters called Unicode that includes international characters. Sometimes we do not want to make entries case sensitive but accept both upper case and lower case as part of input. However, we want to be able to validate it. For example, we may want to accept both "A" and "a" as valid grades entered by the faculty members. Visual Basic provides several ways to accommodate this request. One way is to use a method that can be used to convert the lowercase to uppercase and vice versa. You can use the `ToUpper` or `ToLower` methods to convert the case of input to the desired case. Once you put a period after the `Text` property, IntelliSense will show you all of the available options.

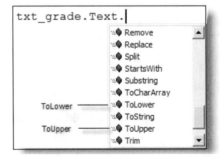

FIGURE 6.2 ToUpper and ToLower methods.

ElseIf **Keyword**

`ElseIf` checks the condition if the previous condition was false. This helps you develop easy-to-follow codes and eliminate additional statements. Here is an example of using the `ElseIf` keyword. The `ElseIf` keyword combines the `If` and the `Else` keywords and creates a new keyword as shown in the following code.

```
If Me.passwordTextBox.Text = "VB" Then
        MessageBox.Show("Welcome to VB Class")
    Else
        If Me.passwordTextBox.Text = "COBOL" Then
            MessageBox.Show("Welcome to COBOL")
        Else : MessageBox.Show("Wrong Input")
        End If
    End If
```

Now we apply the `ElseIf` keyword to the same code:

```
If Me.passwordTextBox.Text = "VB" Then
MessageBox.Show("Welcome to VB Class")
ElseIf ME.passwordTextBox.Text = "COBOL" Then
MessageBox.Show("Welcome to COBOL")
Else : MessageBox.Show("Wrong Input")
End If
```

EXAMPLE 1

In this project, the user will enter valid grades ranging from A to F, I, and W and will see a message box translating the grades into words, such as excellent, above average, and so on. This is a very useful example most books reference to show the features of conditional statements.

Start a new project and call it `Grade`. You need the following controls:

- Three `Labels`
- One `TextBox`
- Three `Buttons`

- **Form1**
  Name: gradeForm
  Text: Grade
- **Label1**
  Name: titleLabel
  Text: Grade Message
  Font: Arial Black, 20.25pt
  Forecolor: Red
- **Label2**
  Name: gradeMessageLabel
  Text: Enter Valid Letter Grades
- **TextBox1**
  Name: gradeTextBox

■ **Button1**
  Name: processButton
  Text: &Process
■ **Button2**
  Name: clearButton
  Text: &Clear
■ **Button3**
  Name: exitButton
  Text: E&xit

Double-click on the processButton and enter the following codes:

```
Private Sub processButton_Click _
(ByVal sender As System.Object, _
ByVal e As System.EventArgs) _
Handles processButton.Click
    'checking for grade A or a
    If (Me.gradeTextBox.Text.ToUpper) = "A" Then
        MessageBox.Show _
        ("Excellent", "Grade Entry", _
        MessageBoxButtons.OK, _
        MessageBoxIcon.Exclamation)
        'checking for grade B or b
    ElseIf (Me.gradeTextBox.Text.ToUpper) _
    = "B" Then
        MessageBox.Show(" Above Average", _
        "Grade Entry", MessageBoxButtons.OK, _
        MessageBoxIcon.Exclamation)
        'checking for grades C or c
    ElseIf (Me.gradeTextBox.Text.ToUpper) = _
    "C" Then
        MessageBox.Show("Average", _
        "Grade Entry", MessageBoxButtons.OK, MessageBoxIcon.Exclamation)
        'checking for grades D or d
    ElseIf (Me.gradeTextBox.Text.ToUpper) _
    = "D" Then
        MessageBox.Show("Below Average", _
        "Grade Entry", MessageBoxButtons.OK, _
        MessageBoxIcon.Exclamation)
        'checking for grades F or f
    ElseIf (Me.gradeTextBox.Text.ToUpper) _
    = "F" Then
        MessageBox.Show("See you later", _
        "Grade Entry", MessageBoxButtons.OK, MessageBoxIcon.Exclamation)
        'checking for grades I or i
    ElseIf (Me.gradeTextBox.Text.ToUpper) _
    = "I" Then
        MessageBox.Show("Not Complete", _
        "Grade Entry", MessageBoxButtons.OK, _
        MessageBoxIcon.Exclamation)
```

```
            'checking for grades W or w
        ElseIf (Me.gradeTextBox.Text.ToUpper) _
        = "W" Then
            MessageBox.Show("Did you drop it?", _
            "Grade Entry", MessageBoxButtons.OK, _
            MessageBoxIcon.Exclamation)
            'checking for invalid input
        Else
            MessageBox.Show("Not valid", _
            "Grade Entry", MessageBoxButtons.OK, _
            MessageBoxIcon.Information)

        End If
    End Sub
```

We have employed the following in this example:

- `If-Then-Else` block
- `ElseIf` keyword
- `ToUpper` method

Each block examines the input and compares it with the set of parameters supplied by the programmer. If the condition is true, the programmer's supplied instructions will be executed. If the input returns a `False` result and doesn't match the parameters, then the control will be given to the `ElseIf` block to deal with the `False` response.

Run the program and enter a valid letter grade. Make sure you enter uppercase, lowercase, and the combination of both cases to see if your program can detect them (see Figure 6.3). Complete the codes for the Clear and Exit buttons.

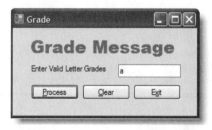

FIGURE 6.3   Grade entry example screenshot.

Let's examine one of the codes closely:

```
If (Me.txtGrade.Text.ToUpper) = "A" Then
    MessageBox.Show("Excellent", _
    "Grade Entry", MessageBoxButtons.OK, _
    MessageBoxIcon.Exclamation)
```

Notice that we placed an uppercase A inside the quotation marks. This can be reversed if you are checking for lowercase characters:

```
If (Me.txtGrade.Text.ToLower) = "a" Then
    MessageBox.Show("Excellent",  _
    "Grade Entry",  _
    MessageBoxButtons.OK, _
    MessageBoxIcon.Exclamation)
```

Note that these two methods do not physically change the input from upper-case to lowercase. The original output is intact. It is only done for the purpose of comparison.

ON THE CD

You can view this solution under the Chapter 6 folder on the companion CD-ROM. The project is saved under its name, grade. Just copy the project folder to your hard drive and double-click on the .sln file.

LOGICAL OPERATORS

Logical operators are used in compound conditional statements. We use them to test the conditions of two or more conditions in one statement. We would like to discuss these common logical operators and their derivatives:

- AND
- OR
- NOT
- AndAlso
- OrElse
- Xor
- IsNot
- Is
- Like

AND **Operator**

Here is the expression:

```
If condition 1 and condition 2 are true then
Statement 1
Statement 2
End if
```

Let's make a change to our previous example:

```
If (Me. userNameTextBox.Text) = "Mike" _
    And (Me. PasswordTextBox.Text) = "Portland" Then
        MessageBox.Show("Valid User", "Welcome!")
    End If
```

As you can see, in order to see the MessageBox, the username must be "Mike" and the password must be "Portland". In other words, both conditions must be true in order to have a True result. When we use the AND logical operator, we need to keep in mind the information given in Table 6.2.

TABLE 6.2 True Table for AND Logical Operator

Expression 1	Operator	Expression 2	Result
True	AND	False	False
False	AND	True	False
False	AND	False	False
True	AND	True	True

As you can see, both statements must be true in order to have a True result. The statement after Then will be executed only if both conditions are true.

EXAMPLE 2

Let's expand the example we used above and add more details to it. In this project, we will receive user names and passwords from users and validate them. There are only five valid user names and passwords. The user name and password must match.

Start a new project, call it passValidation, and add the following controls to it:

- Three Labels
- Two TextBoxes
- Three Buttons

Change the name of these controls according to the following:

- **Form1**
  Name: passValidationForm
  Text: Password Validation

- **Label1**
    - **Name:** titleLabel
    - **Text:** Log in Screen
    - **Font:** Arial Black, 20.25pt
    - **Forecolor:** Red
- **Label2**
    - **Name:** userMessageLabel
    - **Text:** Enter User Name
- **Label3**
    - **Name:** userPassLabel
    - **Text:** Enter Password
- **TextBox1**
    - **Name:** userTextBox
- **TextBox2**
    - **Name:** passTextBox
- **Button1**
    - **Name:** processButton
    - **Text:** &Process
- **Button2**
    - **Name:** clearButton
    - **Text:** &Clear
- **Button3**
    - **Name:** exitButton
    - **Text:** E&xit

Double-click on the processButton and type the following codes:

```
Private Sub processButton_Click _
(ByVal sender As System.Object, _
ByVal e As System.EventArgs) _
Handles processButton.Click
    'matches user names and pawwords with the valid ones
    If Me.userTextBox.Text.ToUpper _
    = "MIKE M" And Me.passTextBox.Text = "VB2005" Then
        MessageBox.Show("Mike-Good to see you!", _
        "Welcome", MessageBoxButtons.OK, _
        MessageBoxIcon.Exclamation)
    ElseIf Me.userTextBox.Text.ToUpper _
    = "DAVID T" And Me.passTextBox.Text _
    = "AA Director" Then
        MessageBox.Show("David-Good to see you!", _
        "Welcome", MessageBoxButtons.OK, _
        MessageBoxIcon.Exclamation)
    ElseIf Me.userTextBox.Text.ToUpper _
    = "BETSY A" And Me.passTextBox.Text = "GEN-ED" Then
        MessageBox.Show("Betsy-Good to see you!", _
```

```
        "Welcome", _
        MessageBoxButtons.OK, _
        MessageBoxIcon.Exclamation)
    ElseIf Me.userTextBox.Text.ToUpper _
    = "PAT H" And Me.passTextBox.Text = "Boss" Then
        MessageBox.Show("Pat-Good to see you!", _
        "Welcome", MessageBoxButtons.OK, _
        MessageBoxIcon.Exclamation)
    ElseIf Me.userTextBox.Text.ToUpper _
    = "MARY J" And Me.passTextBox.Text = "Flex" Then
        MessageBox.Show("Mary-Good to see you!", _
        "Welcome", MessageBoxButtons.OK, MessageBoxIcon.Exclamation)
    Else : MessageBox.Show("Wrong user name or password!", _
    "Warning", MessageBoxButtons.OK, MessageBoxIcon.Question)

    End If
End Sub
```

Complete the Clear and Exit buttons.

Run the project and see how it works. A tool tip has been added to the user name textbox to show valid user names and passwords. User names, such as Mike M, are accepted with uppercase, lowercase, or a combination of both (see Figure 6.4).

FIGURE 6.4 Login screenshot.

ON THE CD
You can view this solution under the Chapter 6 folder on the companion CD-ROM. The project is saved under its name, passValidation. Just copy the project folder to your hard drive and double-click on the .sln file.

OR **Operator**

The OR operator functions differently from the AND logical operator. Table 6.3 shows how it works.

TABLE 6.3 True Table for OR Logical Operator

Expression 1	Operator	Expression 2	Result
True	OR	False	True
False	OR	True	True
False	OR	False	False
True	OR	True	True

As you can see, if one of the expressions is true, the result will be True. Let us change one of the codes we used in our last example:

```
If Me.userTextBox.Text.ToUpper _
= "MIKE M" OR Me.passTextBox = "VB2005" Then
    MessageBox.Show("Mike-Good to see you!", _
    "Welcome", MessageBoxButtons.OK, _
    MessageBoxIcon.Exclamation)
```

If the user name or password is correct, then the MessageBox will be displayed.

NOT **Operator**

The NOT logical operator will reverse the condition, so that the true expression becomes false and vise versa (see Table 6.4).

TABLE 6.4 True Table for NOT Logical Operator

Expression	Operator	Result
True	NOT	False
False	NOT	True

Now change one of the codes we used in our last example:

```
If Not Me.userTextBox.Text.ToUpper = "MIKE M" Then
    MessageBox.Show("Wrong input-User name was: MIKE M", _
    "Warning", MessageBoxButtons.OK, _
    MessageBoxIcon.Stop)
End If
```

As shown in this example, if the user name is not MIKE M, then the MessageBox will be displayed. In this case, the ELSE part of the conditional statement is optional. There are occasions when you do not need to employ the ELSE option.

Is **Operator**

The Is operator is used to determine whether two objects refer to the same object or not. If that is the case, the result of this condition is true. This operator will not compare the values of objects. Here is an example:

```
Dim a As String
Dim b As String
Dim C As String
a = C
b = C

If a Is b Then
MessageBox.Show("Objects Matched", "Matched")
Else
MessageBox.Show("No Match", "Not Matched")

End If
```

IsNot **Operator**

This is a new operator in Visual Basic 2005 and is the opposite of the Is operator. It determines if two objects do not refer to the same object. The following two statements accomplish the same result:

Using Is: If Not a Is b Then

Using IsNot: If a IsNot b Then

Like **Operator**

This operator is used to compare the input against a pattern. If the input includes the pattern, the result is True. Here is a simple example:

```
Dim testString As String
    testString = "G" Like "[C-H]"
    If testString = True Then
        MessageBox.Show("Found")
    End If
```

Xor **Operator**

This is another operator that is available in Visual Basic 2005. The xor operator will evaluate both expressions, so there will be no short-circuiting involved (discussed in the next section). The result is always dependent on both expressions. Here is the true table for xor:

TABLE 6.5 True Table for xor Logical Operator

If First Expression Is	And Second Expression Is	Value of Result Is
True	True	False
True	False	True
False	True	True
False	False	False

SHORT-CIRCUITING LOGICAL OPERATORS

Some logical operators are known as *short circuits*. Short circuit operators evaluate compound statements. If the value of the first expression is dependant on the condition of the second value and the result of the first expression shows the final result, then Visual Basic does not see any need to evaluate the second expression because it will not change the result. We will briefly discuss a few short-circuiting logical operators in this section.

AndAlso **Operator**

This is the same as the AND operator but uses a short-circuiting logic. Table 6.6 shows its behaviors.

TABLE 6.6 True Table for AndAlso Logical Operator

If First Expression Is	And Second Expression Is	Value of Result Is
True	True	True
True	False	False
False	Not evaluated	False

In the third statement, you can see that if the result of the first expression is false, there is no need to evaluate the second expression because regardless of the result of the second expression, the final result will be False. Thus, the second expression will not be evaluated.

OrElse **Operator**

This is another short-circuiting operator that should be mentioned. As shown in Table 6.7, if the result of the first expression is True, the second expression will not be evaluated and the final result will be True.

TABLE 6.7 True Table for OrElse Logical Operator

If First Expression Is	And Second Expression Is	Value of Result Is
True	Not evaluated	True
False	True	True
False	False	False

To see more information, visit the MSDN site at the following URL: *http://msdn2.microsoft.com/en-us/library/wz3k228a.aspx.*

NESTED IF STATEMENTS

It is time to introduce you to a different type of if-then-else selection structure. Under this structure, we will evaluate other conditions if the previous condition is true. We can put new If statements under the Then keyword or under the Else clause. You can *nest* as many If-Then-Else statements within each other as you need. However, nested If statements require careful consideration. If the logic is complicated, the debugging becomes a tedious task. Below is an example of simple nested If statements (see Figure 6.5).

```
Dim numberOfClassesToTakeInteger As Integer
If educationTextBox.Text.ToUpper = "UNDER" Then
    If Integer.Parse(gpaTextBox.Text) >= 3 Then
        numberOfClassesToTakeInteger = 12
        MessageBox.Show("Max Classes", "Class")
    ElseIf Integer.Parse(gpaTextBox.Text) = 2 Then
        numberOfClassesToTakeInteger = 8
        MessageBox.Show("Minimum Classes", "Class")
    Else : numberOfClassesToTakeInteger = 0
        MessageBox.Show("No Class Given", "Class")
    End If
Else : MessageBox.Show("Not Accepted", "Warning")
End If
```

FIGURE 6.5 Nested If structure.

EXAMPLE 3

In this example, we will use a nested if-then-else structure. The user will enter two inputs: educational degree and age. If the educational degree is undergrad, a message will be displayed showing the tuition for undergrad and then check for another condition, which is the age. If the age is less than 18, the student will be advised to contact his advisor. If the educational degree is graduate, a message showing the tuition will be displayed. If the input does not match any of these two, then an error message will be displayed.

Start a new project and call it `nested_if`. Add the following controls to it:

- Two `Labels`
- Two `TextBoxes`
- Three `Buttons`

Rename the objects according to the following:

- **Form1**
  Name: `nestedForm`
  Text: `Nested If`
- **Label1**
  Name: `educationLabel`
  Text: `Enter Educational Program`
- **Label2**
  Name: `ageLabel`
  Text: `Enter Age`
- **TextBox1**
  Name: `educationTextBox`
- **TextBox2**
  Name: `ageTextBox`
- **Button1**
  Name: `processButton`
  Text: `&Process`
- **Button2**
  Name: `clearButton`
  Text: `&Clear`
- **Button3**
  Name: `exitButton`
  Text: `E&xit`

Double-click on the `processButton` and type the following:

```
Private Sub processButton_Click _
 (ByVal sender As System.Object, _
ByVal e As System.EventArgs) _
 Handles processButton.Click
     'Accepts input and checks the value for Under
     If Me.educationTextBox.Text.ToUpper _
     = "UNDER" Then
         'displays this message if the condition is true
         MessageBox.Show _
         ("Tuition for under graduate course is: $1000", "Information")
         'checks for the age if the above condition is true
         If Integer.Parse(Me.ageTextBox.Text) _
         >= 18 Then
             'displays this message if the above condition is true
             MessageBox.Show _
             ("See your academic advisor", _
             "Warning")
         Else
             'displays this message if the above condition is false
             MessageBox.Show("You need to be 18+", _
             "Warning")
         End If
     Else
         'if the input is not equal
         'to under, then this statement will be executed
         If Me.educationTextBox.Text.ToUpper _
         = "GRAD" Then
             'if the input is equal to
             'GRAD then this statement will be executed
             MessageBox.Show("Graduate courses cost $1500", _
             "Information")

         Else
             'if none of the above
             'conditions is true, the following will be executed
             MessageBox.Show("Input must be GRAD or UNDER only", _
             "Warning")
         End If
     End If

 End Sub
```

Hit F5 to run the project. Enter the required input and view the result (see Figure 6.6).

You can view this solution under the Chapter 6 folder on the companion CD-ROM. The project is saved under its name, nestedif. Just copy the project folder to your hard drive and double-click on the .sln file.

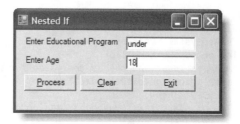

FIGURE 6.6 Example 3 screenshot.

SELECT CASE STATEMENTS

The *select case* selection structure is an alternative that we can use instead of the if-then-else structure. The logic of case structure is cleaner and less confusing. We can utilize select case statements to test conditions, test ranges of data, or take care of validation. Here is the general syntax for case statements.

```
Select Case Expression
Case Expression
Statements that will execute if the condition is true.
More Cases
More Statements that need to be executed.
Case Else
Statements that need to be executed if none of the above is true
End Select
```

Once you become familiar with the features that case statements offer, you will be using them to evaluate multiple conditions. You can use the case statements to evaluate the strings, numeric values, and ranges of inputs and many other purposes. We will be using select case statements in many upcoming projects.

EXAMPLE 4

In this example, we will receive the number of points the students have received and display their grades. Start a new project and call it gradecase. Add the following controls to your form:

- Two Labels
- One TextBox
- Three Buttons

Rename your controls according to the following list:

- **Form1**
  Name: gradeForm
  Text: Grade Conversion
- **Label1**
  Name: titleLabel
  Text: Grade Entry
  Font: Arial Black, 20.25pt
  Forecolor: Red
- **Label2**
  Name: pointsLabel
  Text: Enter the Points
- **TextBox1**
  Name: pointsTextBox
- **Button1**
  Name: processButton
  Text: &Process
- **Button2**
  Name: clearButton
  Text: &Clear
- **Button3**
  Name: exitButton
  Text: E&xit

Here is the breakdown for points and associated grades:

- 90–100: A
- 80–89: B
- 70–79: C
- 60–69: D
- 0–59: F

Double-click on the processButton and type the following:

```
Private Sub processButton_Click _
(ByVal sender As System.Object, _
ByVal e As System.EventArgs) _
Handles processButton.Click
    'declare a variable to
    'accept points and convert them to decimal
    Dim gradeDouble As Double = CDbl(Me.pointsTextBox.Text)
    Select Case gradeDouble
        'convert valid points from 0-100
        Case 90 To 100
            MessageBox.Show("You got an A", "Grade")
        Case 80 To 89
```

```
                    MessageBox.Show("You got a B", "Grade")
                Case 70 To 79
                    MessageBox.Show(" You got a C", "Grade")
                Case 60 To 69
                    MessageBox.Show("you got a D", "Grade")
                Case 0 To 59
                    MessageBox.Show("you got an F", "Grade", _
                    MessageBoxButtons.OK, MessageBoxIcon.Warning)
                    'display error for invalid data
                Case Else
                    MessageBox.Show _
                    ("Enter a number between 0 to 100", _
                    "Warning", MessageBoxButtons.OK, _
                    MessageBoxIcon.Warning)
            End Select
        End Sub
```

As you can see, we are using the case statements to evaluate the range of input by using the To keyword. You probably noticed that the program provides a clean range evaluation.

Now run the program and enter values. It converts the points according to the list we provided. We did not validate the input for blanks at this time.

Complete the Clear and Exit buttons before you save the program (see Figure 6.7).

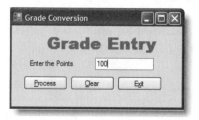

FIGURE 6.7   Example 4 screenshot.

ON THE CD

You can view this solution under the Chapter 6 folder on the companion CD-ROM. The project is saved under its name, gradecase. Just copy the project folder to your hard drive and double-click on the .sln file.

EXAMPLE 5

In this example, we will ask the users to enter characters A, B, C, D, and F. The input can be upper or lower case. The screen will be very similar to the last example, so we are going to display the same controls.

Start a new project and call it letterCheck. Add the following controls to you your form:

- One Label
- One TextBox
- Two Buttons

- **Form1**
  Name: letterForm
  Text: Letter Check
- **Label1**
  Name: letterLabel
  Text: Enter letters A,B,C,D or F Only
- **TextBox1**
  Name: letterTextBox
  MaxLength: 1
- **Button1**
  Name: processButton
  Text: &Process
- **Button2**
  Name: exitButton
  Text: E&xit

Now double-click on the processButton and type the following:

```
Private Sub processButton_Click _
(ByVal sender As System.Object, _
ByVal e As System.EventArgs) _
Handles processButton.Click
    'use Select Case block to accept lower or upper case input
    Select Case (Me.letterTextBox.Text.ToUpper)
        'setting the valid range
        Case "A" To "D", "F"
            MessageBox.Show("You entered valid letters", _
            "Thanks!")
            'displaying error message
        Case Else
            MessageBox.Show("Only A,B,C,D and F are acceptable", _
            "Error!")
    End Select

    Me.letterTextBox.Text = Nothing
    Me.letterTextBox.Focus()
End Sub
```

Run the program and enter letters other than the valid range first. After that, enter valid letters. Note that this range check only looks at the first entry. Later on, you will learn how to check all characters and stop invalid entries (see Figure 6.8). Complete the *Exit* button before saving the project.

FIGURE 6.8   Example 5 screenshot.

ON THE CD

You can view this solution under the Chapter 6 folder on the companion CD-ROM. The project is saved under its name, letterCheck. Just copy the project folder to your hard drive and double-click on the .sln file.

EXCEPTION HANDLING: THE TRY/CATCH BLOCK

By now, you will have noticed that your program may crash as the result of an input that contains a wrong data type or other unexpected input. Visual Basic provides solutions for structured and unstructured exception handling that should be incorporated into your programs. The recommended structured error-handling block that is widely used in programming is known as the Try/Catch block. For unstructured exception handling, Microsoft suggests the On Error method, which is common in programming. We will expand our discussion on the Try/Catch block, which is very effective.

Occasionally serious errors force the program to crash or terminate prematurely. Although the programmer can be blamed for some of these errors, sometimes other factors are the real problem. For instance, the operator could misplace the data files and the program could not access them. It is also possible that the images that are needed by your programs have been moved to other folders and your program fails to locate them.

The Try/Catch block enables the programmer to trap the errors and stop the program from crashing. Here is the structure of Try/Catch:

```
Try
Suspicious program statements
Catch exception variable
Statement to transfer control to
Finally
Statements that will be executed after the process is over
End Try
```

The Try/Catch block should be used in any operation that involves resources such as file loading, calculations, and accessing other blocks and procedures. Remember that Try/Catch is not designed to fix the errors. Let's look at some examples.

EXAMPLE 6

In this example, we will use Try/Catch to trap a divide-by-zero error.

Start a new project, and call it tryCatch. Add the following controls to it:

- Four Labels
- Two TextBoxes
- Two Buttons

Rename the controls accordingly:

- **Form1**
  Name: tryCatchForm
  Text: Try and Catch
- **Label1**
  Name: titleLabel
  Text: Error Trapping Screen!
  Font: Arial Black, 14.25pt
  Forecolor: Red
- **Label2**
  Name: number1Label
  Text: Enter a Number
- **Label3**
  Name: number2Label
  Text: Enter another Number
- **Label4**
  Name: resultMessageLabel
  Text: The Result Was
- **TextBox1**
  Name: number1TextBox
- **TextBox2**
  Name: number2TextBox
- **Button1**
  Name: divideButton
  Text: &Divide
- **Button2**
  Name: clearButton
  Text: &Clear

■ **Button3**

Name: exitButton

Text: E&xit

Double-click on the divideButton and add the following codes to it:

```
Private Sub btnDivide_Click _
(ByVal sender As System.Object, _
ByVal e As System.EventArgs) _
Handles dvideButton.Click
    Dim divide As Double

    Try
    'this section will be executed if there
'is no error in dividing the 'two numbers
        divide = CDbl(Me.number1TextBox.Text) _
        / CDbl(Me.number2TextBox.Text)
        'try to do the calculation
        Me.resultLabel.Text = divide.ToString
        'set the exception variable
    Catch ex As Exception
        'this section will
        'be executed if there is an error
        MessageBox.Show _
        ("You cannot divide by zero or non-numeric characters", _
        "Warning", MessageBoxButtons.OK, _
        MessageBoxIcon.Stop)
        'display this message if error is found in calculation
    Finally
        'do the following after displaying the message. This section will
        'be executed regardless of the outcome.
MessageBox.Show("Now we will reset", _
        "Information")
        Me.number1TextBox.Text = Nothing
        Me.resultLabel.Text = Nothing
        Me.number2TextBox.Text = Nothing
        Me.number2TextBox.Focus()

    End Try
End Sub
```

Complete the Exit and Clear buttons yourself.

The program detects the exception within your program and reports it. Under normal circumstances, unusual data would cause a program crash, but the exception-handling block will catch and report the exception (see Figure 6.9).

ON THE CD You can view this solution under the Chapter 6 folder on the companion CD-ROM. The project is saved under its name, tryCatch. Just copy the project folder to your hard drive and double-click on the .sln file.

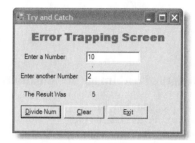

FIGURE 6.9   Example 6 `Try/Catch` screenshot.

Example 7

In this example, we will try to load an image that does not exist. This usually happens because either the name of the file is misspelled or the file is not in the referenced path. The project will examine three different possibilities:

■ A `Button` is used to reference an image that does not exist. This will force Visual Basic to crash.

■ A `Button` uses the same statement as the above example but uses `Try/Catch` to trap the error.

■ A `Button` loads an image that exists and is located in the right directory.

Start a new project, and call it `catchErrors`. Add the following controls to it:

■ Four `Buttons`
■ One `PictureBox`

Rename the control names according to the following list:

■ **Form1**
   Name: `imageForm`
   Text: `Image Load`
■ **Button1**
   Name: `loadButton`
   Text: `&Load Image`
■ **Button2**
   Name: `catchButton`
   Text: `&Try and Catch`
■ **Button3**
   Name: `crashButton`
   Text: `&Crash`

■ **Button4**

Name: exitButton

Text: E&xit

Double-click on the Load Image button and type the following codes:

```
Private Sub loadButton_Click _
(ByVal sender As System.Object, _
ByVal e As System.EventArgs) _
Handles loadButton.Click
    'loading the image to the picturebox
    Me.testPictureBox.Image = Image.FromFile("mike.jpg")
End Sub
```

The referenced button will load the image into the PictureBox.
Now double-click on the Try and Catch button and type the following codes:

```
Private Sub catchButton_Click _
(ByVal sender As System.Object, _
ByVal e As System.EventArgs) _
Handles catchButton.Click
    'Try block starts here
    Try
        'If the operation is normal,
        'this line of code will execute
        Me.testPictureBox.Image = Image.FromFile("mike1.jpg")
        'Error_ex is a programmer supplied variable name
    Catch Error_ex As Exception
        'if the operation detects error,
        'the control will be passed to
        'the following statement
        MessageBox.Show _
        ("The image couldn't be found [Au: OK?yes] in that folder.", _
        "Warning!", MessageBoxButtons.OK, MessageBoxIcon.Information)
    Finally
        'Use of this section is optional
    End Try
End Sub
```

Since the referenced image, mike1.jpg doesn't exist, the message box under the Catch section will be executed.

Double-click on the crashButton and type the same line of code we used under the Try and Catch button. We will not include the Try/Catch code:

```
Private Sub crashButton_Click _
(ByVal sender As System.Object, _
ByVal e As System.EventArgs) _
Handles crashButton.Click
    'trying to load an image that doesn't exist
    Me.testPictureBox.Image = Image.FromFile("mike1.jpg")
End Sub
```

Once we click on this button, the program will crash. Now save the program and run it (see Figure 6.10).

FIGURE 6.10   Example 7 screenshot.

Code the `exitButton` yourself.

You can view this solution under the Chapter 6 folder on the companion CD-ROM. The project is saved under its name, `catchError`. Just copy the project folder to your hard drive and double-click on the .sln file.

DATA VALIDATION

It would be great if we could assume that all users would follow our instructions systematically to enter data. It would be a dream to think that no one would enter invalid data during typing. However, we know this is not possible and sooner or later we will find invalid data entered by the users. The term *data validation* refers to the series of error-trapping features that a programmer can develop to minimize unwanted data. It is not possible to predict all of the data entry problems, but we can minimize the number of invalid entries to a great extent.

Most users enter invalid input unintentionally. It is very common to enter a zero instead of the letter O. Some users forget to fill out some of the fields, and others type correct information in the wrong fields. Whatever the reason is, it will cause problems.

So far you have learned many techniques that can be used to minimize invalid data. Using controls such as `RadioButtons`, `CheckBoxes`, `MaskedTextBoxes`, exception handling blocks like `Try/Catch`, and conditional statements are very useful to having control over input. We are now going to cover several new features that can be applied for data validation.

Error Provider

In Visual programming, visual effects can help the programmer more effectively grab the user's attention. One of the symbols used in Visual Basic is Error Provider. Error Provider is a small red symbol that can be found in the Visual Basic's Toolbox, under the Components category (see Figure 6.11). This class displays a blinking object that appears next to the controls that are associated with the errors. The Error Provider can be turned on and off and is often used for required fields that are not filled by the users.

FIGURE 6.11 Error Provider in the toolbox.

There are many properties that you can employ for your programs. Let us review some of these properties.

BlinkRate

This property allows the programmer to set the rate of the blinking icon.

BlinkingStyle

This property provides different options:

- BlinkIfDifferentError
- AlwaysBlink
- NeverBlink

Icon

This property allows the programmer to pick a different icon for the ErrorProvider object.

You can explore other properties by referring to the language reference.

EXAMPLE 8

In this project, we will show the effect of the Error Provider object. Let's start a new project and call it errorProviderSample. Add the following controls to your form:

- Three Labels
- One TextBox
- One MaskedTextBox
- Three Buttons
- One Error Provider

  Rename your controls according to the following list:

- **Form1**
  Name: errorProviderForm
  Text: Error Provider
- **TextBox1**
  Name: nameTextBox
- **MaskedTextBox1**
  Name: socialSecurityNumberMaskedTextBox
- **Label1**
  Name: titleLabel
  Text: Error Provider
  Font: Arial Black, 20.25pt
  Forecolor: Red
- **Label2**
  Name: nameLabel
  Text: Enter Your User Name
- **Label3**
  Name: socialSecurityLabel
  Text: Enter Social Security
- **Button1**
  Name: processButton
  Text: &Process
- **Button2**
  Name: clearButton
  Text: &Clear

- **Button3**
  Name: exitButton
  Text: E&xit
- **ErrorProvider1**
  Name: nameErrorProvider

Use the MaskedTextBox Smart Tag and set it to Social Security format. Now highlight the ErrorProvider object and review its properties. Change BlinkStyle or BlinkRate if you want.

Double-click on the processButton and type the following codes:

```
Private Sub processButton_Click _
(ByVal sender As System.Object, _
ByVal e As System.EventArgs) _
Handles processButton.Click

    If Me.nameTextBox.Text = "" _
    Or Me.nameTextBox.Text <> _
    "MIKE" Then
        'if the input is blank or not MIKE the
' following will be displayed
        nameErrorProvider.SetError _
        (nameTextBox, "this is a required field")
    Else
        'this line resets the error provider
        MessageBox.Show("Thanks for submitting", "Thanks")
        nameErrorProvider.SetError(nameTextBox, "")
    End If
```

In the above code, the Error Provider will be flashing next to the user name if the input is not valid. If you move your mouse over the icon, a ToolTip supplied by the programer will show (see Figure 6.12).

Complete the Exit and Clear buttons.

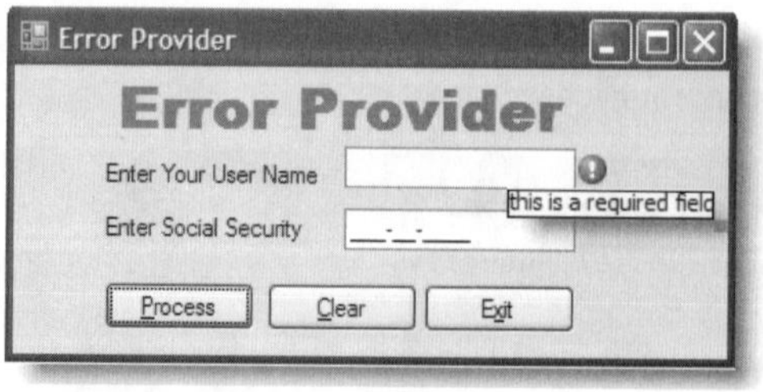

FIGURE 6.12 The ErrorProvider and ToolTip.

You can view this solution under the Chapter 6 folder on the companion CD-ROM. The project is saved under its name, `errorProviderSample`. Just copy the project folder to your hard drive and double-click on the .sln file.

InputBox Function

In the previous chapter, we briefly talked about functions and provided you with an example. In brief, functions are segments of a program that are written to perform specific tasks and can be called on different occasions. In Chapter 7, you will learn how to write your own functions. The function that we are about to introduce is a prewritten one that will be called from the library. There are different types of functions that you can use within your program. One of the useful functions that we will discuss here is `InputBox`. This function provides a predefined dialog box that can be used to communicate with users. The structure of `InputBox` consists of

- Two `Buttons`: OK and Cancel
- A message line
- A title bar
- An input area
- Optional numeric expressions that can be used to determine the edge of the dialog box from the left and top of the form.

This function is very useful for data validation methods. Once the error is detected, we can collect the corrected information in the text area of this function.

`MessageBoxes` and `InputBoxes` have some similarities but are different in nature. The user needs to respond to the `InputBox` before he can do any other task. The user's input will be saved in a variable that we set up. If the user clicks on the Cancel button, a zero-length text will be stored in the variable. Figure 6.13 shows a typical `InputBox` with the `Buttons` and areas of texts. Here is the general syntax for calling the `InputBox` function:

```
Variable=InputBox ("The message to the User", "The title bar message")
```

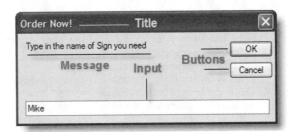

FIGURE 6.13   `InputBox` parts.

EXAMPLE 9

In this example, we will ask the user to type the name of the rubber stamp he wants to buy in the InputBox. There are two rubber stamps for the user to order: OK and SENT.

Start a new project and call it inputBoxSample. Add the following controls to it:

- Two Buttons
- One PictureBox

Rename the controls according to the following:

- **Form1**
  Name: inputOutputForm
  Text: Rubber Stamps Order
- **Button1**
  Name: selectSignButton
  Text: &Click to Order
- **Button2**
  Name: exitButton
  Text: E&xit
- **PictureBox1**
  Name: rubberStampPictureBox
  SizeMode: StretchImage

Double-click on the orderButton and type the following code:

```
Private Sub  selectSignButton _Click _
(ByVal sender As System.Object, _
ByVal e As System.EventArgs) _
Handles  selectSignButton.Click
    'declare a string variable to store user's input
    Dim signOrderString As String
    'store user's input into a variable
    signOrderString = InputBox _
    ("Type in the name of rubber stamp you need" _
    + vbCr + vbCr _
    + "Only OK and SENT Signs are avilable", "Order Now!", _
    "Type in your order")
    'check the user's input to display appropriate image
    If signOrderString.ToUpper = "SENT" Then
        Me.signPictureBox.Visible = True
        Me.signPictureBox.Image = Image.FromFile("SENT.jpg")
    ElseIf signOrderString.ToUpper = "OK" Then
        Me.signPictureBox.Visible = True
        Me.signPictureBox.Image = Image.FromFile("OK.jpg")
        'display an error if the input wasn't valid
    Else
```

```
        MessageBox.Show("Wrong Order. Check and retype!", _
        "Warning")
        Me.signPictureBox.Visible = False
    End If
End Sub
```

Notice that we declared a local string variable called signOrderString:

```
Dim signOrderString As String
```

The task of this variable is to store user's input for later processing. In the next statement, we will use a conditional statement to display an image:

```
If signOrderString.ToUpper = "SENT" Then
Me.signPictureBox.Visible = True
Me.signPictureBox.Image = Image.FromFile("SENT.jpg")
```

We used the IF statement to check the content validity of the signOrderString variable. This will display what the user has entered into the text area of the Input-Box. The VBCR constant that was covered in Chapter 5 is used for carriage control, so you could display the messages in two lines.

The ToUpper method will accept both lowercase and uppercase input from the user. Complete the exitButton codes. Run it and experiment with its features.

You can view this solution under the Chapter 6 folder on the companion CD-ROM. The project is saved under its name, inputBoxSample. Just copy the project folder to your hard drive and double-click on the .sln file. The images for SENT and OK are supplied with the sample program.

String Properties and Methods

Visual Basic 2005, like its predecessors, offers great methods for string manipulations. These features enable you to make data validations tighter. We are going to discuss some of these features here so you can learn how to use them. We encourage you to look up those not discussed here.

String.Length Property

This property allows you to count the number of characters entered by the user. This can be used in a conditional statement to determine how many characters are entered.

```
Dim myString As String = "Hello"
Dim myInteger As Integer
myInteger = myString.Length
MsgBox(myInteger)
```

The MessageBox will show 5.

String.StartsWith Method

This method will check the input against the pattern you have set up.

```
Dim myInputString As String = "Hello World"
If myInputString.StartsWith("Hello") Then
MsgBox("Hello Found")
```

String.EndsWith Method

This is the opposite of the String.StartsWith method and is used to see if the pattern characters are found in the input or not:

```
Dim myInputString As String = "Hello World"
If myInputString.EndsWith("World") Then
MsgBox("World Found")
End If
```

String.PadLeft Method

This method will pad the output with a special character set if it is smaller than the required field. Here is the syntax:

```
String.Papleft(number of required fields," _
fill with this character if the input is not long enough")
    Dim myInputString As String = "300"
    MsgBox(myInputString.PadLeft(5, "*"))
```

The MessageBox will display **300. String.PadRight and will do the same thing for the right side of the input.

Please review the sample that is provided to look at some more examples:

- Chars
- Insert
- Remove
- Replace

You can view this solution under the Chapter 6 folder on the companion CD-ROM. The project is saved under its name, stringMethods. Just copy the project folder to your hard drive and double-click on the .sln file.

Trim Function

Occasionally in data validation you need to deal with the data itself without the leading or tailing blanks. This allows you to measure the actual length of data or insert characters in specific position of it. The Trim function can be used to remove the leading and tailing blanks and represent the data itself. Here is the syntax for the Trim function:

```
Variable=Trim(String)
Here is an example"
    Dim a As String = ("    MIKE    ")
    Dim b As String
    b = Trim(a)
    Label1.Text = b.Length
```

The result is 4 because the leading and tailing is removed. It is also possible to remove only the leading or tailing blanks:

```
    Dim a As String = ("    MIKE    ")
    Dim b As String
    b = LTrim(a)
    Label1.Text = b.Length
```

You can use RTrim to remove the tailing blanks. Visit the MSDN site at the following URL for more information: *http://msdn2.microsoft.com/en-us/library/h9wz3dez.aspx.*

Other Useful Methods for Validation

Isdigit Method and IsNumeric Function

Here are two other features that can identify the nature of input. The IsDigit method is used to see whether the character is a decimal digit or not. It is a boolean method and can return True or False.

```
    Dim myString As Char = "6"c
    If Char.IsDigit(myString) Then
    MsgBox("Found digit")
    End If
```

This will return a True result.

The IsNumeric is another useful function that can be used to determine the nature of the input. This is a boolean function and can return True or False as well. If the input can be categorized as numbers, the result is True.

```
    Dim mystring As String = "300"
    If IsNumeric(mystring) Then
    MsgBox("Number Found")
    End If
```

HAVE MORE CONTROL OVER THE INPUT

Keypress Event and KeyChar Property

Now it is time to introduce another validation tool that our students in the classrooms have real fun with. Under the KeyPress event, we can identify the characters typed by the users. If the character is not among our list, then we can suppress the keyboard so nothing can be typed. The KeyChar property of this event can store the ASCII equivalent of what the user types. By using this property, we can evaluate the input. KeyChar cannot store the values of the keys that do not have ASCII equivalents such as function keys and the Ctrl key. These keys will return null values. Once the user hits a key, KeyChar checks the input against our valid list of approved characters. If the input is valid, the program will display it; otherwise, by using the Handled property, it will hold it. There is also a Handled property that can be set to True or False in a case of exceptions.

EXAMPLE 10

Create a new project and call it keyTrap. Design your Form with three TextBoxes, three Labels, and two Buttons as shown in Figure 6.14.

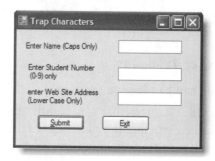

FIGURE 6.14   Example 10 screenshot.

Now double-click on the Enter Name TextBox and from the Method Name window, find KeyPress event. Type the following within its event handler subprocedure:

```
Private Sub nameTextBox_KeyPress _
(ByVal sender As Object, _
ByVal e As System.Windows.Forms.KeyPressEventArgs) _
Handles nameTextBox.KeyPress
    Select Case e.KeyChar
        'allows A-Z caps
        Case CChar("A") To CChar("Z")
            'allows hyphen
        Case CChar(("-"))
            'allows backspace
        Case Chr(CInt("8"))
        Case Else
            'will not show the typed
            'character in the textbox
            e.Handled = True
    End Select
End Sub
```

We are allowing capital characters A–Z. The hyphen can be entered and the backspace can be used to correct errors. Do the same thing for the second and third TextBoxes and type the following under their KeyPress events. Under Student Number type

```
Private Sub studentIdTextBox_KeyPress( _
ByVal sender As Object, _
ByVal e As System.Windows.Forms.KeyPressEventArgs) _
Handles studentIdTextBox.KeyPress
    Select Case e.KeyChar
        'accepts digits only
        Case CChar("0") To CChar("9")
            'allows backspace
        Case Chr(CInt("8"))
        Case Else
            e.Handled = True
    End Select
End Sub
```

Under Web site TextBox KeyPress event type

```
Private Sub webSiteTextBox_KeyPress _
(ByVal sender As Object, _
ByVal e As System.Windows.Forms.KeyPressEventArgs) _
Handles webSiteTextBox.KeyPress
    Select Case e.KeyChar
        'allows lower case
        Case CChar("a") To CChar("z")
            'allows digits
        Case CChar("0") To CChar("9")
            'Accepts these chars
        Case CChar("."), CChar("/"), CChar("\")
            'Allowes backspace
        Case Chr(CInt("8"))
    End Select
End Sub
```

Under the submitButton, make sure no blank is submitted. Save and run the program.

ON THE CD

You can view this solution under the Chapter 6 folder on the companion CD-ROM. The project is saved under its name, keyTrap. Just copy the project folder to your hard drive and double-click on the .sln file.

EXAMPLE 11: COMPREHENSIVE EXAMPLE

In this example, we will utilize most of the concepts we have learned so far. We will create an ice cream order form so the user can pick ice cream, add toppings, see the price, and exit. Here are the conditions:

■ The user needs to pick an ice cream type before he can see the price.

■ There are three ice cream types, four toppings, and three sizes.

■ In order to see the price, the user needs to pick one option from the Ice Cream Type and one from the Ice Cream Size.

Start a new project and call it `iceCreamShop`. Add the following controls to it:

■ Four `GroupBoxes`

■ Six `RadioButtons`

■ Four `CheckBoxes`

■ One `PictureBox`

■ Three `Buttons`

■ Four `Labels`

Rename the controls according to the following:

■ **Form1**
  Name: orderForm
  Text: Ice Cream Online

■ **Label1**
  Name: titleLabel
  Text: Ice Cream Shop
  Font: Arial Black, 20.25pt
  Forecolor: Red

■ **Label2**
  Name: totalLabel
  Text: Total

■ **Label3**
  Name: priceLabel
  Text: Price

■ **Label4**
  Name: iceCreamLabel
  Text: Ice Cream

■ **GroupBox1**
  Name: sizeGroupBox
  Text: Ice Cream Size

■ **GroupBox2**
  Name: toppingGroupBox
  Text: Topping

■ **GroupBox3**
  Name: TypeGroupBox
  Text: Ice Cream Type

■ **GroupBox4**
  Name: processGroupBox
  Text: Process
■ **RadioButton1**
  Name: smallRadioButton
  Text: Small
■ **RadioButton2**
  Name: mediumRadioButton
  Text: Medium
■ **RadioButton3**
  Name: largeRadioButton
  Text: Large
■ **RadioButton4**
  Name: strawberryRadioButton
  Text: Strawberry
■ **RadioButton5**
  Name: chocolateRadioButton
  Text: Chocolate
■ **RadioButton6**
  Name: vanillaRadioButton
  Text: Vanilla
■ **Button1**
  Name: checkoutButton
  Text: &Check Out
■ **Button2**
  Name: resetButton
  Text: &Reset
■ **Button3**
  Name: exitButton
  Text: E&xit
■ **Button4**
  Name: receiptButton
  Text: &Display Receipt
■ **CheckBox1**
  Name: fruitCheckBox
  Text: Fresh Fruit
■ **CheckBox2**
  Name: chocolateCheckBox
  Text: Chocolate
■ **CheckBox3**
  Name: mintCheckBox
  Text: Mint

- **CheckBox4**
  Name: `caramelCheckBox`
  Text: Caramel
- **PictureBox1**
  Name: `iceCreamPictureBox`
  SizeMode: StretchImage
  BorderStype: FixedSingle

Double-click on the `strawberryRadioButton` and type the following:

```
Private Sub strawberryRadioButton_CheckedChanged _
(ByVal sender As System.Object, _
ByVal e As System.EventArgs) _
Handles strawberryRadioButton.CheckedChanged
    'load images
    Try
        Me.iceCreamPictureBox.Image = Image.FromFile("strawberry.tif")
        Me.iceCreamLabel.Text = "Strawberry Ice Cream"
    Catch inputImage As Exception
        MessageBox.Show("Problem loading the image", "Warning")
    End Try
End Sub
```

As you saw before, `Try/Catch` will load the ice cream image. However, if there is a problem, it will catch the error.

Now double-click on the `chocolateRadioButton` and type

```
Private Sub chocolateRadioButton_CheckedChanged _
(ByVal sender As System.Object, _
ByVal e As System.EventArgs) _
Handles chocolateRadioButton.CheckedChanged
    'load images
    Try
        Me.iceCreamPictureBox.Image _
        = Image.FromFile("chocolate.tif")
        Me.iceCreamLabel.Text = "Chocolate Ice Cream"
    Catch inputImage As Exception
        MessageBox.Show _
        ("Problem loading the image", "Warning")
    End Try
End Sub
```

Now double-click on the `vanillaRadioButton` and type

```
Private Sub vanillaRadioButton_CheckedChanged _
(ByVal sender As System.Object, _
ByVal e As System.EventArgs) _
Handles vanillaRadioButton.CheckedChanged
    'Load images
```

```
    Try
        Me.iceCreamPictureBox.Image = Image.FromFile("vanilla.tif")
        Me.iceCreamLabel.Text = "Vanilla Ice Cream"
    Catch inputImage As Exception
        MessageBox.Show("Problem loading the image", "Warning")
    End Try
End Sub
```

Under the `smallRadioButton` type

```
Private Sub smallRadioButton_CheckedChanged _
(ByVal sender As System.Object, _
ByVal e As System.EventArgs) _
Handles smallRadioButton.CheckedChanged
    'check to see if Ice Cream size selected
    If Me.smallRadioButton.Checked Then
        'check to see if any of the
        'radiobuttons within Ice Cream type is selected
        If Me.strawberryRadioButton.Checked Or _
        Me.vanillaRadioButton.Checked _
        Or Me.chocolateRadioButton.Checked Then
            'display the Ice Cream price
            MessageBox.Show("Small Ice Cream $3.00", _
            "Small Ice Cream Price")

        Else
            'display error message
            MessageBox.Show _
            ("Ice Cream type need to be selected", _
            "Warning")
        End If
    Else
    End If
End Sub
```

The comments explain what the code does. Very similar to this code, we will type the following under the other two ice cream Size buttons. Under the Medium radio button type:

```
Private Sub mediumRadioButton_CheckedChanged _
(ByVal sender As System.Object, _
ByVal e As System.EventArgs) _
Handles mediumRadioButton.CheckedChanged
    'check to see if Ice Cream size selected
    If Me.mediumRadioButton.Checked Then
        'check to see if any of the radiobuttons
        'within Ice Cream type is selected
        If Me.chocolateRadioButton.Checked Or _
        Me.strawberryRadioButton.Checked Or _
        Me.vanillaRadioButton.Checked Then
            'display the Ice Cream price
            MessageBox.Show("Medium Ice Cream price is $4.00.", _
```

```
                "Medium Ice Cream Price")
            Else
                'display error message
                MessageBox.Show("Ice Cream type need to be selected", _
                "Warning")
            End If
        Else
        End If
    End Sub
```

Under the `largeRadioButton` type

```
Private Sub largeRadioButton_CheckedChanged _
(ByVal sender As System.Object, _
ByVal e As System.EventArgs) _
Handles largeRadioButton.CheckedChanged
    'check to see if Ice Cream size selected
    If Me.largeRadioButton.Checked Then
        'check to see if any of the
        'radiobuttons within Ice Cream type is selected
        If Me.chocolateRadioButton.Checked Or _
        Me.strawberryRadioButton.Checked Or _
        Me.vanillaRadioButton.Checked Then
            'display the Ice Cream price
            MessageBox.Show("Large Ice Cream $5.00 ", _
            "Large Ice Cream Price")
        Else
            'display error message
            MessageBox.Show("Ice Cream type need to be selected", _
            "Warning")
        End If
    Else
    End If
End Sub
```

Before we proceed with the next one we need to declare the following class-level variable as integer:

```
Dim priceInteger As Integer
```

Now double-click on the `checkOutButton` and type the following:

```
Private Sub checkOutButton_Click _
(ByVal sender As System.Object, _
ByVal e As System.EventArgs) _
Handles checkoutButton.Click
    'if no Ice Cream selected, then display error message
    If Me.chocolateRadioButton.Checked = False And _
    Me.strawberryRadioButton.Checked = False And _
    Me.vanillaRadioButton.Checked = False Then
        MessageBox.Show("You must Select a Ice Cream choice", _
        "Warning")
```

```
ElseIf smallRadioButton.Checked = False And _
Me.mediumRadioButton.Checked = False And _
Me.largeRadioButton.Checked = False Then
    MessageBox.Show("Ice Cream Size not selected")
    '   'make sure Ice Cream is selected
ElseIf chocolateRadioButton.Checked Or _
Me.strawberryRadioButton.Checked Or _
Me.vanillaRadioButton.Checked Then

    'small Ice Cream calculation
    If Me.smallRadioButton.Checked Then
        Me.priceInteger = 3
        If Me.chocolateCheckBox.Checked Then
            Me.priceInteger = Me.priceInteger + 1
        End If
        If Me.caramelCheckBox.Checked Then
            Me.priceInteger = Me.priceInteger + 1
        End If
        If Me.mintCheckBox.Checked Then
            Me.priceInteger = Me.priceInteger + 1
        End If
        If Me.fruitCheckBox.Checked Then
            Me.priceInteger = Me.priceInteger + 1
        End If
        'format the output
        Me.priceLabel.Text = (Me.priceInteger.ToString("c"))

    End If
    'medium Ice Cream calculation
    If Me.mediumRadioButton.Checked Then
        Me.priceInteger = 4
        If Me.chocolateCheckBox.Checked Then
            Me.priceInteger = Me.priceInteger + 1
        End If
        If Me.caramelCheckBox.Checked Then
            Me.priceInteger = Me.priceInteger + 1
        End If
        If Me.mintCheckBox.Checked Then
            Me.priceInteger = Me.priceInteger + 1
        End If
        If Me.fruitCheckBox.Checked Then
            Me.priceInteger = Me.priceInteger + 1
        End If
        Me.priceLabel.Text = (Me.priceInteger.ToString("c"))

    End If

    'large Ice Cream calculation
    If Me.largeRadioButton.Checked Then
        Me.priceInteger = 5
        If chocolateCheckBox.Checked Then
            Me.priceInteger = Me.priceInteger + 1
        End If
```

```
If Me.caramelCheckBox.Checked Then
    Me.priceInteger = Me.priceInteger + 1
End If
If Me.mintCheckBox.Checked Then
    Me.priceInteger = priceInteger + 1
End If
If Me.fruitCheckBox.Checked Then
    Me.priceInteger = Me.priceInteger + 1
End If
Me.priceLabel.Text = (Me.priceInteger.ToString("c"))

        End If

    End If
End Sub
```

We add the topping to the price of each ice cream size and display it in the label area. We also format our output using a different format statement. Later on, you will learn how to make the codes shorter, but for now, let's go with the long one.

Now, double-click on the resetButton and type the following:

```
Private Sub resetButton_Click _
(ByVal sender As System.Object, _
ByVal e As System.EventArgs) Handles resetButton.Click
    'reset all controls
    Me.smallRadioButton.Checked = False
    Me.mediumRadioButton.Checked = False
    Me.largeRadioButton.Checked = False
    Me.chocolateRadioButton.Checked = False
    Me.strawberryRadioButton.Checked = False
    Me.vanillaRadioButton.Checked = False
    Me.chocolateCheckBox.Checked = False
    Me.mintCheckBox.Checked = False
    Me.fruitCheckBox.Checked = False
    Me.caramelCheckBox.Checked = False
    Me.priceLabel.Text = "0"
    Me.iceCreamLabel.Text = "Ice Cream"
    Me.iceCreamPictureBox.Image = Nothing

End Sub
```

Code the exitButton and make sure the displayReceiptButton is disabled. We will be using it later on. Review the codes and run the program again to be familiar with its features (see Figure 6.15).

You can view this solution under the Chapter 6 folder on the companion CD-ROM. The project is saved under its name, iceCreamShop. Just copy the project folder to your hard drive and double-click on the .sln file.

FIGURE 6.15 Ice cream shop screenshot.

PROGRAMMING TIPS

- Try to design easy-to-follow logic for your conditional statements. If you can break the conditional statement into two statements, do so. It is much easier to debug programs this way.
- If you suspect user input might crash the program, use Try/Catch to prevent it.
- Try to utilize the case structure instead of it-then-else as much as possible. Case structure provides clearer logic.

SUMMARY

In this chapter, we covered one of the most important topics in Visual Basic Programming: selection structure. In addition to if-then-else and case statements, we discussed the importance of using Try/Catch to prevent the program from crashing. An example showed you how to work with more conditional statements. The case structure proved an efficient structure to validate users' input. The concept of data validation was covered in detail.

Next

In Chapter 7 we will cover `ComboBoxes`, `ListBoxes`, `MenuStrips`, `ToolStrips`, `ColorDialog`, `FontDialog`, `ImageList`, `ProgressBar`, `StatusStrip`, and many more new features.

DISCUSSION QUESTIONS

1. When do we need to use the `ELSE` statement? Provide an example.
2. Can we use the `IF-THEN-ELSE` statement inside a case structure? If yes, provide an example.
3. What did you learn about `Try/Catch` block? Can we use it inside conditional statements?
4. Can an `InputBox` be used in place of a `MessageBox`? Justify your response.
5. What is the application of the `ELSEIF` statement, and when should it be used in the selection structure?

Exercise 1

Modify Example 1 in this chapter to do the following:

1. Use case structure instead of the if-then-else structure.
2. Use an `InputBox` to receive input instead of using a `TextBox`.
3. Add codes to allow the user to enter letter grades or points.
4. Use `Try/Catch` to block the user's invalid input.

Exercise 2

Modify the ice cream shop program to use case structure instead of if-then-else. Add more toppings and change the prices as well.

Key Terms

- `If-Then-Else`
- Case structure
- `Try/Catch`
- `InputBox`
- Logical operators
- Error Provider

7 COMBOBOX, LISTBOX, MENUSTRIP, TOOLSTRIP, Subprocedures, and Functions

In This Chapter

COMBOBOX AND LISTBOX

In previous chapters, you were introduced to controls such as CheckBox and RadioButtons, which allow users to make choices by clicking on the controls rather than typing the choices in. This method of data collection is efficient and minimizes the chance of errors. You have seen ComboBoxes in Windows and Web applications. It is a tool with a drop-down menu and allows the users to make their choice. ComboBox, which was introduced in Visual Basic 4 and has survived through all Visual Basic upgrades up to now, is a very useful tool. Like RadioButton, ComboBox allows the user to choose one option from a list of many options. These two controls are very similar in nature. If the programmer is concerned about saving space on the form, then he should consider ComboBox rather than ListBox. Both controls use the Items Collection object to store and retrieve values. There are two types of ComboBoxes and ListBoxes:

- Drop-down `ComboBoxes`
- Drop-down `ListBoxes`
- Simple `ListBoxes`
- Simple `ComboBoxes`

We can select any of these styles by using codes such as

```
colorComboBox.DropDownStyle = ComboBoxStyle.DropDown
colorComboBox.DropDownStyle = ComboBoxStyle.DropDownList
colorComboBox.DropDownStyle = ComboBoxStyle.Simple
```

We will discuss the two most commonly used controls: drop-down `ComboBox` and drop-down `ListBox`. Figure 7.1 shows the different elements of `ComboBox` and we will review them individually:

- Size Handle
- `TextBox`
- Drop-down `ListBox`
- Tasks Pane

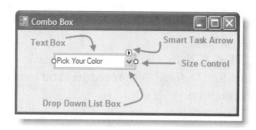

FIGURE 7.1 `ComboBox` elements.

Size Handle

Size Handle is used to change the size of the control. You can resize the control by dragging the Size Handle vertically or horizontally.

TextBox

The `TextBox` section of the `ComboBox` has dual functions. It can be used to display the `ComboBox`'s heading and as a placeholder for the users' input. Once the user selects an item, it will be displayed in this text area.

The Tasks Pane and String Collection Editor

Once a `ComboBox` or `ListBox` is selected, you can click on the Smart Task arrow (Delta-shaped arrow) located in the upper-right corner of the control to open the `ComboBox` or `ListBox` Tasks Pane (see Figure 7.2). You have seen the Smart Task arrow known as Smart Tag in many other controls. It makes it more convenient for you to use the Smart Tag rather than going to the Properties window and finding those properties. As you can see, there are two options within the Tasks Pane:

- Edit Items
- Use Data Bound Item `CheckBox`

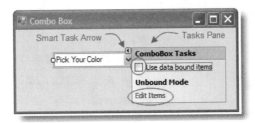

FIGURE 7.2 *Tasks Pane.*

By clicking on Edit Items, you can access the String Collection Editor. This editor can be used to add items to your `ComboBox` item collections. These items will appear in the drop-down list when the down arrow is pressed or the F4 key is hit (see Figure 7.3). You can also fill your `ComboBox` using the `Items` property in the Properties box.(see Figure 7.4).

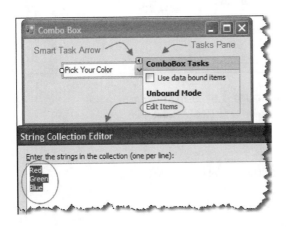

FIGURE 7.3 Edit Item dialog box.

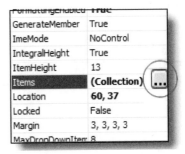

FIGURE 7.4 Adding items through the `Items` property.

The Tasks Pane is a Visual Basic 2005 feature, which is added to the ComboBox and ListBox controls. Checking the Data Bound Item's CheckBox will open a different setting. This screen deals with databases and is used when the content of database fields should be displayed in a ComboBox. We will discuss this option of the ComboBox later (see Figure 7.5).

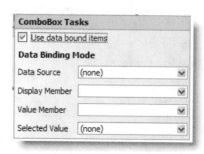

FIGURE 7.5 Data Bound Item's CheckBox opened.

Drop-Down ListBox

The drop-down ListBox can be used to view the list of options within the ComboBox at the run time. Once the user clicks on this arrow, the hidden items will be displayed or the user can also hit F4 to display the list of options (see Figure 7.6).

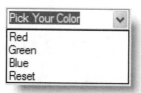

FIGURE 7.6 Using the drop-down arrow to show items.

There are two ways to put the items in the ComboBox:

- Through the String Collection Editor
- By using the Add method

When we add items to the Item Collection at the design time, the same items will be in the ComboBox every time we call it up. However, in some cases, we want the users to provide their own options or populate the ComboBox with database data. If that is what we want, we should use the Add method to allow the users to add items dynamically and interactively. We will show you how to use String Collection Editor and the Add method in this chapter.

EXAMPLE 1

Let's start a new project and call it ComboBoxExample. This project will let the user pick the BackColor of the Form by using a ComboBox.

Add the following controls to the new form:

- Three Labels
- One ComboBox
- Two Buttons
- One ListBox

Change the control names according to the following:

- **Form1**
  Name: ComboBoxForm
  Text: Combo Box
- **Label1**
  Name: TitleLabel
  Text: Screen Color
  Font: Arial Black, 20.25pt, style=Bold
  Backcolor: White
- **ComboBox1**
  Name: colorComboBox
  Text: Pick Your Color
- **ListBox1**
  Name: colorListBox
- **Label2**
  Name: backColorLabel
  Text: Background Color
- **Label3**
  Name: textColorLabel
  Text: Text Color
- **Button1**
  Name: exitButton
  Text: E&xit

■ **Button2**
    Name: countButton
    Text: &Number of Items

Let us use the String Collection Editor at the design time and add items to the ComboBox collection. The ComboBox's Item Collection object will store the items we add at the design time. Highlight the colorComboBox and click on the Smart Task arrow (Smart Tag) on the top-right corner of the control to open the Tasks Pane. Once the Tasks Pane is open, you can click on Edit Items to access the String Collection Editor. This is demonstrated in Figure 7.2, above.

Visual Basic will open a text editor that you can use to add your items. Add the following:

■ Red
■ Green
■ Blue
■ Reset

SelectedIndex, Text, and Count Properties

Now the question is how Visual Basic knows which item the user has picked. The answer is that when the user selects an item, an integer value corresponding to that item will be stored in the SelectedIndex property of the ComboBox. The index starts from zero and is incremented by one the more items that are added. However, since we start from zero, the highest index is always one number less than the number of items we have in our ComboBox. The Count property, on the other hand, reports the actual number of items in each collection. For example, the items we are using will have the index numbers shown in Figure 7.7.

FIGURE 7.7 Index numbers for items.

Now, based on the value of SelectedIndex, we can tell what the user has selected. Double-click on the colorComboBox subprocedure and add the following code:

```
Private Sub colorComboBox_SelectedIndexChanged _
(ByVal sender As System.Object, _
ByVal e As System.EventArgs) _
Handles colorComboBox.SelectedIndexChanged
    'use the index of the combo box to detect what is picked

    Select Case Me.colorComboBox.SelectedIndex
        Case 0
        Me.BackColor = Color.Red
        Case 1
        Me.BackColor = Color.Green
        Case 2
        Me.BackColor = Color.Blue
        Case 3
        Me.BackColor = Color.Empty
    End Select
End Sub
```

We are using the case structure to detect the integer number stored in the selectedIndex property of the ComboBoxes and ListBoxes. Once the user picks an item, the BackColor of the screen will be changed to the user's choice. It is also possible to detect the user's choice by evaluating the Text property of the ComboBox and ListBox.

Add the following items to the ColorListBox using the same method you used to add items to the colorComboBox:

- Orange
- Purple
- Dark salmon
- Reset

Now double-click on the colorListBox, and add the following code:

```
Private Sub colorListBox_SelectedIndexChanged _
(ByVal sender As System.Object, _
ByVal e As System.EventArgs) _
Handles colorListBox.SelectedIndexChanged
    'use the text property to detect what is picked
    Select Case Me.colorListBox.Text.ToUpper
        Case "ORANGE"
            Me.ForeColor = Color.Orange
        Case "PURPLE"
            Me.ForeColor = Color.Purple
        Case "DARKSALMON"
            Me.ForeColor = Color.DarkSalmon
        Case "RESET"
            Me.ForeColor = Color.Empty
    End Select
End Sub
```

As stated before, occasionally we may have to use the Text property instead of the SelectedIndex. SelectedIndex works for programmers' supplied items. However, in interactive programming, the users can supply the items, and in order to react to them, we need to use the Text property. We will look at an example later on.

Now, double-click on the NumberOfItemsButton and add the following:

```
Private Sub countButton_Click _
(ByVal sender As System.Object, _
ByVal e As System.EventArgs) _
Handles countButton.Click
    'Display the number of items
    Dim count As String = Me.colorComboBox.Items.Count
    MessageBox.Show("The number of items in combobox is: " _
    + count, "Number of Items", _
    MessageBoxButtons.OK, MessageBoxIcon.Information)
End Sub
```

Complete the exitButton code, save the program, and run it. Use the dropdown arrow and click on each item to see the result (see Figure 7.8).

FIGURE 7.8   Screenshot of Example 1.

ON THE CD
You can view this solution under the Chapter 7 folder on the companion CD-ROM. The project is saved under its name, comboboxExample. Just copy the project folder to your hard drive and double-click on the .sln file.

Add, RemoveAt, Remove, Insert, and Clear Methods

As mentioned earlier, in addition to adding items at the design time, we can add items to the ComboBox at runtime. We will accomplish this task by using the Add method, which allows us to add items while the program is running. The general format for adding items to the ComboBox and ListBox is

```
ComboBox.Items.Add(value)
```

Here are some examples:

```
ComboBox1.Items.Add("Mike")
ComboBox1.Items.Add("TextBox1.Text)
ComboBox1.Items.Add(stringValue)
```

We can also remove items from these two objects by using three different methods:

- RemoveAt
- Remove
- Clear

The RemoveAt method allows us to remove an item by referencing its index. Here is the general syntax:

```
ComboBox.Items.RemoveAt(Index)
```

Here are some examples:

```
ComboBox1.Items.RemoveAt(SelectedIndex)
ComboBox1.Items.RemoveAt(5)
```

The Remove method allows us to remove an item by referencing a string value. Here is the general syntax:

```
ComboBox.Items.Remove(String)
```

Here are some examples:

```
ComboBox1.Items.Remove("Mike")
ComboBox1.Items.Remove(TextBox1.Text)
ComboBox1.Items.Remove(StringValue)
ComboBox1.Items.Remove(ComboBox1.text)
```

The Clear method removes all items from the ComboBox:

```
ComboBox.Items.Clear()
```

Here is an example:

```
ComboBox1.Items.Clear()
```

We can use the Insert method to add an item in the specific position of the list. Here is the syntax:

```
ComboBox.Items.Insert(InsertPosition,Value)
```

Here is an example:

```
ComboBox1.Items.Insert(1,"Mike")
```

EXAMPLE 2

In this example, we want to create a phone book so you can add names and phone numbers to the ComboBox. We will also demonstrate how to insert items or remove items from the ComboBox.

Start a new project and call it comboDynamic. Add the following controls to your new form:

- Seven Buttons
- One Label
- One ComboBox

Here is what we need:

- **Form1**
  Name: phoneBookForm
  Text: Personal Directory
- **Label1**
  Name: phoneLabel
  Text: Phone Book
  Font: Arial Black, 20.25pt, style=Bold
  BackColor: Black
  ForeColor: White
- **Button1**
  Name: addSavedButton
  Text: &Add Saved Phone Numbers
- **Button2**
  Name: interactiveButton
  Text: &Interactive Entry
- **Button3**
  Name: removeItemButton
  Text: &Remove Items by Index
- **Button4**
  Name: clearAllButton
  Text: &Clear All

■ **Button5**

   Name: insertButton

   Text: &Specific Insert

■ **Button6**

   Name: removeByNameButton

   Text: &Delete by Name

■ **Button7**

   Name: exitButton

   Text: E&xit

Now we need to add codes.

Adding Strings

Double-click on the addSavedPhoneNumbersButton and add the following codes:

```
Private Sub addSavedButton_Click _
(ByVal sender As System.Object, _
ByVal e As System.EventArgs) Handles addSavedButton.Click
    'clearing the combobox before adding items
    Me.phoneNumberComboBox.Items.Clear()
    'adding two items at runtime
    Me.phoneNumberComboBox.Items.Add("Mike-503-000-0000")
    Me.phoneNumberComboBox.Items.Add("Heidi-503-000-0000")

End Sub
```

Let us examine the code closely. Look at the first line of code:

```
Me.phoneNumberComboBox.Items.Clear()
```

This will clear the ComboBox. If this line of code is not there, duplicate items will be added to the ComboBox if the user clicks on this button more than once.
   The second line of code will add the items to the ComboBox:

```
phoneNumberComboBox.Items.Add("Mike-503-000-0000")
```

Now double-click on the *Interactive Entry* button and add the following code:

```
Private Sub interactiveButton_Click _
(ByVal sender As System.Object, _
ByVal e As System.EventArgs) _
Handles interactiveButton.Click
    'adding items interactively
    'We add what the user has typed in the combobox text area
    me.phoneNumberComboBox.Items.Add _
    (phoneNumberComboBox.Text)
    Me.phoneNumberComboBox.Text = Nothing
End Sub
```

As you can see, instead of adding a string value, we used the text that the user entered into the text area of the ComboBox.

RemoveAt **Method**

We now want to explore the different Remove methods we discussed before. Double-click on the Remove Items by Index button and add the following code:

```
Private Sub removeItemButton_Click _
(ByVal sender As System.Object, _
ByVal e As System.EventArgs) _
Handles removeItemButton.Click
    'removing an item using the index. If there is no more item to remove
    'then catch the error
    Try
        Me.phoneNumberComboBox.Items.RemoveAt _
        (Me.phoneNumberComboBox.SelectedIndex)
        Me.phoneNumberComboBox.Text = "Name-Phone Number"
    Catch ex As Exception
        MessageBox.Show("Nothing to remove!", "Warning", _
        MessageBoxButtons.OK, MessageBoxIcon.Information)
        Me.phoneNumberComboBox.Text = "Name-Phone Number"
    End Try
End Sub
```

As shown in this code, we try to remove the item at the specified index position. If the operation cannot be performed, the error message will be displayed. This can be very helpful if the user clicks on this button when the ComboBox is empty.

Remove **Method**

As stated before, in addition to the RemoveAt method, it is possible to use the Remove method to remove an item. Double-click on the Delete by Name button and add the following:

```
Private Sub removeByNameButton_Click _
(ByVal sender As System.Object, _
ByVal e As System.EventArgs) Handles removeByNameButton.Click
    'removes an Item by string
    Try
        Me.phoneNumberComboBox.Items.Remove("Heidi-503-000-0000")
    Catch ex As Exception
        MessageBox.Show("Nothing to remove!", "Warning", _
        MessageBoxButtons.OK, MessageBoxIcon.Information)
        Me.phoneNumberComboBox.Text = "Name-Phone Number"
    End Try
End Sub
```

As you can see, a specific string was removed from the list.

Insert **Method**

Occasionally we want to insert an item in the specific location of our ComboBox. Here is the syntax:

```
ComboBox.Items.Insert(Index, String)
```

Double-click on the Specific Insert button and add the following codes:

```
Private Sub insertButton_Click _
(ByVal sender As System.Object, _
ByVal e As System.EventArgs) _
Handles insertButton.Click
    'Get the input from the user and place
    ' it on the second location of the item list
    Dim responseString As String
    responseString = InputBox _
    ("Enter the name & Phone number separated by a hyphen", _
    "Phone Entry")
    Me.phoneNumberComboBox.Items.Insert(1, responseString)
End Sub
```

The user's input will be inserted in the second position of the list

Clear **Method**

We will now use the Clear method to reset the items. This will remove all items from the ComboBox.

```
Private Sub clearAllButton_Click _
(ByVal sender As System.Object, _
ByVal e As System.EventArgs) _
Handles clearAllButton.Click
    'This will clear the entire list
    Dim response As DialogResult
    response = MessageBox.Show _
    ("This will clear all items. Do you want to proceed?", _
    "Warning", MessageBoxButtons.YesNo, MessageBoxIcon.Information)
    If response = Windows.Forms.DialogResult.Yes Then
        Me.phoneNumberComboBox.Items.Clear()
    End If
End Sub
```

Complete the Exit subprocedure and run the project (see Figure 7.9).

You can view this solution under the Chapter 7 folder on the companion CD-ROM. The project is saved under its name, comboDynamic. Just copy the project folder to your hard drive and double-click on the .sln file.

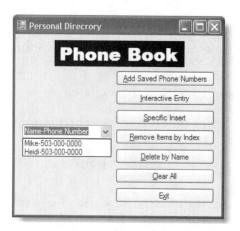

FIGURE 7.9 Screenshot of Example 2.

ListBox and ComboBox Differences

Although there are many similarities between ComboBox and ListBox, they also have some differences, which include:

- ComboBox has a Text property, which can be used for various reasons.
- ListBox has a MultiColumn property that can be set to True to display items in different columns to avoid vertical scrollbar.
- ListBox offers the SelectionMode property. This property allows the user to select more than one item at a time.

Using MultiColumn and Selectedindex

In general, we can set the MultiColumn property to True or specify the number of columns we want to have. Here is how it is done:

```
descriptionListBox.MultiColumn = True
```

In the next example, we will be using these two properties and demonstrating their features.

EXAMPLE 3

In this example, we want to have a photo album so when the user clicks on the name of each picture it will be displayed in the picture box. At the same time, a short description of the picture will be displayed in the descriptionListBox. The descriptionListBox is designed to display the items in columns. This control is also set to let the user select more than one item at once.

We have used similar examples with `RadioButtons` in previous chapters, but now we want to use a `ListBox` to do the job. In addition, we show new features of it. Start a new project and call it `listboxExample`. Add the following controls to your new form:

- Two `ListBoxes`
- One `PictureBox`
- One `Label`
- Two `Buttons`

We need the following:

- **Form1**
  Name: `listBoxForm`
  Text: `List Box`
- **Label1**
  Name: `photoLabel`
  Text: `Kids Photo Album`
  Font: `Arial Black, 20.25pt, style=Bold`
  ForeColor: Red
- **Button1**
  Name: `clearButton`
  Text: `&Clear All`
- **Button2**
  Name: `exitButton`
  Text: `E&xit`
- **PictureBox1**
  Name: `photoPictureBox`
- **ListBox1**
  Name: `kidsListBox`
- **ListBox2**
  Name: `descriptionListBox`

Now click on the *Smart Task* arrow and change the `PictureBox`'s `SizeMode` property to `StretchImage`.

In this project, we populate the `ListBox` by placing the code within the `listBox-Form_load` subprocedure:

```
Private Sub listBoxForm_Load _
(ByVal sender As System.Object, _
ByVal e As System.EventArgs) Handles MyBase.Load
```

```
            'Sets the description List Box into columns
            Me.descriptionListBox.MultiColumn = True
            'lets user to select more than one Item
            Me.descriptionListBox.SelectionMode = _
            SelectionMode.MultiExtended
            'populate the listbox
            Me.kidsListBox.Items.Add("First Kid")
            Me.kidsListBox.Items.Add("Second Kid")
            Me.kidsListBox.Items.Add("Together")
        End Sub
```

As you can see, three items will be added to `kidsListBox`. Notice that we set the `MultiColumn` property to 2. This statement forces the items to be displayed in two columns.

Now double-click on the `kidsListBox` and type the following code into the `SelectedIndexChanged` subprocedure:

```
        Private Sub kidsListBox_SelectedIndexChanged _
        (ByVal sender As System.Object, _
        ByVal e As System.EventArgs) _
        Handles kidsListBox.SelectedIndexChanged
            'clear DescriptionListBox
            Me.descriptionListBox.Items.Clear()
            'Populate the DescriptionListBox
            Me.descriptionListBox.Items.Add(" These two kids are sisters ")
            Me.descriptionListBox.Items.Add(" They love each other ")
            Me.descriptionListBox.Items.Add(" They watch TV together ")
            Me.descriptionListBox.Items.Add(" They argue as well! ")
            Me.descriptionListBox.Items.Add(" One will be a journalist ")
            Me.descriptionListBox.Items.Add(" The other one will be an artist ")

            'proceed if no error found
            Try
                Select Case Me.kidsListBox.SelectedIndex
                    'load images to the picturebox
                    Case 0
                        Me.photoPictureBox.Image = Image.FromFile("bea.jpg")

                    Case 1
                        Me.photoPictureBox.Image = Image.FromFile("sa.jpg")
                    Case 2
                        Me.photoPictureBox.Image = Image.FromFile("beasa.jpg")
                End Select
                'display error message if picture not found
            Catch errorTrap As Exception
                MessageBox.Show("The image couldn't be found", _
                "Warning", MessageBoxButtons.OK, _
                MessageBoxIcon.Information)
            End Try

        End Sub
```

In the first part of this code, we fill the `descriptionListBox`. In the second part, we detect the user's selection by evaluating the `SelectedIndex` property. As you saw before, if the image does not exist, a message will be displayed.

Double-click on the `clearButton` and type the following:

```
Private Sub clearButton_Click _
(ByVal sender As System.Object, _
ByVal e As System.EventArgs) _
Handles clearButton.Click
    'reset the Listbox and Picturebox
    Me.kidsListBox.Items.Clear()
    Me.photoPictureBox.Image = Nothing
    Me.descriptionListBox.Items.Clear()
End Sub
```

Complete the project by coding the `ExitButton` and then run it (see Figure 7.10).

FIGURE 7.10 Example 3 screenshot.

 You can view this solution under the Chapter 7 folder on the companion CD-ROM. The project is saved under its name, `listboxExample`. Just copy the project folder to your hard drive and double-click on the .sln file.

SEARCHING, SORTING, AND FINDING ITEMS

`Contains` Method

The `Contains` method can be used to search the collection for a specific key value. If the key matches any of the collections items, it returns a `True` result. This method can be used to prevent duplicate items being added to the `ComboBox`. We will examine this method in the following example.

The syntax for using this method is

```
Object.Items.Contains(searched element)
```

Contains carries a boolean value:

True: The object contained the searched element.

False: The object didn't contain the searched element.

Sorted **Property**

Once values are added to a ComboBox, there might be a need to sort the content alphabetically and place the new added items in appropriate positions within the collection. The sort is case sensitive, and uppercase and lowercase characters are treated differently. Only ascending sorting will be performed on characters. If you decide to turn off this feature by setting the value of the property to False, then all new added items will be appended to the end of ComboBox. Here is the syntax for the Sorted property:

```
Object.Sorted=True
```

Here is an example:

```
shoppingComboBox.Sorted = True
```

DropDownStyle **Property**

The DropDownStyle property allows you to select the way your ComboBox should behave. You can set this property to several different styles. If you set it to DropDown, users can type in the TextBox area of the ComboBox and be able to edit their typing. However, if you set it to DropDownList, the user can only find values that are stored within the ComboBox. Once the user types the first character of a valid value, which would be included in the ComboBox, the value will be displayed in TextBox area of the ComboBox. By typing the same character over again, you will be able to find other values that start with that character. For example, if the values within the ComboBox are: Mike, Betsy, Mary, Jamie, by typing an *M* the first time the value Mike will be displayed. If you type another *M* in the text area of the ComboBox, Mary will be displayed. Here is the syntax:

```
ComboBox.DropDownStyle = ComboBoxStyle.DropDownList
```

Here is a sample code:

```
shoppingComboBox.DropDownStyle = ComboBoxStyle.DropDownList
```

EXAMPLE 4

In this example, we will add items to a ComboBox and catch the duplicates once the user wants to add the items to the list. In addition, we will search the ComboBox for specific elements. The items are sorted alphabetically in ascending order and you can find values by typing their first character.

Let's start a new project and call it shoppingList. Add the following controls to it:

- Three Labels
- Four Buttons
- One TextBox
- One ComboBox

We need the following:

- **Form1**
  Name: shoppingForm
  Text: Search Combo
- **Label1**
  Name: titleLabel
  Text: Shopping List
  Font: Arial Black, 20.25pt, style=Bold
- **Lable2**
  Name: addItemLabel
  Text: Enter Shopping List
- **Label3**
  Name: viewLabel
  Text: View Shopping List
- **Button1**
  Name: addButton
  Text: &Add to List
- **Button2**
  Name: searchButton
  Text: &Search
- **Button3**
  Name: clearButton
  Text: &Clear
- **Button4**
  Name: exitButton
  Text: E&xit
- **TextBox1**
  Name: addItemTextBox
- **ComboBox1**
  Name: shoppingComboBox

Double-click on the Form and add the following to the Form_Load subprocedure:

```
Private Sub shoppingForm_Load _
(ByVal sender As System.Object, _
ByVal e As System.EventArgs) Handles MyBase.Load
    'Populating the combobox
    Me.shoppingComboBox.Items.Add("Pizza")
    Me.shoppingComboBox.Items.Add("Milk")
    Me.shoppingComboBox.Items.Add("Fruit")
    Me.shoppingComboBox.Items.Add("Meat")
    Me.shoppingComboBox.Items.Add("Ice Cream")
    'Sort the ComboBox
    Me.shoppingComboBox.Sorted = True
    'change the style of ComboBox to DropDown
    Me.shoppingComboBox.DropDownStyle = ComboBoxStyle.DropDownList
End Sub
```

As you can see, we add items to the ComboBox, set the Sorted property to True, and set the ComboBox's DropDownStyle to DropDownList.

Now double-click on the Add to List button and add the following:

```
Private Sub addButton_Click _
(ByVal sender As System.Object, _
ByVal e As System.EventArgs) _
Handles addButton.Click
    If Me.addItemTextBox.Text = Nothing Then
        MessageBox.Show("Blank is not acceptable", _
        "Warning", MessageBoxButtons.OK, _
        MessageBoxIcon.Information)
        'adding to the combobox if not duplicate
    ElseIf Me.shoppingComboBox.Items.Contains(addItemTextBox.Text) Then
        MessageBox.Show("Duplicate Entry. Cannot Add", _
        "Warning!", MessageBoxButtons.OK, _
        MessageBoxIcon.Information)
    Else : Me.shoppingComboBox.Items.Add(addItemTextBox.Text)
    End If
End Sub
```

Once the user enters the data, Visual Basic searches through the existing items. If the entered string is not found, it will be added to the ComboBox. Otherwise, a message will be displayed.

Now let us add the following codes under the searchButton:

```
Private Sub searchButton_Click _
(ByVal sender As System.Object, _
ByVal e As System.EventArgs) _
Handles searchButton.Click
    'Will search for the element
    Dim mySearchString As String
    mySearchString = InputBox _
    ("Enter the shopping item you need to search", _
    "Searching Items")
    If Me.shoppingComboBox.Items.Contains(mySearchString) Then
```

```
        MessageBox.Show("Item Found " _
        + mySearchString, "Found it!", _
        MessageBoxButtons.OK, _
        MessageBoxIcon.Information)
      Else : MessageBox.Show("Item not Found " _
      + mySearchString, "Warning!", MessageBoxButtons.OK, _
      MessageBoxIcon.Information)
      End If
  End Sub
```

The above codes will search the existing items to find the searched element. If it is found, a message will be displayed to confirm a successful search. Otherwise, a message will be displayed to announce an unsuccessful search.

Complete the Exit and Clear buttons and run the project. Type an M in the text area of the shoppingComboBox and see what happens. Test all buttons for their functions (see Figure 7.11).

FIGURE 7.11 Example 4 screenshot.

ON THE CD

You can view this solution under the Chapter 7 folder on the companion CD-ROM. The project is saved under its name, shoppingList. Just copy the project folder to your hard drive and double-click on the .sln file.

MENUSTRIP

Visual Basic 2005 has enhanced the mainMenu tool that was available through Visual Basic.NET. It is now called MenuStrip. MenuStrip is a container that can hold menu items and can be used for many Windows applications and Web projects and you have seen menu components in many Windows and Web applications. You can add the MenuStrip component to your form by using your toolbox. As discussed in Chapter 2, the Toolbox is divided into categories. You can find MenuStrip under the Menus & ToolBars tab. You will find some similarities between MenuStrips, ComboBoxes, and ListBoxes.

Once the control is added to your form, you can add members to it. You can choose from several styles:

- MenuItem
- ComboBox
- TextBox

Start a new project and call it menu. Add a MenuStrip control to your Form. You will notice that the MenuStrip sits in the Component Tray area. Once you highlight it, it should look like Figure 7.12.

Menu Designer

Menu Designer has a TextBox labeled "Type Here" and allows you to build your menu items and add your menus and submenus. You can choose from MenuItem, ComboBox, and TextBox options available under the MenuStrip designer drop down. If you click on the arrow button, you should be able to see these options (see Figure 7.13).

FIGURE 7.12 MenuStrip control.

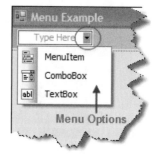

FIGURE 7.13 MenuStrip options.

Tasks Pane

MenuStrip has its own Tasks Pane that allows us to access many features that are normally available via the Properties box. To open the Tasks Pane, click on the Smart Task arrow located in the upper-right corner of the control. Among the available features are Edit Items, Embed in ToolStripContainer, Insert Standard Items, RenderMode, Dock, and GripStyle (see Figure 7.14).

FIGURE 7.14   MenuStrip *Tasks Pane.*

Edit Items

Edit Items will take you to the Item Collection Editor for MenuStrip and allows you to add, remove, or edit the items. This is very useful when you want to move a menu item to a different position or insert a new item between existing members (see Figure 7.15).

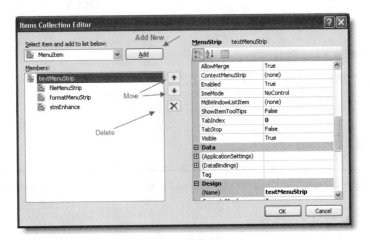

FIGURE 7.15   MenuStrip Item Collection Editor.

Embed in `ToolStripContainer`

Instead of placing your ToolStrip directly into the Form, you can place it in a ToolStripContainer. The panels allow you to place the controls around the Form but inside the containers. This is a new feature added to the 2005 edition. When it is added to the ToolStripContainer, it provides its own options (see Figure 7.16).

Insert Standard Items

Insert Standard Items is another feature in the MenuStrip Tasks Pane. If you select this feature, a standard menu with File, Edit, Tools, and Help will be added to your menu bar. This will provide basic design components and allows users to add to it or change it according to their needs (see Figure 7.17).

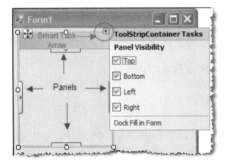

FIGURE 7.16   ToolStripContainer panels.

FIGURE 7.17   Standard Items added to the Form.

RenderMode Property

The RenderMode property allows you to pick one of three choices as the default theme for your Form: System, Professional, or MangerRenderMode. We have picked Professional with a blue color for the menu project in Example 5.

Dock Property

The Dock property allows you to pick the location of your MenuStrip on the screen. If you click on None, it allows you to move the MenuStrip where you need it (see Figure 7.18).

GripStyle Property

This property makes the grip, which is used to make the controls visible or invisible. You can choose from two options: Hidden and Visible.

Separators

A separator is a menu item that separates groups of menu items from each other. You can add a separator to your menu by clicking on the drop-down arrow next to

FIGURE 7.18 Dock panel.

the menu entry TextBox and choosing Separator from the list of options. You need to move the mouse over the control to see the drop-down arrow.

The top of Figure 7.19 shows you how to select a separator from the drop-down options. The bottom of the image shows a separator, which is added to a menu.

It is also possible to convert an existing menu item to a separator. To accomplish this task, just select a menu item that you want to convert to a separator and right-click on it. From the Context menu, select the Convert To option. You will see another drop-down list, in which Separator is an option (see Figure 7.20). Figure 7.20 also shows a few other options, including Enabled, Checked, and Set Image. Let us briefly explain them.

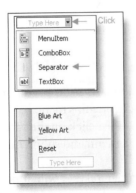

FIGURE 7.19 Separator demonstration.

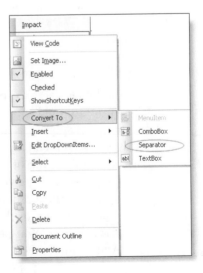

FIGURE 7.20 Converting an existing item to a separator.

Enabled **Property**

This property can be used to make an item enabled or disabled. The possible values are True and False. This is useful when you want to force users to select a series of actions in a specific sequence. You can make an item enabled by setting its property to True. If the item is not available and it is displayed in gray, it means the property of it is set to False.

Here is the syntax to change this property through the codes:

```
Menuitem.Enabled=True
```

Checked **Property**

This property is used to put a checkmark next to the menu item. This is a visual reminder to the user that the item is already selected. Here is the syntax to do this through codes:

```
Menuitem.Checked=True
```

Set Image **Property**

The Image property allows us to pick an image that will show up on the left side of the menu item. We can do this at design time or through codes:

```
Menuitem.Image = Image.FromFile("Name.Extension")
```

EXAMPLE 5

Start a new project and call it menuStripDemo. Add the following controls to it:

- One MenuStrip
- One PictureBox

Add the MenuStrip to your Form by using the Toolbox. As soon as you highlight it, a menu bar should appear on the top of your form. Inside this menu bar, you will see a TextBox displaying a label that reads "Type Here." Just click on the TextBox and start typing your menu items. The MenuStrip provides a menu and submenu. On the first TextBox on the top of the MenuStrip, type "&File."

As soon as you type your main menu item, another TextBox will appear right below it. Type your submenu item, which is "E&xit." Once you are done with this, click on a blank spot of the menu bar, just next to the &File menu item. A new TextBox will appear. You need to type "&Images" in the new TextBox (see Figure 7.21). Add menus and submenus according to the chart in Figure 7.22.

FIGURE 7.21 Menus and submenu.

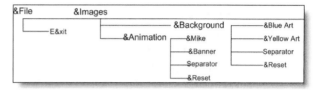

FIGURE 7.22 Project menu structure.

In this project, we will be using the following concepts so you can apply what you have learned about menus and submenus:

- Menu
- Submenu
- Shortcut
- Set image
- Separator
- Enabled property
- Checked property

In this project, we will be using menu items to change the background images and load animations into the PictureBox. You can find animations that come with Visual Studio 2005 or you can download those included in the accompanying CD-ROM. To load the animations that are supplied with Visual Studio 2005, you need to search within the following folder: C:\Program Files\Microsoft Visual Studio 8\Common7\VS2005ImageLibrary\VS2005ImageLibrary\animations. Notice that we are using access keys for all menus and submenus.

Naming the Menu Items

As stated before, menus and toolbars have gone through major revisions in Visual Basic 2005. Among these changes is menu items naming. In Visual Basic 2005, the Text property of the menu item is used to create a unique item name. For example, an &Clear submenu item will have the following name: ClearToolStripMenuItem. This change will minimize the need for applying the naming convention on MenuStrips. Let's add the following menu and submenus (child menus).

- **Form1**
  Name: menuForm
  Text: Menu Strip

■ **MenuStrip1**
   Name: MenuStrip1
■ **PictureBox1**
   Name: animationPictureBox
   SizeMode: AutoSize

Menu Items

Figure 7.22 showed you the structure for adding menu and submenu items. Here are your menu items:

■   &File
■   &Images

Submenu Items

Here are your submenu items. The following will go under the &File menu item:

■   E&xit

The following will go under the &Images menu item:

■   &Background
■   &Blue Art
■   &Yellow Art
■   Separator
■   &Reset
■   &Animation
■   &Mike
■   &Banner
■   Separator
■   &Reset

Now we need to add codes to each menu item. First, open the menuForm sub-procedure and add the following:

```
Private Sub menuForm_Load _
(ByVal sender As System.Object, _
ByVal e As System.EventArgs) _
Handles MyBase.Load
    'Making the picturebox invisible
    Me.animationPictureBox.Visible = False
    'Declaring the file location variables
    Dim fileLocationString As String
```

```
Dim filelocationString1 As String
'assigning file locations to the variables
fileLocationString = _
"C:\Program Files\Microsoft Visual Studio 8\" + _
"Common7\vs2005imagelibrary\" + _
"vs2005imagelibrary\bitmaps\misc\Expand_large.bmp"
filelocationString1 = _
"C:\Program Files\Microsoft Visual Studio 8\" + _
"Common7\vs2005imagelibrary\vs2005imagelibrary\" + _
"bitmaps\misc\warning.bmp"

Try
    'displaying the images next to the menu items
    Me.ExitToolStripMenuItem.Image = _
    Image.FromFile(filelocationString1)
    Me.BackgroundToolStripMenuItem.Image = _
    Image.FromFile(fileLocationString)
    Me.AnimationToolStripMenuItem.Image = _
    Image.FromFile(fileLocationString)
Catch ex As Exception
    'display if images couldn't be loaded
    MessageBox.Show("Images couldn't be loaded", "Warning", _
    MessageBoxButtons.OK, MessageBoxIcon.Information)
    End Try
End Sub
```

First we set the Visible property of the PictureBox. This helps make it visible only when the user clicks on the menu item. In the next two statements, we declared two variables so we can store the location of our image files in them. This is not required but will help us use them later without the need to retype the entire path. The next two statements show how to store the value of the file locations to variables. The Try/Catch exception handler will help us catch errors if the requested files are not found. If files are found, the images will be displayed in designated areas.

Now add the following statements under the Blue Art menu item by double-clicking on it:

```
Private Sub blueArtToolStripMenuItem_Click _
(ByVal sender As System.Object, _
ByVal e As System.EventArgs) _
Handles blueArtToolStripMenuItem.Click
    'display checkmark next to Blue Art menu item and clear
    'checkmarks from Yellow Art menu item
    Me.blueArtToolStripMenuItem.Checked = True
    Me.yellowArtToolStripMenuItem.Checked = False
    'Cover the form's background with this image
    Me.BackgroundImage = Image.FromFile("back1.tif")
End Sub
```

We will display a checkmark next to the item that the user clicks and clear any checkmark that was displayed in any other menu item. This allows us to see the last menu item that was used by the user. The next statement covers the background of the Form with the image we are loading. It is a good idea to add a Try/Catch exception handler to prevent a program crash.

Add the following statements under the Yellow Art menu items:

```
Private Sub yellowArtToolStripMenuItem_Click _
(ByVal sender As System.Object, _
ByVal e As System.EventArgs) _
Handles yellowArtToolStripMenuItem.Click
    'display checkmark next to Yellow Art menu item and clear
    'checkmarks from Blue Art menu item
    Me.blueArtToolStripMenuItem.Checked = False
    Me.bellowArtToolStripMenuItem.Checked = True
    'Cover the form's background with this image
    Me.backgroundImage = Image.FromFile("back2.tif")
End Sub
```

The above statements are very similar to what you did for the Blue Art menu item. In the next step, we will make the Reset menu item disabled. We will use the Background menu item's MouseMove event procedure to accomplish this task. Based on this code, if none of the menu items, Blue Art and Yellow Art, are selected, then the Reset menu item will be disabled. Add the following under the MouseMove subprocedure of the Background menu item:

```
Private Sub backgroundToolStripMenuItem_MouseMove _
(ByVal sender As Object, _
ByVal e As System.Windows.Forms.MouseEventArgs) _
Handles backgroundToolStripMenuItem.MouseMove
    'once the user moves the mouse over this menu item
    'the checked property of two submenu items are evaluated.
    'if none of them is checked, then the reset menu item
    'will be disabled so it cannot be used
    If Me.blueArtToolStripMenuItem.Checked = _
    False And Me.YellowArtToolStripMenuItem.Checked = False Then
        Me.resetToolStripMenuItem.Enabled = False
    Else
        'if any of these two menu items is checked, then the reset
        'menu item is enabled
        Me.resetToolStripMenuItem.Enabled = True
    End If
End Sub
```

The last menu item in the Background group is the Reset menu item. Type the following:

```
Private Sub ResetToolStripMenuItem1_Click _
(ByVal sender As System.Object, _
ByVal e As System.EventArgs) _
Handles ResetToolStripMenuItem1.Click
```

```
    'remove the checkmarks from Mike and Banner animation
    'menu items.
    Me.mikeToolStripMenuItem1.Checked = False
    Me.bannerToolStripMenuItem.Checked = False
    'Reset the animationpicturebox to default
    Me.animationPictureBox.Image = Nothing
    'makes the animationpicturebox invisible
    Me.animationPictureBox.Visible = False
End Sub
```

As you can see from the comments, we changed everything back to default.

Now we need to complete the other sections, which are very similar to what we did here. Add the following codes under the Animation menu item MouseMove subprocedure:

```
Private Sub animationToolStripMenuItem_MouseMove _
(ByVal sender As Object, _
ByVal e As System.Windows.Forms.MouseEventArgs) _
Handles animationToolStripMenuItem.MouseMove
    'once the user moves the mouse over this menu item
    'the checked property of two submenu items are evaluated
    'if none of them is checked, then the reset menu item
    'will be disabled so it cannot be used
    If Me.mikeToolStripMenuItem1.Checked = _
    False And Me.BannerToolStripMenuItem.Checked = False Then
        Me.resetToolStripMenuItem1.Enabled = False
    Else
        'if any of these two menu items is checked, then the reset
        'menu item is enabled
        Me.ResetToolStripMenuItem1.Enabled = True
    End If
End Sub
```

This is similar to what we did with the Background menu item. We need to type the following under the Mike menu item's subprocedure:

```
Private Sub mikeToolStripMenuItem1_Click _
(ByVal sender As System.Object, _
ByVal e As System.EventArgs) _
andles mikeToolStripMenuItem1.Click
    'display checkmark next to Mike menu item and clears
    'checkmarks from Banner menu item
    Me.mikeToolStripMenuItem1.Checked = True
    Me.BannerToolStripMenuItem.Checked = False
    'make the Picturebox visible
    Me.animationPictureBox.Visible = True
    'display Mike animation
    Me.animationPictureBox.Image = Image.FromFile("mike.gif")
End Sub
```

The following goes under the Banner submenu item's subprocedure:

```
Private Sub bannerToolStripMenuItem_Click _
(ByVal sender As System.Object, _
ByVal e As System.EventArgs) _
Handles bannerToolStripMenuItem.Click
    'display checkmark next to Banner menu item and clears
    'checkmarks from Mike menu item
    Me.mikeToolStripMenuItem1.Checked = False
    Me.BannerToolStripMenuItem.Checked = True
    Me.animationPictureBox.Visible = True
    'display banner animation  which is under the Banner
    Me.animationPictureBox.Image = Image.FromFile("banner.gif")
End Sub
```

Type the following under Reset, which is part of the Animation group:

```
Private Sub resetToolStripMenuItem1_Click _
(ByVal sender As System.Object, _
ByVal e As System.EventArgs) _
Handles resetToolStripMenuItem1.Click
    'remove the checkmarks from Mike , Banner and animation
    'menu items.
    Me.mikeToolStripMenuItem1.Checked = False
    Me.bannerToolStripMenuItem.Checked = False
    'Reset the animationpicturebox to default
    Me.animationPictureBox.Image = Nothing
    'makes the animationpicturebox invisible
    Me.animationPictureBox.Visible = False
End Sub
```

Please complete the Exit menu item, save the program, and run it. Figure 7.23 shows the screenshot.

FIGURE 7.23   Example 5 screenshot.

ON THE CD

You can view this solution under the Chapter 7 folder on the companion CD-ROM. The project is saved under its name, menuStripDemo. Just copy the project folder to your hard drive and double-click on the .sln file.

TOOLSTRIP

ToolStrip is a new tool that comes with Visual Basic 2005 to replace the previous ToolBar control used by many programmers. ToolBar can still be used in Visual Basic programs, but ToolStrip contains new enhancements. Like menus, ToolStrip is another container that holds other controls such as TextBox, ComboBox, and Button. You can adopt ToolStrip and customize it to develop professional-looking forms. You may also include images to resemble other professional Windows programs.

Once you add this control, it places itself on the top of the Form by default. By using the Properties box or its Smart Task arrow, you can change these default values by using its Tasks Pane. We will examine this tool by providing an example later in the chapter.

IMAGELIST

ImageList is an image container that can hold images and be used by the program at runtime. Think of an ImageList as a slide tray that you use in a slide projector. The slide tray contains many slots that can be used to hold slides. If the slide tray can hold 100 slides, then you can arrange your slides as you desire. You can use a specific sequence for placing slides onto the tray in order to remember them later. If you want to replace the slides, you can take out one slide from a specific slot, say slot number 85, and replace it with another slide. ImageList does much the same thing. You can place your images in the ImageList (slide tray) and refer to each one by its index number (slot).

The advantage of an ImageList is that it uses a single library of images instead of a group of scattered pictures all around the hard drive. We can use one ImageList for several controls and assign the images at runtime. If the control we are planning to use, such as a Button, has the ImageList property, then ImageList can be used by that control (see Figure 7.24). Like MenuStrip and ToolStrip, ImageList has its own *Smart Task* arrow that takes you to its Tasks Pane (see Figure 7.25).

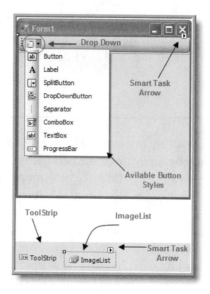

FIGURE 7.24 Adding `ToolStrip` and `ImageList` to a `Form`.

FIGURE 7.25 The `ImageList` *Tasks Pane.*

COLOR DIALOG BOX

You have learned how to change the background color of the `Form` and other controls through many examples in this book. You have also learned how to use different fonts for your projects. In this chapter, we will be using some of the useful dialog boxes that can make programming tasks much easier. You can apply these tools to let users choose their options from pop-up dialog boxes. It is also more convenient for programmers to use these dialog boxes rather than coding all possible inputs.

The Color dialog box allows users to select colors from a pallet and create their own custom colors. You have probably seen this color pallet in many Windows and Web applications. The Color dialog allows you to let users have full control using this dialog box or have limited options. Here are a few options.

AllowFullOpen **Property**

You can use this property to keep users from defining custom colors. The two possible values for this property are True and False. If you set this property to False, the user can only choose from available colors and will not be able to make custom colors. The default value for this property is True. Here is a sample code:

```
ColorDialog1.AllowFullOpen = True
```

Color **Property**

The color the user selects will be stored in this property. If the user does not select any color, the value of this property will be the default color, which is Black. Here is a sample code:

```
TextBox1.ForeColor = ColorDialog1.Color
```

SolidColorOnly **Property**

This property, which can have True or False values, can be used to restrict users from selecting solid colors only. Here is an example:

```
ColorDialog1.SolidColorOnly = True
```

AnyColor **Property**

When you select this property, any basic colors that are available can be selected. Here is an example:

```
ColorDialog1.AnyColor = True
```

ShowHelp **Property**

If this property is set to True, the user will see a Help button that can be used to get help for the Color dialog box. Otherwise, the Help button will not be available to the user.

ShowDialog **Method**

This method is used to display the built-in Color dialog box and waits until the user makes a selection. The user's selection will be stored in the Color property of the dialog box. Here is an example (see Figure 7.26):

```
ColorDialog1.ShowDialog()
```

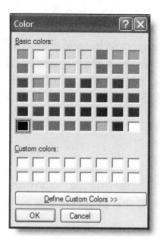

FIGURE 7.26 Color pallet.

FONT DIALOG BOX

The Font dialog box can be used to display all fonts that are installed on the user's computer and allow him to choose the Typeface Name, Style, Point Size, Effects, and Script. You can set the dialog box to show screen fonts, print fonts, or both. As with the Color dialog box, you have many options, such as restricting users from making specific changes. Here are some examples.

FontMustExist Property

When this property is set to True, if the user specifies a font that does not exist, an error message will be displayed. Here is an example:

```
FontDialog1.FontMustExist = True
```

MinSize and MaxSize Properties

By setting these two properties, you can specify a range for the fonts that will be shown in the Size drop-down list. If the user specifies a value that is out of range, there will be an error message. Here is an example:

```
FontDialog1.MaxSize = 36
FontDialog1.MinSize = 24
```

ShowDialog **Method**

Like the Color dialog box, this method is used to display the built-in font dialog box and waits until the user makes a selection. Here is an example:

```
FontDialog1.ShowDialog()
```

ShowHelp **and** ShowEffect **Properties**

If these two properties are set to False, they will not appear on the Font dialog box. Here is how we can use them (see Figure 7.27):

```
FontDialog1.ShowHelp = True
FontDialog1.ShowEffects = True
```

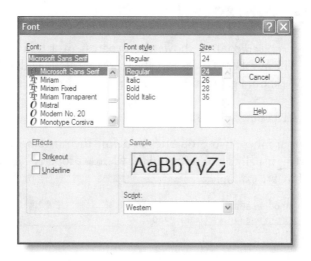

FIGURE 7.27 Font dialog box with MinSize 24 and MaxSize 36.

STATUSSTRIP

StatusStrip, which replaces and enhances the previous control called StatusBar, can be used to provide useful information about the objects that are placed on the Form or provide information about the system. Generally, StatusStrip is used to show time, data, cap lock, num lock, and other related information. This control will sit at the bottom of the Form by default but can be moved to any location using the docking feature available in its Tasks Pane. StatusBar can still be used for backward and compatibility reasons. Like many other controls discussed in this chapter,

StatusStrip uses an Item Collection Editor to add, remove, or revise Buttons. Four types of controls can be placed on StatusStrip:

- Buttons
- ProgressBars
- DropDowns
- Labels

You can add these controls either by right-clicking on the controls or by using the Smart Tag. Among the possible controls above, ProgressBar is new so we will highlight some of its features.

PROGRESSBAR CONTROL

The ProgressBar control shows the progress of a task by displaying segmented blocks. The number of blocks will be increased along with the length of the progress value. We should get familiar with some of its properties:

Maximum and Minimum Properties

You can use these two properties to define the range of an operation. The Minimum property is usually set to zero, and the Maximum property can represent the completed task. Here are examples:

```
progressBar.Minimum = 0
progressBar.Maximum = 60
```

Style Property

This property allows you to choose a style from three available styles: Blocks, Continues, and Marquee.

Value Property

The progress of the task can be identified by the Value property of the ProgressBar. We will use this value to show the status bar blocks:

```
progressBar.Value = 50
```

Step Property

This property is used to increment the value of the ProgressBar:

```
progressBar.Step = 10
```

PerformStep **Method**

We use this method to increase the value of the ProgressBar by the number we assigned to the Step property:

```
progressBar.PerformStep()
```

Increment **Method**

This method will increment the Value property of the ProgressBar by the given number:

```
progressBar.Increment(6)
```

EXAMPLE 6

In this example, we will be adding the following tools to our project and practicing the features we referenced before: ToolStrip, StatusStrip, ColorDialog, FontDialog, and ImageList. Start a new project and call it imagelistToolstrip and use the following names:

■ **Form1**
   Name: toolStripForm
   Text: Tool Strip
■ **Label1**
   Name: textEntryLabel
   Text: Enter Text
■ **TextBox1**
   Name: textEntryTextBox
   MultiLine: True

You need to add the following controls to your form. Just use the Toolbox and add the controls listed below. You will find ToolStrip and StatusStrip under the Menus and Toolbars tab. The ImageList and Timer can be found under the Component tab. The ColorDialog and FontDialog controls are located under the Dialog tab.

■ One ToolStrip
■ One TextBox
■ One ImageList
■ One StatusStrip
■ One ColorDialog
■ One FontDialog

- One `Label`
- One `Timer`

Other than the `Label` and the `TextBox`, these controls will be placed in the Component Tray.

We will be using the `ToolStrip` Tasks Pane to add eight buttons to our toolbar. These buttons will enable the user to apply `Cut`, `Paste`, and `Copy` methods. In addition, we will be using the `TextAlign` property to align the text to Center, Right, and Left. It will also provide tools for changing the controls' colors and fonts by using Color and Font dialog boxes. You will also learn how to use an `ImageList`.

Loading the Image List

Now load the `ImageList` with images. We want to use *Center, Right, Left, Cut, Paste,* and *Copy* icons from the Visual Basic vs2005ImageLibrary folder, which is located on your hard drive: C:\Program Files\Microsoft Visual Studio 8\Common7\ VS2005ImageLibrary\VS2005ImageLibrary\bitmaps\commands\16color. The easiest way to add images to the `ImageList` is to right-click on the `ImageList` control located in the Component Tray and select Choose Images from the Context menu (see Figure 7.28). This will take you to the Images Collection Editor. This editor allows you to add, move, and remove images (see Figure 7.29). You can also access this editor by using the `Image Collection` property within the Properties box or by using the Smart Tag provided on the top of the `ImageList` control.

FIGURE 7.28 Choose *Images* option from *Context* menu.

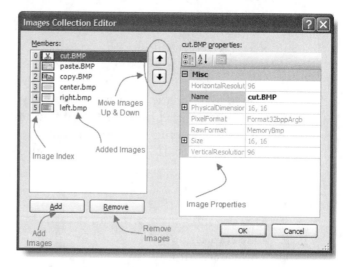

FIGURE 7.29 Images Collection Editor.

It is also possible to add images to the ImageList at runtime:

```
ImageList1.Images.Add(Image.FromFile("path:\Graphics\SelectedFile.bmp"))
```

Now you need to locate these six image files within your hard drive. By default, they are located in the folder that was referenced before. Once you have located the bitmap files and added them to the ImageList, then you are ready to use it. The names and the appearances of the images may be different, but that should not matter. Use your own discretion to choose the files you feel are appropriate for this application. When all of the images are added, click on the OK button to exit the Images Collection Editor.

If you look at Figure 7.29, you will notice a number on the left side of the image. That index number can be used to reference a specific image. We will be using the index numbers of each image to assign them to each button.

Adding Buttons to the ToolStrip

Highlight the ToolStrip bar on the top of the form. Click on the Add button of the ToolStrip to add buttons (see Figure 7.30). When you click on the Add ToolStripButton, you will see a drop-down list appear, as shown on the right side of Figure 7.30. Add the following:

- Eight Buttons
- One ComboBox

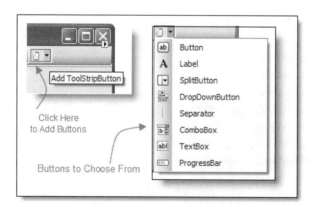

FIGURE 7.30 Adding buttons to the tool strip and available options.

Rename the controls according to the following:

- **ToolStrip1**
  Name: menuToolStrip
- **ToolStripButton1**
  Name: exitToolStripButton
  Text: E&xit
  ToolTipText: Exits the Program
- **ToolStripButton2**
  Name: cutToolStripButton
  Text: C&ut
  DisplayStyle: ImageAndText
  ToolTipText: Cuts Selected Text
- **ToolStripButton3**
  Name: pasteToolStripButton
  Text: &Paste
  DisplayStyle: ImageAndText
  ToolTipText: Pastes Text
- **ToolStripButton4**
  Name: copyToolStripButton
  Text: &Copy
  DisplayStyle: ImageAndText
  ToolTipText: Copies Selected Text
- **ToolStripButton5**
  Name: centerToolStripButton
  Text: C&enter
  DisplayStyle: ImageAndText
  ToolTipText: Aligns Center
- **ToolStripButton6**
  Name: rightToolStripButton
  Text: &Right
  DisplayStyle: ImageAndText
  ToolTipText: Aligns Right
- **ToolStripButton7**
  Name: leftToolStripButton
  Text: &Left
  DisplayStyle: ImageAndText
  ToolTipText: Aligns Left
- **ToolStripComboBox1**
  Name: fontColorToolStripComboBox
  Text: Text Color
  ToolTipText: Color and Font dialog

Assigning Images to ToolStrip Buttons

Now we need to assign the images we stored in our ImageList to the Buttons we added to the ToolStrip. Double-click on the Form and add the following in the Form_load subprocedure:

```
Private Sub toolStripForm_Load _
(ByVal sender As System.Object, _
ByVal e As System.EventArgs) _
Handles MyBase.Load
    'Assign the Imagelist images to Toolstrip buttons
    Me.menuToolStrip.ImageList = menuImageList
    'assign each button an image from the imagelist
    Me.cutToolStripButton.ImageIndex = 0
    Me.pasteToolStripButton.ImageIndex = 1
    Me.copyToolStripButton.ImageIndex = 2
    Me.centerToolStripButton.ImageIndex = 3
    Me.rightToolStripButton.ImageIndex = 4
    Me.leftToolStripButton.ImageIndex = 5
```

First we assigned the ImageList to the ToolStrip by typing

```
Me.menuToolStrip.ImageList = menuImageList
```

Then we assigned the images that we stored in the ImageList to the Buttons that we placed on the ToolStrip. As discussed before, we use the index of these images to assign them to the buttons.

Now add the following codes into the toolStripForm_Load subprocedure, just after what you typed before:

```
'add items to the combobox
    Me.fontColorToolStripComboBox.Items.Add("Color Dialog Box")
    Me.fontColorToolStripComboBox.Items.Add("Font Dialig Box")
    Me.fontColorToolStripComboBox.Items.Add("Reset")
    'display the current date in Date label
    Me.DateToolStripStatusLabel.Text = "Date " & Today.ToString
```

Now that we have populated the ImageList and renamed all of our controls, we are ready to enter codes.

More Properties and Methods for TextBox

In this project, we will also use more of the TextBox control features:

■ The Cut method copies the selected text to the clipboard and deletes the selection from the TextBox.

■ The Copy method copies the selected text to the clipboard and keeps the original in the TextBox.

- The Paste method is used to transfer the content of the clipboard to the TextBox or other objects.
- The AlignText property is used to align the text to Center, Right, or Left.

Detecting the User's Choice

Now we need to know which Button the user clicks in order to react to it. Double-click on the ToolStrip control and add the following code to the ItemClicked subprocedure:

```
Private Sub menuToolStrip_ItemClicked _
(ByVal sender As System.Object, _
ByVal e As System.Windows.Forms.ToolStripItemClickedEventArgs) _
Handles menuToolStrip.ItemClicked

    Select Case Me.menuToolStrip.Items.IndexOf(e.ClickedItem)
        'detect each selection and take action
        Case 0
            'first button is clicked
            MessageBox.Show _
            ("The program will be terminated", "Warning", _
            MessageBoxButtons.OK, MessageBoxIcon.Warning)
            Me.Close()

        Case 1
            'Cut the text

            Me.textEntryTextBox.Cut()
        Case 2
            'Paste the text
            Me.textEntryTextBox.Paste()
        Case 3
            'Copy the text
            Me.textEntryTextBox.Copy()
        Case 4
            'Align Center
            Me.textEntryTextBox.TextAlign = _
            HorizontalAlignment.Center
        Case 5
            'Align Right
            Me.textEntryTextBox.TextAlign = _
            HorizontalAlignment.Right
        Case 6
            'Align Left
            Me.textEntryTextBox.TextAlign = _
            HorizontalAlignment.Left
    End Select

End Sub
```

The code should be self-explanatory since we have already explained the nature of these methods and properties. We have also provided comments to help you identify these features.

Type the following under the fontColorToolStripComboBox_SelectedIndexChanged:

```
Private Sub fontColorToolStripComboBox_SelectedIndexChanged _
(ByVal sender As Object, _
ByVal e As System.EventArgs) _
Handles fontColorToolStripComboBox.SelectedIndexChanged
    'detect the user's action
    Select Case Me.fontColorToolStripComboBox.SelectedIndex
        Case 0
            'Show color Dialog Box
            Me.menuColorDialog.ShowDialog()
            Me.textEntryTextBox.ForeColor = _
            Me.menuColorDialog.Color
        Case 1
            'show Font dialog
            Me.menuFontDialog.ShowDialog()
            Me.textEntryTextBox.Font = _
            Me.menuFontDialog.Font
        Case 2
            'Reset the color and font
            me.textEntryTextBox.ForeColor = _
            Color.Empty
            Me.menuFontDialog.Reset()
            Me.textEntryTextBox.Font = _
            Me.menuFontDialog.Font

    End Select
End Sub
```

In the above code, we used a ColorDialog and FontDialog to change the ForeColor and Font properties of the TextBox.

Adding StatusStrip **Control**

It is time to add a StatusStrip to your project. We want to add three buttons to this StatusStrip. Find StatusStrip, which is located under the Menus & ToolBars tab in your Toolbox, and add it to your form. Once the StatusStrip is added to your form, just click on the StatusBar on your form and by clicking on the Menu Designer drop-down arrow, add the following Buttons to your StatusStrip (see Figure 7.31):

■ Two ToolStrip StatusLabels
■ One ToolStrip ProgressBar

Name these three buttons as follows:

■ **ToolStripLabel1**
   Name: timeToolStripStatusLabels
   Text: Time

- **ToolStripLabel2**
  Name: dateToolStripLabel
  Text: Data
- **ToolStripProgressBar1**
  Name: secondToolStripProgressBar

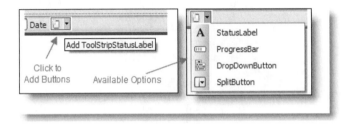

FIGURE 7.31 Adding Buttons to the StatusStrip and available options.

Adding a Timer Control

We will be introducing the Timer control in Chapter 8 and will give you many examples to show its features. For this project, we only use one of its features, which is showing the time. You have used this control before so you should be familiar with its nature:

- **Timer1**
  Name: toolStripTimer

Add the following statements under the toolStripForm_Load subprocedure, just under other statements you added before:

```
'set the interval to one millisecond
Me.toolStripTimer.Interval = 1000
'start the timer
Me.toolStripTimer.Start()
```

The above code includes what you have already completed, and the comments explain their function. Now double-click on the Timer and add the following codes:

```
Private Sub toolStripTimer_Tick _
(ByVal sender As System.Object, _
ByVal e As System.EventArgs) _
Handles toolStripTimer.Tick
    'display time of the day in Time label
    Me.timeToolStripStatusLabel.Text = "Time " + TimeOfDay.ToString
```

```
            'set the progress bar's minimum value to 0
            Me.secondToolStripProgressBar.Minimum = 0
            'set the progress bar's maximum value to 60
            Me.secondToolStripProgressBar.Maximum = 60
            'set the step value to 10 so it will be
            'increased by 10 every second
            Me.secondToolStripProgressBar.Step = 10
            'increments the value of progressbar by
            'the value of the step
            Me.secondToolStripProgressBar.PerformStep()
            'display the seconds changes in progressBar
            Me.secondToolStripProgressBar.Value = Now.Second
        End Sub
```

This code should also be self-explanatory. Now complete the exitButton, save your program, and run it. Type something in the TextBox and try all the Buttons (see Figure 7.32).

FIGURE 7.32 Example 6 screenshot.

You can view this solution under the Chapter 7 folder on the companion CD-ROM. The project is saved under its name, imagelistToolstrip. Just copy the project folder to your hard drive and double-click on the .sln file.

CONTEXTMENU

The ContextMenuStrip is a pop-up menu that is activated when the user right-clicks on the Form. This shortcut menu can be used to provide more options for the user. ContextMenuStrips and MenuStrips are very similar in nature. The difference is that one appears on the top of the form and the other will pop up on demand. Visual Basic 2005 has added more functionality to the ContextMenu that has been used in previous versions. Although ContextMenu has been replaced by this new control, the compiler still recognizes it for backward compatibility. An example will show how `ContextMenu` works.

EXAMPLE 7

Create a new project and call it `contextMenuExample`. Add the following controls to it:

- **Form1**
  Name: `contextMenuForm`
  Text: `Context Menu`
  Size: `364, 303`
- **Label1**
  Name: `nameLabel`
  Text: `Enter Name`
- **TextBox1**
  Name: `nameTextBox`
- **Button1**
  Name: `exitButton`
  Text: `E&xit`

Now, from the Toolbox, add a `ContextMenuStrip` control to your form. This new control, like the tool bar you used before, sits in the Component Tray area of the form. Highlight the `ContextMenuStrip` control and add items to your menu as you did for the `MenuStrip` before (see Figure 7.33).

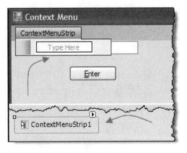

FIGURE 7.33 `ContextMenuStrip` design.

The `Form` and all controls that you place on it can use their own `ContextMenuStrip`, so in this project, we will be using two `ContextMenus`: one for the `Form` and the other one for the `TextBox`. It is also possible to share one `ContextMenuStrip` with several controls. Add the following to the `ContextMenuStrip` (see Figure 7.34):

- &Form Size
- &BackColor
- &Blue
- &Green
- &Reset

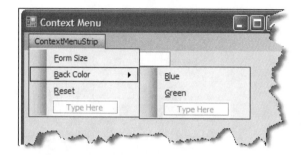

FIGURE 7.34 Adding items to the ContextMenuStrip.

Add another ContextMenuStrip to your Form and add the following items to it:

- &ForeColor
- &Red
- &Green
- &BackColor
- &Black
- &Yellow
- &Reset

Now highlight the Form and find the ContextMenuStrip property. Assign it to ContextMenuStrip1 (see Figure 7.35).

The drop down for the Form's ContextMenuStrip shows two ContextMenus. We will use the second one later. We just told Visual Basic that if the user right-clicks on the form, this menu should pop up. Now we should add codes for each menu item. Highlight ContextMenuStrip1 and double-click on the Form Size menu item that appears on the top of the form. Each menu item has its own subprocedure. Add the following code to the Form Size subprocedure:

```
Private Sub formSizeToolStripMenuItem_Click _
(ByVal sender As System.Object, _
ByVal e As System.EventArgs) Handles _
```

```
formSizeToolStripMenuItem.Click
    'Change the size of the form
    Me.Size = New Size(300, 200)
End Sub
```

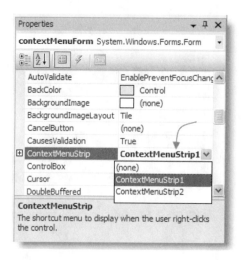

FIGURE 7.35 Assigning `ContextMenuStrip1` to the `Form`.

Once the user picks the Form Size option from the pop-up menu, the `Form`'s size will change from the original (364, 303) to a new size (300, 200). The `New` keywords will get a new instance of the object, which you will learn about in later chapters.

Let's add codes for all the other options. Under the Blue menu item, which is under the `BackColor` menu item, add the following:

```
Private Sub blueToolStripMenuItem_Click _
(ByVal sender As System.Object, _
ByVal e As System.EventArgs) _
Handles blueToolStripMenuItem.Click
    'change the form's back color to blue
    Me.BackColor = Color.Blue
End Sub
```

Under the Green submenu, type the following:

```
Private Sub greenToolStripMenuItem_Click _
(ByVal sender As System.Object, _
ByVal e As System.EventArgs) _
Handles greenToolStripMenuItem.Click
    'change the form's back color to green
    Me.BackColor = Color.Green
End Sub
```

For Reset, we change everything back to normal:

```
Private Sub resetToolStripMenuItem_Click _
(ByVal sender As System.Object, _
ByVal e As System.EventArgs) _
Handles ResetToolStripMenuItem.Click
    'Reset the form's size and back color
    Me.Size = New Size(364, 303)
    Me.BackColor = Color.Empty
End Sub
```

Now, hit F5 and right-click on the Form. You should see something resembling Figure 7.36.

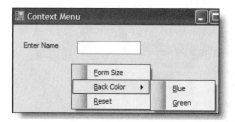

FIGURE 7.36 ContextMenuStrip in action.

ON THE CD

You can view this solution under the Chapter 7 folder on the companion CD-ROM. The project is saved under its name, contextMenuExample. Just copy the project folder to your hard drive and double-click on the .sln file. Follow the same instructions to assign the second ContextMenuStrip to the nameTextBox. You can review the code from the accompanying CD-ROM if you need help.

CALLING SUBPROCEDURES AND FUNCTIONS

Up until now, we have been using the subprocedures that were provided by the specific event of the controls. It is also possible to create our own subprocedures and functions and call them when we need them. In addition, we can share the event procedures of other controls and use them if needed.

Call Statement

The Call statement is used to transfer the control from the calling statement to the functions or subprocedures:

```
Call procedureName (ArgumentList)
```

Use of the Call keyword is optional but some programmers use it for readability. Inside the parentheses, we will list the arguments. Arguments are variables or expressions that are used to pass values when the procedure is called. We separate different arguments by commas. Some subprocedures do not have any arguments, so we will keep the parentheses empty. Calling other subprocedures becomes handy when we share one subprocedure with the other subprocedures within our project.

EXAMPLE 8

Let's use Call in a simple example to show you how it works. In this project, we will be sharing the Button's click subprocedure with a MenuStrip's subprocedure. Create a new project and call it callSub. Here is what we need:

- **Form1**
  Name: callForm
  Text: Calling Sub
  Size: 224, 100
- **Button1**
  Name: exitButton
  Text: E&xit
- **MenuStrip1**
  Name: callMenuStrip

Add &File as the main menu item and E&xit as a submenu item. Now, double-click on the exitButton and add the following:

```
Private Sub exitButton_Click _
(ByVal sender As System.Object, _
ByVal e As System.EventArgs) Handles exitButton.Click
    'Exit the program
    Dim response As DialogResult
    response = MessageBox.Show _
    ("Do you want to exit the program", _
    "Warning", MessageBoxButtons.YesNo, _
    MessageBoxIcon.Information)
    If response = Windows.Forms.DialogResult.Yes Then
        Me.Close()
    Else
        MessageBox.Show("Thanks for staying", _
        "Thanks", MessageBoxButtons.OK)
    End If
End Sub
```

We have used this code before, so it should not require any explanation. Here is what we need to put under the Exit menu collection:

```
Private Sub exitToolStripMenuItem_Click _
```

```
(ByVal sender As System.Object, _
ByVal e As System.EventArgs) _
Handles exitToolStripMenuItem.Click
    'call exit button from another sub procedure
    Call Me.exitButton_Click(sender, e)
End Sub
```

In the above statement, we are referencing the arguments Sender and E as they appear within the `exitButton_click` subprocedure. Save and run the program and select Exit from the menu (see Figure 7.37).

FIGURE 7.37   Example 8 screenshot.

ON THE CD

You can view this solution under the Chapter 7 folder on the companion CD-ROM. The project is saved under its name, `callSub`. Just copy the project folder to your hard drive and double-click on the .sln file.

CREATING DEFINED SUBPROCEDURES AND FUNCTIONS

Occasionally you may need to create your own subprocedure and call it from different locations of your project. Like all other subprocedures, user-defined subprocedures will have the following format:

```
[Modifiers]Sub SubProcedureName _
(list of arguments)
Statements…
End Sub
```

User-defined subprocedures follow the same rules as event procedures. Procedure modifiers such as the name of the procedure and access modifiers such as `Private` are very similar to event procedures. A subprocedure's access modifier is public by default. In Visual Basic 2005, all executable codes must be defined within the identifier's procedures, and only namespace declarations can appear outside the procedures.

As stated before, subprocedures are a series of statements that are grouped between `Sub` and `End Sub` to do a specific task. It is especially useful when more than one subprocedure uses these statements. We can divide procedures in Visual Basic into two types: subprocedures and function procedures. These are very similar in nature, but one distinct difference is that subprocedures execute the statements that are assigned to them but will not return values. On the other hand, functions will return values after the completion of their tasks. In general, we use function procedures for performing calculations, while subprocedures are used more for declaration purposes.

Subprocedures with No Arguments

Some subprocedures do not require any arguments, so the calling statement does not need to reference any argument inside parentheses. Here is an example of that:

```
Private Sub clearAll()
TextBox1.text=Nothing
TextBox2.Text=Nothing
End Sub
```

The calling statement would call this subprocedure like this:

```
Call clearAll()
```

Subprocedures with Arguments, Passing by Values, and Passing by Reference

When we declare arguments in our program, they reserve spaces in our computer memory. When we share these variables with other procedures, we can just pass the values of them. Other procedures can use the values of our variables without having a chance to change them. This is known as *passing by values*. However, as stated above, each argument has a specific address in the memory of the computer as well. It is also possible to pass arguments using their memory location. This is known as *passing by reference*. Visual Basic 2005 provides the mechanisms for both. When you pass arguments by reference, you give the authority to the receiving procedure to modify the arguments to their advantage. We use two keywords to distinguish the passing of arguments: ByVal and ByRef. It is very important that you carefully choose the method of passing arguments to avoid problems.

We will explore these two types of passing by giving a nonprogramming example. In a job interview, you could tell the interviewer that you have a bachelor degree in information systems and technology. The information that you passed to the interviewer is similar to passing by value. However, if you would have provided further details such as the year of your graduation and the name and location of school from which you graduated, then that would be like passing by reference. In general, passing by reference is more convenient for the receiving procedures, and passing by value is more protective for the passed arguments. We suggest that you investigate this further by reviewing the help files that come with your Visual Basic 2005 software. A great article can be found at the following location: *http://msdn2. microsoft.com/en-us/library/ddck1z30.aspx*.

As an example of how passing by reference and passing by value can be used, here is what we have in the calling subprocedure:

```
Dim valueOneInteger As Integer=10
Dim valueTwoInteger As Integer=10
Dim resultInteger As Integer
Call calculateAverage(valueOneInteger, valueTwoInteger, resultInteger)
MessageBox.Show(resultInteger, "Average plus Incentive")
```

Here is what we have included in the called subprocedure:

```
Private Sub calculateAverage _
(ByVal valueOne As Integer, _
ByVal valueTwo As Integer, _
ByRef valueThree As Integer)
valueThree = (valueOne + valueTwo) / 2
```

We have matching variable types for the three referenced variables that are declared within the subprocedure. Two of the variables are referenced by value and one is referenced by reference. After the subprocedure is called and the statements with it are executed, the control will be passed to the statement that appears after the Call statement. In our case, after the subprocedure is executed, the following statement will have the control:

```
MessageBox.Show(resultInteger, "Average plus Incentive")
```

When the above code is executed, a MessageBox will be displayed with the number 10 in it. You will see more examples on this later.

Function Procedures

Function procedures return values to the calling subprocedures. You may notice similarities between subprocedures and functions. Here is the general format for function definition:

```
[Modifiers] Function FunctionName(ParameterList)
    Statements
Returen
End Function
```

Here is an example of calling a function:

```
Dim averageDouble As Double
MessageBox.Show(calculateAverage(3, 4, averageDouble), _
    "Average Result")
```

In addition, here is how we declare the function:

```
Private Function calculateAverage _
(ByVal valueOne As Integer, _
ByVal valueTwo As Integer, ByVal averageResult As Double)
    averageResult = (valueOne + valueTwo) / 2
    Return AverageResult
End Function
```

We will see this example in action in Example 9, below.

Module Declarations

All declarations we have talked about are valid in a single-Form project. However, as you will see later, most projects are composed of several forms. To share our variables and constants among all forms we need to declare them as *public* or *friend* and reference the class name that defines them. This works fine for small projects. However, it is also possible to share our variables and constants with the Module Forms.

Module Forms are not meant to display controls. They are designed to include codes. You can declare public and private variables within your module as well. Private variables will be accessed only from within the Module. Like many other procedures, the Module will have its own block:

```
[Access Modifier] Module ModuleName
Statements
End Module
```

Here is how you can add a Module Form to your project. Click on the Project tab and select Add Module from the drop-down list (see Figure 7.38). You will see the Add New Item dialog box (see Figure 7.39).

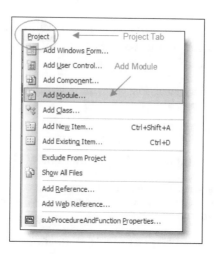

FIGURE 7.38 Adding a Module to the project.

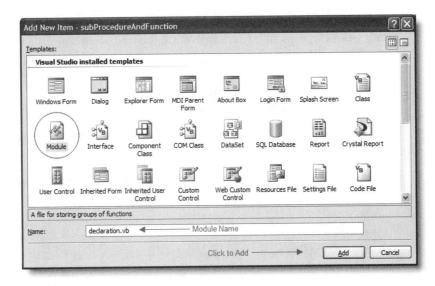

FIGURE 7.39 *Add New Item* dialog box.

Make sure the Module icon is selected. You will be using this in Example 9. By clicking the OK button, you will add the new Module to your Form. You will be able to see the added Module among the other Visual Basic files (see Figure 7.40). If you double-click on your Module, you will see its code block (see Figure 7.41).

FIGURE 7.40 Added Module Form with the other files.

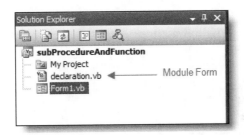

```
Public Module declaration
     'declare public variables
     Public incentiveInteger As Double = 30
     Public resultInteger As Double
End Module
```

FIGURE 7.41 Module code block.

EXAMPLE 9

In this example, we will be demonstrating the following concepts we have learned in this section:

- Subprocedures with no arguments
- Subprocedures with arguments (`ByVal` and `ByRef`)
- Function procedure
- `Module Form`

Start a new project and call it `subProcedureAndFunction`. We need the following:

- One `MenuStrip`
- Two `Labels`
- Two `TextBoxes`
- One `Module Form`
- One `Button`

Rename them according to the following:

- **Form1**
  Name: `subForm`
  Text: `Sub Procedures and Functions`
- **Label1**
  Name: `valueOneLabel`
  Text: `Enter a number`
- **Label2**
  Name: `valueTwoLabel`
  Text: `Enter another Number`
- **TextBox1**
  Name: `valueOneTextBox`
- **TextBox2**
  Name: `valueTwoTextBox`
- **Button1**
  Name: `submitButton`
  Text: `&Submit`
- **MenuStrip1**
  Name: `subMenuStrip`

Using the Menu Strip Editor, add the following to your menu bar:

- &File
- E&xit
- &Value and Reference
- &Enter Two Values
- &Process
- &Show Function
- Module1
- Name: declaration

Now create a subprocedure and call it `exitProgram`. Type the following in the new procedure:

```
'creating a sub procedure called exitProgram
Private Sub exitProgram()
    'terminate the program
    MessageBox.Show("You Terminated the Program" _
    , "Warning", MessageBoxButtons.OK, _
    MessageBoxIcon.Information)
    Me.Close()
End Sub
```

Double-click on the Exit menu item and add the following:

```
Private Sub exitToolStripMenuItem_Click _
(ByVal sender As System.Object, _
ByVal e As System.EventArgs) _
Handles exitToolStripMenuItem.Click
    'call sub procedure to exit the program
    Me.exitProgram()
End Sub
```

We are using `Me.exitProgram()` to call the subprocedure we just created. Now create a new subprocedure and call it `disableTextAndButton`:

```
'a sub procedure that disables the fields
Private Sub disableTextAndButton()
    Me.valueOneTextBox.Enabled = False
    Me.valueTwoTextBox.Enabled = False
    Me.submitButton.Enabled = False
End Sub
```

We will be using this subprocedure several times in this project. Let us call it from within the `SubForm_Load`:

```
Private Sub subForm_Load _
(ByVal sender As System.Object, _
ByVal e As System.EventArgs) Handles MyBase.Load
    'call a sub procedure to disable the textboxes
    'and the button
```

```
            Me.disableTextAndButton()
        End Sub
```

We are calling this subprocedure to disable the TextBoxes and the Button:

```
        Me.disableTextAndButton
```

Now double-click on the declaration module you added to your project and type the following:

```
        Public Module declaration
        'declare public variables
            Public incentiveDouble As Double = 30
            Public resultDouble As Double
        End Module
```

As stated before, the declaration in this module is available to all procedures. We will be using these variables shortly. Double-click on the Enter Two Numbers menu item and add the following:

```
        Private Sub enterTwoValuesToolStripMenuItem_Click _
        (ByVal sender As System.Object, _
        ByVal e As System.EventArgs) _
        Handles enterTwoValuesToolStripMenuItem.Click
            'call a sub procedure to enable the textboxes
            'and the button
            Me.enableTextandButton()
            'clear all fields
            Me.resetAll()
        End Sub
```

We are calling the two subprocedures we created before. Now create a new subprocedure and call it calculateAverageNumbers:

```
        'a sub procedure that calculates the inputs
        'two by value and one by reference
        Private Sub calculateAverageNumbers _
        (ByVal valueOne As Double, _
        ByVal valueTwo As Double, _
        ByRef valueThree As Double)
            'add two user's input and get the average
            'add the average to the incentivedouble
            'that is declared in the Module
            valueThree = (valueOne + valueTwo) / 2 + incentiveDouble
            'the result of calculation will be stored
            'in valueThree variable. Since resultDouble
            'is the matching variable that is declared
            'in the module, it can be displayed outside
            'this sub procedure

        End Sub
```

We have defined the variables by values and by reference. We will also utilize the variable we declared within our module. The values that are entered by the user will get into this subprocedure through the valueOne and valueTwo variables that were declared in this subprocedure. Now double-click on the submitButton and type the following:

```
Private Sub submitButton_Click _
(ByVal sender As System.Object, _
ByVal e As System.EventArgs) _
Handles submitButton.Click
    'accept valid input and assign them
    'to variables
    Try
        Dim valueOneDouble As Double = _
        Double.Parse(Me.valueOneTextBox.Text)
        Dim valueTwoDouble As Double = _
        Double.Parse(Me.valueTwoTextBox.Text)
        MessageBox.Show("Click on Process menu item now", _
        "Input Submitted")
        'call calculate sub procedure and pass the user's input
        'note that the resultDouble variable is
        'declared in the module and is visible
        'to all procedures
        Me.calculateAverageNumbers(valueOneDouble, _
        valueTwoDouble, resultDouble)
        'call to disable the textbox and button
        Me.disableTextAndButton()

    Catch ex As Exception
        'reject invalid data
        MessageBox.Show("You need to enter valid values", _
        "Warning", MessageBoxButtons.OK, _
        MessageBoxIcon.Information)
        'call a sub procedure to clear everything
        Me.resetAll()

    End Try
End Sub
```

As you can see from the comments, we validated the input before sending them to the calculateAverageNumbers subprocedure. Once we get acceptable data, we will send the values to this subprocedure to calculate the average. We also have some housekeeping tasks that are explained in the comments.

Double-click on the processButton and type in the following:

```
Private Sub processToolStripMenuItem_Click _
(ByVal sender As System.Object, _
ByVal e As System.EventArgs) _
Handles processToolStripMenuItem.Click
    'display the average from the sub procedure
```

```
MsgBox(resultDouble, MsgBoxStyle.OkOnly, _
"The Average Plus Incentive")

End Sub
```

We have displayed the result of the calculation through a public variable that is declared within our module. As you know, subprocedures do not return values.

Now we need to complete the last part of our project: the function procedure. Let us declare a function and call it `CalculateAverage`.

```
'declare a function to calculate two numbers average
Private Function calculateAverage _
(ByVal valueOne As Double, ByVal _
valueTwo As Double, ByVal averageResult As Double) _
As Double 'store the result of calculation in aveResult
    averageResult = (valueOne + valueTwo) / 2
    'the result is returned to the calling sub procedure
    'and stored in averageDouble variable
    Return averageResult
End Function
```

Now double-click on the Show Function menu item and add the following to its subprocedure:

```
Private Sub showFunctionToolStripMenuItem_Click _
(ByVal sender As System.Object, _
ByVal e As System.EventArgs) _
Handles showFunctionToolStripMenuItem.Click
    'call a sub to disable the data entry section
    Me.disableTextAndButton()
    'declare a variable to receive information from function
    Dim averageDouble As Double
    'display the result of function in a message box
    'we pass values 3 and 4 and the result will be stored in
    'averageDouble variable

    MsgBox(calculateAverage(3, 4, averageDouble), _
    MsgBoxStyle.OkOnly, "Average")

End Sub
```

The result of the calculation is returned to the calling procedure and we can use it to display the data.

Now save your project and run it (see Figure 7.42).

You can view this solution under the Chapter 7 folder on the companion CD-ROM. The project is saved under its name, `subProcedureAndFunction`. Just copy the project folder to your hard drive and double-click on the .sln file.

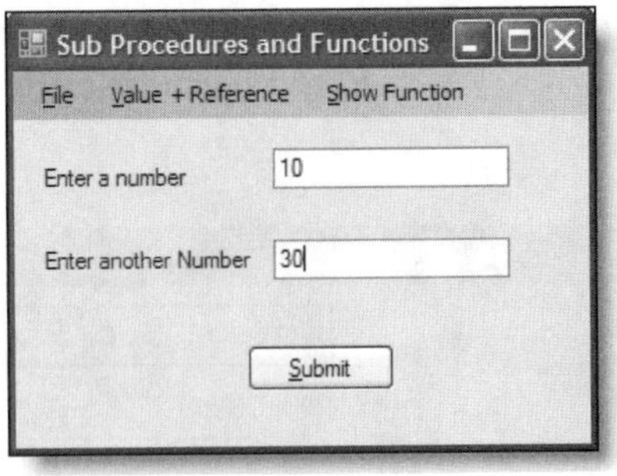

FIGURE 7.42   Project 9 screenshot.

EXAMPLE 10: COMPREHENSIVE EXAMPLE

In this example, we want to utilize a few of the tools we learned in this chapter. The example shows some complete routines that can be used as models to complete other sections. The Exercise section will suggest other components that may also be added to the project.

This Discount Book Store allows users to place orders for the books they want. First, the user needs to pick a book category from the three available book categories. This selection will display an image for that category and will show the name of the books that are available within that category. Once you select the book, an image for the book and the book price will be displayed.

At this stage, you can add the book to your shopping cart. Since this is a discount bookstore, you are allowed to buy one copy of each book. You will receive an error message if you try to add more than one copy of the book. Once you have added your selected books to the shopping cart combo box, you can see the total price. You can remove single items from your cart or remove all items at once, but you cannot remove any item if the cart is empty.

Let's start a new project and call it book_order. Add the following controls to your form:

- Four GroupBoxes
- Seven Labels
- One Panel
- Two PictureBoxes
- One ListBox
- Three RadioButtons
- One ComboBox
- One MenuStrip
- Five Buttons

Let's arrange these controls on our form according to the following screenshot shown in Figure 7.43. We need to rename these controls as follows.

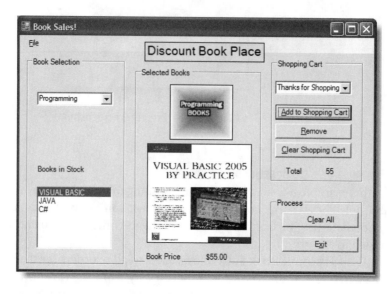

FIGURE 7.43   Shopping design structure.

- **Form1**
  Name: booksForm
  Text: Book Sales!
- **ToolTip1**
  Name: bookToolTip
- **Label1**
  Name: titleLabel
  Text: Discount Book Place
  Font: Microsoft Sans Serif, 14.25pt
- **Label2**
  Name: avilableBookLable
  Text: Book in Stock
- **Label3**
  Name: bookPriceLabel
  Text: Book Price
- **Label4**
  Name: priceLabel
  Text: Price

- **Label5**

  Name: costLabel

  Text: Total

- **Label6**

  Name: totalLabel

  Text: Cost

- **GroupBox1**

  Name: catGroupBox

  Text: Book Selection

- **GroupBox2**

  Name: bookPickGroupBox

  Text: Selected Books

- **GroupBox3**

  Name: cartGroupBox

  Text: Shopping Cart

- **GroupBox4**

  Name: processGroupBox

  Text: Process

- **ListBox1**

  Name: booksListBox

- **ComboBox1**

  Name: cartComboBox

  Text: Thanks for Shopping

- **MenuStrip1**

  Name: bookMenuStrip

- **FileToolStripMenuItem**

  Name: tlsmnuFile

  Text: &File

- **ClearToolStripMenuItem**

  Name: tlsmnuClear

  Text: C&lear

- **ExitToolStripMenuItem**

  Name: tlsmnuExit

  Text: E&xit

- **ComboBox2**

  Name: booksComboBox

  Text: Book Catagories

- **Button1**

  Name: addToCartButton

  Text: &Add to Shopping Cart

  ToolTipText: Click to add selected book

■ **Button2**

Name: removeFromCartButton

Text: &Remove

ToolTipText: Click to Remove selected book

■ **Button3**

Name: btnClearCart

Text: &Clear Shopping Cart

ToolTipText: Click to clear your shopping cart

■ **Button4**

Name: clearCartButton

Text: C&lear All

ToolTipText: Click to reset the form

■ **Button5**

Name: exitButton

Text: E&xit

ToolTipText: Click to exit the program

This program is very similar to the Ice Cream Shop program in Chapter 6. We will show you how this program works and you can complete the rest of the codes by yourself.

Double-click on the Book Categories ComboBox and add the following code:

```
Private Sub booksComboBox_SelectedIndexChanged _
(ByVal sender As System.Object, _
ByVal e As System.EventArgs) _
Handles booksComboBox.SelectedIndexChanged
    Select Case booksComboBox.SelectedIndex
        Case 0
            'if programming is selected, then the following will
            'be added to the list box
            Me.booksListBox.Items.Clear()
            Me.catPictureBox.Image = Nothing
            Me.bookPictureBox.Image = Nothing
            Me.booksListBox.Items.Add("VISUAL BASIC")
            Me.booksListBox.Items.Add("JAVA")
            Me.booksListBox.Items.Add("C#")
            Me.catPictureBox.Image = Image.FromFile("programming.jpg")
            Me.priceLabel.Text = Nothing
        Case 1 'if Networking selected, then these will added
            Me.booksListBox.Items.Clear()
            Me.catPictureBox.Image = Nothing
            Me.bookPictureBox.Image = Nothing
            Me.priceLabel.Text = Nothing
            Me.booksListBox.Items.Add("LAN Networks")
            Me.booksListBox.Items.Add("Windows Networking")
            Me.booksListBox.Items.Add("More about Networking")
            Me.catPictureBox.Image = Image.FromFile("Networking.jpg")
```

```
            Me.priceLabel.Text = Nothing
        Case 2 'Web Programming
            Me.catPictureBox.Image = Nothing
            Me.bookPictureBox.Image = Nothing
            Me.booksListBox.Items.Clear()
            Me.booksListBox.Items.Add("Web Programming")
            Me.booksListBox.Items.Add("JavaScript")
            Me.booksListBox.Items.Add("ASP")
            Me.catPictureBox.Image = Image.FromFile("html.jpg")
            Me.priceLabel.Text = Nothing

    End Select
```

This code will detect the user's selections. If the Programming item is selected, then the following books will be added to the Book in Stock ListBox:

- Visual Basic
- JAVA
- C#

Prior to displaying the book names, we first clear the PictureBoxes, the ListBox, and the Book Price Label. This will clear these controls before we display the new items. This code will display the programming image and the names of the above books. You will find many similarities between the previous code and the code just listed. This code will populate the networking books into the Book in Stock ListBox.

Now double-click on the Book in Stock ListBox and add the following code:

```
Private Sub booksListBox _SelectedIndexChanged _
(ByVal sender As System.Object, _
ByVal e As System.EventArgs) _
Handles booksListBox.SelectedIndexChanged
    'if Programming selected, then display
    'selected programming books
    'and prices. This goes for all
    Select Case booksListBox.Text
        Case "VISUAL BASIC"
            Me.bookPictureBox.Image = _
            Image.FromFile("Visualbasic.jpg")
            Me.priceLabel.Text = ("$55.00")
        Case "JAVA"
            Me.bookPictureBox.Image = _
            Image.FromFile("Java.jpg")
            Me.priceLabel.Text = ("$45.00")
        Case "C#"
            Me.bookPictureBox.Image = _
            Image.FromFile("csharp.jpg")
            Me.priceLabel.Text = ("$85.00")
        Case "LAN Networks"
            Me.bookPictureBox.Image = _
```

```
                         Image.FromFile("Networks.jpg")
                         Me.priceLabel.Text = ("$35.00")
                 Case "Windows Networking"
                         Me.bookPictureBox.Image = _
                         Image.FromFile("Windows.jpg")
                         Me.priceLabel.Text = ("$45.00")
                 Case "More about Networking"
                         MessageBox.Show("No image availabe", _
                         "Sorry!", MessageBoxButtons.OK, _
                         MessageBoxIcon.Information)
                         Me.priceLabel.Text = ("$75.00")
                 Case "Web Programming"
                         Me.bookPictureBox.Image = _
                         Image.FromFile("webprogramming.jpg")
                         Me.priceLabel.Text = ("$95.00")
                 Case "JavaScript"
                         Me.bookPictureBox.Image = Image.FromFile("JavaScript.jpg")
                         Me.priceLabel.Text = ("$105.00")
                 Case "ASP"
                         Me.bookPictureBox.Image = Image.FromFile("ASP.jpg")
                         Me.priceLabel.Text = ("$35.00")
         End Select

     End Sub
```

In the above code, we placed a series of codes for every possible situation. For example, if the user has clicked on the Programming ComboBox, three items will be added to the Book in Stock ListBox. By looking at the index of the ListBox, we can tell which item was selected by the user and react to it accordingly.

In this project, we also want to use a Module and place a function in it. This function will be called to perform the calculations. As described in Chapter 5, this is a module-level function that can be seen anywhere within the project.

Create a Module and put this code inside it:

```
Module Module1

Public Sub checkPrices(ByVal cartComboBox As ComboBox, _
     ByVal costLabel As Label)
     'this function will be called to perform calculations
     Dim PriceInt32 As Int32
     If Me.cartComboBox.Items.Contains("VISUAL BASIC") Then
         PriceInt32 += 55
         Me.costLabel.Text = PriceInt32.ToString
     End If
     If Me.cartComboBox.Items.Contains("JAVA") Then
         PriceInt32 += 45
         Me.costLabel.Text = PriceInt32.ToString
     End If
     If Me.cartComboBox.Items.Contains("C#") Then
         PriceInt32 += 85
```

```
        Me.costLabel.Text = PriceInt32.ToString
    End If
End Sub

End Module
```

Now double-click on Add to Shopping Cart and add the following codes:

```
Private Sub addToCartButton_Click _
(ByVal sender As System.Object, _
ByVal e As System.EventArgs) _
Handles addToCartButton.Click
    'if the user hasn't
    'selected any item the following will be performed
    If Me.booksListBox.SelectedItem Is Nothing Then
        MessageBox.Show _
        ("Please select a book before adding to the Cart.", _
        "Select Book!", MessageBoxButtons.OK, _
        MessageBoxIcon.Information)
        'if the user adds duplicates
    ElseIf Me.cartComboBox.Items.Contains _
    (Me.booksListBox.SelectedItem()) Then
        MessageBox.Show _
        ("The discount applys to one book only", "Warning", _
        MessageBoxButtons.OK, MessageBoxIcon.Information)
        'if he has selected an item, then the following
        'will be performed
    Else : Me.cartComboBox.Items.Add(booksListBox.Text)

    End If
    'set label value to 0

    Me.costLabel.Text = "0"

    'call a module to check prices
    checkPrices(cartComboBox, costLabel)

End Sub
```

The above code is very similar to the Ice Cream Shop program as well. First, we make sure the user has selected a book to be added to the cart. Then we check to see if the item is a duplicate item or not. If these two conditions are not satisfactory, then we will display an error message. After this validation, we will add the selected book to the shopping cart. Remove uses the same function that we used for add.

Now double-click on the removeButton and add the following code:

```
Private Sub removeFromCartButto_Click( _
ByVal sender As System.Object, _
ByVal e As System.EventArgs) _
Handles removeFromCartButton.Click
    'remove items from the cart
```

```
Try
    Me.cartComboBox.Items.RemoveAt _
    (Me.cartComboBox.SelectedIndex)
    Me.cartComboBox.Text = "Thanks for Shopping!"
    Me.costLabel.Text = "0"

    'call a Module to check prices
    checkPrices(cartComboBox, costLabel)

Catch ex As Exception
    MessageBox.Show("Calculation error", "Warning")
End Try
End Sub
```

We have also added a subprocedure to add the books to the shopping cart by double-clicking on the ListBox items. This is done by choosing the ListBox Double Click event.

```
Private Sub booksListBox_DoubleClick _
(ByVal sender As Object, _
ByVal e As System.EventArgs) _
Handles booksListBox.DoubleClick
    'add books when items are double clicked
    Me.addToCartButton_Click(sender, e)
End Sub
```

We are adding a conditional statement here as well. If the cart is empty, the user cannot remove an item. Otherwise, the items will be removed from the cart and the value of the price will change as the result of this transaction.

Now double-click on Clear Shopping Cart and add the following codes. This code will remove all items from the ComboBox:

```
Private Sub clearCartButton_Click _
(ByVal sender As System.Object, _
ByVal e As System.EventArgs) _
Handles clearCartButton.Click
    'remove all items from the combobox
    Me.cartComboBox.Items.Clear()
    Me.costLabel.Text = "0"
End Sub
```

We are confident that you can finish the rest of this project. Complete the Clear and Exit buttons. Run the program and test its features.

ON THE CD You can view this solution under the Chapter 7 folder on the companion CD-ROM. The project is saved under its name, bookOrder. Just copy the project folder to your hard drive and double-click on the .sln file.

PROGRAMMING TIPS

- Decide which tool is appropriate for your application. For example, ListBox and ComboBox share many similarities, but in some cases one works better for a specific application than the other. Which one to pick becomes your decision.
- Use ComboBoxes, CheckBoxes, ListBoxes, and RadioButtons to minimize users' entry errors. You need to provide adequate tips to prevent confusion, so using ToolTips is highly recommended.

SUMMARY

In this chapter, we covered ComboBox, ListBox, MenuStrip, ImageList, and ToolStrip and demonstrated how to add and remove items from them. These tools are very useful in both Windows and Web applications. The provided examples show step-by-step instructions on how to create and use these tools. In addition to these features, this chapter also includes examples on searching the ComboBox and ListBox. We also discussed subprocedures and functions and explained their natures.

Next

In Chapter 8 you will be introduced to the concept of loop. We will cover Do Loops, For Each Loops, Timer and For/Next Loops. You will learn how to move objects using the Timer control.

DISCUSSION QUESTIONS

1. What are the differences between ListBox and ComboBox? When should we use one in place of the other?
2. How do we prevent duplicating items in a ComboBox? Please explain.
3. What is the difference between a menu and submenu? Briefly explain.
4. What are the advantages of using a ComboBox?
5. What is the major difference between a subprocedure and a function? Please explain.

Exercise

Modify the Book_Order sample program in the following ways:
1. Add more MenuStrip items to include Add and Remove options.
2. Complete the networking and Web section so they can be included in book-price calculations.
3. Add Try/Catch to all of the calculations subprocedures to prevent errors.

Key Terms

- ComboBox
- ListBox
- ImageList
- Removing item
- Inserting item
- MenuStrip
- ProgressBar
- ToolStrip
- Function
- Module
- Subprocedure

8 Repetition Structures

In This Chapter

LOOPS

In Chapter 6, you learned about If-Then-Else, case, and other decision-making statements. In this chapter, we will introduce a new topic: *iteration*. *Loop*, or *repetition*, is used when a set of instructions need to be repeated as long as a condition exists. Let us look at a simple example:

1. Start driving from California toward Oregon.
2. As long as you are not tired, keep driving.
3. If you get tired, check into a hotel and stay over night.
4. Call your spouse every hour before midnight.

The first statement is considered a *sequence structure* because there is no condition involved. The second statement is considered a loop. This loop can continue as long as the condition is true. It means that as long as you are not tired, you will keep driving. As soon as you get tired, this condition becomes false and you stop driving. This loop stops as soon as the condition becomes false (see Figure 8.1).

Now look at another example. In this example, we look at payroll processing. To issue your paycheck, we do the following:

1. Read the first record in the file.
2. If the hours worked are greater than 40, proceed with the overtime calculations.
3. If not, process regular pay.
4. Print paychecks.

Read the next record. If it is not the end of the file, then repeat the previous actions again (see Figure 8.2). As long as the end of the file has not been detected, the computer will read records from the file, processes them, and produce paychecks. Once the end of the file is detected, the process will stop.

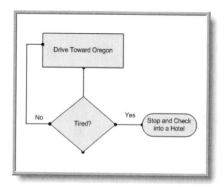

FIGURE 8.1 Repetition example: driving.

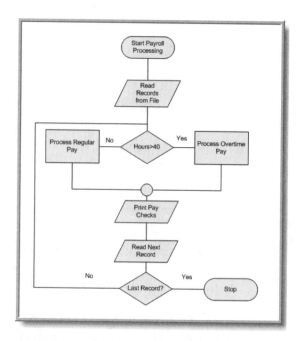

FIGURE 8.2 Repetition example: payroll.

FOR / NEXT **LOOPS**

Occasionally we know the number of times a loop should be repeated. If you look at the driving example above, you should notice the following statement: "Call your spouse every hour before midnight." In this statement, we have a range of the possible numbers of times you could call your spouse. The syntax is

```
For variable As data_type = Staring value To Ending Value [Step]
statements
Next Variable
```

We will analyze the syntax:

- `For` is required to start the loop. The statements must appear within the `For`/`Next` block.
- `Next` is another required keyword. It is customary to put the incrementing variable after `Next`, but that is optional. `Next` is used as the end-of-loop indicator.
- `Variable` is required to increment the number. This acts as a counter for the loop.
- `Data type` is only required if the variable has not been declared before. You could declare the variable in a separate statement.
- `Starting value` is required. This should be a numeric expression.
- `End value` is required to stop the counter. This should be expressed as a numeric expression as well.
- `Step` is another numeric expression used to increment the loop. If the loop needs to be incremented by one, there is no need for this expression. The `Step` is optional but very powerful for manipulating data.
- `Statements` are required to show the effect of the loop.

Here is an example:

```
For counter As Integer = 1 To 5
    Me.TextBox1.Text _
    &= counter & _
    ControlChars.CrLf
Next
```

The result is 1, 2, 3, 4, 5.

EXAMPLE 1

Let us start a new project and call it `forNextExample1`. In this example, we will place loop statements in the `Form_Load` subprocedure to display repeated texts in five lines.
Add the following controls to your form:

- One TextBox
- One ListBox
- Two Buttons

Change the controls' names according to the following:

- **Form1**
  Name: forNextForm
  Text: For Next Loop
- **TextBox1**
  Name: loopTextBox
  MultiLine: True
  ScrollBar: Vertical
- **ListBox1**
  Name: loopListBox
- **Button1**
  Name: clearButton
  Text: &Clear
- **Button2**
  Name: ExitButton
  Text: E&xit

Now double-click on the Form and type the following codes in the Form_Load subprocedure:

```
Private Sub forNextForm_Load _
(ByVal sender As System.Object, _
ByVal e As System.EventArgs) _
Handles MyBase.Load
    'Will display these lines 5 times in the textbox and list box
    For myCounterInteger As Integer = 1 To 5
        Me.loopTextBox.Text _
        &= " This is line number " _
        & myCounterInteger & _
        ControlChars.CrLf
        Me.loopListBox.Items.Add _
        ("This is line number  " & myCounterInteger)
    Next myCounterInteger
End Sub
```

The following statements are going to be repeated five times:

```
Me.loopTextBox.Text _
&= " This is line number " _
& myCounterInteger & _
ControlChars.CrLf
```

```
Me.loopListBox.Items.Add _
("This is line number  " & myCounterInteger)
```

Complete the Clear and Exit buttons and run the project (see Figure 8.3).

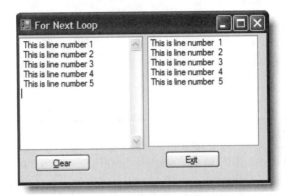

FIGURE 8.3   Example 1 screenshot.

You can view this solution under the Chapter 8 folder on the companion CD-ROM. The project is saved under its name, `forNextExample1`. Just copy the project folder to your hard drive and double-click on the .sln file.

USING STEPS IN FOR/NEXT LOOPS

For/Next loops can be used to increment numeric values based on given steps. *Steps* are numeric expressions that are used to increment or decrement values. Here are some examples:

```
For counter As Integer = 1 To 10 Step 3
    Me.TextBox1.Text _
    &= counter & _
    ControlChars.CrLf
Next
```

The output would be 1, 4, 7, and 10.
Here is another example:

```
For counter As Integer = 10 To 1 Step -2
    Me.TextBox1.Text _
    &= counter & _
    ControlChars.CrLf
Next
```

The output of this operation is 10, 8, 6, 4, and 2.

Signs can play an important role in loop constructions:

```
For counter As Integer = -5 To 2 Step 2
    Me.TextBox1.Text _
    &= counter & _
    ControlChars.CrLf
Next
```

The result is −5, −3, −1, and 1.

EXIT FOR

Occasionally, we want to jump out of the loop if the element we are looking for is found. As we know, in the For/Next loop we set up a cycle that needs to be completed regardless of the result. Let us clarify this by giving an example. You have a list of employees that contains 500 names and you set up a loop to search this list to find your own name. Let us assume that your name is located within the first 10 names. Although your name is found and reported, the loop still continues until the counter value becomes 500. In this case, if the record is found and the condition is satisfied, it is not necessary to continue the loop to the end. To stop searching after the condition is satisfied; we use the Exit For statement to stop the loop.

```
For myNameRcordInteger As Integer = 1 To 2000
If myNameRcordInteger = 100 Then
    MsgBox("Record found at row number" & myNameRcordInteger)
    Exit For
End If
Next
```

As soon as myNameRcordInteger is found, the loop is terminated.

FOR EACH LOOPS

The For Each loop will perform a series of statements every time an element is found within a collection. For example, let us say you have created a ListBox that will be used as a quarterly calendar and shows all seven days of the week for three months. Each item of this ListBox represents a day of the week and you would like to search it for a specific day of the week. For each time that day is found, you would like to see a reminder. The general syntax is like this:

```
For Each element as Data Type in Collection
    Statements
```

```
Exit For
     Statements
Next element
```

This is what we want:

```
FOR EACH Sunday in Calendar
Display a reminder
NEXT
```

Here is another example. You are searching a `ListBox` for the name Sara. Once the record is found, you want to display a message and exit the loop.

```
For Each mysearch As Object In Me.forNextListBox.Items
    'if found, display a message and then exit loop
    If mysearch.ToString = "Sara" Then
        MessageBox.Show(mysearch.ToString & " Found", _
        "Search Result")
        'exit the loop
        Exit For
    End If
Next
```

LISTBOX MULTISELECTION **FEATURE**

In Chapter 7, we covered many features offered by `ListBox` and `ComboBox`. We now want to turn our attention to another feature that is included in `ListBox`. In some projects, we want the users to be able to select multiple items from the `ListBox`. Here is what we need to do. `ListBox` has a property called `SelectionMode`. The following options are available for setting this property:

None: Does not allow the user to select any item.

One: Allows the user to select only one item.

MultiSimple: Allows the user to select multiple items. With this option, the user can click on the desired items and select them.

MultiExtended: Similar to `MultiSimple`, except that it allows the user to use Ctrl, Shift, and arrow keys to select multiple items.

We have selected the `MultiExtended` option for our `ListBox`. This is a useful feature when we need to have default selections or attract the user's attention to specific items. It can also be used to receive multiple selections from users (see Figure 8.4).

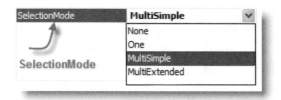

FIGURE 8.4 `ListBox MultiSelection` options.

EXAMPLE 2

In this example, we want to practice what we have learned so far. The user can select one or a group of names from the `ListBox` and add them to a `TextBox`. He would be also able to select multiple names, search the entire `ListBox`, and sort the names. The finished screen should look like Figure 8.5.

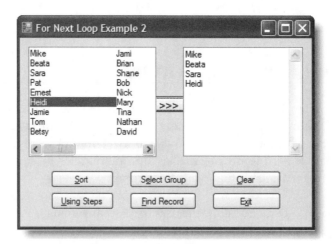

FIGURE 8.5 Example 2 finished screenshot.

Start a new project and call it `forNextExample2`. Add the following controls to your form:

- One `ListBox`
- One `TextBox`
- Seven `Buttons`

In this project, we first populate the ListBox by using the Form_Load event subprocedure. We also add more items to our ListBox using the For/Next loop. By using the For/Next loop, we will extract items from the ListBox and display them in a TextBox. This is a common practice in most online shopping Web sites. This project also finds our desired names interactively.

Change the control names according to the following:

- **Form1**
  Name: forNextForm
  Text: For Next Loop Example 2
- **TextBox1**
  Name: forNextTextBox
  Multiline: True
  ScrollBar: Vertical
- **ListBox1**
  Name: forNextListBox
  MultiColumn: True
  SelectionMode: MultiExtended
- **Button1**
  Name: addToListButton
  Text: >>>
  Font: Microsoft Sans Serif, 11.25pt
- **Button2**
  Name: sortButton
  Text: &Sort
- **Button3**
  Name: stepButton
  Text: &Using Steps
- **Button4**
  Name: findAllButton
  Text: &Find Record
- **Button5**
  Name: selectGroupButton
  Text: S&elect Group
- **Button6**
  Name: exitButton
  Text: E&xit
- **Button7**
  Name: clearButton
  Text: Clear

Double-click on the Form and add the names of some of your friends and family members into the Form_Load event subprocedure.

```
Private Sub forNextForm_Load _
(ByVal sender As System.Object, _
ByVal e As System.EventArgs) _
Handles MyBase.Load
    'populate the listbox with the following constants
    Me.forNextListBox.Items.Add("Mike")
    Me.forNextListBox.Items.Add("Beata")
    Me.forNextListBox.Items.Add("Sara")
    Me.forNextListBox.Items.Add("Pat")
    Me.forNextListBox.Items.Add("Ernest")
    Me.forNextListBox.Items.Add("Heidi")
    Me.forNextListBox.Items.Add("Jamie")
    Me.forNextListBox.Items.Add("David")
    Me.forNextListBox.Items.Add("Betsy")
    'use for next loop to add 5 more items
    For addItemInteger As Integer = 0 To 4
        Me.forNextListBox.Items.Add("Name " & addItemInteger)
    Next

End Sub
```

This code will add these items to the ListBox. The following code will add five more items to the ListBox.

```
    'use for next loop to add 5 more items
For addItemInteger As Integer = 0 To 4
    Me.forNextListBox.Items.Add("Name " & addItemInteger)
    Next
```

We used a loop to add these items to the ListBox. The addItemInteger variable is incremented by the loop and adds the names to the ListBox.

To understand this concept better, let us examine the code more closely. As soon as we start the loop, the value of the addItemInteger variable will be 0, and consequently item 0 will be added to the ListBox. In reality, this is how the computer sees our statement:

```
Me.forNextListBox.Items.Add("Name " & 0)
```

When this statement is executed, the Next clause will repeat the loop, and as a result, this time the value of the addItemInteger variable will be 1, which corresponds to the ListBox Item 1:

```
Me.forNextListBox.Items.Add("Name " & 1)
```

This will continue until the value of the addItemInteger variable is equal to 4, and that is when the loop stops. In the program that you downloaded from the companion CD-ROM, `forNextExample2`, we have added more names to the `ListBox` to force the scrollbar to appear, but you do not need to add as many names to understand how the code works.

Now, double-click on the `addButton` (>>>) and type the following statements:

```
Private Sub addToListButton_Click _
(ByVal sender As System.Object, _
ByVal e As System.EventArgs) _
Handles addToListButton.Click

    'Use the For/Next statement to search all items within
    'the ListBox

    For counter As Integer = 0 To Me.forNextListBox.Items.Count - 1
        If Me.forNextListBox.GetSelected(counter) = True Then
            'extracts all selected items
            Me.forNextLoopTextBox.Text &= _
            Me.forNextListBox.Items(counter).ToString & _
            ControlChars.CrLf
        End If
    Next
End Sub
```

The following statements will search the entire `ListBox`:

```
For counter As Integer = 0 To Me.forNextListBox.Items.Count — 1
Next
```

Adding this conditional statement will extract all selected items and display them in the `TextBox`.

Now double-click on the `sortButton` and type the following statement:

```
Private Sub sortButton_Click( _
ByVal sender As System.Object, _
ByVal e As System.EventArgs) _
Handles sortButton.Click
    'sorts the ListBox
    Me.forNextListBox.Sorted = True
End Sub
```

We used the *Sort* feature in Chapter 7, so you are familiar with it. Double-click on the `usingStepsButton` and type the following codes:

```
Private Sub selectGroupButton_Click(ByVal sender As System.Object, _
ByVal e As System.EventArgs) _
Handles usingStepsButton.Click
    Me.forNextLoopTextBox.Text = Nothing

    'using the step option to skip items
```

```
    For counter As Integer = 0 To 7 Step 2
        Me.forNextLoopTextBox.Text _
        &= Me.forNextListBox.Items(counter).ToString & _
        ControlChars.CrLf
    Next
End Sub
```

In this code, we are using the Step option. Based on this code, only items 0, 2, 4, and 6 will be displayed, and the rest will be skipped.

Double-click on the findRecordButton and add the following codes:

```
Private Sub findRecordButton_Click _
(ByVal sender As System.Object, _
ByVal e As System.EventArgs) _
Handles findRecordButton.Click

    'get user's input
    Dim myInputString As String
    'store user's input
    myInputString = InputBox _
    ("Enter a name to search the list box", _
    "Your input needed")
    'search for the user's input
    For Each mysearch As Object In Me.forNextListBox.Items
        'if found, display message and then find the next item

        If mysearch.ToString = myInputString Then

            MessageBox.Show(myInputString + " Found", _
            "Search Result")
            'You could inesrt Exit For Here
        End If
    Next
End Sub
```

In this statement, we did not use the Exit For statement. We placed a comment to indicate where it should be inserted if needed. However, by placing the Exit For clause, you will terminate the loop. What if the name you are looking for is listed in two or more items? If that is a possibility, the Exit For clause will force the loop to terminate prematurely, right after the first occurrence of the name and you will not be able to see the other occurrences of your data.

Now double-click on the selectGroupButton and add the following:

```
Private Sub selectGroupButton_Click _
(ByVal sender As System.Object, _
ByVal e As System.EventArgs) _
Handles selectGroupButton.Click
    'The following items will be selected
    'once the the buttom is clicked
    For myIndex As Integer = 1 To 15 Step 2
```

```
            Me.forNextListBox.SetSelected(myIndex, True)
            Me.forNextListBox.SetSelected(myIndex, True)
            Me.forNextListBox.SetSelected(myIndex, True)
            Me.forNextListBox.SetSelected(myIndex, True)
        Next
    End Sub
```

Now complete the exitButton and clearButton and run the project. Try to add one item at a time or use the Ctrl and Shift keys to select multiple items and add them to the TextBox.

You can view this solution under the Chapter 8 folder on the companion CD-ROM. The project is saved under its name, forNextExample2. Just copy the project folder to your hard drive and double-click on the .sln file.

CONTINUE **KEYWORD**

You saw that the Exit For clause is used to force a loop to stop. Visual Basic 2005 introduces a new keyword: Continue. Unlike Exit For, the Continue statement allows the program to skip to the next iteration point of the loop. An example will clarify this further:

```
For myValueInteger As Integer = 1 To 10
    If myValueInteger < 5 Then
        MsgBox(myValueInteger)
    End If
    MsgBox("If Statement Ended")
Next
```

In this statement, we see one MessageBox that shows the value of myValueInteger followed by the MessageBox showing the loop ended. However, the intention could be to skip the second MessageBox as long as the value of myValueInteger is less than 5. If this is the intention, we will change the above statement to the following:

```
For myValueInteger As Integer = 1 To 10
    If myValueInteger < 5 Then
        MsgBox(myValueInteger)
        Continue For
    End If
    MsgBox("If Statement Ended")
Next
```

Now the second MessageBox will pop up as soon as the value of myValueInteger is greater than 5.

The Continue statement is available for the For/Next loop, Do Loop, and While/EndWhile loops. You need to be careful about using this statement in your nested conditional statements because it may not work as you expect.

CHECKEDLISTBOX

In previous chapters, we introduced ComboBox, ListBox, RadioButton, and CheckBox. At that time we chose not to discuss another tool, which belongs to the same category. This tool is CheckedListBox, which behaves like ListBox in many ways but has a unique feature that can be utilized effectively. CheckedListBox adds a CheckBox to each item that can be checked or unchecked. We can detect the CheckBox that is checked by creating a loop. Let us look at an example.

EXAMPLE 3

This example is very similar to our last project, with the exception that we are using the CheckedListBox control. We are also going to apply some of the validation techniques we discussed before. The user can check the items he wants to add to his shopping list or add them by clicking on the Add button; they would be added to the ListBox. The user can order one item from the available list, so duplicate items will not be added to the ListBox. We have prechecked the CPU as a suggested item. We also let the user remove the ordered items from the ListBox or reset the entire list.

ON THE CD

In this project, we also added an arrow image to the Add button. The image is located on the accompanying CD-ROM, under Chapter 8 in the CheckedListBox-Example folder. As always, the images are placed in the bin\Debug Folder.

Start a new project and call it CheckedListBoxExample. Add the following controls to your form:

■ Three Labels
■ Four Buttons
■ One CheckedListBox
■ One ListBox

Since this project is very similar to the last one, we just reference the suggested names for important controls. Name the rest of them according to the naming conventions.

■ **Form1**
   Name: checkedListBoxForm
   Text: Order Form
■ **ListBox1**
   Name: orderListBox
   Size: 120, 121
■ **CheckedListBox1**
   Name: availableCheckedListBox
   BorderStyle: Fixed3D

CheckOnClick: True

Collections: Extra Hard Drive, CD or DVD Drive, LCD Monitor, Wireless Card, Keyboard & Mouse

Size: 120, 123

■ **ListBox1**

Name: avilableCheckedListBox

As you learned in previous chapters, we need to populate the CheckedListBox by using the String Collection Editor at design time or by using the Add method at runtime. We will populate the items at design time. Highlight the CheckedListBox and find the Items property. Click on the Collection dialog box to get to the editor. Type the computer part options as specified in the program specifications (see Figure 8.6).

FIGURE 8.6 String Collection Editor for this project.

Now double-click on the Form and type the following under the form_load event handler subprocedure:

```
Public Class checkedListBoxForm
Private Sub frmCheckedListBox_Load _
    (ByVal sender As System.Object, _
    ByVal e As System.EventArgs) Handles MyBase.Load
    'add a prechecked item to the checkedlistbox at
    'the runtime
    Me.avilableCheckedListBox.Items.Add("CPU BOX", True)
End Sub
```

This code will add another option to the CheckedListBox. The True keyword will make the option prechecked.

Now double-click on the addButton and type in the following codes:

```
Private Sub addButton_Click _
(ByVal sender As System.Object, ByVal e As System.EventArgs) _
Handles addButton.Click
    'declare the variable as searching parameter
    Dim Index As Object
    'search through the checkedlistbox and
    ' find any checked item
    For Each Index In Me.avilableCheckedListBox.CheckedItems
        'if it is found, add them to the list box but
        'after catching the duplicate items
        If Me.orderListBox.Items.Contains(Index) Then
            MessageBox.Show("You Already added " _
            + Index.ToString, "warning!", _
            MessageBoxButtons.OK, _
            MessageBoxIcon.Exclamation)
        Else : Me.orderListBox.Items.Add(Index)

        End If
    Next
End Sub
```

In this statement, the For Each loop will search the CheckedListBox. If any of the options are checked, then the item will be added to our ListBox. Notice that we block duplicate entries to the ListBox.

Now double-click on the clearItemButton and type the following:

```
Private Sub clearButton_Click _
(ByVal sender As System.Object, _
ByVal e As System.EventArgs) Handles clearButton.Click
    'remove selected items. If no item can be removed
    'display a warning
    Try
        Me.orderListBox.Items.RemoveAt(Me.orderListBox.SelectedIndex)
    Catch Ex As Exception
        MessageBox.Show("Cannot remove", "Warning")
    End Try

End Sub
```

This statement removes the selected items from the ListBox. You will notice that Try/Catch is used to prevent the user from trying to remove an item that does not exist. This is helpful when the user accidentally clicks on this Button when the list is already empty.

Complete the Exit and Clear buttons, save your project, and run it (see Figure 8.7).

ON THE CD

You can view this solution under the Chapter 8 folder on the companion CD-ROM. The project is saved under its name, checkedListBoxExample. Just copy the project folder to your hard drive and double-click on the .sln file.

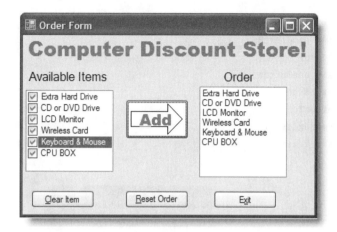

FIGURE 8.7   Example 3 screenshot.

BOOLEAN EXPRESSIONS

In Chapter 5, we introduced the boolean data type. We chose not to give you an example at that time, but now that you are familiar with conditional statements, we can provide an example so you will be able to utilize it in your projects. The boolean data types can represent two values: `True` or `False`. The boolean variables can examine the states of boolean values. The default value for boolean variables is `False`.

EXAMPLE 4
Start a new project and call it `booleanTest`. Add the following controls to your form:

- One `Label`
- One `TextBox`
- Two `Buttons`
- One `ListBox`

The form should look like Figure 8.8.

- **Form1**
  Name: booleanForm
  Text: Boolean
- **Label1**
  Name: nameLabel
  Text: Enter Names. END to Finish

- **TextBox1**

  Name: nameTextBox
- **Button1**

  Name: addButton

  Text: &Add
- **Button2**

  Name: exitButton

  Text: E&xit

FIGURE 8.8 Example 4 screenshot.

In this project, we will accept data from the user and add them to the ListBox. This process continues until the user enters "End" in the TextBox. At that time, the Exit button becomes visible and the user can click on it. We hide the Add button at the same time.

In the program's declaration area, declare a module-level variable as public with a boolean data type:

```
Public Class booleanForm
'declare a module level Boolean variable
Private ButtonVisible As Boolean = False
```

Double-click the form and type the following in the Form_load subprocedure:

```
Private Sub booleanForm_Load _
(ByVal sender As System.Object, _
ByVal e As System.EventArgs) Handles MyBase.Load
    'Hide the exit button
    Me.exitButton.Visible = False
End Sub
```

As you can see, in the above code, we are hiding the Exit button from the user. Now, double-click on the TextBox and type the following in its textChanged subprocedure:

```
Private Sub nameTextBox_TextChanged(ByVal sender _
As System.Object, _
ByVal e As System.EventArgs) Handles _
nameTextBox.TextChanged
    'if the user types end, the exit button will become
    'visible
    If Me.nameTextBox.Text.ToUpper = "END" Then
        'set the boolean variable to true
        buttonVisible = True
        'set the Add button invisible and Exit button
        'Visible
        Me.addButton.Visible = False
        Me.exitButton.Visible = True
    End If
End Sub
```

In the above codes, we accept inputs from the user and add them to the List-Box. However, as soon as the user types "End," we hide the Add button and unhide the Exit button.

Now double-click on the addButton and type the following codes:

```
Private Sub addButton_Click(ByVal sender _
As System.Object, ByVal e As System.EventArgs) _
Handles addButton.Click
    'add the user's input to the listbox and
    'clear the textbox
    Me.nameListBox.Items.Add(Me.nameTextBox.Text)
    Me.nameTextBox.Text = Nothing
    Me.nameTextBox.Focus()
End Sub
```

As you can see, first, we add the input to the ListBox and then we clear the TextBox to accept more data. Complete the exitButton code and run the project. add names and at the end type "End."

ON THE CD

You can view this solution under the Chapter 8 folder on the companion CD-ROM. The project is saved under its name, booleanTest. Just copy the project folder to your hard drive and double-click on the .sln file.

TIMER CONTROL

The Timer control is a class that allows methods be executed at given intervals. In many ways, timers are similar to loops, so we will discuss this control in this section. Recall that we briefly used this control in Chapter 7, but now we expand our discussion.

`Timer` has some useful properties and methods that programmers can use to their advantage:

Interval: Consider this property as your watch's tick function. You can set this property to perform specific tasks on each tick. You can also set the distance between each tick by setting the `Interval` property. The value of this property is measured by milliseconds; each 1000 milliseconds equals 1 second.

Start: This method is used to set the `Enabled` property to `True`.

Stop: This method sets the `Enabled` property to `False`. It is the opposite of the `Start` method.

Enabled: This property is used to let the `Timer` run or stop.

AutoRestart: If this property is set to `False`, the `Timer` stops at the end of the event.

EXAMPLE 5

Start a new project and call it `timer_1`. Add the following controls to it:

- Two `Labels`
- Three `Buttons`
- One `Timer`

In this project, we will show the time of day. By using Stop and Start buttons, we can control the `Timer`. Add the following controls to your form and name them properly (see Figure 8.9):

FIGURE 8.9 Example 5 screenshot.

- **Timer1**
  Name: myTimerTimer
  Enabled: True
  Interval: 1000

Double-click on the Timer control and add the following:

```
Private Sub myTimerTimer_Tick _
(ByVal sender As System.Object, _
ByVal e As System.EventArgs) _
Handles myTimerTimer.Tick
    'Display the time of the day
    Me.timerLabel.Text = TimeOfDay.ToString

End Sub
```

Now double-click on the stopButton and type the following:

```
Private Sub stopButton_Click _
(ByVal sender As System.Object, _
ByVal e As System.EventArgs) _
Handles stopButton.Click
    'Stop the timer
    Me.myTimerTimer.Stop()
End Sub
```

With this code, we have stopped the timer.
Now double-click on the startButton and type the following code:

```
Private Sub startButton_Click _
(ByVal sender As System.Object, _
ByVal e As System.EventArgs) _
Handles startButton.Click
    'Start the timer
    Me.myTimerTimer.Start()
End Sub
```

Now complete the exitButton and run the project.

ON THE CD
You can view this solution under the Chapter 8 folder on the companion CD-ROM. The project is saved under its name, Timer_1. Just copy the project folder to your hard drive and double-click on the .sln file.

Now that you are familiar with the function of the Timer, let us try another example.

EXAMPLE 6
Start a new project and call it timer_2. Add the following controls to your form:

■ Two Labels
■ Two Buttons
■ One TextBox
■ One Timer

In this project, we want the user to type the given text within 15 seconds. If the text is not entered within 15 seconds, the Process button will go away and the Exit button will appear. If the user types the text within 15 seconds but it is not what we wanted, an error message will be displayed. If the correct text is typed within 15 seconds, a welcome message will be displayed.

Figure 8.10 shows the screenshot for this project. Design your screen similar to it. Here are some of the controls and suggested names.

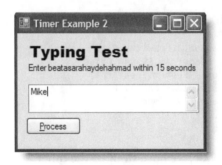

FIGURE 8.10   Example 6 screenshot.

■ **Timer1**

   Name: timer2Timer

   Enabled: True

   Interval: 15000

■ **TextBox1**

   Name: timerTextBox

   Scrollbar: Vertical

Double-click on the `Timer` control and type the following codes:

```
Private Sub timer2Timer _Tick _
(ByVal sender As System.Object, _
ByVal e As System.EventArgs) _
Handles timer2Timer.Tick
    'if the input is not entered within 15 seconds,
    'then this message will be displayed and the Process
    'button will be hidden and the Exit button will be visible
    Me.timer2Timer.Stop()
    MessageBox.Show("You didn't type fast enough", _
    "Log off please", _
    MessageBoxButtons.OK, MessageBoxIcon.Exclamation)
    Me.processButton.Visible = False
    Me.exitButton.Visible = True
End Sub
```

As this code shows, if the user cannot enter the text within 15 seconds, an error message will be displayed and the Exit button will show up.

Now double-click on the processButton and type the following:

```
Private Sub processButton_Click _
(ByVal sender As System.Object, _
ByVal e As System.EventArgs) Handles processButton.Click
    'the input is validated to find beatasarahaydehahmad
    ' in the textbox
    'if found, the user receives a welcome message
    If Me.timerTextBox.Text = " beatasarahaydehahmad" Then
        Me.timer2Timer.Enabled = False
        MessageBox.Show("Welcome to my program!", _
        "Welcome!", MessageBoxButtons.OK, _
        MessageBoxIcon.Information)
        'if not found, the following message will
        'be displayed
    Else
        MessageBox.Show("Did you follow the instructions", _
        "Warning!", MessageBoxButtons.OK, _
        MessageBoxIcon.Error)
        timer2Timer.Enabled = True
    End If
End Sub
```

The above code is self-explanatory and you should be able to follow it. Now complete the exitButton.

ON THE CD

You can view this solution under the Chapter 8 folder on the companion CD-ROM. The project is saved under its name, Timer_2. Just copy the project folder to your hard drive and double-click on the .sln file.

Now that you are familiar with the function of the timer, let us try another example.

MOVING OBJECTS

It is possible to move an object around on the Form. This can be accomplished by increasing or decreasing the Left and Top properties of the object. In other words, if you want to move the object to the right side of Form, you increase the value of the object's Left property. It may sound confusing but it is very simple. By increasing the value of the Left property, you increase the distance of the object from the left side of the Form and move it toward the right side of the Form. In contrast, if you decrease the value of the Left property, you will move the object to the left. The same rule applies to the Top property of the object. In order to move the object to the top of the Form, you need to decrease the value of the Top property (see Figure 8.11). Let's look at an example.

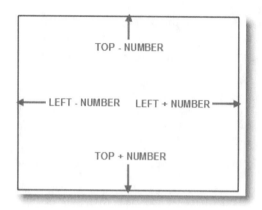

FIGURE 8.11   The top and left territories.

EXAMPLE 7

Start a new project and call it `timer_3`. Add the following controls to your form:

- One `Label`
- Three `Buttons`
- One `PictureBox`
- One `Timer`

In this project, we will move the image from one side of the form to the other side using a `Timer` control (see Figure 8.12). Add the objects to your form and name them. Here are some specifications for some of the controls.

FIGURE 8.12   Project 7 screenshot.

- **Form1**

  Name: timerForm

  Text: Move the Object

  MaximumSize: 300,300

  MinimumSize: 300,300

- **Timer1**

  Name: MoveTimr

  Enabled: False

  Interval: 100

Place the Label on the form and then drag the PictureBox over it to cover the label. Now right-click on the PictureBox and select Bring to Front from the list of options. This option removes the transparency of Label (see Figure 8.13).

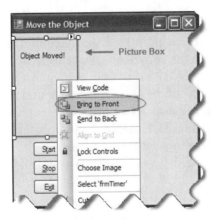

FIGURE 8.13 *Bring to Front* option.

Double-click on the Form and add the following codes in the Form_load subprocedure:

```
Private Sub timerForm_Load _
(ByVal sender As System.Object, _
ByVal e As System.EventArgs) Handles MyBase.Load

    'load the image into the picturebox.
    Try
        Me.movePictureBox.Image = _
        Image.FromFile("kid1.tif")
    Catch badpic As Exception
        MessageBox.Show("Couldn't locate the image", "Warning", _
```

```
                MessageBoxButtons.OK, MessageBoxIcon.Error)
        End Try

    End Sub
```

This statement loads the image into the PictureBox.
Double-click on the Timer control and add the following:

```
Private Sub moveButton_Tick _
(ByVal sender As System.Object, _
ByVal e As System.EventArgs) _
Handles moveButton.Tick
    'as long as it hasn't got to position 150,
    ' keep adding to the value of left
    If Me.movePictureBox.Left < 150 Then
        Me.movePictureBox.Left = Me.movePictureBox.Left + 1
    End If

End Sub
```

As you set the size of the Form, the maximum and minimum size for height and width was 300. In the above code, we tell Visual Basic to keep raising the value of the Left property of the PictureBox as long as the left side of the picture has not passed position 150 of the Form. This may sound confusing, but as soon as you run the project, you will notice that the PictureBox keeps moving from the left side of the Form to the right side. However, as soon as the left side of the PictureBox reaches position 150 of the form, it stops moving.

Now double-click on the startButton and add the following code:

```
Private Sub MoveTimer_Click _
(ByVal sender As System.Object, _
ByVal e As System.EventArgs) Handles MoveTimer.Click
    'Start the timer
    Me.moveTimer.Start()
End Sub
```

Code the *Stop* and *Exit* buttons. Save and run your project.

ON THE CD

You can view this solution under the Chapter 8 folder on the companion CD-ROM. The project is saved under its name, Timer_3. Just copy the project folder to your hard drive and double-click on the .sln file.

EXAMPLE 8

This project is similar to the last one. However, we add new features to it to give you some new ideas. Start a new project and call it timer_4. Add the following controls to your form:

■ One `PictureBox`
■ Three `Buttons`
■ One `Timer`

Because this project is similar to the last project you worked on, we just list controls that have different settings than the last one:

■ **PictureBox1**
Name: movePictureBox
Size: 35, 38
Location: 24, 28
ImageMode: StretchImage
BorderStyle: FixedSingle

There is no need for a `Label` control in this project. The other controls are the same as in the last project.

Double-click on the `Form` and type the following code in the `Form_load` subprocedure:

```
Private Sub moveForm_Load _
(ByVal sender As System.Object, _
ByVal e As System.EventArgs) Handles MyBase.Load
    'will load the image into the picturebox
    Try
        Me.movePictureBox.Image = Image.FromFile _
        ("kid2.tif")
    Catch ex As Exception
        MessageBox.Show _
        ("The image couldn't be found", "Warning", _
        MessageBoxButtons.OK, MessageBoxIcon.Exclamation)
    End Try

End Sub
```

This code is very similar to the one you used in the last example. Double-click on the `Timer` control and add the following codes:

```
Private Sub moveTimer_Tick _
(ByVal sender As System.Object, _
ByVal e As System.EventArgs) Handles moveTimer.Tick
    'as long as it hasn't got to position 150,
    ' keep adding to the value of left
    If Me.movePictureBox.Left < 150 Then
        Me. movePictureBox.Left = Me.movePictureBox.Left + 3
    End If
    'as long as the vertical postition 100
    'hasn't reached, continue the process
```

```
If Me.movePictureBox.Top < 100 Then
    Me.movePictureBox.Top = Me.movePictureBox.Top + 1
    Me.movePictureBox.Height = Me.movePictureBox.Top
    Me.movePictureBox.Width = Me.movePictureBox.Top
End If

End Sub
```

In the first section of the code, we changed the incrementing parameter from 1 to 3. This will speed up the movement of the object. We also added another conditional statement, which examines the distance between the object and the bottom of the Form. At the start time, we set the position of the PictureBox to 28. That was the distance between the PictureBox and the top of the Form. The conditional statement will increase the value of the top property of the PictureBox and move it down until it gets to position 100 and stop it there. Notice that we have included three different tasks within the moveTimer:

- Moving the object horizontally
- Moving the object vertically
- Zooming the image

Complete the Start, Stop, and Exit buttons and run the project (see Figure 8.14).

FIGURE 8.14 Example 8 screenshot.

You can view this solution under the Chapter 8 folder on the companion CD-ROM. The project is saved under its name, Timer_4. Just copy the project folder to your hard drive and double-click on the .sln file.

DO **LOOPS**

Although all loops are designed to repeat a set of instructions, the For/Next loop is perfect when we know how many times the loop will be executed. It is faster to develop and easier to understand, but there are occasions when we want to set up a boolean condition and repeat the loop as long as the condition exists. This takes us back to our previous example about driving from California to Oregon. In this section, we will introduce you to other types of loop structures: Do While and Do Until.

The Do loops repeat the instructions as long as the condition is True or until the condition becomes True. The Do loops are designed for operations that can be repeated an indefinite number of times. The Do conditional block gives you more flexibility than the While/End block. There are two ways we can use Do statements.

Here is the general syntax for Do While and Do Until:

```
Do |While | Until| Condition
Set of statements
[Exit Do]
Set of statements
Loop
```

The condition will be tested before the instructions are executed. When the condition is tested first, there is a chance that the loop does not run even one time. However, when we test the condition at the end, we can guarantee that the loop will be executed at least once.

It is also possible to test the condition at the end:

```
Set of statements
[Exit Do]
Set of statements
Do |While | Until| Condition
```

In this code:

- We can use either the While or Until keywords but not both of them at once.
- Do is required to process the loop.
- Loop is required to end the Do loop block.
- The While keyword is needed if the Until keyword is not used. It will repeat the loop while the test condition is True.
- The Until keyword is required if the While keyword is not used. It will repeat the loop until the test condition is True.
- Statements are optional.

Unlike the For/Next loop, this loop structure should be utilized when the loop will be repeated for an indefinite number of times.

EXAMPLE 9

Let's use an example very similar to Example 1, which dealt with the For/Next loop. Start a new project and call it dowhile_until. Add the following controls to your form:

■ One TextBox
■ Four Buttons

In this project, we will use three loop structures to display incremented numbers in a TextBox. Figure 8.15 shows the screenshot for the completed project.

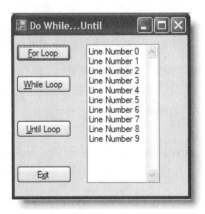

FIGURE 8.15   Example 9 screenshot.

Double-click the forLoopButton and add the following codes:

```
Private Sub forLoopButton_Click _
(ByVal sender As System.Object, _
ByVal e As System.EventArgs) _
Handles forLoopButton.Click
    Me.loopTextBox.Text = Nothing
    'repeat this loop for 10 times

    For Counter As Integer = 0 To 9
        Me.loopTextBox.Text _
        &= "Line Number " & Counter & vbCrLf
    Next

End Sub
```

As you saw earlier in this chapter, this code will display the incremented value of the counter in the TextBox. We will use the same method for utilizing the While and Until keywords.

DoWhile

Now, double-click on the `whileLoopButton` and add the following in the subprocedure:

```
Private Sub whileButton_Click _
(ByVal sender As System.Object, _
ByVal e As System.EventArgs) _
Handles whileButton.Click
    Me.loopTextBox.Text = Nothing
    'will continue this loop as long as the counter
    'is less than 10
    Dim counter As Integer = 0
    Do While counter < 10
        Me.loopTextBox.Text _
        &= "Line Number " & counter & vbCrLf
        counter = counter + 1
    Loop
End Sub
```

The loop will be repeated as long as the value of the counter is less than 10. If the value of the `counter` variable in the above statement is greater than 10, this loop will never be executed. For example, if you set the value of the counter to 10 and run the project, no output will be displayed.

Pretest and Posttest

Occasionally you need to make sure the loop is executed at least once. To change the above statements, you can place the testing condition at the end of the block:

```
Do
    Me.loopTextBox.Text _
    &= "Line Number " & counter & vbCrLf
    counter = counter + 1
Loop While counter < 10
```

This loop will be executed at least once. The concept of evaluating the test condition before or after executing the loop block is known as *pretest* and *posttest*. Pretest means evaluating the test condition before executing the Do block, and posttest means evaluating the test condition after the execution of the conditional block. It is up to the programmer to decide which one should be used.

Do Until

A similar code will be placed under the `untilLoopButton`:

```
Private Sub untilButton_Click _
(ByVal sender As System.Object, _
ByVal e As System.EventArgs) _
Handles untilButton.Click
    Me.loopTextBox.Text = Nothing
    'will continue this loop until the value
    'of the counter is greater than 9
```

```
Dim counter As Integer = 0
Do Until counter > 9
    Me.loopTextBox.Text _
    &= "Line Number " & counter & vbCrLf
    counter = counter + 1
Loop

End Sub
```

You can change the above pretest structure to the following posttest structure:

```
Dim counter As Integer = 0
Do
    Me.txtLoop.Text _
    &= "Line Number " & counter & vbCrLf
    counter = counter + 1
Loop Until counter > 9
```

Complete the `exitButton` and run the project.

ON THE CD You can view this solution under the Chapter 8 folder on the companion CD-ROM. The project is saved under its name, `Dowhile-until`. Just copy the project folder to your hard drive and double-click on the .sln file.

INFINITE LOOPS

Constructing a flawless loop is a challenge to many students. Based on the author's experience, most students experience several infinite loops before they become proficient in this task. Finding the appropriate test condition is one of the prerequisites for constructing a loop. Because of the complicated nature of the loop structure, it is possible for programmers to trap themselves in an endless loop. Under this condition, the loop continues forever and there is no condition to provide an exit for the loop. This is known as an *infinite loop*. Let us look at what an endless loop does.

EXAMPLE 10

Start a new project and call it `endless_loop`. Figure 8.16 shows the screenshot for the project. Add the following controls to your form:

- One `Label`
- Two `Buttons`

Double-click on the `processButton` and type the following:

```
Private Sub processButton_Click _
(ByVal sender As System.Object, _
```

```
ByVal e As System.EventArgs) Handles processbutton.Click
    'start an endless loop
    Dim test As Integer = 0
    Do
        Dim input As String
        input = InputBox("Enter a number ", "Input Data")
        test = 1
    Loop Until test < 1
End Sub
```

FIGURE 8.16   Example 10 screenshot.

Now run the project and click on the Process button. The InputBox will pop out endlessly. To get out of the loop, you can either stop it by clicking on the Stop icon on the Visual Basic toolbar or use Ctrl-Alt-Delete and close the program. In most cases, programmers can predict areas that may cause infinite loop and provide a mechanism to get out of it.

ON THE CD

You can view this solution under the Chapter 8 folder on the companion CD-ROM. The project is saved under its name, Endless_loop. Just copy the project folder to your hard drive and double-click on the .sln file.

Exit Do

This keyword can be used to get out of the loop. Add this statement to the program you just executed and run it again:

```
Do
    Dim input As String
    input = InputBox("Enter a number ", "Input Data")
    test = 1
    Exit Do
Loop Until test < 1
```

The InputBox will be executed only once.

FROMNAME **METHOD**

In this project, we will introduce the FromName method. This method is a color method that lets you create colors using the valid identifiers. We will be using a sample to show you how to use this method.

Here is the syntax for it:

```
returnValue=Color.FromName(SpecifiedColorName)
```

EXAMPLE 11

Start a new project and call it dowhile_example2. Add the following controls to your form:

- One Label
- Two Buttons
- One ComboBox

Change the name and other characteristics of the controls according to the following:

- **Form1**
  Name: loopForm
  Text: Do While Example 2
- **Label1**
  Name: loopLabel
  Text: Press to Enter Color
- **ComboBox1**
  Name: loopComboBox
  Text: Favorite Colors
- **Button1**
  Name: processButton
  Text: &Process
- **Button2**
  Name: exitButton
  Text: E&xit

In this project, we will accept valid colors from the user and place them in the ComboBox. Once the valid color is entered, the BackColor of the Form will change to the user's choice. Duplicate colors are invalid; they will be detected and rejected. The InputBox will be displayed over and over to receive valid input from the user. Figure 8.17 shows the screenshot.

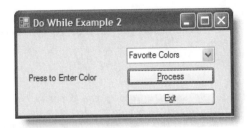

FIGURE 8.17 Example 11 screenshot.

Double-click on the processButton and type the following code:

```
Private Sub processButton_Click _
(ByVal sender As System.Object, _
ByVal e As System.EventArgs) Handles processButton.Click
    Dim colorString As String
    Dim confirmExitString As DialogResult
    Dim confirmString As DialogResult
    confirmString = System.Windows.Forms.DialogResult.Yes
    'start the loop and continue as long as the user
    'clicks on the Yes button of the message box
    Do While confirmString = System.Windows.Forms.DialogResult.Yes
        'Get the input from the user
        colorString = InputBox _
        ("What are your Favorite Colors", "input required")

        'If the input already exists in the combobox
        'display a messagebox to the user and inform him
        'about the existance of the entry
        'If the input does not exist and it is not blank
        ' it will
        ' be added to the combobox.   '

        Try
            Me.BackColor = Color.FromName(colorString)
            If Me.loopComboBox.Items.Contains(colorString) Then
                MessageBox.Show _
                ("The color you entered already exist", _
                "Please enter another one")
                confirmString = MsgBox("Do you want to Continue?", _
                MsgBoxStyle.YesNo)
            ElseIf colorString <> "" Then
                Me.loopComboBox.Items.Add(colorString)
                confirmString = MessageBox.Show _
                ("Do you want to Continue?", "warning" _
                , MessageBoxButtons.YesNo)

            End If
        Catch ex As Exception
```

```
                    MessageBox.Show _
                        ("the color you entered is not known to me", "Warning")
                End Try

            Loop

            'thank the user for using the program
            'if the user wants to quit, let him do so.
            confirmExitString = MsgBox("Thank You, Do you want to Exit?", _
            MsgBoxStyle.YesNo)

            If confirmExitString = System.Windows.Forms.DialogResult.Yes Then
                Me.Close()
            End If
        End Sub
```

As you can see, the program has several conditional statements. The Do While
loop repeats all of the instructions as long as the test condition is True, which is
when the user clicks on the Yes button in the MessageBox. The other condition is the
Try/Catch condition, which makes sure the valid color name is entered by the user.
The other conditions are self-explanatory and you can follow the logic. You can
also see how the FromName method is used to accept valid color names. This method
increases the efficiency of the programmer's work and minimizes the need for un-
necessary codes.

Now complete the exitButton and run the project.

You can view this solution under the Chapter 8 folder on the companion CD-
ROM. The project is saved under its name, dowhile_example2. Just copy the project
folder to your hard drive and double-click on the .sln file.

We do not discuss the While and End While loop structures in this book. Look
them up if you are interested in knowing what they do.

PROGRAMMING TIPS

- When you design a loop and you want to make sure that it executes at least
  once, use the pretest style rather than posttest.
- Try to utilize Exit Do to avoid infinite loops.

SUMMARY

In this chapter, we examined ways to construct loops. We discussed many loop
structures including the For/Next, Do While, and Do Until loop structures. We also

demonstrated how timers can be used to repeat the instructions in a way similar to loops. The `Continue` and `Exit` loop statements were covered in detail.

Next

In Chapter 9 you will learn how to create objects at runtime. You will also follow the step-by-step instructions to create your own classes. Similar instructions will help you develop structures and use them within your program.

DISCUSSION QUESTIONS

1. What is the difference between pretest and posttest structures?
2. When do we get stuck in infinite loops?
3. Explain the differences between `For/Next` loops and `Do` loops.
4. Is there any difference between `Exit For` and `Continue For` statements? Please explain.
5. Explain the nature of the `FromName` method and `Timer` control and suggest applications that you can develop for them.

Exercise

Using the `Do/While`, `Try/Catch`, and boolean variables, create a project that accepts input from the user and places it in a `TextBox`. Try to apply the `Continue` statement to your codes.

Key Terms

- Boolean
- `For/Next` loop
- `Do/While`
- `Do/Until`
- `Timer` control

9 Object-Oriented Programming

In This Chapter

- Getting Familiar with the Object-Oriented Environment
- Creating Your Own Classes
- Constructors
- Using the Class
- Instantiating and Creating Objects
- Using the Class Properties
- Object Browser
- Destructors and Garbage Collectors
- View Class Diagram Tool
- Structures

GETTING FAMILIAR WITH THE OBJECT-ORIENTED ENVIRONMENT

In Chapter 1, we discussed the elements of object-oriented programming and explained them briefly. Through other chapters, you learned how to use the Toolbox and drag and drop instances of classes into your form. You became familiar with different tools and their applications. You wrote codes to handle different events associated with these objects and you set their properties according to the application requirements.

In Visual Basic, you can use objects without using the Toolbox and you can create your own classes and generate different events and properties for them. Why do we need to learn this when we can drag and drop objects from the Toolbox? Here is an example to justify the need. Let us say you want to create an application that allows the user to decide what objects should be on a form. This interactive program will ask questions about the type of objects and their properties such as size, color, and location and use this information to create the object according to the users' request. As you see, we do not have access to the Toolbox at the runtime. Occasionally, you would like to add controls to your form programmatically rather than by using the Toolbox. In addition, you may want to create your own class and add properties, methods, and events to it. In this chapter, we will examine all of these features.

Adding Control by Codes

There are many applications for adding the controls to your form programmatically. Before we look at an example, let's be familiar with some new terms:

`Controls.Add` **method:** This method is used to add a new control to a form. In our example, we will use this to add a new `Button` to our `Form`.

`WithEvent` **keyword:** This keyword is used to declare a variable that is used to refer to an instance of a class. We can use the event handler to react to different events.

`New` **keyword:** We have used the `New` keyword briefly before. It is used to instantiate an object. As you may remember from the previous chapters, we used the `New` keyword to instantiate objects, and we will be using this keyword again in this chapter.

EXAMPLE 1

In this example, we want to add a `Button` to a `Form`, add events to it, and use the `Click` event subprocedure to add codes (see Figure 9.1). *Remember that we want to accomplish this task through codes, not the Toolbox.*

FIGURE 9.1 Adding a `Button` to a `Form`.

Start a new project and call it `object_1`. Use the following parameters:

■ **Form1**
  Name: objectForm
  Text: Objects
  Size: 300, 163

On the `Form`'s declaration area, declare a `Form`-level variable as follows:

```
Dim buttonExit As New Button
```

As you saw before, this statement will create a new instance of the `Button` class. In other words, it allows us to create a `Button` called `buttonExit` on our form.

Now double-click on the `Form` and type the following statements in the `object-Form_load` subprocedure:

```
Private Sub objectForm_Load _
(ByVal sender As System.Object, _
ByVal e As System.EventArgs) Handles MyBase.Load
    'adding the control to our form
    Me.Controls.Add(exitButton)
    'assigning values to the button properties
    With Me.exitButton
        'setting the text property to "E&xit"
        .Text = "E&xit"
        'Setting the alignment of the text within the button
        .TextAlign = ContentAlignment.MiddleCenter
        'setting the location
        .Location = New System.Drawing.Point(20, 60)
        'setting the size
        .Width = 90
        .Height = 30
    End With
End Sub
```

What did we do here? Here is the sequence of actions:

1. We added the control to our form by using the `Controls.Add` method.
2. We set the `Text` property of the new `Button` to `E&xit`. The text can be activated by the Alt key and the underlined character of the text, which is x.
3. We aligned the text to the center and the middle of the `Button`.
4. We told Visual Basic that the `Button` should appear in the location point of (20, 60). The first parameter (20) is the horizontal location on the `Form`, and the second number (60) is the vertical location on the `Form`. If we do not set this parameter, Visual Basic will place the `Button` in the default location, which is (0, 0).
5. We set the `Button` size to (90, 30). If we do not set this property, the default value (75, 23) will be assumed.
6. We can set other properties as well, but let us leave it as it is and hit F5 to run the program. Notice that a `Button` appears on the form and that the `Button` is not functioning. There are two simple explanations for this:
   - We have not developed the codes to perform a task when the user clicks on the `Button`.

- The Button does not have any event handler to react to the user's click action.

In order to add codes for this Button we need a subprocedure, and to have a subprocedure for this Button, we need an event. We mentioned a new term in the beginning of this chapter: the WithEvent keyword. We will use it to add events to this new Button. To accomplish this task, we need to make a minor change to the Form-level declaration that we made before:

```
Dim exitButton As New Button
```

We must change this statement to the following to add events to the new Button:

```
Dim WithEvents exitButton As New Button
```

As you see, we made a very small modification. While you are in the code editor, click on the *Class Name* drop-down window and select exitButton class from the list of options (see Figure 9.2). While the exitButton class name is selected, open the Method Name drop-down window and select Click from the list of options (see Figure 9.3). Once you click on the Click event, a new subprocedure will be added to the form. Add the following statement to the Click subprocedure of the new Button:

```
Private Sub exitButton_Click _
(ByVal sender As Object, _
ByVal e As System.EventArgs) _
Handles exitButton.Click
    'declaring a string variable
    Dim strResponse As DialogResult = _
    MessageBox.Show _
    ("Are you sure you wish to exit the program?", _
    "Exit", MessageBoxButtons.YesNo, MessageBoxIcon.Exclamation)
    'storing the user input to strResponse variable
    'and reacting to it
    If strResponse = DialogResult.Yes Then
    Me.Close()
    End If
End Sub
```

Now click on the Exit button and it should display the message. Let's add a few more controls to our project. We want to add one more Button, two Labels, and one TextBox to our current Form. To accomplish this task, we will add the following codes to our form declaration area:

```
'adding events to the new object
Dim WithEvents TestButton As New Button
Dim passwordTextBox As New TextBox
Dim headerLabel As New Label
Dim passwordLabel As New Label
Dim characterChar As Char = "*"
```

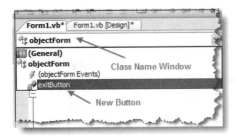

FIGURE 9.3 Adding `Click` event to the `Button` class.

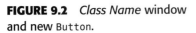

FIGURE 9.2 *Class Name* window and new `Button`.

Now we need to move the object to the second half of the `Form` to make room for the new objects we are adding. Let us change the parameters for the Exit button as follows:

```
exitButton. Location = New System.Drawing.Point(20, 140)
```

As you can see, we changed the vertical value of the system drawing point to move the object down the form. Now let's add the following statements to the `Form_Load` subprocedure. These statements appear right after the codes you used to add a `Button` to your `Form`:

```
'adding a label to the form
    Me.Controls.Add(headerLabel)
    'setting the properties for the label
    With Me.headerLabel
        .Text = "Object at Runtime"
        .TextAlign = ContentAlignment.MiddleCenter
        .Location = New System.Drawing.Point(8, 8)
        .Width = 460
        .Height = 60
        .Font = New System.Drawing.Font _
        ("Arial" _
        , 16, FontStyle.Bold, GraphicsUnit.Point)

    End With
```

This is very similar to what we did before. Now let's add another `Label`:

```
'adding another label to the form
    Me.Controls.Add(passwordLabel)
    'setting the properties for the label.
    With Me.passwordLabel
        .Text = "Enter Password"
        .Location = New System.Drawing.Point(20, 100)
        .Width = 420
```

```
        .Height = 50
    End With
```

Now that another `Label` is added, let's add a `TextBox` to our `Form`. Again, as we did for all the other controls so far, we will add the following statements in the `Form_Load` subprocedure:

```
'adding a textbox to the form
    Me.Controls.Add(passwordTextBox)
    'setting the properties of the textbox
    With Me.passwordTextBox
        .Text = ""
        .PasswordChar = "*"
        .Location = New System.Drawing.Point _
        (130, 100)
        .Width = 90
        .Height = 30
    End With
```

Now it is time to add another `Button` to our `Form`:

```
'adding another button to the form
    Me.Controls.Add(TestButton)
    'setting the properties for the button
    With Me.TestButton
        .Text = "&Test"
        .TextAlign = ContentAlignment.MiddleCenter
        .Location = New System.Drawing.Point(130, 140)
        .Width = 90
        .Height = 30

    End With
```

The last thing we need to do is add codes to the `Click` subprocedure of the second `Button` we added. The Test button will be used to validate the passwords the users enter. Here is what we have in our program:

```
Private Sub TestButton_Click _
(ByVal sender As Object, _
ByVal e As System.EventArgs) _
Handles TestButton.Click
    'using the click event of the
    ' button to validate the input.
    Select Case Me.passwordTextBox.Text
        Case "Mike", "Sara", "Beata", "Heidi"
            MessageBox.Show _
            ("Welcome to my program", "Welcome")
        Case Else
            MessageBox.Show _
            ("Wrong Password", _
            "Warning!", MessageBoxButtons.OK, _
```

```
            MessageBoxIcon.Error)
        End Select
    End Sub
```

Now hit F5 and run your project. Type a valid password in the TextBox, click on the Test button, and witness your success (see Figure 9.4).

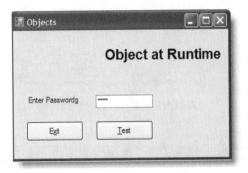

FIGURE 9.4 Example 1 at runtime.

ON THE CD
You can view this solution under the Chapter 9 folder on the companion CD-ROM. The project is saved under its name, Objects_1. Just copy the project folder to your hard drive and double-click on the .sln file.

CREATING YOUR OWN CLASSES

In Example 1, we showed you how to use existing classes at runtime. However, occasionally we want to create our own classes and create objects based on them. This is a little different from what we did in Example 1.

EXAMPLE 2

To add a user-defined class to your project, do the following:

1. Fire up your Visual Basic program and create a new project called myclass_1.
2. From the menu bar, click on the Project option and select Add Class from the drop-down menu (see Figure 9.5).
3. From the Add New Item dialog box, pick the Class icon and type "glasses" in the Name dialog box. Now click on the Add button (see Figure 9.6).

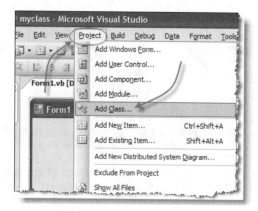

FIGURE 9.5   Adding a class to your form.

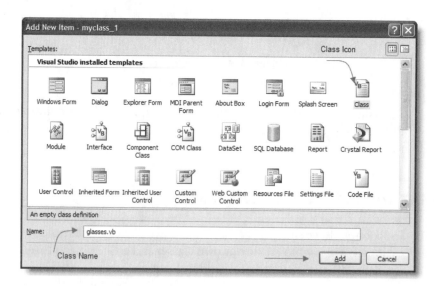

FIGURE 9.6   Using the *Add New Item* dialog box to add a class.

Now, if you view the Solution Explorer window, you should be able to see the Glasses class file that we added to our project (see Figure 9.7).

Once you are done with this process, you can double-click on the new user-defined class and add codes to it. Like the Form class, the Glasses class file has a Visual Basic file extension. Once you open this new class file, you can type codes between the Class and End Class block (see Figure 9.8).

We called our new class Glasses because we want to create a class to store the name of glasses we offer for sale, the price, and color. Glasses types, price, and color will be

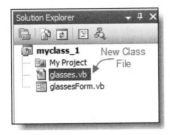

FIGURE 9.8 `Class` and `End Class` block.

FIGURE 9.7 Viewing the class filename in *Solution Explorer*.

considered the properties. This class will work with a method that we created called `Calculate`. The user-defined classes will involve some or all of the following steps:

- Creating the class (we have already done it in our last practice)
- Adding properties to our new class
- Adding methods
- Creating new objects using our new class
- Using inheritance
- Using instances

The example we will be working on involves creating a `Glasses Sales` class. Within that class, we will design the constructor, properties, and methods.

Class File

In our last practice, we showed you how to create a class file. However, we did not do anything with it. As you saw before, we created objects by using their associated *classes*. Objects have properties and methods. Classes are like rubber stamps that we use to instantiate new objects. In our example, we used the properties of an object to store values. We used event procedures to write methods for these objects. However, the object came with these features and we did not have to create them. The case is a little different here because we have to create our own classes. The class file that we created can contain multiple class declarations.

Declaring Class Variables

Within our class file, just right below the `Public Class glasses` clause, we can declare instance variables. This is very similar to what we did with variables before. Recall that variables can store values temporarily. We need to declare these classes' variables as `Private` variables so they will deal with their own data.

Adding Instance Fields

You have learned that by instantiating a class, we can create objects. However, when these objects are created, we need to store the values of the new objects' properties in some variables. These variables are known as *instance variables* or *instance fields*.

```
'create instance variables
Private glassesTypeString As String
Private glassesColorString As String
Private glassesPriceInteger As Integer = 1
Private discountedPrice As Double
```

You can access these variables from within the class only. To comply with the encapsulation rules, we have defined these variables as `Private` so they can be accessed locally.

Shared Variables or Properties and Methods

Until now, you have been using members of a class through objects. You can access members of a class by using the class name and a dot. After this step, you can access the properties and methods associated with that class. In order to access these shared methods and properties, you need to have an instance of the class. However, occasionally you want to use these properties without an instance of them. In this case, the user will use the shared members of a class without its instance. For example, you can access the shared properties of `TimeDate`'s class from any other class:

```
Label1.Text = DateTime.Today
```

As you can see, there is no need to create an instance of the `TimeDate` class.

With this in mind, we need to create some shared variables. It is important to know that the instance variables we declared are different from class-shared variables. The `Shared Property` subprocedure can interact with the variables we declare within each subprocedure. We can use shared methods and shared properties as well.

Shared variable and shared Property mean the same thing. We use one shared variable for all instances of a class. Since the changes we make to the values of the shared properties apply to every instance of the class, we should not use the shared properties if there are instances that are set to be independent from each other. In some programming languages, shared properties are known as static property members. In order to use a shared method, you do not need to create an instance of the class before using it. You can use it directly from within the class.

To create a shared variable, we will add the `Shared` keyword to the variable. Add the following code under the instance variables you declared under the `Glasses` class before. In this project we haven't used shared variables.

Defining Properties

We define properties for our classes by using a property procedure within the class. These Private variables will be used to store the values for our class properties. Many options are available for declaring property procedures. Let us look at the general syntax; then we will explain different options:

```
[Default] [modifiers] Property property-name As data type
Get
    ' Get procedure.
    Return expression
End Get
Set[(ByVal variable name As data type)]
    ' Set Procedure.
Property Value = new value
End Set
End Property
```

In the above syntax, notice two procedures: Get and Set. The Get procedure will return a value that can be accessed by another class. This value could be the one that you have assigned to the property in the Get statement or the Return statement. The Value keyword is used by the Set procedure to access the property value that comes to the procedure.

The Return statement is required to allow the class to retrieve the data within the Get procedure. Based on this general syntax, we will define properties for our class:

```
'Defining the glassType property
Property glassesType() As String
    Get
        Return glassesTypeString
    End Get
    Set(ByVal Value As String)
        glassesTypeString = Value
    End Set
End Property
```

The property procedures are declared as Public by default.

We will do the same thing for other properties as well. Here is what we need for the glassColor property:

```
'Defining the glassColor property
Property glassesColor() As String
    Get
        Return glassesColorString
    End Get
    Set(ByVal Value As String)
        glassesColorString = Value
    End Set
End Property
```

Here is what we need for the `Price` property:

```
'Defining the price property
Property glassesPrice() As Integer
    Get
        Return glassesPriceInteger
    End Get
    Set(ByVal value As Integer)
        glassesPriceInteger = value
    End Set
End Property
```

Put the following for the `total` property:

```
'Defining the total property

Property total() As Double
    Get
        Return discountedPrice
    End Get
    Set(ByVal Value As Double)
        discountedPrice = Value
    End Set
End Property
```

Defining Class Method

As discussed in previous sections, methods are either subprocedures or functions. By default, methods are defined as `Public` and are accessible to the forms of other classes. If you need to make the subprocedure available to only the class, you will define it as a `Private` subprocedure. However, we have declared our method in a `Module`. Add a `Module` form and add the following to it:

```
Module callclass
'we create a method to calculate the price
Public Function calculate _
(ByVal glassesPriceInteger As Integer) As Double
    Dim discountDecimal As Double = 0.5
    Return (discountDecimal * glassesPriceInteger)
End Function

End Module
```

CONSTRUCTORS

In order to initialize the class we have added to our project, we need to create constructors. If we do not define our own constructors, the default ones will be used. We should use this `Public` subprocedure any time we create a new class. The parameterized constructors are subprocedures that allow parameters to pass between the class and client objects, which are instantiated from the class. The keyword New is a required phrase in the constructor subprocedures. Adding the parameters makes it possible for the instances to have the required information during the initialization process. Once the constructor is defined, the Common Language Runtime will execute it when the client wants to access it. In our example, the constructor is defined as follows:

```
'creating constructor
Sub New(ByVal glassesTypeString As String, _
    ByVal glassesColorString As String, _
    ByVal glassesPriceInteger As Integer)
    Me.glassesType = glassesTypeString
    Me.glassesColor = glassesColorString
    Me.glassesPrice = glassesPriceInteger
    'Calling a method within a module
    discountedPrice = calculate(glassesPriceInteger)
```

USING THE CLASS

Now let us get back to our project and add controls to our form:

- **Form1**

  Name: glassesForm

  Text: Glasses on Sale!

  Size: 463; 204

- **Label1**

  Name: titleLabel

  Text: Mike's Glasses Store

  Size: 141; 20

  Font: Microsoft Sans Serif; 12pt

- **Lable2**

  Name: glassesTypeLabel

  Text: Glasses Type

- **Label3**

  Name: glassesColorLabel

  Text: Glasses Color

- **Label3**

  Name: glassesUnitPriceLabel

  Text: Unit Price

- **Label4**

  Name: glassesDiscountLabel

  Text: Discount Price

- **Label5**
  Name: glassesTypeOutLabel
  Text: Glasses Type
- **Label6**
  Name: glassesColorOutLabel
  Text: Glasses Color
- **Label7**
  Name: glassesUnitPriceOutLabel
  Text: Unit Price
- **Label8**
  Name: glassesDicountedPriceOutLabel
  Text: Discount Price
- **Button1**
  Name: exitButton
  Text: E&xit

Figure 9.9 shows what the form should look like.

FIGURE 9.9   Class form design.

INSTANTIATING AND CREATING OBJECTS

The whole purpose of defining a class is to create objects based on it. You will see that we create an object by instantiating the class and assigning values to our constructor arguments. Here is a module-level declaration:

```
Public Class glassesForm
'define object variable and
'object instantiation. We are also passing values
'for the arguments we have defined in our constructor

Private objglasses As glasses = _
New glasses("Sun Glasses", "Blue", 10)
```

As you can see in this statement, we are assigning values to the following properties:

- glassestype, which is Sun Glasses
- glassesColor, which is Blue
- glassesPrice, which is 10

USING THE CLASS PROPERTIES

We have made all the preparations for using the class. Here is what we type under the glassesForm_load subprocedure:

```
Private Sub glassesForm_Load _
(ByVal sender As System.Object, _
ByVal e As System.EventArgs) _
Handles MyBase.Load

    'We display the value of our class properties in different labels
    Me.glassesTypeOutLabel.Text = _
    objglasses.glassesType
    Me.glassesColorOutLabel.Text = _
    objglasses.glassesColor
    Me.glassesUnitPriceOutLabel.Text = _
    objglasses.glassesPrice.ToString
    Me.glassesDicountedPriceOutLabel.Text = _
    objglasses.total.ToString

End Sub
```

Now let us add the closing statement under the exitButton:

```
Private Sub exitButton_Click(ByVal sender As System.Object, _
ByVal e As System.EventArgs) Handles exitButton.Click
    'Terminate the program
    Me.Close()
End Sub
```

Now let's run the program. Figure 9.10 shows what you should see.

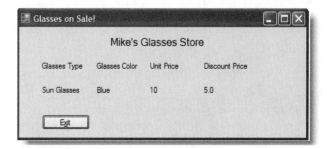

FIGURE 9.10   Class program running.

Here is the complete code for the class:

```vb
Public Class glasses
'create instance variables
Private glassesTypeString As String
Private glassesColorString As String
Private glassesPriceInteger As Integer = 1
Private discountedPrice As Double

'creating constructor
Sub New(ByVal glassesTypeString As String, _
    ByVal glassesColorString As String, _
    ByVal glassesPriceInteger As Integer)
    Me.glassesType = glassesTypeString
    Me.glassesColor = glassesColorString
    Me.glassesPrice = glassesPriceInteger
    'Calling a method within a module
    discountedPrice = calculate(glassesPriceInteger)

End Sub
'Defining the glassType property
Property glassesType() As String
    Get
        Return glassesTypeString
    End Get
    Set(ByVal Value As String)
        glassesTypeString = Value
    End Set
End Property
'Defining the glassColor property
Property glassesColor() As String
    Get
        Return glassesColorString
    End Get
    Set(ByVal Value As String)
        glassesColorString = Value
    End Set
End Property

'Defining the price property
Property glassesPrice() As Integer
    Get
        Return glassesPriceInteger
    End Get
    Set(ByVal value As Integer)
        glassesPriceInteger = value
    End Set
End Property
'Defining the total property

Property total() As Double
    Get
        Return discountedPrice
```

```
        End Get
        Set(ByVal Value As Double)
            discountedPrice = Value
        End Set
    End Property

End Class
```

You can view this solution under the Chapter 9 folder on the companion CD-ROM. The project is saved under its name, `myclass_1`. Just copy the project folder to your hard drive and double-click on the .sln file.

OBJECT BROWSER

It is time to talk about an important tool: the *Object Browser*. This tool allows us to locate the objects, properties, methods, and events in your Visual Basic application. You can use this tool to locate user-defined objects or other objects that you can use in your project. To access the Object Browser, click on the View tab on your toolbar and select Object Browser from the list of drop-down options (see Figure 9.11). You can also use the Object Browser button on the toolbar (see Figure 9.12).

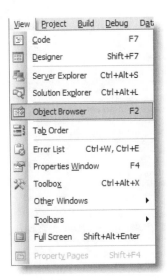

FIGURE 9.11 Accessing the Object Browser through the View Tab.

FIGURE 9.12   Locating the *Object Browser* button.

The Object Browser tool provides useful information that can be utilized by the programmers (see Figure 9.13). The Object Browser is divided into three panes: Object Pane, Member Pane, and Description Pane. Each item within each pane is identified by a symbol or icon. (see Figure 9.14).

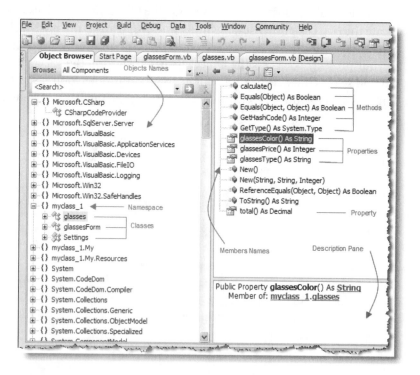

FIGURE 9.13   Object Browser panes.

To explore the Object Browser, you can select the class we created and view the properties and methods within it. If you want to locate the method or property in your project, double-clicking on its name will take you to its location within the class.

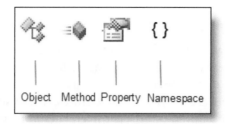

FIGURE 9.14   Icons in the Object Browser.

DESTRUCTORS AND GARBAGE COLLECTORS

In our example, we created a constructor and used it in our project. Visual Basic.NET offers a new feature that enables its Garbage Collector to find objects that are no longer in use and release resources. Visual Basic 2005 uses a *destructor* procedure to control the release of system resources. The `Finalize` destructor is called to destroy the unneeded object. This concept is beyond the scope of this book but you can review it at the following URL: *http://msdn2.microsoft.com/en-us/library/hks5e2k6.aspx*.

VIEW CLASS DIAGRAM TOOL

In the Solution Explorer toolbar is an icon called View Class Diagram, which can be used to see the structure of a class in a visual format or create a class in this format. It allows us to modify an existing class and create classes, properties, and the other concepts we have discussed in visual format. We created our class in the traditional way, but you may want to try the same steps using View Class Diagram (see Figure 9.15).

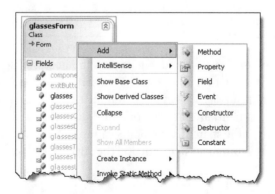

FIGURE 9.15   *View Class Diagram.*

STRUCTURES

So far, you have been working with data types that are available in Visual Basic. In most cases, these data types are adequate for our needs. However, occasionally we need to create our own data types and use them in our project. You will see some similarities between classes and structures. These similarities are in the areas of properties, procedures, interface implementation, and more. Both are considered containers that can hold different data types. Containers are used to hold closely related information such as students' information. Although the collected data are related to students, they cannot be stored in a single data type. When we use class or structure, we can keep these related data close to each other and treat them as class or structure members. We can access them individually in our program.

Despite their similarities, classes and structures have major differences as well. Here are some of the differences:

- Structures are value type–based, while classes are based on reference types.
- Classes support inheritance and polymorphism, while structures do not.
- Structures are more limited to handling events than are classes.

The inheritance item is an important difference. Regardless of these differences, structures are used for their faster results in some areas. In general, if you work with a small amount of data, most likely structures will be a better choice than classes. Unlike with classes, you do not need to use the New keyword to create a new instance of the structures.

Structure Declaration

We start declaring our structure by using the Structure statement, which consist of the keyword Structure, a name, and the End Structure statement:

```
Private|Public|Friend|Protected Structure Name
Variable Declaration
End Structure
```

We have the option of using any of the accessibility keywords listed in the above general code model. However, the default accessibility for structures is Public. Between the Structure keyword and the End Structure block, we need to declare at least one element, and at least one of them must be a nonshared member. The initialization of the structure elements cannot take place within the structure block, so you need to initialize them outside the structure block.

EXAMPLE 3
In this example, we will be looking at the following:

- `Declare` structures
- `Declare` structure members
- `Declare` structure type variables
- Loading the structure with the user's input
- Reading and displaying the data that is stored in structures

Create a new project and call it `Structure`. We need the following:

- **Form1**
  Name: `StructureForm`
  Text: `Structure`
- **Label1**
  Name: `courseNameLabel`
  Text: `Enter Course Name`
- **TextBox1**
  Name: `courseNameTextBox`
- **Label2**
  Name: `courseNumberLabel`
  Text: `Enter Course Number`
- **TextBox2**
  Name: `courseNumberTextBox`
- **Label3**
  Name: `courseTuitionLabel`
  Text: `Enter Course Tuition`
- **Button1**
  Name: `addToStructureButton`
  Text: `&Add to Structure`
- **Button2**
  Name: `readFromStructure`
  Text: `&Read from Structure`
- **Button3**
  Name: `clearButton`
  Text: `&Clear`
- **Button4**
  Name: `exitButton`
  Text: `E&xit`
- **ListBox1**
  Name: `structureListListBox`

Step 1: Structure Declaration

To accomplish this task, you need to add the following statements under the `Form`'s declaration area:

```
Public Class structureForm
'Declare the structure to hold course information
Structure courses
    'declare the structure's members which
    'include Course Number, Course Name and
    'Course tuition
    Public courseNumberInteger As Integer
    Public courseTuition As Decimal
    Public CourseName As String
End Structure
```

As you can see, structure members appear between `Structure` and `End Structure` statements. The name of the structure is `Courses`.

Step 2: Create an Instance of the New Structure You Defined

In this step, we will create an instance of the new structure we created. We can use the new instance to store the data that is supplied by the user. Here is how it is done:

```
'declaring a variable as course structure type.
'This is a new instance of the structure we declared
Dim onlineCourses As courses
```

This statement should be placed right under the `End Structure` block. Notice that we didn't use the `New` keyword to create an instance of our `Courses` structure. The new instance is called `OnlineCourses`.

Step 3: Load the New Instance of Our Structure with Data

In this step, we store the data in the properties of our structure. The users supply the data through a `Form` interface that we have designed. We can refer to these properties any time we need them. Now, double-click on the `addToStructureButton` and type the following in its subprocedure:

```
Private Sub addToStructureButton_Click _
(ByVal sender As System.Object, _
ByVal e As System.EventArgs) Handles addToStructureButton.Click
    'making the listbox visible
    Me.structureListListBox.Visible = False
    'loading the structure with the
    'users input
    Try
        Me.onlineCourses.CourseName = _
    Me.courseNameTextBox.Text
    Me.onlineCourses.courseNumberInteger = _
Integer.Parse(Me.courseNumberTextBox.Text)
        Me.onlineCourses.courseTuition = _
Decimal.Parse(Me.courseTuitionTextBox.Text)
        'if data type doesn't match, display a message
    Catch ex As Exception
```

```
        MessageBox.Show("Error in processing-check your input", _
            "Warning", MessageBoxButtons.OK, MessageBoxIcon.Information)
    End Try
    Me.structureListListBox.Items.Clear()
End Sub
```

We have added some housekeeping codes on the top of the procedure. The main segment is located within the Try/Catch block. We are filling the properties with the data that are supplied by the user. The only validation we have added is to catch wrong type values. To make it easier to follow, we did not want to impose other types of validations.

Step 4: Read the Values from the Structure

This step is the opposite of what we did in our last step. Now we extract the data that is stored in the properties of the onlineCourses structure. Double-click on the readFromStructureButton and add the following:

```
Private Sub readFromStructure_Click _
(ByVal sender As System.Object, _
ByVal e As System.EventArgs) Handles readFromStructure.Click
    'clear the listbox and make it visible
    Me.structureListListBox.Items.Clear()
    Me.structureListListBox.Visible = True
    'display the members of structure in the listbox
    Me.structureListListBox.Items.Add("Course Name " _
    & Me.onlineCourses.CourseName)
    Me.structureListListBox.Items.Add("Course Number " _
    & Me.onlineCourses.courseNumberInteger)
    Me.structureListListBox.Items.Add("Course Tution " _
    & Me.onlineCourses.courseTuition)

End Sub
```

You can easily follow the process. Pay attention to the line break symbols used in the above codes and most other codes used in this book.

Step 5: Complete other Housekeeping Tasks

This includes completing the Clear and Exit buttons. We will list the entire code here so you can compare it with your own:

```
Public Class structureForm
'Declare the structure to hold course information
Structure courses
    'declare the structure's members which
    'include Course Number, Course Name and
    'Course tuition
    Public courseNumberInteger As Integer
    Public courseTuition As Decimal
```

```
        Public CourseName As String
    End Structure
    'declaring a variable as course structure type.
    'This is a new instance of the structure we declared
    Dim onlineCourses As courses

    Private Sub structureForm_Load _
    (ByVal sender As System.Object, _
    ByVal e As System.EventArgs) Handles MyBase.Load
        'making the listbox invisible at the time
        'of data entry
        Me.structureListListBox.Visible = False
    End Sub


    Private Sub addToStructureButton_Click _
    (ByVal sender As System.Object, _
    ByVal e As System.EventArgs) Handles addToStructureButton.Click
        'making the listbox visible
        structureListListBox.Visible = False
        'loading the structure with the
        'users input
        Try
            Me.onlineCourses.CourseName = _
    Me.courseNameTextBox.Text
            Me.onlineCourses.courseNumberInteger = _
    Me.courseNumberTextBox.Text
            Me.onlineCourses.courseTuition = _
    Me.courseTuitionTextBox.Text
            'if data type doesn't match, display a message
        Catch ex As Exception
            MessageBox.Show("Error in processing-check your input", _
            "Warning", MessageBoxButtons.OK, MessageBoxIcon.Information)
        End Try
        Me.structureListListBox.Items.Clear()
    End Sub

    Private Sub readFromStructure_Click _
    (ByVal sender As System.Object, _
    ByVal e As System.EventArgs) Handles readFromStructure.Click
        'clear the listbox and make it visible
        Me.structureListListBox.Items.Clear()
        Me.structureListListBox.Visible = True
        'display the members of structure in the listbox
        Me.structureListListBox.Items.Add("Course Name " _
        & Me.onlineCourses.CourseName)
        Me.structureListListBox.Items.Add("Course Number " _
        & Me.onlineCourses.courseNumberInteger)
        Me.structureListListBox.Items.Add("Course Tuition " _
        & Me.onlineCourses.courseTuition)

    End Sub

    Private Sub clearButton_Click( _
    ByVal sender As System.Object, _
    ByVal e As System.EventArgs) Handles clearButton.Click
```

```
        'call a sub procedure to clear the textboxes and listbox
        Call clear()
    End Sub
    Private Sub clear()
        'Clear the textboxes and listbox
        Me.courseNameTextBox.Text = Nothing
        Me.courseNumberTextBox.Text = Nothing
        Me.courseTuitionTextBox.Text = Nothing
        Me.structureListListBox.Visible = False

    End Sub
    Private Sub exitButton_Click _
    (ByVal sender As System.Object, _
    ByVal e As System.EventArgs) Handles exitButton.Click
        'terminate the program
        Me.Close()
    End Sub
    End Class
```

Complete the project, save it, and hit F5 to run it. Figure 9.16 shows you what you should see.

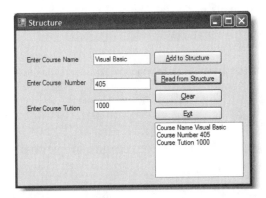

FIGURE 9.16   Structure program with Add and Read features.

You can view this solution under the Chapter 9 folder on the companion CD-ROM. The project is saved under its name, structure. Just copy the project folder to your hard drive and double-click on the .sln file.

SUMMARY

In this chapter, we covered classes, properties, methods, constructors, and structures. We showed you the step-by-step process of making your own classes and structures. We also explained many object-oriented terms such as Garbage Collector and shared properties.

Next

In Chapter 10 we will cover arrays and collections. We will show you how to create arrays and loop trough them and how to prevent errors. You will also learn about multidimensional arrays and collections.

DISCUSSION QUESTIONS

1. What is the `WithEvent` keyword? What does it do in an object-oriented environment?
2. What is the difference between a class and a structure? Please explain.
3. Can we have more than one class file in a project? Please explain.
4. What kind of help we can get from the Object Browser?
5. Is there a way to design classes, properties, and methods using visual tools? Please explain.

Exercise 1

Modify Example 1 and add a `ComboBox` and a `ListBox` and place items within them at runtime.

Exercise 2

Use the View Class Diagram tool to design a simple class with properties and methods.

Key Terms

- View Class Diagram
- Structure
- Class
- Constructors
- Properties
- Methods
- Garbage Collector

10 ░ Arrays and Collections

In This Chapter

- ■ Arrays
- ■ Collections

ARRAYS

In previous chapters, we introduced you to `ListBox` and `ComboBox`. Understanding those concepts will make it easier to understand the concept of arrays. In the `ListBox` example, we referred to each `ListBox` item by its index. An array is very similar to that, with one major difference. We do not store our values in the property of a control. In fact, we do not add a new control to our form in order to store array values. We create a series of variables that carry the same names, and each variable can hold a date. As with `ListBox` and `ComboBox`, we refer to each item of our array by using its index. Each variable in an array is called an *array element,* and the index that identifies each element is known as the *subscript.*

Array Dimensions, Subscripts, and Elements

The number of subscripts in an array identifies the *dimension,* or *rank,* of the array. The subscript can be a numeric value, a numeric constant, or a variable. We store these values in the main memory of the computer. There are many ways to declare an array.

Array Size

The total number of elements in an array is known as array size. The array size ranges from zero to the highest subscript that is declared by the programmer. An array with a zero subscript does not represent a zero-length array. It is good to know that even an empty array, which has zero length, still exists and in Visual Basic's eyes, is not equal to nothing. To calculate the total size of the array, we need to add up the length of all dimensions that are declared within an array. We can find the size of the array by using the array's Length property. Although arrays that are declared by specific dimensions are know as *fixed-size* arrays, their size can be changed by using the Redim keyword, which we will discuss later. The size of an array does not represent the amount of storage needed for each array. The total number of elements included within an array indicates the length of its dimensions.

Array Type

Once we declare an array type, all of the elements that are stored within it must have the same type. However, the array could be declared as an object, which allows its members to be of a different type.

Lbound **and** Ubound

The lowest available subscript in an array is called Lbound. The value is always an integer and returns zero value. The highest subscript in an array is called Ubound. We will be demonstrating these two functions later.

Declaring an Array

Here is the general format used to declare an array:

```
Dim ArrayName (upperSubscript) as Type
```

We can declare our arrays by using a Dim, Public, Private, or Friend. The subscript shows the maximum number of elements we want to store in our array. Here are some examples:

```
Dim colorString (3) as String
```

In the above statements, we can store five string values in our array. The range of elements will be from zero to four: 0, 1, 2, 3, and 4. The lower subscript is always zero. The type of our array is string, so only the string data type can be stored in the array elements.

Here are two other array declarations:

```
Dim averageDecimal (4) as Decimal
Dim  CreditInteger (4) as Integer
```

These are very similar to the first declaration. However, the data types for these two statements are different.

One-Dimensional Arrays

The simplest form of array is a *one-dimensional array*. With this form of array, each element of the array represents one data element. This is very similar to one column of a spreadsheet table. Figure 10.1 shows how our `colorString` array that we declared above is represented.

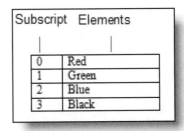

FIGURE 10.1   One-dimensional array with subscript and elements.

EXAMPLE 1

Start a new project and call it `array_sample`.

Change your form parameters according to the following:

■ **Form1**
  Name: `arraySampleForm`
  Text: `Array Sample`
  Size: `320, 224`

Add the following controls to your form:

■ **Label1**
  Name: `subscript0Label`
  Text: `Subscript 0`
■ **Label2**
  Name: `subscript1Label`
  Text: `Subscript 1`
■ **Label3**
  Name: `subscript2Label`
  Text: `Subscript 2`
■ **Label4**
  Name: `subscript3Label`
  Text: `Subscript 3`

- **TextBox1**

  Name: subscript0TextBox

  Text: Subscript 0
- **TextBox2**

  Name: subscript1TextBox

  Text: Subscript 1
- **TextBox3**

  Name: subscript2TextBox

  Text: Subscript 2
- **TextBox4**

  Name: subscript3TextBox

  Text: Subscript 3
- **ListBox1**

  Name: arrayList
- **Button1**

  Name: exitButton

  Text: E&xit

At the module level, let us declare our array by placing the following statement:

```
Public Class arraySampleForm
'Declare an array with 4 elements
Dim colorString(3) As String
```

Now we want to load our array with data and display them in the TextBoxes we placed on our page. Type the following statements under the form_Load subprocedure:

```
Private Sub arraySampleForm_Load _
(ByVal sender As System.Object, _
ByVal e As System.EventArgs) _
Handles MyBase.Load
    'Load the array with data
    colorString(0) = "Red"
    colorString(1) = "Green"
    colorString(2) = "Blue"
    colorString(3) = "Black"
    'Display the array's content in the textboxes
    Me.subscript0TextBox.Text = colorString(0)
    Me.subscript1TextBox.Text = colorString(1)
    Me.subscript2TextBox.Text = colorString(2)
    Me.subscript3TextBox.Text = colorString(3)
    'Display the array's content in the ListBox
    Me.arrayListBox.Items.Add(colorString(0))
    Me.arrayListBox.Items.Add(colorString(1))
    Me.arrayListBox.Items.Add(colorString(2))
    Me.arrayListBox.Items.Add(colorString(3))
End Sub
```

Type the following under the `exitButton`:

```
    Private Sub exitButton_Click(ByVal sender As System.Object, ByVal e As
System.EventArgs) Handles exitButton.Click
        'terminate the program
        Me.Close()
    End Sub
```

Now run the project. The content of our array is displayed in the `TextBoxes` we placed on our form (see Figure 10.2).

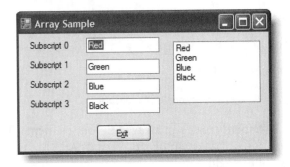

FIGURE 10.2   Loading and displaying the array.

You can view this solution under the Chapter 10 folder on the companion CD-ROM. The project is saved under its name, `array_sample`. Just copy the project folder to your hard drive and double-click on the .sln file.

EXAMPLE 2: OBJECT TYPE

We want to declare an array with a specified type so that all elements within the array will have the same type. However, it is possible to store values from different data types in an array. If we are not sure about the type of data we want to store in our array and the values might have mixed types, then we should declare our array with an object type.

Start a new project and call it `arrayObject`. We need the following:

- **Form1**
  Name: `arrayObjectForm`
  Text: `Displaying Object Type`
- **Label1**
  Name: `arrayLabel`
  Text: `Display Array`

- **ListBox1**
  Name: `arrayListBox`
- **Button1**
  Name: `processButton`
  Text: `&Process`
- **Button2**
  Name: `clearButton`
  Text: `&Clear`
- **Button3**
  Name: `exitButton`
  Text: `E&xit`

As you did for the last project, add the following statement:

```
Public Class objectTypeForm
'Declare Object Type array
Dim BookInformation(3) As Object
```

This statement creates an array with four elements. The type is declared as object, so any type of data can be stored in it. Add the following statement into the Form_load subprocedure of the Form:

```
Private Sub objectTypeForm_Load(ByVal sender As System.Object, _
ByVal e As System.EventArgs) Handles MyBase.Load
    'Loading the array
    BookInformation(0) = "Visual Basic 2005 by Practice"
    BookInformation(1) = "Mike Mostafavi"
    BookInformation(2) = 49.95
    BookInformation(3) = 500

End Sub
```

We have stored three types of data in our array: string, decimal, and integer. The array represents the book's name, the author's name, the price of the book, and the number of pages in the book.

Now add the following statements under the processButton:

```
Private Sub processButton_Click _
(ByVal sender As System.Object, _
ByVal e As System.EventArgs) _
Handles processButton.Click
    'Displaying the array using a loop
    Me.arrayListBox.Items.Clear()
    Dim index As Integer
    For index = 0 To 3
        Me.arrayListBox.Items.Add(BookInformation(index))
    Next
End Sub
```

In the first statement, we cleared the content of the ListBox before we displayed new data. The next statement reads the contents of our array one by one and displays them in the ListBox. We use a For/Next loop to accomplish this task.

Add the following statement under the clearButton:

```
Private Sub clearButton_Click _
(ByVal sender As System.Object, _
ByVal e As System.EventArgs) _
Handles clearButton.Click
    'Clear the ListBox
    Me.arrayListBox.Items.Clear()
End Sub
```

Code the exitButton and run the project (see Figure 10.3).

FIGURE 10.3   Object type array.

You can view this solution under the Chapter 10 folder on the companion CD-ROM. The project is saved under its name, arrayObject. Just copy the project folder to your hard drive and double-click on the .sln file.

Out of Range Subscripts

The subscript represents the highest number of elements an array can hold. Referring to a subscript that is greater than what you have specified in your Dim statement will cause an error. Let's look at an example and evaluate the code.

EXAMPLE 3

Create a new project and call it outOfRangeArray. Change your form parameters according to the following:

- **Form1**
  Name: errorForm
  Text: Subscript Error
- **Label1**
  Name: arrayLabel
  Text: List of Elements
- **ListBox1**
  Name: arrayListBox
- **Button1**
  Name: exitButton
  Text: E&xit

Your form should look like Figure 10.4.

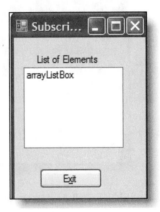

FIGURE 10.4 outOfRangeArray
Form **design.**

As we did before, place the following statement in an appropriate place:

```
Public Class errorForm
'Declare an array with 4 elements in it
Dim errorInteger(3) As Integer
```

Place the following statements under the Form_load subprocedure:

```
Private Sub errorForm_Load _
(ByVal sender As System.Object, _
ByVal e As System.EventArgs) Handles MyBase.Load
    'Load the array with values
    errorInteger(0) = 100
```

```
        errorInteger(1) = 200
        errorInteger(2) = 300
        errorInteger(3) = 400
        'Read the array and display the content of it in the listBox
        Dim index As Integer
        For index = 0 To 4
            Me.arrayListBox.Items.Add(errorInteger(index))
        Next
    End Sub
```

The loop we have set up will try to read one element beyond the maximum number of elements we have declared in our DIM statement. There is no syntax error in the above statement, but once you try to run this project, the program will crash owing to a logical error that we explained in Chapter 3 (see Figure 10.5).

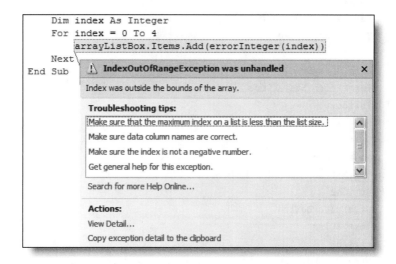

FIGURE 10.5 Out of Range error message.

In the above code, the IndexOutOfRangeException occurs because the index was outside the bounds of our array. We can fix the problem by changing the current loop statement to the following:

```
    For index = 0 To 3
            Me.arrayListBox.Items.Add(errorInteger(index))
        Next
```

You can view this solution under the Chapter 10 folder on the companion CD-ROM. The project is saved under its name, outOfRangeArray. Just copy the project folder to your hard drive and double-click on the .sln file.

Array Lookup

One of the advantages of an array is the Lookup feature. This is also known as *Table Search* or *Table Lookup*. We can store valid data in the array element and use it as a validation tool. For example, we can store states' abbreviation codes in our array. Once the user enters a state's two-letter abbreviation code, we can search our array to see if the state code that the user has entered is valid or not. The following example will show how this task can be accomplished:

Example 4

Create a new project and call it arrayLookUpProject. Change your Form parameters according to the following:

- **Form1**
  Name: arrayLookupForm
  Text: Array Lookup
- **Label1**
  Name: arrayLabel
  Text: Enter State Code
- **TextBox1**
  Name: lookupTextBox
- **Button1**
  Name: processButton
  Text: &Process
- **Button2**
  Name: clearButton
  Text: &Clear
- **Button3**
  Name: exitButton
  Text: E&xit

Place the following statement in an appropriate location as you did in the last few projects:

```
Public Class arrayLookupForm
'Create an array with 5 elements
Dim states(4) As String
```

Type the following statements under the Form_load subprocedure:

```
Private Sub arrayLookupForm_Load _
(ByVal sender As System.Object, _
ByVal e As System.EventArgs) Handles MyBase.Load
    'Load the array with values
```

```
    states(0) = "OR"
    states(1) = "WA"
    states(2) = "CA"
    states(3) = "ID"
    states(4) = "NY"

End Sub
```

Now type these statements under the processButton:

```
Private Sub processButton _Click _
(ByVal sender As System.Object, _
ByVal e As System.EventArgs) Handles processButton.Click
    'Declare the index and boolean variables
    Dim index As Integer
    Dim BooleanIndex As Boolean
    'Search the array to find user's input by using a loop
    For index = 0 To 4
        'If it is found then set the boolean variable to True
        If Me.lookupTextBox.Text.ToUpper = states(index) Then
            BooleanIndex = True
        End If
    Next
    'If the value is found, first display a message,
    'then set the backcolor of textbox to Green and forecolor of textbox
    'to White

    If BooleanIndex Then
        MessageBox.Show("The state was found!" "Good News!")
        Me.lookupTextBox.BackColor = Color.Green
        Me.lookupTextBox.ForeColor = Color.White
    Else
        'If the text is not found,
        'then display a message and turn the backcolor to default
        MessageBox.Show("The state couldn't be found","Sorry")
        Me.lookupTextBox.Text = Nothing
        Me.lookupTextBox.BackColor = Color.Empty
    End If
    'set the focus to the textbox
    Me.lookupTextBox.Focus()
End Sub
```

Add the following under the clearButton:

```
Private Sub clearButton_Click _
(ByVal sender As System.Object, _
ByVal e As System.EventArgs) Handles clearButton.Click
    'Reset the textbox forecolor and backcolor
    Me.lookupTextBox.Text = Nothing
    Me.lookupTextBox.BackColor = Color.Empty
    Me.lookupTextBox.ForeColor = Color.Empty
End Sub
```

Complete the exitButton and run the project.

Once the user enters a value in the lookup TextBox and presses on the Process button, the loop searches the array for a matching value. If the value the user has entered is found within the array, the value of the boolean variable will be set to True. The user will be informed by a MessageBox that will be displayed. At the same time, the background color of the TextBox changes to green and the ForeColor becomes white. However, if the entered value is not found within the array, the boolean variable will be set to False and the user will receive a MessageBox telling him that his entry was not found in the array (see Figure 10.6).

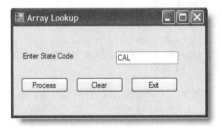

FIGURE 10.6 Array *Lookup*.

ON THE CD   You can view this solution under the Chapter 10 folder on the companion CD-ROM. The project is saved under its name, arrayLookUpProject. Just copy the project folder to your hard drive and double-click on the .sln file.

Multidimensional Array

Using a one-dimensional array is fine, and you saw one simple application for it. However, occasionally we need to use a multidimensional array for business purposes. You can visualize a spreadsheet as a multidimensional array with rows and columns. We can expand our state abbreviation example to come up with a two-dimensional array. Let us say that once the user's entry for a state's two-letter code is found, we want to display the whole state name (see Figure 10.7).

State Abbreviation	State Name
OR	OREGON
WA	WASHINGTON
CA	CALIFORNIA
ID	IDAHO
NY	NEW YORK

FIGURE 10.7 Two-dimensional array.

Two-dimensional arrays can be declared as follows:

```
DIM Array Name (rows, columns) as Data Type
```

Here is an example:

```
Dim stateString(4, 1) As String
```

As you can see, our two-dimensional array will have five rows and two columns. Here is how we can load our array:

```
stateString (0, 0) = "OR"
stateString (0, 1) = "Oregon"
stateString (1, 0) = "WA"
stateString (1, 1) = "Washington"
stateString (2, 0) = "CA"
stateString (2, 1) = "California"
stateString (3, 0) = "ID"
stateString (3, 1) = "Idaho"
stateString (4, 0) = "NY"
stateString (4, 1) = "New York"
```

It is also possible to declare this two-dimensional array as follows:

```
Dim statesString(,) As String = {{"OR", "OREGON"}, _
{"WA", "WASHINGTON"}, {"CA", "CALIFORNIA"}, _
  {"ID", "IDAHO"}, {"NY", "NEW YORK"}}
```

The above statements will produce the same output.

EXAMPLE 5

Create a new project and call it `multidemensionalArray`. This project is very similar to our array `Lookup` project we wrote for a one-dimensional array project. However, in this project, we will search a two-dimensional array to find an entry. We need the following:

▪ **Form1**
   Name: twoDimArrayForm
   Text: Two Dimensional Array
   Size: 368, 264
▪ **Label1**
   Name: titleLabel
   Text: Table Search
▪ **Label2**
   Name: stateCodeLabel
   Text: Enter State's Two-Letter Code

- **TextBox1**

   Name: stateCodeTextBox
- **Label3**

   Name: stateNameLabel

   Text: State Name
- **Label4**

   Name: stateFoundLabel

   BorderStyle: Fixed3D

   FlatStyle: PopUp
- **Button1**

   Name: searchButton

   Text: &Search
- **Button2**

   Name: clearButon

   Text: &Clear
- **Button3**

   Name: exitButton

   Text: E&xit

In this simple project, we will search our two-dimensional array for the user's entry. If the entry is found, we will display the state's complete name. If the entry is not found, a message will be displayed. Let's put the following statement in the form's declaration area:

```
Public Class twoDimArrayForm
 'Declare a two Dimensional array with no size specified
 ' and load it with values at the same time
 Dim statesString(,) As String = {{"OR", "OREGON"}, _
 {"WA", "WASHINGTON"}, {"CA", "CALIFORNIA"}, _
 {"ID", "IDAHO"}, {"NY", "NEW YORK"}}
```

As you can see, we did not specify any size for our array. The values are loaded along with the array declaration.

Now add the following statements under the searchButton:

```
Private Sub searchButton_Click _
(ByVal sender As System.Object, _
ByVal e As System.EventArgs) Handles searchButton.Click
    'Declare the search-index variables
    Dim index1Integer, index2Integer As Integer
    Dim foundBoolean As Boolean

    'Find the TextBox entry in the states array
    For index1Integer = 0 To 4
        For index2Integer = 0 To 4
```

```
            If statesString(index1Integer, 0) _
            = Me.stateCodeTextBox.Text.ToUpper Then
                Me.stateFoundLebel.Text = _
                statesString(index1Integer, 1)
                foundBoolean = True
            End If
        Next
    Next

    'Show a message if the value of the TextBox was not found
    If Not foundBoolean Then
        MessageBox.Show _
        (Me.stateCodeTextBox.Text & " couldn't be found. Try again.", _
            "Two-Dimensional Array", _
            MessageBoxButtons.OK, _
            MessageBoxIcon.Information)
        Me.stateCodeTextBox.Focus()
        Me.stateCodeTextBox.Text = Nothing
    End If
End Sub
```

In the above codes, we are using a nested For/Next conditional statement to search through a multidimensional array.

Now complete the Clear and Exit buttons and run the project (see Figure 10.8).

FIGURE 10.8 Two-dimensional array project in running state.

ON THE CD

You can view this solution under the Chapter 10 folder on the companion CD-ROM. The project is saved under its name, multiDemensionalArray. Just copy the project folder to your hard drive and double-click on the .sln file.

EXAMPLE 6

Start a new project and call it arraySize. We need the following:

- **Form1**
  Name: arraySizeForm
  Text: Array Size
- **Label1**
  Name: arraySizeLabel
  Text: Array Size
- **Label2**
  Name: arrayLenLabel
- **Label3**
  Name: arrayLowSubscriptLabel
  Text: Low Subscript
- **Label4**
  Name: arrayLowSubLabel
- **Label5**
  Name: arrayHighSubscriptLabel
  Text: High Subscript
- **Label6**
  Name: arrayHighSubLabel
- **ListBox1**
  Name: arrayListBox
- **Button1**
  Name: processButton
  Text: &Process
- **Button2**
  Name: exitButton
  Text: E&xit

Double-click on the processButton and type the following:

```
Private Sub processButton_Click _
(ByVal sender As System.Object, _
ByVal e As System.EventArgs) Handles processButton.Click
    'Declare an array and the counter variables
    Dim arrayInteger(10), counter As Integer
    'Initialize the array by using a loop
    For counter = LBound(arrayInteger) To UBound(arrayInteger)
        'increment the value of the subscript
        arrayInteger(counter) = counter + 1
        'display the arrays elements in the listbox
        Me.arrayListBox.Items.Add(arrayInteger(counter) - 1)
    Next
    'display the length, lbound and Ubound subscripts
    Me.arrayLenLabel.Text = arrayInteger.Length
    Me.arrayLowSubLabel.Text = LBound(arrayInteger)
    Me.arrayHighSubLabel.Text = UBound(arrayInteger)
End Sub
```

We used Lbound and Ubound as our loop variables. Complete the Exit button's code, save the project, and run it (see Figure 10.9).

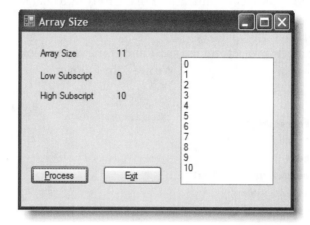

FIGURE 10.9 Showing the array size and subscripts.

 You can view this solution under the Chapter 10 folder on the companion CD-ROM. The project is saved under its name, arraySize. Just copy the project folder to your hard drive and double-click on the .sln file.

Redim **and** Preserve **in Dynamic Arrays**

In our previous examples, we specified the number of elements that could be stored in an array, but occasionally we need to change the size of our array after it is declared. This could happen in an interactive program in which users supply the elements of our arrays. We can change the size of our dynamic array in two ways:

```
Redim Variable-Name(subscript)
Redim Preserve Variable-Name(subscript)
```

In the first statement, we changed the size of our array. However, the Redim statement clears the content of our array, and we lose the data we previously stored in it. Redim variables can only be used within procedures, not by themselves, so before we use them, we need to declare our arrays by using Dim and other keywords we referenced above.

In the second statement, we change the size of the array but we *preserve* the data that was stored in it. The content of the array will be copied into the new resized array. We can make the size of the array smaller or larger than the original size, which frees up space but also results in data loss.

The Preserve modifier allows us to retain the information while we are resizing the arrays, but then we can only change the last dimension of our array, and the other dimensions need to stay unchanged. The Redim statement cannot be used to change the number of dimensions of an array or its data type.

EXAMPLE 7

Create a new project and use Redim and Preserve and look at the result. Name your new project redimAndPreserve. We need the following:

- **Form1**
  Name: redimPreserveForm
  Text: Redim and Preserve
- **Label1**
  Name: customerNameLabel
  Text: Enter Name
- **TextBox1**
  Name: customerNameTextBox
- **Label2**
  Name: addedNamesListBox
- **Button1**
  Name: redimButton
  Text: &Redim
- **Button2**
  Name: exitButton
  Text: E&xit

Now add the following statements under the form declaration area:

```
Public Class redimPreserveForm
'Declare the array with one element
Private arrayCustomerString(0) As String
```

These statements declare our array. Now double-click on the redimButton and add the following statements:

```
Private Sub redimButton_Click _
(ByVal sender As System.Object, ByVal e As System.EventArgs) _
Handles redimButton.Click
    'Name entry is required
    'declare variables
    Dim nameString As String = Me.customerNameTextBox.Text.Trim
    Dim numberOfElementsInt32, IndexInt32 As Int32
    'checking for blanks
    If nameString = Nothing Then
```

```
        MessageBox.Show("Name is required.", _
            "ReDim Array", _
            MessageBoxButtons.OK, _
            MessageBoxIcon.Information)
        Me.customerNameTextBox.Focus()
        Exit Sub
    End If


    'ReDim and Preserve the array arrayCustomerString
    numberOfElementsInt32 = UBound(arrayCustomerString)
    If arrayCustomerString(0) Is Nothing Then
        numberOfElementsInt32 = 0
        ReDim arrayCustomerString(numberOfElementsInt32)
    Else
        numberOfElementsInt32 += 1
        ReDim Preserve arrayCustomerString(numberOfElementsInt32)
    End If


    'Load the array arrayCustomerString with values
    'from(CutomerNameTextBox)
    arrayCustomerString(numberOfElementsInt32) = nameString


    'Load the ListBox addedNamesListBox with data
    ' from the ArrayCustomerString
    With Me.addedNamesListBox
        .Items.Clear()

        For IndexInt32 = LBound(arrayCustomerString) _
        To UBound(arrayCustomerString)
            .Items.Add(arrayCustomerString(IndexInt32))
        Next IndexInt32

        .SelectedIndex = IndexInt32 - 1
    End With
    'Clear the CustomerNameTextBox and focus to it.
    Me.customerNameTextBox.Clear()
    Me.customerNameTextBox.Focus()
End Sub
```

In this subprocedure, we accept data from the user, validate it to make sure it is not blank, add it to our array, resize the array with the Redim statement, and preserve the modifier and display the data in the ListBox.

Complete the exitButton, save your project, and run it. Enter values to the TextBox and click on *Add*. Figure 10.10 shows the screenshot for the running program with added data. You will see many similarities between this example and one of the examples we demonstrated in Chapter 7, but that example did not use arrays.

ON THE CD You can view this solution under the Chapter 10 folder on the companion CD-ROM. The project is saved under its name, redimAndPreserve. Just copy the project folder to your hard drive and double-click on the .sln file.

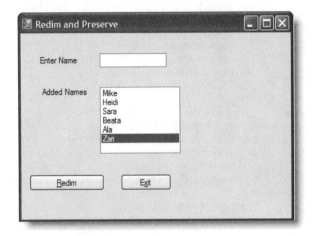

FIGURE 10.10   Redim and Preserve program screenshot.

Array **Class**

Under the .NET Framework, the Array class supports arrays. The Array class is a member of the System namespace, so we can use the System.Array properties and methods in our array projects. Once you type System.Array., the dot notation will show you all valid methods (see Figure 10.11).

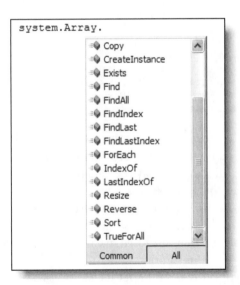

FIGURE 10.11   System.Array. lists of methods.

Let us look at a simple example to show some of these methods and properties.

EXAMPLE 8: USING RANK, For Each LOOP, Sort, Reverse, IndexOf, AND MORE
In this example, we will be using some of the methods and properties of the array. Start a new project, and name it `arraySort`. Let's have the following:

- **Form1**
  Name: arrayForm
  Text: Array's Methods and Properties
- **ListBox1**
  Name: arrayListBox
- **Button1**
  Name: sortButton
  Text: &Sort
- **Button2**
  Name: reverseButton
  Text: &Reverse
- **Button3**
  Name: rankButton
  Text: &Display Rank
- **Button4**
  Name: arrayIndexOfButton
  Text: &Index
- **Button5**
  Name: forEachButton
  Text: &For Each Loop
- **Button6**
  Name: exitButton
  Text: E&xit

Double-click on the `sortButton` and add the following statements:

```
Private Sub sortButton_Click _
(ByVal sender As System.Object, ByVal e As System.EventArgs) _
Handles sortButton.Click
    'This section will sort the array in ascending order
    Me.arrayListBox.Items.Clear()
    Array.Sort(arraySortString)
    Dim index As Integer
    For index = 0 To 3
        Me.arrayListBox.Items.Add(arraySortString(index))
    Next
End Sub
```

In this subprocedure, we are using the `Array.Sort` method to sort the content of the array in an ascending order. We will display the sorted elements in the `arrayListBox`.

Now double-click on the `reverseButton` and type in the following statements:

```
Private Sub reverseButton_Click _
(ByVal sender As System.Object, _
ByVal e As System.EventArgs) Handles reverseButton.Click
    'This section sorts the array in descending order
    Me.arrayListBox.Items.Clear()
    Array.Reverse(arraySortString)
    Dim index As Integer
    For index = 0 To 3
        Me.arrayListBox.Items.Add(arraySortString(index))
    Next
End Sub
```

These codes will sort the elements of the array in descending order by using the `Array.Reverse` method and display them in the `arrayListBox`.

Double-click on the `displayRankButton` and use the `rank` property to display the number of dimensions in the array.

```
Private Sub rankButton_Click _
(ByVal sender As System.Object, _
ByVal e As System.EventArgs) Handles rankButton.Click
    'Displaying array rank"
    MessageBox.Show("The Array Rank is: " _
    & arraySortString.Rank, "Array rank")
End Sub
```

In the following statements that we add under the `indexButton`, we use an array method called `IndexOf`. This method allows us to search the array to find an object. Once it is found, it reports the index of the first occurrence of the object within the array. Double-click on the `indexButton` and add the following:

```
Private Sub arrayIndexOfButton_Click _
(ByVal sender As System.Object, _
ByVal e As System.EventArgs) Handles arrayIndexOfButton.Click
    'Searching the array using Indexof
    Dim SearchString As String
    SearchString = InputBox("Enter the name you are looking for" _
    , "Searching the array")
    Dim searchIndex As Integer
    'Search the array for user's input and report its index if found
    searchIndex = (Array.IndexOf(arraySortString, _
    SearchString.ToUpper))
    If searchIndex < 0 Then
        'If the object is not found,
        ' then display the following message
```

```
        MessageBox.Show("The value couldn't be found", "Not Found")
    Else
        'If found, report the index
        MessageBox.Show("The element has an index of " _
        & searchIndex, "Found!")
    End If
End Sub
```

Now, we need to use a For Each loop to search the array. You were introduced to this loop in Chapter 7. Here is another application of it. Double-click the forEachButton and type the following:

```
Private Sub forEachButton_Click _
(ByVal sender As System.Object, _
ByVal e As System.EventArgs) Handles forEachButton.Click
    'Searching the array using For Each loop
    Dim SearchString As String
    SearchString = InputBox("Enter the name you are looking for" _
    , "Searching the array")

    For Each mysearch As String In arraySortString
        If mysearch = SearchString.ToUpper Then
            MessageBox.Show(mysearch & " Was found", _
            "Search was successful")
        End If

    Next
End Sub
```

Now complete the exitButton and run the project (see Figure 10.12).

FIGURE 10.12 Example 8,
ArraySort screenshot.

You can view this solution under the Chapter 10 folder on the companion CD-ROM. The project is saved under its name, arraySort. Just copy the project folder to your hard drive and double-click on the .sln file.

COLLECTIONS

In simple language, *collection* means gathering related objects in one place in order to manage them. You have been working with Forms and placing objects on them and you have learned that you can refer to any of those object as you wish. How does the Form keep track of objects you place on it? The answer is simple. There is one object called Control Collection and all objects are represented by it. In addition to this object is a class called Collection. By using this class, you can create your own collections and access them any time you wish.

Creating Your Own Collection

Here are a few steps we need to take in order to create our own collection.

Step 1: Declaration of Collection Variables

Declare the Collection variable as we did when creating all other objects and instantiate the object. Here is an example:

```
Dim shoes As New Collection
```

Step 2: Declaration of Members

Declare the members that need to be added to the collection:

```
Dim jogging, tennis, basketball As String
```

Step 3: Assigning Values to Members

Assign values to the member's variables:

```
jogging = "White Large"
tennis = "Black Small"
basketball = "Red Medium"
```

Step 4: Adding Members to the Collection using the Add Method

Add these new members to our collection using the Add method. We can also pick a uniqe string value that identifies each member. Each member has an index number that shows the sequence of the member within the collection (see Figure 10.13).

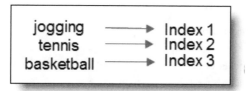

FIGURE 10.13 Collection's index.

In this example, the index starts with *one,* not zero. This is called a one-based collection. There are other collections that have a zero-based index. Controls Collection is an example of zero-based collection. Here is an example of one-based collection:

```
shoes.Add(jogging, "LARGE")
shoes.Add(tennis, "SMALL")
shoes.Add(basketball, "MEDIUM")
```

There are three members in this collection. We will use the collection's Count property to report the number of members in each collection.

Step 5: Access the Members

Loop through the members that you added to the collection in order to display them. Here is an example:

```
For Each mystring In shoes
Me.collectionListBox.Items.Add(mystring)
    Next
```

EXAMPLE 9

Start a new project and practice what we learned in this section. Name your new project Collections. We need the following:

- **Form1**
  Name: collectionForm
  Text: Collection
- **GroupBox1**
  Name: searchGroupBox
  Text: Search
- **Label1**
  Name: searchLabel
  Text: Enter Search String

- **TextBox1**
  Name: searchTextBox
- **Button1**
  Name: searchButton
  Text: &Search
- **GroupBox2**
  Name: operationGroupBox
  Text: Operation
- **Button2**
  Name: clearButton
  Text: &Clear
- **Button3**
  Name: exitButton
  Text: &Exit
- **GroupBox3**
  Name: removeGroupBox
  Text: Remove From Collection
- **ComboBox1**
  Name: removeComboBox
  Text: Remove Shoes From Collection
- **GroupBox4**
  Name: displayGroupBox
  Text: Display Collection
- **Button4**
  Name: displayButton
  Text: &Display
- **ListBox1**
  Name: collectionListBox
- **Label2**
  Name: countLabel
  Text: Count
- **Label3**
  Name: countOutLabel
  Text: Member Count
- **ToolTip1**
  Name: collectionToolTip

Figure 10.14 shows the Form design.

Double-click the Form and place the following codes under the Form's general declaration area:

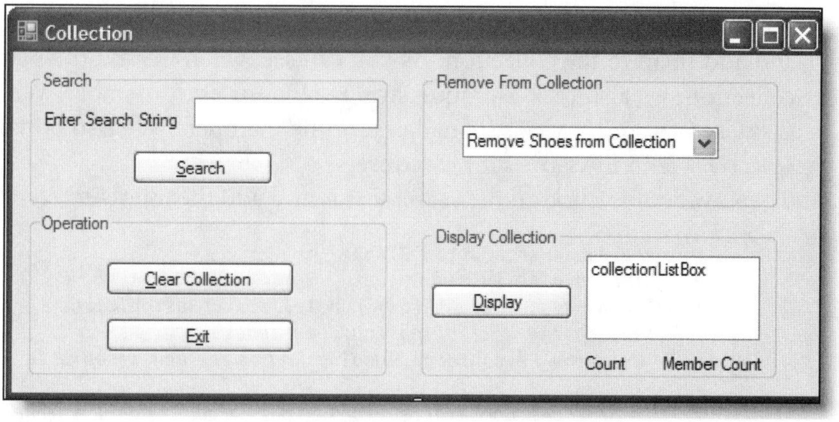

FIGURE 10.14 Example 9 Form design.

```
Public Class collectionForm
'Declare the shoes as collection type
Dim shoes As New Collection
'Declare the member variables
Dim jogging, tennis, basketball As String
'Declare a search String
Dim mystring As String
```

We have declared our new collection, called shoes, and we declared our member variables as string type.

Now type in the following statements under the Form's Click subprocedure:

```
Private Sub Form1_Load _
(ByVal sender As System.Object, _
ByVal e As System.EventArgs) Handles MyBase.Load
    'assign values to members
    jogging = "White Large"
    tennis = "Black Small"
    basketball = "Red Medium"
    'add new members to the collection. Also
    'add a unique string key to each members'variables
    Me.shoes.Add(jogging, "LARGE")
    Me.shoes.Add(tennis, "SMALL")
    Me.shoes.Add(basketball, "MEDIUM")
    'Populate the remove ComboBox with new items
    Me.removeComboBox.Items.Add("Remove Jogging Shoes")
    Me.removeComboBox.Items.Add("Remove Tennis Shoes")
    Me.removeComboBox.Items.Add("Remove Basketball Shoes")

End Sub
```

As explained within the comments, first we assign values to members' variables and add them to the collection. As you can see, when we add the members to the collection, we also pick a unique string value for each member. We have picked LARGE, MEDIUM, and SMALL as string keys for the members. We also populated the re-moveComboBox in the same subprocedure.

Now double-click on the searchButton and add the following statements:

```
Private Sub searchButton_Click _
(ByVal sender As System.Object, _
ByVal e As System.EventArgs) Handles searchButton.Click
    'search the collection for user input.
    'Only the keys: large, medium and small are acceptable

    If Me.shoes.Contains(searchTextBox.Text.ToUpper) = True Then
        MessageBox.Show("The Following Item Was Found " _
        ControlChars.CrLf + Me.searchTextBox.Text, _
        "Item Found", MessageBoxButtons.OK, _
        MessageBoxIcon.Information)
    Else
        MsgBox("The desired customer is not in the collection.")
    End If

End Sub
```

As you can see, we accept the users' input and check it against three values: large, medium, and small. Appropriate MessageBoxes will be displayed if the search is successful or is not. To help the users, add the following string to the SearchTextBox ToolTip property:

```
Possible Input: Large, Medium and Small
```

Remove Method

You have learned how to declare a collection and add members to it. Now we need to discuss the Remove method. By using the Remove method, we can remove a member from the collection. We can accomplish this task in two ways:

- Using the index
- Using the key string

To use the index, we simply reference the member's index number. For example, to remove the first member, which is the jogging shoes, we reference index one:

```
shoes.Remove(1)
```

We can also remove an item by using the string key we added to the items during the add process:

```
shoes.Remove("LARGE")
```

Once you remove a member from the collection, the index value will be adjusted automatically to show the removal.

Now double-click on the `removeComboBox` and type the following:

```
Private Sub removeComboBox_SelectedIndexChanged _
(ByVal sender As System.Object, _
ByVal e As System.EventArgs) _
Handles removeComboBox.SelectedIndexChanged
    'remove the members using the string key
    Try
        Select Case removeComboBox.SelectedIndex
            Case 0
                Me.shoes.Remove("LARGE")
                MessageBox.Show("Jogging Shoes Removed", _
                "Warning", MessageBoxButtons.OK, _
                MessageBoxIcon.Information)
            Case 1
                Me.shoes.Remove("MEDIUM")
                MessageBox.Show("Tennis Shoes Removed", _
                "Warning", MessageBoxButtons.OK, _
                MessageBoxIcon.Information)

            Case 2
                Me.shoes.Remove("SMALL")
                MessageBox.Show("Basketball Shoes Removed", _
                "Warning", MessageBoxButtons.OK, _
                MessageBoxIcon.Information)
        End Select

    Catch ex As Exception
        MessageBox.Show("The referenced item couldn't be found", _
        "Warning", MessageBoxButtons.OK, _
MessageBoxIcon.Information)
        End Try

End Sub
```

In the above statements, we use the string key to remove an item from the collection.

As stated before, we can display all members or a specific member any time we wish. Now we want to use a `For/Each` loop to display all items and at the same time use the `Count` property to show the number of members in the collection.

Double-click on the `displayButton` and add the following statements:

```
Private Sub displayButton_Click _
(ByVal sender As System.Object, _
ByVal e As System.EventArgs) _
Handles displayButton.Click
```

```
'clear the collectionListBox before displaying data
collectionListBox.Items.Clear()
'loop through the members and display them
For Each mystring In shoes
    Me.collectionListBox.Items.Add(mystring)
Next
'Using the Count property, display the number of members in the
'collection
Me.countOutLabel.Text = shoes.Count

End Sub
```

Now, in order to use the Clear property, we will add the following statements under the clearButton:

```
Private Sub clearCollectionButton_Click _
    (ByVal sender As System.Object, _
    ByVal e As System.EventArgs) _
    Handles clearCollectionButton.Click
        'clear the collection
        MessageBox.Show("All items within the collection will be cleared", _
        "Warning")
        Me.shoes.Clear()
    End Sub
```

Now complete the exitButton, save your project, and run it. Figure 10.15 shows the screenshot.

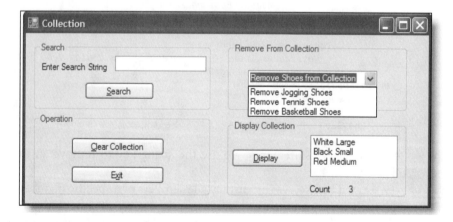

FIGURE 10.15 Example 9 at runtime.

ON THE CD

You can view this solution under the Chapter 10 folder on the companion CD-ROM. The project is saved under its name, collection. Just copy the project folder to your hard drive and double-click on the .sln file.

SUMMARY

In this chapter, we discussed one-dimensional and multidimensional arrays and collections. The size of arrays, Redim, IndexOf, and many other features of arrays were explained. Through hands-on exercises, you became familiar with Out of Range arrays as well. Many features of array and collection were highlighted and you had a chance to examine them step-by-step.

Next

In Chapter 11 we will cover multiple-Form environments and you will be introduced to My namespace, Splash Form, Login Form, Inherited Form, and Multiple Document Interface (MDI).

DISCUSSION QUESTIONS

1. Do you see any similarities between arrays, collections, classes, and structure? Please explain.
2. What is the function of Redim in array construction? When should we use it?
3. When do we get an Out of Range exception error? How can we prevent it?
4. What are Lbound and Ubound. List their characteristics.
5. What is object type array? Please explain.

Exercise

Using the array, create an interactive program that gets state abbreviation codes from the user. The program should display the corresponding state name for the user.

Key Terms

- Arrays
- Collections
- Elements
- Subscripts
- Lbound
- Ubound
- Array size
- Array type
- Array lookup

11 Multiple-Form Environments

In This Chapter

- Exchanging Data among `Forms`
- Scope and Lifetime of Variables
- Adding a New `Form` to the Project
- `Show`, `Hide`, and `ShowDialog` Methods
- `Form` Templates
- `TabControl`
- `TableLayoutPanel`
- Displaying Web Pages in Windows `Forms`
- Adding an Existing `Form`
- Developing a Multiple-Document Interface (MDI)
- Inherited `Forms`

MULTIPLE-FORM PROJECTS

The projects in previous chapters were single-`Form` projects, and we have been placing controls into the default `Form` that was generated by the system. In real life, this is unrealistic and most projects will have more than one `Form`. In this chapter, we will show you how to create multiple-`Form` projects.

Those of you who have been programming in older versions of Visual Basic and have created multiple-`Form` projects will find the changes and enhancements in the new version a real treasure.

Before we introduce you to this new concept, we need to expand our discussion of `My` namespace, particularly, one of the `My` objects, called `My.Forms`. This is instrumental to the concept we are going to present. Let's get familiar with some of the `My` objects and see some examples.

My **Namespace**

You might remember that we referenced the My namespace in previous chapters and briefly explained what it can do in the programming environment. We will be utilizing the power of this namespace in this chapter.

The My namespace was developed to allow you to access the system resources in a shorter amount of time. The new classes that go under My namespace enable you to utilize system resources within your solution. As you may remember, the new classes are Application, Computer, Forms, Resources, Settings, and User. Here are some examples:

My.Computer

The My Computer object can be a great resource for accessing computer resources, such as files, audio components, and other related resources. To show the operating system that is used on your computer, we can use the following:

```
MessageBox.Show(My.Computer.Info.OSFullName, "Operating System in use")
```

To show the amount of physical memory we can use

```
MessageBox.Show _
(My.Computer.Info.TotalPhysicalMemory.ToString, "Total Memory")
```

The following code will load an image from your computer clipboard:

```
PictureBox1.Image = My.Computer.Clipboard.GetImage
```

My.Application

The My Application object is designed to provide information about the application you are currently using. The following statement displays the copyrights for your application:

```
MessageBox.Show(My.Application.Info.Copyright, "Application Copyright")
```

The next statement will provide the name for the current solution you are using:

```
MessageBox.Show(My.Application.Info.ProductName, "Application Name")
```

My.User

You can use this object to verify the users' information before you let them use your program. The following statement gathers the user's name.

```
MessageBox.Show(My.User.Name, "User Name")
```

The next example uses the `IsInRole` method to confirm that the user is an adminstrator:

```
MessageBox.Show _
(CStr(My.User.IsInRole(ApplicationServices.BuiltInRole.Administrator)))
```

My.Forms

This object helps programmers gather and use information about the windows Forms. This will display an instance of the Form called myform:

```
My.Forms.myform.Show()
```

As you would probably guess, this will hide the Form:

```
My.Forms.myform.Hide()
```

You can look up other My examples and definitions in MSDN resources at: *http://msdn.microsoft.com/msdnmag/issues/05/07/My/*.

Multiple-Form Projects

Most projects in Visual Basic consist of multiple Forms. Visual Basic 2005 comes with many new templates you can choose from and add to your applications. You have been introduced to three types of Forms so far:

- Class Forms
- Module Forms
- Windows Forms

We will be using different types of Forms in this chapter to familiarize you with their nature. However, let us refresh our minds about what we covered in Chapter 5. It is important to know the variables Scope and Lifetime before we can write codes to exchange data among Forms.

EXCHANGING DATA AMONG FORMS

Before we can add new Forms to our project, we need to remember what we discussed in order to learn new rules that will help us manage our projects effectively. As you may remember from Chapter 5, we defined several types of variables that can be used in a Form. Here is the summary of what we discussed:

Public Variables: Can be accessed from within or outside the project

Private Variables: Are visible to the block they has been declared in

Friend Variables: Can be accessed through codes by the same project or assembly

Protected Variables: Can be accessed within the class that they have been declared in

Looking at this list, we can eliminate the `Private` and `Protected` variables because they cannot be used outside of the class.

SCOPE AND LIFETIME OF VARIABLES

We also discussed the scope and lifetime of variables. Here is a summary of that discussion:

Block: The scope of a variable that is declared within the `IF` statement block is within the `IF` block. The lifetime of this variable will end when the procedure ends.

Procedure: The scope of a variable that is declared outside the `IF` blocks but within a procedure is the end of the procedure. When the procedure ends, the lifetime of the variable stops as well.

Module/Class: The scope of a variable that is declared outside procedures but within the class or module is any procedure that is placed inside that module. The variables must be declared within the `Class/End Class` or `Module/End Module` statements. The variable lifetime that is declared within a module will end when the program ends. The lifetime of the variables, which are declared within a class, ends when the Garbage Collector cleans up the object.

Project: The scope of the `Public` variables that are declared within modules is all procedures within the project. Once the program is terminated, the lifetime of the variable ends.

Remembering these rules will help you more carefully declare variables that are used to exchange data. Depending on your program, you may want to give limited access to your variables and make some of them local access only.

ADDING A NEW FORM TO THE PROJECT

Adding a new `Form` to the project can be accomplished in several ways:

- Use the toolbar and select Add Items, Windows Form.
- Use the Project Menu tab and select Windows Form from it.
- Use the shortcut Shift-Ctrl-A.
- Right-click on your solution name in the Solution Explorer and point the mouse to the Add menu option. On the new expanded submenu select the Windows Form menu item (see Figure 11.1).

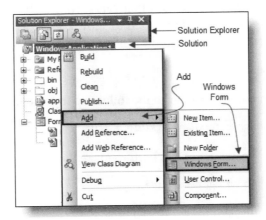

FIGURE 11.1 Adding new Form using Solution Explorer.

Once this is done, you will see the Add New Item dialog box (see Figure 11.2).

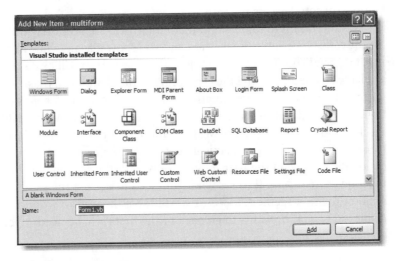

FIGURE 11.2 Add New Item dialog box.

In the Add New Item dialog box, you will notice many different templates. Among those, you may recall the class and module Forms that you used in previous projects.

SHOW, HIDE, **AND** SHOWDIALOG **METHODS**

The Show method can access other Forms from within a current form. As you saw before, the Show method was used to show a MessageBox. Using the Show method in this project will accomplish the same task and will display the Form.

```
My.Forms.formName.Show
```

This method is similar to the following statement:

```
My.Forms.formName.Visible = True
```

The opposite statement, used to make the Form invisible is

```
My.Forms.formName.Hide
```

The equivalent to that would be

```
My.Forms.formName.Visible = False
```

Contrary to its predecessors, Visual Basic 2005 will create a new instance of the referenced Form as soon as the Show Method is executed. In previous versions of VB.NET, you needed to create a new instance of the Form by using the New keyword before you could access the Form.

It is important to understand that *hiding* the Form is entirely different from *closing* the Form. Once you close the Form and you show it again, you will notice the user's input is gone. This is because once you close the Form, it will be disposed and loses all available resources. Hiding the Form, on the other hand, will make the Form invisible. Once you unhide it, the information will appear again. It depends on your application. You may decide to hide a Form under one condition and close it for another.

If you use the Show method without hiding the current Form, the user will see two Forms on the screen. He can activate each Form by clicking on it and enter data. Occasionally, you want the user to work only with the second Form but don't want to hide the current Form. If this is what you need to do, use the ShowDialog method instead of the Show method. ShowDialog will force the user to work only with the new displayed Form. If he wants to go back to the first Form, he needs to close the second Form first.

EXAMPLE 1

Start a new project and call it `multiform`. Create the following:

- **Form1**
  Name: mainForm
  Text: Main Control
- **Button1**
  Name: secondFormButton
  Text: &Access Second Form
- **Button2**
  Name: showPropertyButton
  Text: &Show Property
- **Button3**
  Name: showVariableButton
  Text: &Display Variables
- **Button4**
  Name: hideFormButton
  Text: &Hide Second Form
- **Button5**
  Name: exitButton
  Text: E&xit Application

Now add the following items to your project:

- A Windows Form (using Shift-Ctrl-A or any of the other methods explained above)
- A module file

Here they are:

- **Form2**
  Name: inputForm
  Text: Input Data
  StartPosition: CenterScreen
- **Label1**
  Name: enterMessageLabel
  Text: Enter Text
- **TextBox1**
  Name: inputTextBox
- **Button1**
  Name: exitButton
  Text: E&xit

■ **Module**
Name: shareModule

We want to practice the concepts we have learned. Figure 11.3 shows what these two Forms are going to look like. You can navigate through the Forms by clicking on their tabs or the drop-down list that is provided to you. Once you move your mouse over the tab, the ToolTip will show you its location (see Figure 11.4). We have made the sizes of these Forms small so they will not shrink too much at print time. However, you may change them to any size you want.

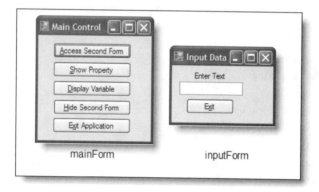

FIGURE 11.3 Finished project Form layout.

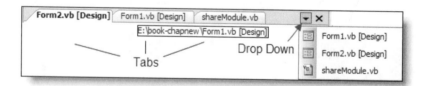

FIGURE 11.4 Tabs, ToolTip, and drop-down list.

Double-click on the accessSecondFormButton and type the following:

```
Private Sub secondFormButton_Click _
(ByVal sender As System.Object, _
ByVal e As System.EventArgs) _
Handles secondFormButton.Click
    'use the show method to display the form
    My.Forms.inputForm.Show()
End Sub
```

As this code shows, the `Show` method is used to display the `Form`. Now double-click on the `hideSecondFormButton` and type the following:

```
Private Sub hideFormButton_Click _
(ByVal sender As System.Object, _
ByVal e As System.EventArgs) _
Handles hideForm.Click
    'using Hide method to hide the application
    My.Forms.inputForm.Hide()
End Sub
```

Unlike the first subprocedure, we are hiding the `Form` by using the `Hide` method, which was explained before.

Once you are done with this, click on `Form2` tab and add a `Label`, a `TextBox`, and a `Button` as described in the project specs. We want to demonstrate how you can directly access the values of the object properties you placed on the second `Form`. Later, we will show how you can access the same values though a module. We talked about modules in Chapter 7 and had you do a project on them as well.

Double-click the `showPropertyButton` and type the following:

```
Private Sub showPropertyButton_Click _
(ByVal sender As System.Object, _
ByVal e As System.EventArgs) _
Handles showPropertyButton.Click
    'display the TextBox's text property value
    MessageBox.Show("User Input " _
    & inputForm.inputTextBox.Text, _
    "Access Property", MessageBoxButtons.OK, _
    MessageBoxIcon.Information)
End Sub
```

We access the `Text` property of the `TextBox` we placed on the second `Form` by referencing the *Form Object Name*.

Now double-click on the `inputForm` and declare the following `Public` variable:

```
Public Class inputForm
'declare a public string variable
Public myFormString As String = _
"You accessed second form's Public variable"
```

Since this `String` variable is declared as `Public`, we can access it from within all other `Forms`.

Now double-click on the `Share` module and add the following declaration:

```
Module shareModule
'declare a Friend String Variable
Friend userInputString As String = _
inputForm.inputTextBox.Text
End Module
```

This variable is declared as `Friend` and is inside a module, so it is available to both `Forms`.

We want to test both `Forms`, so we will put the following under the `displayVariablesButton`:

```
Private Sub showVariableButton_Click _
(ByVal sender As System.Object, _
ByVal e As System.EventArgs) _
Handles showVariableButton.Click
    'showing the value of variable coming from the module
    MessageBox.Show("User Input " & _
    userInputString, "Access Variable within the Module", _
    MessageBoxButtons.OK, MessageBoxIcon.Information)
    'showing a public variable declared within the second form
    MessageBox.Show(inputForm.myFormString, _
    "Varible defined within the form", _
    MessageBoxButtons.OK, MessageBoxIcon.Information)
End Sub
```

The preceding subprocedure will display a variable that is declared within the second `Form` and within the module.

Now code the Exit button for both `Forms`. Remember that the Exit button (`Me.Close`) on the second `Form` will only close the second `Form`, but the Exit button on the first `Form` will close both `Forms`. Save the project and hit F5 to run it.

Here are a few tests that we want you to do:

1. Once the main `Form` is displayed, click on the Show Property button first. The `MessageBox` does not display any value. Now click the Display Variables button. The first `MessageBox` does not show any value because the user has not entered any text yet. However, the second `MessageBox` shows the `Public` variable that is declared within the second `Form`. Can you tell why?
2. Click on Access Second Form to display the `Form`. Type text in the `TextBox` and then click on the Show Property button. The text that you typed now is displayed in the `MessageBox`. Click on the Display Variables button. This time the text you typed in the `TextBox` is displayed in the `MessageBox`. The second `MessageBox` still shows the `Public` variable declared within the second `Form`.
3. Click on the Hide Second Form button. Once again, click on Show Property and Display Variables and you will find the same information that was displayed before. Click on Access Second Form. You should see that the same `Form` with the text that you typed is displayed again.
4. This time, click on the second `Form`'s Exit button and then click on Access Second Form. The text you typed before is gone now, and Show Property shows nothing. However, Show Variables displays the value of the text you typed before.

ON THE CD
You can view this solution under the Chapter 11 folder on the companion CD-ROM. The project is saved under its name, `multipleForm`. Just copy the project folder to your hard drive and double-click on the .sln file.

FORM **TEMPLATES**

While you were adding a Windows `Form` to your project, you also probably noticed a few other `Form` templates. These templates are premade `Forms` that can easily be adopted, modified, and used in your program. Among those, we want to adopt the following:

- Splash screen template
- Login template
- About template

Splash Screen Template

You have seen many Web pages and Windows application programs that display a splash screen while the program is loading. This screen provides basic information, such as copyrights, version number, project team members, and the platform. On most Web pages, you will see a splash screen with a progress bar that informs you that the application is loading. In general, the splash screen is displayed as long as it takes to load the main program. If the main program takes longer to load, it affects the loading time of the splash screen.

Splash screens do not need to be selected from the preconfigured templates. You can pick any `Form` and designate it as a splash screen. However, the templates expedite the process. You can modify the template according to your needs.

Like other `Forms`, you can add a Splash Screen `Form` from the Add New Item dialog box, which we explained before. To designate a page as a Screen Splash, select the solution name and right-click on it. Select the Properties item from the menu (see Figure 11.5).

Once you get into the Properties page, click on the Application tab (see Figure 11.6). A few areas within the Property page require your attention:

Assembly Name Property: This is the name of the application when it is compiled. Change the name if you wish. The new name will appear on several of your files. Look at the EXE files in the Bin\Debug folder once you change this name and notice the files under the new name.

Root Namespace: This is the root name for all of the files in your solution. For example, the name of our program is `multipleform_2`. A class that is outside any namespace would have a name like `multipleform_2.SplashScreen1`.

FIGURE 11.5 Getting into the *Properties* of a solution.

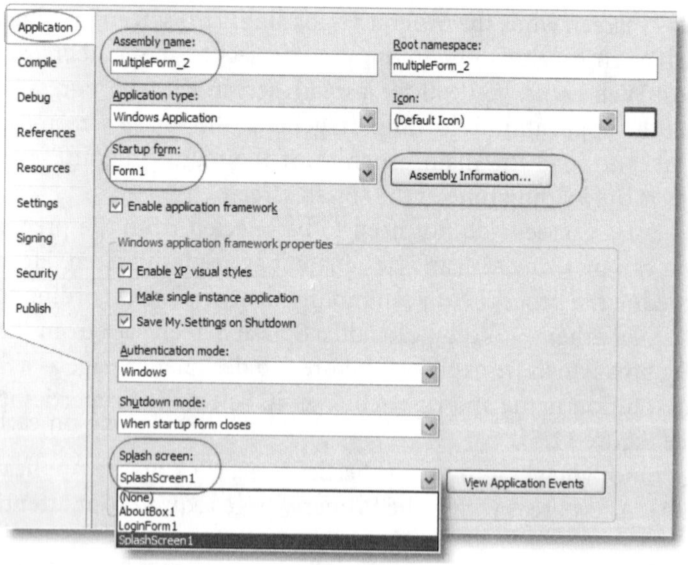

FIGURE 11.6 *Solution Property* page.

Startup Form's Drop Down: This allows you to select the Form that should be loaded at the startup. This can be useful if you want to pick a Form other than the default one to start your project with.

Assembly Information Button: This allows you to provide information for the user of your program. You can provide information such as company name, copyright, description, and other information so it can be picked by the My.Application.Info class. You saw a demonstration of this at the beginning of this chapter.

Splash Screen: Located under the Windows Application Framework Properties GroupBox, this can be utilized to select a Form such as a Splash Screen.

Login Template

This template has User Name and Password TextBoxes, and you can revise them to fit your needs.

About Template

Almost every Web page and Windows application has an About page. The About Form provides information about the organization, the product, or the developers. The About Form is a standard Form containing basic information.

TABCONTROL

In Chapter 4, we talked about Panel and GroupBox, and now is the time to introduce a similar tool. TabControl is used to divide a page into several pages called tab pages. It is very similar to a dictionary or phone book, in that it uses a label or tab to divide different sections. Each tab can contain its own properties that affect its tab page. By using the TabPage Collection, you can add as many tabs as needed and align them on the top, bottom, left, or right. TabControl allows you to change the color of each section and make them distinct from each other. You can add TabControl by expanding the *Containers* tab within your Toolbox. We want to utilize this control in our example.

The user can navigate through tab pages by clicking on each tab. Although the controls that you place on the Forms appear to be on different pages, they are still a part of the Form collection and must have unique names. You can add and remove tabs by using the *Smart Task* arrow that is included with the TabControl (see Figure 11.7).

FIGURE 11.7   TabControl *Smart Task* arrow.

TABLELAYOUTPANEL

This is very similar to the Panel control that we covered in Chapter 4. However, this control enables you to add rows and columns. This is actually a table that allows you to control its features at the design time and runtime. The Windows Form can be set to the TableLayoutPanel child. When controls are added to the TableLayoutPanel, they can be set to expand horizontally or vertically. This grid-type control can be used to arrange the controls in uniform format. Add a Splash Screen Form to your project and review its design and properties. Like many other controls, TableLayoutPanel has a Smart Tag that gives you access to several tasks. We will be using this control in our next example.

EXAMPLE 2

Let us use a simple multiple-Form project to get familiar with this new concept. Call your new project multipleForm_2. Add the following Forms to it:

- About Form
- Login Form
- Splash Screen Form

Your project will have four Forms. Make sure you set the splash screen as the Splash Screen Form in the Property page. You need to select the login Form as your startup Form. You can accomplish these tasks by using the Solution Properties page, explained before. You can look at Figure 11.5 one more time and review the materials in that figure that we discussed.

Rename the default first Form (Form1) displayForm. Add a TabControl to the displayForm and resize it so it will cover the entire Form. You need four tabs in your TabControl: Exit, Enter Grade, Calculated Grade, and Report Grade (see Figure 11.8). Rename your tabs accordingly. Now click on the Exit tab to activate it and add the following Label and Button to it:

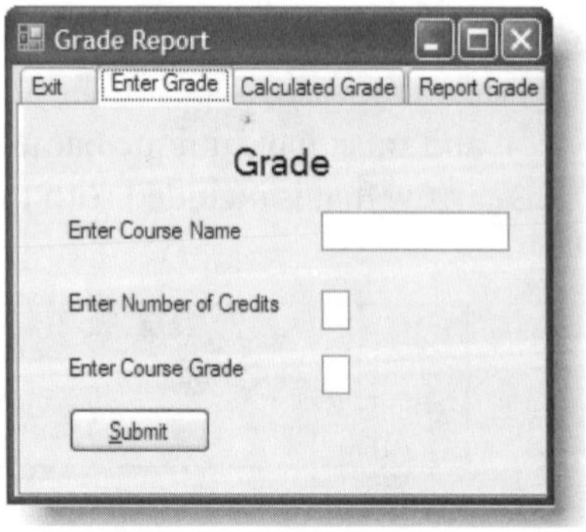

FIGURE 11.8 Adding tabs to the TabControl.

■ **Label1**
  Name: exitLabel
  Text: Click to Exit this form
■ **Button1**
  Name: gobackButton
  Text: &Go to Login Form

Change the BackColor of this tab to your favorite color. Now click on the Grade Entry tab and add the following:

■ **Label1**
  Name: titleLabel
  Text: Grade
  Font: Microsoft Sans Serif, 14.25pt
■ **Label2**
  Name: enterNameLabel
  Enter: Enter Course Name
■ **Label3**
  Name: numberOfCreditLabel
  Enter: Enter Number of Credits
  Label4
  Name: courseGradeLabel
  Text: Enter Course Grade
■ **TextBox1**
  Name: courseNameTextBox
■ **TextBox2**
  Name: creditTextBox
  MaxLength: 1
  Height: 20
  Width: 15
■ **TextBox2**
  Name: gradeTextBox
  MaxLength: 1
  Height: 20
  Width: 15
■ **Button1**
  Name: submitButton
  Text: &Submit

Now click on the Calculated Grade tab and add the following:

■ **Label1**

   Name: gpaLabel

   Text: GPA

■ **Label2**

   Name: gpaReportLabel

   Text: GPA for Course

Now we want you to design the last tab, which is the Report Grade tab, and add a `TableLayOut` control to the `TabPage`. Your table should have two rows and three columns. Once the table is added, you can use its Smart Task arrow to add or remove columns and rows. Add seven labels according to the following: Rename the Title `Label` and three heading `Labels` on your own. You need to name the bottom `Labels` according to the names listed on Figure 11.9.

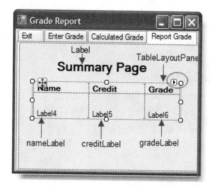

FIGURE 11.9 `TableLayoutPanel` and `Labels` inside it.

Go into the code editor and add the following code in the `Form`'s declaration area:

```
Public Class displayForm
Private gradeValueInteger As Integer
```

This variable will be available anywhere in the current `Form`.

Now find the `KeyPress` event in the Methods Name window for `creditTextBox` and enter the following in its `KeyPress` event subprocedure:

```
Private Sub creditTextBo_KeyPress _
(ByVal sender As Object, _
ByVal e As System.Windows.Forms.KeyPressEventArgs) _
Handles creditTextBox.KeyPress
```

```
    Select Case e.KeyChar
        'Accept characters between 1 to 4 only
        Case CChar("1") To CChar("4")
            'Let Backspace pass
        Case Chr(CInt("8"))
        Case Else
            e.Handled = True
    End Select
End Sub
```

As you have seen before, these statements force the users to enter only the requested values.

We can be more conservative and add more statements, but we will leave it as it is for now. Now find the KeyPress event for gradeTextBox.

```
Private Sub gradeTextBox_KeyPress _
(ByVal sender As Object, _
ByVal e As System.Windows.Forms.KeyPressEventArgs) _
Handles gradeTextBox.KeyPress
    Select Case e.KeyChar
        'only A-D and F are acceptable
        Case CChar("A"), CChar("a")
            gradeValueInteger = 4
        Case CChar("B"), CChar("b")
            gradeValueInteger = 3
        Case CChar("C"), CChar("c")
            gradeValueInteger = 2
        Case CChar("D"), CChar("d")
            gradeValueInteger = 1
        Case CChar("F"), CChar("f")
            gradeValueInteger = 0
            'Let Backspace pass
        Case Chr(CInt("8"))
        Case Else
            e.Handled = True
    End Select
End Sub
```

This subprocedure is very similar to the last code block, in which we forced users to enter valid grade letters into the grade TextBox.

Now double-click on the submitButton and enter the following:

```
Private Sub submitButton_Click _
(ByVal sender As System.Object, _
ByVal e As System.EventArgs) _
Handles submitButton.Click
    'Make sure that the input is not blank

    'calculate the grade and display the result
    'in the calculated tab page. Also, display
    'the input in the Report tab page as wll.
```

```
If Me.courseNameTextBox.Text <> _
    Nothing And Me.creditTextBox.Text <> _
    Nothing And Me.gradeTextBox.Text <> Nothing Then
    Try

        Dim gradeDecimal As Decimal
        gradeDecimal = Decimal.Parse(CStr(gradeValueInteger)) * _
        Decimal.Parse(creditTextBox.Text) / _
        Decimal.Parse(creditTextBox.Text)
        Me.gpareport.Text = gradeDecimal.ToString
        Me.nameLabel.Text = Me.courseNameTextBox.Text.ToUpper
        Me.creditLabel.Text = Me.creditTextBox.Text
        Me.gradeLabel.Text = Me.gradeTextBox.Text.ToUpper
    Catch inputError As Exception
        'display an error message if there
        'was an exception
        MessageBox.Show("The input wasn't acceptable", _
        "Warning", MessageBoxButtons.OK, _
        MessageBoxIcon.Information)
    End Try

Else
    MessageBox.Show("Blank is not acceptabe", _
    "Warning", MessageBoxButtons.OK, _
    MessageBoxIcon.Information)
End If
End Sub
```

Now click on the *Exit* tab to activate it. Double-click on the goToLoginFormBut-ton and add the following:

```
Private Sub gobackButton_Click _
(ByVal sender As System.Object, _
ByVal e As System.EventArgs) _
Handles gobackButton.Click
    'return the control to Login form
    My.Forms.loginForm.Show()
    'close the current form
    Me.Close()
End Sub
```

The Login Form is a basic Form with two TextBoxes: User Name and Password. Make the image, which is located on the left side of the Form, a little farther from the top so there is enough room for the MenuStrip. Now add a MenuStrip to the Login Form with the following items:

- &File
- E&xit
- &About
- &About Us

Add codes under the OKButton in the Login Form:

```
Private Sub OK_Click _
(ByVal sender As System.Object, _
ByVal e As System.EventArgs) _
Handles OK.Click
    'validate the password
    Select Case passwordTextBox.Text
        Case "Mike", "Heidi", "VisualBasic"
            'show the Displayform
            My.Forms.displayForm.Show()
            'Focus on the first textbox on
            'the(display)form
            My.Forms.displayForm.courseNameTextBox.Focus()
            'hide the Login form
            Me.Hide()
        Case Else
            'display error message if the
            'input is not the right password
            System.Windows.Forms.MessageBox.Show _
            ("Your input" & _
            passwordTextBox.Text, "Warning", _
            MessageBoxButtons.OK, _
            MessageBoxIcon.Information)
    End Select
End Sub
```

You are validating the user's input for the correct passwords. If the password is correct, you hide the Login Form and display the main Form, which is the displayForm. Now add the following Form under the About submenu item. This will direct the user to your main Form:

```
Private Sub AboutUsToolStripMenuItem_Click _
(ByVal sender As System.Object, _
ByVal e As System.EventArgs) _
Handles AboutUsToolStripMenuItem.Click
    'show the About form
    My.Forms.displayForm.Show()
End Sub
End Class
```

Save your project and test it. The splash screen pops up and stays there for a few seconds. Once it disappears, the Login Form will be displayed. While the Login Form is displayed, you can display the About Form.

ON THE CD You can view this solution under the Chapter 11 folder on the companion CD-ROM. The project is saved under its name, multipleForm_2. Just copy the project folder to your hard drive and double-click on the .sln file.

Form Events and Methods

In previous chapters, you became familiar with some of the Form's events including:

- FormLoad
- FromClosed

The Form object has many other events that you might want to utilize in your projects. You can view the Form events by clicking on the down arrow in the Method Names window. In Chapter 3, you learned how to add codes under the FormClosed event subprocedure. Once the user closed the Form by using the X button, a MessageBox appeared and warned the user about this action. That exercise demonstrated the FormClosed event but did not really do anything specific. In the real world, it is important that you close the Form through the Exit button. This allows you to perform some housekeeping tasks before you close the Form. If the user closes the Form by clicking on the X button, your housekeeping tasks will not be completed. In the next example, we will be utilizing the FormClosed event subprocedure to return the control to the calling Form.

DISPLAYING WEB PAGES IN WINDOWS FORMS

Introducing the WebBrowser Control

We will talk about Web Forms in later chapters. However, in this chapter, we want to introduce another interesting control: the WebBrowser class. This is a new class in the .NET Framework 2.0 and has many capabilities that can be utilized by developers. This class offers many useful properties and methods that are also new in this version. Like many other controls that we have discussed so far, you can add a WebBrowser control to your Form by using the Toolbox. Although in the previous version of .NET Framework you could add a WebBrowser control to your Windows Form, it did not provide the features that are available in the WebBrowser class. The WebBrower keeps track of the URLs you visit and allows you to access them as you have seen in Internet Explorer (IE). Among the new properties and methods are the following:

- URL
- Navigate
- GoBack
- GoForward
- GoHome
- Refresh

■   Stop
■   AllowNavigation

You can find many more events, properties, and methods if you search the MSDN library. They are beyond the scope of this chapter.

URL **Property**

This property can be set at the design time or runtime. If the URL is valid, the Web-Browser will navigate the referenced address to display the page. Here is an example:

```
WebBrowser1.Url = New System.Uri("http://www.beasa.com")
```

URI stands for Uniform Resource Identifier, which is used to identify resources on the Internet.

Navigate **Method**

This method is very similar to the URL property explained above. It will load the specified page into the WebBrowser. Here is an example:

```
WebBrowser1.Navigate("http://www.beasa.com")
```

GoBack **Method**

This method is used to display a page that was visited prior to the current page. It can be used as a boolean expression to test the page's status. The CanGoBack property can be used to evaluate the action. If no page was visited prior to the current page, then the value of CanGoBack will be False. The following statement can be placed under the backButton:

```
If navigateWebBrowser.CanGoBack = True Then
    backButton.Enabled = True
Else
    backButton.Enabled = False
End If
```

GoForward **Method**

This method is the opposite of the GoBack method and can be used to display the next page if it is available. The CanGoForward property can be used to check the condition of GoBack:

```
If navigateWebBrowser.CanGoForward = True Then
    forwardButton.Enabled = True
Else
```

```
        forwardButton.Enabled = False
    End If
```

GoHome **Method**

Within your IE browser options, you can define your home page. This home page is loaded any time the browser is fired up. The GoHome method will force your defined home page to be loaded into the browser. This is the same as your IE *Home* button. Here is an example:

```
    navigateWebBrowser.GoHome()
```

Refresh **Method**

This method will be used to reload the page you just visited. This is useful if the page did not load properly or if it loaded incompletely.

```
    navigateWebBrowser.Refresh()
```

Stop **Method**

Similar to IE, this method will cancel the loading of the current page if it is still loading and stops the background sound:

```
    navigateWebBrowser.Stop()
```

AllowNavigation **Property**

You can set this property to allow or disallow the WebBrowser to navigate new links or not. This is after the initial page is loaded. If the page that you called has a link that requires a new browser window, the control will be given to your default Internet browser. You can write an event handler subprocedure to control this action.

EXAMPLE 3

In this example, we will add more Forms to the Ice Cream Shop project we developed in Chapter 6. As you may remember, we had an order Form that was used to get ice cream orders, display the images for each ice cream, and display the price. We also had a button called Display Receipt, which was disabled. We will utilize the disabled button to display a receipt. The receipt will collect data from two Forms: the logInForm and orderForm. We also have put together a simple Web page that will be loaded in the Web site Form.

The new project will have three new Forms:

- loginForm
- websiteForm
- receiptForm

Add these Forms to your project. For the loginForm, you will use the Login template that is located under the Add New Item dialog box. You will add a few more controls to the loginForm:

- One Label
- One MaskedTextBox
- Two Buttons

The Label is used to identify the MaskedTextBox. The MaskedTextBox is formatted to accept phone numbers. One of the Buttons has a caption of "Visit Our Website" and the other one reads, "Email Your Order." Now your websiteForm has four Buttons: OK, Visit Our Web site, Email Your Order, and Cancel. We will talk about some new terms before we start coding.

Application.StartUpPath Property

In Chapter 4, we briefly talked about the Windows.Forms.Application.StartUpPath property and used it in our application but did not provide details. This property is used to find the path that the application program started from and append it to the name of the file we are trying to load. This could be an image file, a Web page, or a data file. As suggested before, we can place our files in the \bin\Debug folder of our application. This works fine in most cases and we do not need to specify the full path for the location of our files. However, occasionally we need to be specific about the path. Specifying the full path is not a problem as long as the application has not been relocated. Once it is moved to other computers, the path becomes obsolete and cannot be used any longer. To prevent portability issues, we use this property. The StartUpPath property returns the path of the location that contained the EXE file to run the application. We have developed a Web site that is located in the \bin\Debug folder. To reference it, we have to use the following path on our machine: C:\Documents and Settings\Administrator\Desktop\iceCreamShop\iceCreamShop\bin\Debug\mike_ice_cream_shop.htm. Unless you install this application in the same referenced location of your computer hard drive, it will not work. The following statement is equal to what we used above:

```
Windows.Forms.Application.StartupPath & "\mike_ice_cream_shop.htm"
```

Of course, you can omit the Windows.Forms phrase to make it shorter.
The StartUpPath property returns the following value:

```
C:\Documents and Settings\Administrator\Desktop\iceCreamShop\
iceCreamShop\bin\Debug
```

Why? Because the iceCreamShop.exe file is located in that location, and we can add the value of this property to the name of the file that is also located with that folder.

AutoCompleteMode and AutoCompleteSource Properties

These new properties add more capabilities to your TextBox and ComboBox. Using them allows the TextBox or ComboBox to use the entered prefix to search the most frequently used names in the source and automatically display them. As you entered a URL in the search window of your browser, you may have noticed that similar URLs started showing up in the window. Most likely, you can pick your desired URL from within the suggested URLs displayed for you. These could be the name of the files, URLs, addresses, or commands that you used before and are saved in the Source. The AutoCompleteMode will offer the following options:

None: No automatic completion is performed.

Suggest: Suggested completion strings will be populated in the drop-down list.

Append: The remaining of the closest matching characters will be appended to the entered characters. The appended characters will be highlighted.

SuggestAppend: This performs both Suggest and Append.

The AutoCompleteSource property identifies the source that should be used for autocompletion. The following options are available:

- FileSystem
- HistoryList
- AllUrl
- RecentlyUsedList
- AllSystemSources
- FileSystemDirectories
- CustomeSource
- ListItems
- None

We will be using the AllUrl property as the source for autocompletion in our project.

Add the following controls to your websiteForm:

- One Label
- One ComboBox
- One Web browser
- Seven Buttons

Name these controls according to the Naming Conventions. The ComboBox is used to type in the URL. One of the Buttons will be used as the *Go* button to navigate the link. The other Buttons will be used for the following: Home, Refresh, Back, Forward, Stop, and Close. The Label is used as the caption for the ComboBox.

We will talk about the receiptForm later. Now we need to add codes to our program. On the loginForm, double-click on the OKButton and add the following:

```
Private Sub okButton_Click _
(ByVal sender As System.Object, _
ByVal e As System.EventArgs) _
Handles okButton.Click
    'validate the password to move to the order form
    If Me.passwordTextBox.Text = "iceCream" Then
        My.Forms.orderForm.Show()
        Me.Hide()
    End If
End Sub
```

With this code, we will display the orderForm and hide the loginForm after validating the password.

Now double-click on the visitOurWebsiteButton and add the following:

```
Private Sub webSiteButton_Click _
(ByVal sender As System.Object, _
ByVal e As System.EventArgs) _
Handles webSiteButton.Click
    'load the webpage that is located in the
    '\bin\Debug folder
    My.Forms.websiteForm.navigateWebBrowser.Navigate _
    (Windows.Forms.Application.StartupPath & _
    "\mike_ice_cream_shop.htm")
    'Show the website form
    My.Forms.websiteForm.ShowDialog()
End Sub
```

As you can see, we are using the Navigate method to load a Web page that is located in the \bin\Debug folder. In the above code, we have also utilized the Application.StartupPath property and the ShowDialog method. The name of the Web page is *mike_ice_cream_shop.htm*.

The Email Your Order button is very similar to the one we used in Chapter 4. Here is the code for it:

```
Private Sub emailOrderButton_Click _
(ByVal sender As System.Object, _
ByVal e As System.EventArgs) _
Handles emailOrderButton.Click
    'use the process.start to send emails
    Process.Start _
    ("mailto:mike.Mostafavi@beasa.com")
End Sub
```

Now add the following code under the Form_load event subprocedure:

```
Private Sub LoginForm_Load _
(ByVal sender As System.Object, _
ByVal e As System.EventArgs) _
Handles MyBase.Load
    'load the icecream image at under the Form_load event
    Me.logoPictureBox.Image = _
    Image.FromFile _
    (Windows.Forms.Application.StartupPath & _
    "\vanilla.tif")
End Sub
```

This code should be self-explanatory because you have used it before. Complete the *Cancel* button.

We are now ready to code the websiteForm. Add the following codes under the Form_load subprocedure:

```
Private Sub websiteForm_Load _
(ByVal sender As System.Object, _
ByVal e As System.EventArgs) _
Handles MyBase.Load
    'set the AutoCompleteMode and AutoCompleteSource
    'Properties
    Me.navigateComboBox.AutoCompleteMode _
    = AutoCompleteMode.Suggest
    Me.navigateComboBox.AutoCompleteSource _
    = AutoCompleteSource.AllUrl

End Sub
```

As you can see, we are applying the AutoCompleteMode and AutoCompleteSource in the code.

Add the following code under the WebBrowser CanGoForwardChange event subprocedure:

```
Private Sub navigateWebBrowser_CanGoForwardChanged _
(ByVal sender As Object, _
ByVal e As System.EventArgs) _
Handles navigateWebBrowser.CanGoForwardChanged
    'If it can go forward, make the ForwardButton
    'enabled. Otherwise disable the button
```

```
      If Me.navigateWebBrowser.CanGoForward = True Then
          Me.forwardButton.Enabled = True
      Else
          Me.forwardButton.Enabled = False
      End If
End Sub
```

If there were a next page that could be displayed, the Button would be enabled. Now type the following code under CanGoBackChanged event subprocedure:

```
Private Sub navigateWebBrowser_CanGoBackChanged _
(ByVal sender As Object, _
ByVal e As System.EventArgs) _
Handles navigateWebBrowser.CanGoBackChanged
    'If it can go back, make the backButton
    'enabled. Otherwise disable the button
    If Me.navigateWebBrowser.CanGoBack = True Then
        Me.backButton.Enabled = True
    Else
        Me.backButton.Enabled = False
    End If
End Sub
```

Now double-click on the goButton and add the following code:

```
Private Sub navigateButton_Click _
(ByVal sender As System.Object, _
ByVal e As System.EventArgs) _
Handles navigateButton.Click
    'Make sure the combobox is not blank
    If Me.navigateComboBox.Text = Nothing Then
        MessageBox.Show("Please Enter a URL", "Warning")
        'if the input doesn't have http://,
        'append it to the string
    ElseIf Me.navigateComboBox.Text.StartsWith("http://") _
    = False Then
        Me.navigateComboBox.Text = _
        "http://" & Me.navigateComboBox.Text
    End If
    Try
        'Navigate the URL entered by the user
        Me.navigateWebBrowser.Url = _
        New Uri(Me.navigateComboBox.Text)
    Catch ex As Exception
    End Try

End Sub
```

This code checks the URL to make sure it is not blank. If the input does not include HTTP:// as starting characters, it will be added to it. The next statement will check for exceptions.

Complete the codes for the Home, Refresh, Back, Forward, Stop, and Close buttons. We gave you the required codes in this chapter.

It is time to design the `receiptForm`. We would like to display the following information:

- User name
- Ice cream type
- Phone number
- Order total

Figure 11.10 shows the screenshot for the output. As you will notice, the Print button is disabled. This portion will be completed later.

FIGURE 11.10   `receiptForm` design.

Now we want to enable the Display Receipt button. Add the following code under the conditional statement that we wrote for calculating the price of ice cream:

```
Me.receiptButton.Enabled = True
```

These statements are under the `checkoutButton`. Once the price is displayed in the `priceLabel`, this `Button` will be enabled. Now we need to add the following statements under the `displayReceiptButton`:

```
Private Sub receiptButton_Click _
(ByVal sender As System.Object, _
ByVal e As System.EventArgs) _
Handles receiptButton.Click
    'display the user name and phone number from
    'the loginForm
```

```
        My.Forms.receiptForm.userNameReceiptLabel.Text _
        = My.Forms.loginForm.userNameTextBox.Text
        My.Forms.receiptForm.iceCreamNameLabel.Text _
        = Me.iceCreamLabel.Text
        My.Forms.receiptForm.phoneMaskedTextBox.Text _
        = CStr(My.Forms.loginForm.phoneMaskedTextBox.Text)
        'display the ice cream type and
        'price from the orderForm
        My.Forms.receiptForm.totalPriceLabel.Text _
        = Me.priceLabel.Text
        'show the receiptForm and hide the orderForm
        My.Forms.receiptForm.Show()
        Me.Hide()
    End Sub
```

As you can see, we are extracting data from two Forms to display in the receipt-Form.

We also would like to trap the FormClosing event subprocedure:

```
    Private Sub orderForm_FormClosing _
    (ByVal sender As Object, _
    ByVal e As System.Windows.Forms.FormClosingEventArgs) _
    Handles Me.FormClosing
        'clear the password and display the loginForm
        My.Forms.loginForm.passwordTextBox.Text = Nothing
        My.Forms.loginForm.Show()

    End Sub
```

Similar statements should be put under the Exit buttons of the orderForm and ClosingForm event subprocedure.

You can view this solution under the Chapter 11 folder on the companion CD-ROM. The project is saved under its name, iceCreamShop. Just copy the project folder to your hard drive and double-click on the .sln file.

ADDING AN EXISTING FORM

Occasionally you will develop Forms that can be used in other projects as well. These items could be password Forms that include many validations or modules that contain complicated calculations. There is no need to redevelop these items. You can easily add the existing items to your projects. To accomplish this task, do the following:

1. Click on the *Project* menu or simply hit Ctrl-D.
2. Select the item you want to add to your project from the Add Existing Item dialog box.

DEVELOPING A MULTIPLE-DOCUMENT INTERFACE (MDI)

You have learned how to add Forms to your projects, how to access them, and how to close them. You added Forms as you needed and controlled them individually. This is known as single document interface, or SDI. SDI is very popular among developers. However, you need to be familiar with another type of interface that is called multiple-document interface (MDI).

When you use MDI, you identify one Form as parent and all other additional Forms as child Forms. Unlike the SDI Forms that function on their own, MDI Forms are under the domain of parent Forms. You should not be confused about the nature of these Forms. Both are developed using the techniques we have discussed so far. However, we need to make small changes to the Form properties to identify the parent and child Forms.

Arranging MDI Forms by Using the LayoutMdi Method

You can arrange the child Forms within your MDI parent Form by using the Layout-Mdi method. This method allows you to choose from Cascade, TileHorizontal, and TileVertical. During this process, the MdiLayout enumeration for the parent MDI Form will be set. Here is an example:

```
Me.LayoutMdi(System.Windows.Forms.MdiLayout.Cascade)
```

EXAMPLE 4

In this example, we will show you how to create and maintain an MDI project. Create a new project and call it mdiProject. Rename the Form mainForm and add a new Form to your project. Rename the new Form additionalForm.

Select the mainForm and you should see a property called isMdiContainer. If we set the value of this property to True, it means the mainForm is the parent Form and all new Forms that are created are child Forms and will appear within this Form. We will identify the mainForm as the parent by adding the following statement in the Form_load subprocedure:

```
Private Sub mainForm_Load_1 _
(ByVal sender As System.Object, _
ByVal e As System.EventArgs) _
Handles MyBase.Load
    'make the mainForm a Parent form
    Me.IsMdiContainer = True
End Sub
```

Add controls to the additionalForm at runtime to practice the techniques we learned in previous chapters. Add the following class-level declaration to the additionalForm declaration area:

```
Public Class additionalForm
'Declare new instances of controls
Private nameLabel As New Label
Private WithEvents nameTextBox As New TextBox
Private WithEvents exitButton As New Button
```

As you learned before, we are creating new instances of the Label, TextBox, and Button.

Now add the following statements under the Form_load event subprocedure:

```
Private Sub addtionalForm_Load _
(ByVal sender As System.Object, _
ByVal e As System.EventArgs) _
Handles MyBase.Load
    'Add a label to the form
    Controls.Add(nameLabel)
    nameLabel.Location = New System.Drawing.Point(25, 25)
    nameLabel.Text = "Enter Your Name"
    'Add a TextBox to the form
    Controls.Add(nameTextBox)
    nameTextBox.Location = New System.Drawing.Point(130, 25)
    nameTextBox.Size = New System.Drawing.Size(129, 250)
    'Add a Button to the form
    Controls.Add(exitButton)
    exitButton.Location = New System.Drawing.Point(25, 60)
    exitButton.Text = "E&xit"
End Sub
```

As you learned before, create a Click event procedure for the Exit button and code it.

Now add a MenuStrip to the mainForm and add the following menu items to it:

- &File
- &Additional Forms
- E&xit

Double-click on the Additional Forms menu item and add the following:

```
Private Sub AdditionalFormsToolStripMenuItem_Click _
(ByVal sender As System.Object, _
ByVal e As System.EventArgs) _
Handles AdditionalFormsToolStripMenuItem.Click
    'create a new instance of the additionalForm
    Dim newadditionalForm As New addtionalForm

    'make the additionalForm a child form
    newadditionalForm.MdiParent = Me
    'use a cascade layout
    Me.LayoutMdi(System.Windows.Forms.MdiLayout.Cascade)
```

```
        'show the form
        newadditionalForm.Show()
    End Sub
```

The Form identified as the parent has a darker background.

Code the Exit menu item and save and run your project. As soon as you click on the Additional Form's menu item, a new Form will be created.

You may want to limit the number of Forms that are added to the parent Form by setting a counter (see Figure 11.11).

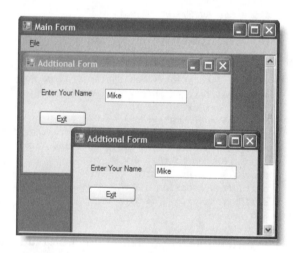

FIGURE 11.11   Screenshot for Example 4.

ON THE CD
You can view this solution under the Chapter 11 folder on the companion CD-ROM. The project is saved under its name, mdiProject. Just copy the project folder to your hard drive and double-click on the .sln file.

INHERITED FORMS

You can use the Inheritance Picker dialog box to create a Form that has inherited the characteristics of another Form. The inherited Form will carry the layout and behavior of the original Form. This is useful for customized Forms that developers have created and need to get duplicates from. This is known as *visual inheritance*. In order to create inherited Forms you need to build your project into an executable or DLL as the first step. Follow these steps to create an inherited Form:

1. Click on the Project menu tab and pick Add Windows Form.
2. From the Add New Item dialog box, point to Inherited Form and then click on the Add button.
3. From the Inheritance Picker dialog box, point to the file to inherit from and click on the OK button. If the file is located in another location, you need to click on Browse to find it.

The inherited Form is added to the Solution Explorer. There are glyph symbols on all the controls on the inherited Form. The borders that appear around the selected controls indicate the level of security the control has inherited from the original Form.

SUMMARY

In this chapter, we covered the multiple-Form environment and showed you how to exchange data between different Forms. In addition, we explained the My namespace and provided examples of all of its classes. The Splash and Login Forms were added to the existing Forms to give a realistic appearance to your projects. We also showed you how to add Web pages to your Windows projects and we introduced you to MDI Forms.

Next

In Chapter 12, you will learn how to print. The concept of graphics and shapes are explained, and you will learn how to print the content of a ComboBox. The Using block will be employed in an example as well.

DISCUSSION QUESTIONS

1. What is the role of a module in a multiple-Form environment? Is it necessary or more convenient?
2. What are the major differences between SDI and MDI?
3. Explain the function of the Show and Hide methods.
4. Name five of the most useful methods we covered for the browser control.
5. What is the main advantage of Application.StartupPath?

Exercise

Create a project that has three Forms. The first Form is a Login Form and the second one is data entry. Use the MaskedTextBox control and Keychar property to validate the users' control. Display the input in the third Form.

Key Terms

- My Namespace
- Single-document interface
- Multiple-document interface
- Adding existing Form to project
- Application.StartupPath
- WebBrowser control

12 Introduction to Printing, Graphics, Shapes, and More

In This Chapter

- System.Drawing Namespace, Paint Event, Pen Class, and Brush Class
- Using Block
- DrawLine Method and Shapes in Visual Basic 2005
- Using Loops to Print ComboBoxes

In Chapter 3, we showed you how to print your codes, and now it is time to discuss the process of adding output functionality to your projects. Many printing features can be added to your projects to give them a professional look.

PRINT METHOD

We use the PrintDocument.Print method to print our documents. We use this method to initiate the printing process. Like designing a Form, printing requires planning. We need to use a layout that is easy to follow. We can enhance our printed outputs by adding other components such as dialog boxes that are available to us. We will discuss them individually.

PrintDocument Component

An instance of this class can be added to your solution by using the Toolbox. It offers many properties, events, and methods that can be used in your program. By setting the provided properties, we can tell the printer what the output should look like.

PrintPage, BeginPrint, and EndPrint Events

The Print method is used to start the printing process. During this process, for every printing phase, the BeginPrint, PrintPage, and EndPrint events are raised to perform the job. As soon as the `Print` method starts the process, the `BeginPrint` event is raised to respond to the request. In the `PrintPage` event subprocedure, you will specify the requirements for your output. If you need to print more than one page, the `Print-Page` event will be called for each additional page.

Once printing is complete, the `EndPrint` event will occur. It sounds like a complicated concept but it is not. As soon as you learn how to apply it, it will become a routine task. In addition, most of these tasks are done automatically.

PrintDialog

This dialog box provides options for printing jobs. You see the Print dialog box any time you want to send a document to the printer. This dialog box offers options such as Printer Name, Print Range, Print to File, Printer Setting, Show Help, Number of Copies, and more. As developers, we can specify the options the user can see in the Print dialog box.

PrintPreviewDialog

This is another feature that can be added to a project. You have probably seen this feature when you wanted to print a spreadsheet or any other document. The Print Preview dialog box allows you to view the document on your screen before it is sent to the printer. You can make the required adjustments and then print the document.

PageSetupDialog

This dialog is used to specify the margins, spacing, borders, and other requirements for your print job. We use the properties that are available in this class to specify our needs.

PrintPreviewControl

This control can be added to your document to customize your printing needs. You can use it to preview your printouts. It has many properties that are available to developers.

Graphics **Object and** DrawString **Method**

We have briefly explained the printing process and the available dialog boxes. However, in order to print, we need to specify the fonts, the specific location of the page, and other information. The event arguments include the `Graphics` object that uses X and Y coordinators to find the specific locations of the page. The X coordinator is used to specify horizontal location, and the Y coordinator is used find vertical locations. We use the `DrawString` method to draw lines of text in specific locations. We also provide `Font` and `Brush` objects to facilitate this task.

GDI and `e.Graphics.DrawString`

Microsoft Windows uses a graphical device interface (GDI) to display and print documents. The GDI allows us to develop our programs without worrying about how our output is displayed or printed. As some of you may remember from the old days, in order to display enhanced fonts on the screen, you needed to be an expert in the monitor features and utilize them in your program. The most frustrating part of programming was portability issues. Fortunately, programmers do not need to worry about them anymore.

The `Graphics` class encapsulates the drawing surface and the GDI to facilitate your printing. The `Graphics` class has many methods that can be used to print documents. One of these methods is the `e.Graphics.DrawString` method, but this method cannot function by itself. It needs to get help from the fonts, the `Color` class, String, and so on to accomplish the task. (We will talk about this process later.) When we want to print a document, we normally use different fonts to differentiate between the elements of our output. For example, you may want the title to be large and bold. You may want to have different fonts and font styles for the headings of the columns and other similar requirements. It is possible to define these fonts' categories once and reuse them within the program many times.

`SYSTEM.DRAWING` NAMESPACE, `PAINT` EVENT, `PEN` CLASS, AND `BRUSH` CLASS

We have talked about the `Graphics` class to show you some of its features, but there are more features to be covered. You will see other applications for graphics methods later on. We will be using the `System.Drawing` namespace in several examples. This namespace allows us to access the GDI and create basic drawings. One of its properties is known as `PageBounds`, which identifies the total area of the paper.

The `Pen` class is designed to draw lines, while the `Brush` class is used to fill shapes. To create shapes, we need to use the `Form`'s `Paint` event subprocedure. We will show you an example of these features.

Here is an example of the `System.Drawing.Font` class:

```
Dim titleFont As New System.Drawing.Font _
("Arial", 18, System.Drawing.FontStyle.Bold)
```

In this statement, we are creating a new instance of the `Font` class, with the following characteristics:

- New instance name: `titleFont`
- Font name: Arial

- Font size: 18
- Font style: Bold

The DrawString method needs to have additional information to perform the print tasks. In addition to what we declared, we would also need the following:

- Brush color
- String
- Horizontal and vertical locations
- Font

Here is how the DrawString method can be used to address these needs:

```
e.Graphics.DrawString("User Address", titleFont, _
    System.Drawing.Brushes.Black, 270, 27)
```

Let's translate what we put in the code to make sure it meets all requirements:

- Brush color: Black
- String: "User Address"
- Font: titleFont (Arial, 18, Bold)
- Horizontal location: 270
- Vertical location: 27

USING BLOCK

Visual Basic 2005 introduces a new block, which is similar to the Try/Catch block. The Try/Catch block offers more control for exception handling but has some similarities to the Using block. The intention was to make sure all system resources are disposed after you get out of the block. This is more useful for database connections and other resources that are used in your program and need a large memory space. The Using block releases these resources after completion to reduce overhead. The general format for this block is

```
Using resource As New resource

'statements that are using the above resource
End Using
```

As you can see, the block starts with the Using keyword and ends with the End Using keyword. We will be taking advantage of this new block in our next example.

EXAMPLE 1: SIMPLE PRINTING

Let us utilize our learning by developing a very simple example. Later, we will add print functionalities to the Ice Cream Shop program we developed in previous chapters.

Start a new project and call it `printingProject`. Add two `Labels`, two `TextBoxes`, and two `Buttons`. The `Label` is used to ask for the name and the address of the user, and the `TextBoxes` are used to store the names and addresses. The `Buttons` will be used to print the entered texts and exit the program.

Add the following dialog boxes to your solution:

- `PrintDocument`
- `PrintDialog`
- `PrintPreviewDialog`

Like many other components you used before, these objects will land in the Component Tray of your solution (see Figure 12.1).

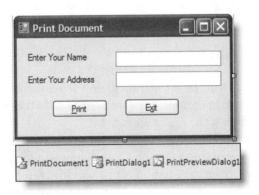

FIGURE 12.1 Print `Form` and added objects.

Adding Codes

The first thing we need to do is to create an instance of the `PrintDocument` class that we discussed before:

```
Public Class printingForm
'Create a new instance of PrintDocument class
Private WithEvents documentToPrint _
As New System.Drawing.Printing.PrintDocument
```

You can tell where this declaration should be inserted by now. We can use this instance within our project more than once.

Double-click the `printButton` that you added to your project and type the following codes:

```
Private Sub printButton_Click _
(ByVal sender As System.Object, _
ByVal e As System.EventArgs) _
Handles printButton.Click
    'allow the user to select a range for printing
    Me.myDocumentPrintDialog.AllowSomePages = True
    'let the document be previwed
    Me.myDocumentPrintPreviewDialog.Document = _
    Me.documentToPrint
    Me.myDocumentPrintPreviewDialog.ShowDialog()
    'Let the help be available to the users
    Me.myDocumentPrintDialog.ShowHelp = True
    'Display the PrintDialog and let the user decide
    Me.myDocumentPrintDialog.Document = _
    Me.documentToPrint
    'if the user decides to print, print the document
    Dim result As DialogResult = _
    Me.myDocumentPrintDialog.ShowDialog()
    If (result = Windows.Forms.DialogResult.OK) Then
        Me.documentToPrint.Print()

    End If
```

We are showing how different dialog boxes can be added to the project to provide more printing options. Now we need to code the most important section of the program, which is the `PrintPage` event.

As you may remember, we created a new instance of the `PrintDocument` class and called it `documentToPrint`. In the Class Name window, locate `documentToPrint` and select it. Now, from the Method Name window, select the `PrintPage` event. Type the following statements under the event subprocedure (see Figure 12.2):

```
Private Sub documentToPrint_PrintPage _
(ByVal sender As Object, _
ByVal e As System.Drawing.Printing.PrintPageEventArgs) _
Handles documentToPrint.PrintPage
    'applying the Using Block to define new instances
    'of Font class.

    Using titleFont As New _
    System.Drawing.Font("Arial", 18, FontStyle.Bold)
        'print the title using titleFont
        e.Graphics.DrawString _
        ("User Address", titleFont, _
        System.Drawing.Brushes.Black, 270, 27)
    End Using
```

```
Using headingFont As New _
System.Drawing.Font("Arial", _
12, FontStyle.Bold)
    'Print the caption for User
    'Name using headingFont
    e.Graphics.DrawString _
    ("Name: ", headingFont, _
    System.Drawing.Brushes.Black, 10, 100)
    'Print the caption for User
    'address using headingFont
    e.Graphics.DrawString _
("Address: ", headingFont, _
System.Drawing.Brushes.Black, 10, 130)
End Using

Using dataFont As New System.Drawing.Font _
("Arial", 10, System.Drawing.FontStyle.Regular)
    'Printing the users input for Address using
    'dataFont
    e.Graphics.DrawString _
    (Me.nameTextBox.Text, dataFont, _
    System.Drawing.Brushes.Black, 200, 100)
    e.Graphics.DrawString _
    (Me.addressTextBox.Text, dataFont, _
    System.Drawing.Brushes.Black, 200, 130)

    End Using
End Sub
```

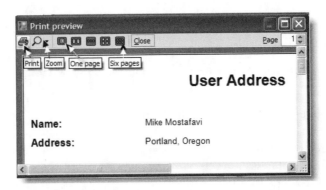

FIGURE 12.2   `PrintPreview` screen with Toolbar.

ON THE CD

You can view this solution under the Chapter 12 folder on the companion CD-ROM. The project is saved under its name, `printingProject`. Just copy the solution folder to your hard drive and double-click on the .sln file.

DRAWLINE METHOD AND SHAPES IN VISUAL BASIC 2005

In Visual Basic 6, you could have created shapes such as circles, rectangles, and ellipses in less than a few minutes. In Visual Basic 2005, things are done differently. In the current version, you need to specify the Brushes you want to use and the location on the Form where the shape needs to be placed and be specific about other requirements. The DrawLine method allows us to use a Pen and specify the thickness of it and where it needs to be used. Here are some examples of this:

```
e.Graphics.FillRectangle _
(Brushes.BlueViolet, _
10, 110, 150, 100)
```

In this statement, we created a rectangle with the following specification:

- Width: 150
- Height: 100
- Horizontal position: 10
- Vertical position: 110
- Fill color: Blue Violet

Here is an example of a circle:

```
e.Graphics.FillEllipse _
(Brushes.Red, 0, 0, 100, 100)
```

We can use the DrawLine method to connect two points. Here is an example of drawing a line:

```
Dim pen1 As New System.Drawing.Pen(Color.White, 5)
e.Graphics.DrawLine(pen1, 10, 120, 160, 120)
```

Here is what we understand from this:

- Pen color: Red
- Pen thickness: 5
- Horizontal location 1: 10
- Vertical location 1: 120
- Horizontal location 2: 160
- Vertical location 2: 120

Here is how we can draw a rectangle:

```
e.Graphics.DrawRectangle(Pens.Purple, 15, 15, 70, 70)
```

Here is the Form's Paint event subprocedure on which we placed all of these codes (see Figure 12.3):

```
Private Sub drawForm_Paint _
(ByVal sender As Object, _
ByVal e As System.Windows.Forms.PaintEventArgs) _
Handles Me.Paint
    'create a filled rectangle
    e.Graphics.FillRectangle _
    (Brushes.BlueViolet, _
    10, 110, 150, 100)
    'Create a filled circle
    e.Graphics.FillEllipse _
    (Brushes.Red, 0, 0, 100, 100)
    'set the pen and choose color and thickness
    Dim pen1 As New System.Drawing.Pen(Color.White, 10)
    'draw a line
    e.Graphics.DrawLine(pen1, 10, 120, 160, 120)
    'draw a rectangle
    e.Graphics.DrawRectangle(Pens.White, 15, 15, 70, 70)

End Sub
```

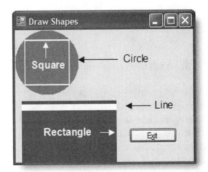

FIGURE 12.3 Line and shape examples.

You can view this solution under the Chapter 12 folder on the companion CD-ROM. The project is saved under its name, graphicsPractice. Just copy the solution folder to your hard drive and double-click on the .sln file.

USING LOOPS TO PRINT COMBOBOXES

In Example 1, we printed the content of two TextBoxes. That was very easy. In the real world we need to print the contents of arrays, data files, ComboBoxes, ListBoxes, and so on. As you learned in previous chapters, we can use a loop to display the content of ComboBoxes on the screen. We can use the same trick to print them. We will be using the logic we used before. We just insert the printing requirements into it.

EXAMPLE 2

Let's start a new project and call it printingComboBox. Add the following to your Form: One Label, one ComboBox, and three Buttons (see Figure 12.4).

FIGURE 12.4 Example 3 screenshot.

Double-click the addToCartButton and add the following:

```
Private Sub addToButton_Click _
(ByVal sender As System.Object, _
ByVal e As System.EventArgs) _
Handles addToButton.Click
    'add user's input to combobox
    cartComboBox.Items.Add(cartComboBox.Text)
End Sub
```

This will add the user's input to the ComboBox. Now click on the printButton and add these statements:

```
Private Sub printButton_Click _
(ByVal sender As System.Object, _
ByVal e As System.EventArgs) _
Handles printButton.Click
    'assign dialogboxes to our document
    Me.myDocumentPrintPreviewDialog.Document = _
        Me.documentToPrint
    Me.myDocumentPrintPreviewDialog.ShowDialog()
    Me.myDocumentPrintDialog.Document = _
        Me.documentToPrint
End Sub
```

This is very similar to what we used in our last exercise and does not need any explanation. Now type the following under the `PrintPage` event handler:

```
Private Sub documentToPrint_PrintPage _
(ByVal sender As Object, _
ByVal e As System.Drawing.Printing. _
PrintPageEventArgs) _
Handles documentToPrint.PrintPage
    'print the heading and draw a line under it
    Using titleFont As New Font("arial", 14, FontStyle.Bold)
        e.Graphics.DrawString _
            ("Item", titleFont, Brushes.Black, 100, 90)
        Dim pen1 As New System.Drawing.Pen(Color.Red, 2)
        e.Graphics.DrawLine(pen1, 0, 120, _
        850, 120)
    End Using
    'Loop through combobox and print them
    Using comboFont As New _
    System.Drawing.Font("arial", 10, _
    FontStyle.Regular)

        Dim lineInteger As Integer = 1

        For Each lookupString As Object In _
        Me.cartComboBox.Items
            'print the text and increment the vertical spacing
            'to make room for the next line
            e.Graphics.DrawString _
            (lookupString.ToString, _
            comboFont, Brushes.Black, _
            100, 110 + (15 * lineInteger))

            lineInteger = lineInteger + 1

        Next
    End Using

End Sub
```

Here is what we did:

1. We printed the Item word on the top of the column.
2. We drew a line under it across the paper.
3. The thickness of the line was 2 and its color was red.
4. We looped through the `ComboBox` and printed each item.
5. We incremented the vertical spacing so it would print the next item in the next line.

ON THE CD You can view this solution under the Chapter 12 folder on the companion CD-ROM. The project is saved under its name, `printingComboBox`. Just copy the solution folder to your hard drive and double-click on the .sln file.

Enhancements Using `PageBounds.Width` and `e.HasMorePages` Properties

The project works as intended. However, we could enhance it a little more. We manually inserted the width of the paper we wanted to draw a line on. We specified 850 as the width of the paper:

```
Dim pen1 As New System.Drawing.Pen(Color.Red, 2)
e.Graphics.DrawLine(pen1, 0, 120, _
850, 120)
```

We could rewrite the code this way:

```
Dim pen1 As New System.Drawing.Pen(Color.Red, 2)
e.Graphics.DrawLine(pen1, 0, 120, _
e.PageBounds.Width, 120)
```

The `PageBounds.Width` can automatically calculate the width of our paper. The other thing that we could do is set a page counter for our little program. We could print a specific number of lines in each page and then move to the next page. You can create logic for the `PrintPageEventArgs.HasMorePages` property and print a specific number of lines per page:

```
e.HasMorePages=True
```

Create logic for it.

EXAMPLE 3

In this example, we will add print capabilities to the Ice Cream Shop project we have been working on. In the previous chapter, we added a Receipt Form to our project. However, we purposely disabled the Print button so we could complete it now. Figure 12.5 shows the screenshot for it.

Open the IceCreamShop solution and add the following to it:

■ PrintDocument
■ PrintDialog
■ PrintPreviewDialog

We can modify the codes we used before to print the receipt for our customers. Notice that we have made small changes in our previous codes to accomplish this task. Here is what you need to do:

FIGURE 12.5 Receipt screenshot.

1. Select your Receipt `Form`.
2. Highlight the Print button and look for its `Enabled` property and change it to `True`.

Now double-click the `Form` and add the following in the `Form`'s declaration area:

```
Public Class receiptForm
Private WithEvents documentToPrint _
As New System.Drawing.Printing.PrintDocument
```

This is what we have done for all the other projects. Now double-click on the `printButton` to add these codes:

```
Private Sub printButton_Click _
(ByVal sender As System.Object, _
ByVal e As System.EventArgs) Handles printButton.Click
    'assign dialogboxes to our document
    Me.myDocumentPrintPreviewDialog.Document = _
        Me.documentToPrint
    Me.myDocumentPrintPreviewDialog.ShowDialog()
    Me.myDocumentPrintDialog.Document = _
        Me.documentToPrint
End Sub
```

This code should look familiar and does not require explanation. Now add the following to the `PrintPage` event handler:

```
Private Sub documentToPrint_PrintPage _
(ByVal sender As Object, _
ByVal e As System.Drawing.Printing. _
PrintPageEventArgs) Handles documentToPrint.PrintPage
    'print the Title
```

```
Using titleFont As New Font _
("arial", 18, FontStyle.Bold)
    e.Graphics.DrawString _
    ("Customer Receipt", titleFont, _
    System.Drawing.Brushes.Black, 270, 27)
    'draw line under Customers name
    Dim pen1 As New System.Drawing.Pen(Color.Red, 2)
    e.Graphics.DrawLine(pen1, 0, 120, _
    e.PageBounds.Width, 120)

End Using

'Declare fonts for headings and print them
Using headingFont As New _
System.Drawing.Font("Arial", _
12, FontStyle.Bold)
    'Print the caption for User
    'Name using headingFont
    e.Graphics.DrawString _
    ("Name: ", headingFont, _
    System.Drawing.Brushes.Black, 10, 100)
    'Print the caption for the ice cream type
    ' using headingFont
    e.Graphics.DrawString _
("Product: ", headingFont, _
System.Drawing.Brushes.Black, 10, 130)
    'Print heading for Phone number
    e.Graphics.DrawString _
    ("Phone Number ", headingFont, _
    System.Drawing.Brushes.Black, 10, 160)
    'print heading for the total
    e.Graphics.DrawString _
("Total Charge ", headingFont, _
System.Drawing.Brushes.Black, 10, 190)
End Using
'declare smaller fonts
Using dataFont As New System.Drawing.Font _
("Arial", 10, System.Drawing.FontStyle.Regular)
    'Printing users receipt details
    'dataFont
    e.Graphics.DrawString _
    (userNameReceiptLabel.Text, dataFont, _
    System.Drawing.Brushes.Black, 200, 100)
    e.Graphics.DrawString _
    (iceCreamNameLabel.Text, dataFont, _
    System.Drawing.Brushes.Black, 200, 130)
    e.Graphics.DrawString _
    (phoneMaskedTextBox.Text, dataFont, _
    System.Drawing.Brushes.Black, 200, 160)
    e.Graphics.DrawString _
    (totalPriceLabel.Text, dataFont, _
    System.Drawing.Brushes.Black, 200, 190)
```

```
        End Using
    End Sub
```

This code is very similar to what we did before. We just added more details to it (see Figure 12.6).

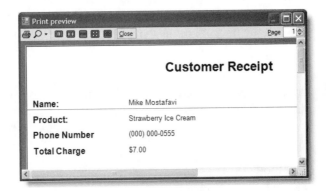

FIGURE 12.6 Print Preview of the receipt.

You can view this solution under the Chapter 12 folder on the companion CD-ROM. The project is saved under its name, `iceCreamShop`. Just copy the solution folder to your hard drive and double-click on the .sln file.

SUMMARY

In this chapter, we showed you how to set up and format your output and print reports. In addition, we demonstrated how to draw line and shapes. We explained the nature of *Print* dialog boxes and utilized them in the sample projects. We used loops to read the contents of `ComboBoxes` and print them.

Next

In Chapter 13, we cover stream text files and show you how to read them into your program. We also explain how these files can be saved on your system. We then explain tables and databases and through a step-by-step process help you connect your applications to SQL or Access databases.

DISCUSSION QUESTIONS

1. How many dialog boxes are provided for printing? Name them and briefly explain their nature.
2. Is it possible to draw shapes in Visual Basic? Please comment.
3. Name the most important method for printing.
4. How do you set up a page break in Visual Basic printing?
5. What is the purpose of the Using block? Please explain.

Exercise

Create a multiple-Form project. Transfer information from one form to another one. Extract data from both Forms and print them.

Key Terms

- Print method
- Print document component
- GDI
- Using block
- *Print Preview* dialog box

13   Files, Tables, and Databases

In This Chapter

- Multitier Applications
- Dealing with Data
- Introducing `IO.StreamReader`
- Introducing `IO.StreamWriter`
- Relational Databases
- Using a Database, SQL Server, and Access Database
- ADO.NET 2.0
- `BindingNavigator` Control
- `DataGridView` Control
- Server Explorer

MULTITIER APPLICATIONS

In Chapter 1 and Chapter 9, we touched on the concept of object-oriented programming and covered its many features. In this chapter, we will include databases in our applications so you will become familiar with this important concept as well. In previous chapters, we recognized data as an important asset that is integrated into our projects. So far, we have been working on the user interface, the code behind the application, and now we will add databases to it. In object-oriented programming, these three components are known as *three multitier applications*. The three logical tiers are the following objects:

User Interface: The `Forms` are designed and needed controls are added.

Business Objects: The inputs are validated, sorted, calculated, and accessed.

Data: The input is stored and retrieved in your Grade Book (see Figure 13.1).

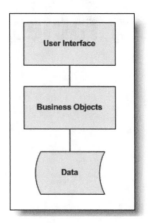

FIGURE 13.1   Multitier application logical tiers.

Think of the multitier applications as the players on a soccer team. They perform individually but need to work as a team to be successful. The multitier applications facilitate the smooth distribution of the applications among other users. Each tier is designed independently and can change without affecting the other two tiers. As a result, in a case of expansion, we do not need to redesign the entire program because the changes affect only one tier. At the same time, these three tiers work together to make the distribution of the software smooth. Obviously, without the business object, the data cannot be accessed, and without the user interface, the data will not be available to the users.

The concept of the multitier application is not new. However, since the release of the .NET it has received more attention. The .NET technology provides the required support for this architecture, but designing the applications that can be recognized as multitier requires planning and expertise.

DEALING WITH DATA

You may have asked yourself when you would learn to save your data permanently. You will learn that now and we will discuss data files, databases, tables, records, and other related topics in this chapter. However, before we proceed, we need to understand a few essential terms. We normally cover these terms in our introductory computer classes, but it is not a bad idea to discuss them here and refresh your memory. Let us talk about the way people keep track of their daily lives. They may keep track of their classes, grades, teachers' names, and other information by writing them down in a notebook. They could organize this notebook like a table, with columns and rows, or just divide the items by lines, spaces, or any other divider. They could have used the same notebook to make a shopping list or jot down notes about things to do. Figure 13.2 shows what a typical notebook would look like.

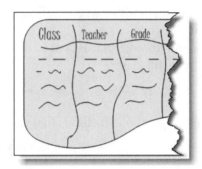

FIGURE 13.2   Your notebook organization.

If you wanted to be more organized, you could have typed the information in a Notepad document and saved it on your hard drive as a text file. It is not important how you do it. It is important that the data is available to you and that you can access it at any time. Once you type your information into a text file document, you can access it faster and more easily. This text file is known as a *flat data file*.

Flat Data Files

A flat data file is the simplest method to store data. You can store memos, addresses, phone numbers, and other information in it. Flat files, which are transportable among different computers and operating systems, can be used as system input and output files. All computers have the mechanism to process flat data files, which have ASCII format. A flat file is a single file that can represent some form of data structures. The Visual Basic 2005 software provides the needed mechanism to read and write these files. We need to be familiar with the process of *read/write* before we introduce you to more complicated file-handling mechanisms.

INTRODUCING IO.STREAMREADER

Through Visual Basic tools, you can read existing files from your hard drive and view them in your application. You can also resave the file under the same name or any other name. This can be accomplished by the tools referenced above. IO.StreamReader is a class that is designed to read the content of your standard text file. There are other tools that are availabe to read relational databases. We will talk about them later in this chapter.

The IO.StreamReader class is a good tool for accessing text files. It is designed to read lines of text and transfer them to the buffer of the computer. Our application program can retrieve the transferred data. IO.StreamReader has many methods that can be used within our code.

We need to use an instance of this class to read texts. Here is the general syntax for instantiating from this class:

```
Dim streamReaderIO As IO.StreamReader
```

Here are some of the public methods that are available for the IO.StreamReader class:

- Close
- ReadLine
- ReadToEnd

Close **Method**

This method is used to close the StreamReader object. The system resources will be released after the execution of this method. Here is an example:

```
streamReaderIO.Close()
```

ReadLine **Method**

This method is used to read a line of text. A line of text is a string of characters followed by a line feed. When the end of the input stream is detected, then the value of the line feed would be null (Nothing in Visual Basic). The displayed text read from the stream will not include the line feed. Here is an example:

```
dataTextBox.Text = streamReaderIO.ReadLine
```

ReadToEnd **Method**

We use this method when we want to read the entire stream from any given position to the end. Here is an example:

```
dataTextBox.Text = streamReaderIO.ReadToEnd
```

If the memory is not sufficient to hold the string that is read into memory, an OutOfMemoryException will occur.

INTRODUCING IO.STREAMWRITER

This class is used to write characters into a stream. There are many methods for this class as well. Here are a few of them:

- Close
- Write
- WriteLine

We explained the function of the Close method before, so let us discuss the other two terms:

Write Method

This method is used to write specified text to the stream. Here is an example:

```
streamWriterIO.Write("Mike")
```

WriteLine Method

This method is similar to the Write method, with the exception that it will have a line terminator at the end of the text. Here is an example:

```
streamWriterIO.WriteLine(textEntryTextBox.Text)
```

Creating a New File

The StreamWriter can be used to create new files. This is useful when the output file is set to be generated dynamically at the runtime. Here is an example:

```
Dim streamWriterIO As New _
    IO.StreamWriter("C:\myfile.txt")
        With streamWriterIO
            .Write("Hello ")
            .WriteLine(Date.Now)
            .Close()
        End With
```

A new file with the name myfile.txt will be created and the output will be similar to the following:

```
Hello 2/3/2006 12:08:43 AM
```

OpenFileDialog

This class is used to prompt the user to open an existing file. We need to use the ShowDialog method to prompt the user. Here are some of the available properties for this dialog box:

- Filter
- FileName
- InitialDirectory
- FilterIndex

Filter Property

This property allows us to display the files with specific extensions. Here is an example:

```
openFileDilogBox.Filter = "(*.txt)|*.txt|All Files (*.*)|*.*"
```

This filter will show all files, and *.txt is the selection option under the File of Type ComboBox.

FileName Property

This property will show the string in the File Name ComboBox:

```
openFileDilogBox.FileName = "Text Files"
```

InitialDirectory

This property will set the initial search directory for the user:

```
openFileDilogBox.InitialDirectory = _
    "C:\Documents and Settings\Administrator\Desktop"
```

FilterIndex

This property will allow you to display a selected File of Type filter as the default option:

```
openFileDilogBox.Filter = "(*.txt)|*.txt|All Files (*.*)|*.*| RTF Files
(*.*)|*.rtf"
openFileDilogBox.FilterIndex = (3)
```

In this example, RTF files, as the third index, will be shown as the first option in the File of Type window.

SaveFileDialog

This class is designed to let you choose the location in which you want to save your file. SaveFileDialog and OpenFileDialog have many similar public properties including the Filter, FileName, FileIndex, and InitialDirectory. We want to reference a new public property for the SaveFileDialog, which is the DefaultExt property.

DefaultExt Property

This property allows us to add a default extension to the file we are saving. Here is an example:

```
saveFileDialogBox.DefaultExt = "txt"
```

EXAMPLE 1

Create a new solution and call it readAndWriteStream. In this project, we will open text files and read the contents into a TextBox. We will have the following controls (see Figure 13.3):

- One TextBox
- Four Buttons
- One OpenFileDialog
- One SaveFileDialog

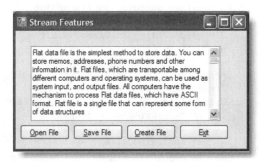

FIGURE 13.3   Example 3 screenshot.

Change the properties for the following controls:

- **TextBox1**
  Name: dataTextBox
  Multiline: True
  ScrollBars: Both

- **OpenFileDialog**
  Name: openFileDilogBox
- **SaveFileDialog**
  Name: saveFileDialogBox

Rename the other controls according to the naming conventions. Double-click on the openFileButton and add the following:

```
Private Sub readButton_Click _
(ByVal sender As System.Object, _
ByVal e As System.EventArgs) _
Handles readButton.Click

    'a dialogbox will prompt the user to pick a file
    With Me.openFileDilogBox
        'displaying Text Files in the File Name ComboBox
        .FileName = "Text Files"
        'setting the filters
        .Filter = _
        "(*.txt)|*.txt|All Files(*.*)|*.*| RTF Files (*.*)|*.rtf"
        'Selecting the Deskcop as the initial search directory
        .InitialDirectory = _
        "C:\Documents and Settings\Administrator\Desktop"
        'RTF file will be the default file type
        .FilterIndex = (1)
    End With

    'open the file and display its content in the textbox.
    Try
        Dim resultDialog As DialogResult = _
        Me.openFileDilogBox.ShowDialog

        resultDialog = Windows.Forms.DialogResult.OK
        'read the file to end
        Using streamReaderIO As New IO.StreamReader _
        (Me.openFileDilogBox.FileName)
            Me.dataTextBox.Text = String.Empty
            Me.dataTextBox.Text = streamReaderIO.ReadToEnd
            streamReaderIO.Close()
        End Using
    Catch ex As Exception
        MessageBox.Show("Error in Reading", "Warning", _
        MessageBoxButtons.OK, MessageBoxIcon.Information)

    End Try

End Sub
```

In these statements, we use the OpenFileDialog with selected properties such as Filter and InitialDirectory to open a file and read the content of it into a TextBox.

We used an instance of the IO. StreamReader and the OpenFileDialog along with the parameters such as InitialDirectory, FileName, and Filter.

Now double-click on the saveFileButton and add the following code:

```
Private Sub saveButton_Click _
(ByVal sender As System.Object, _
ByVal e As System.EventArgs) _
Handles saveButton.Click
    'a dialogbox will prompt the user
    With Me.saveFileDialogBox
        'displaying Text Files in the File Name ComboBox
        .FileName = "Text Files"
        'setting the filters
        .Filter = _
        "(*.txt)|*.txt|All Files(*.*)|*.*| RTF Files (*.*)|*.rtf"
        'Selecting the Desktop as the initial search directory
        .InitialDirectory = _
        "C:\Documents and Settings\Administrator\Desktop"
        'txt file will be the default file type
        .FilterIndex = (1)
        'the saved file will have the TXT extension.
        .DefaultExt = "txt"

    End With
    Try
        Dim resultDialog As DialogResult = saveFileDialogBox.ShowDialog

        'Saving the file
        Using streamWriterIO As New IO.StreamWriter _
        (Me.saveFileDialogBox.FileName)

            streamWriterIO.Write(dataTextBox.Text)
            streamWriterIO.Close()
        End Using
    Catch ex As Exception
        MessageBox.Show("Error in Saving", "Warning", _
        MessageBoxButtons.OK, MessageBoxIcon.Information)
    End Try

End Sub
```

This code is very similar to the Open File code you saw before. Instead of IO. StreamReader, we use IO.StreamWriter to save the file.

Now we want to code the createFileButton. Double-click on this Button and add the following statements:

```
Private Sub createButton_Click _
(ByVal sender As System.Object, _
ByVal e As System.EventArgs) _
Handles createButton.Click
    'creates a new file
```

```
Using streamWriterIO As New _
IO.StreamWriter("C:\myfile.txt")
    'Write to the file
    With streamWriterIO
        'use Write and writeline
        .Write("Hello")
        .WriteLine(Date.Now)
        'close
        .Close()
    End With
End Using
End Sub
```

This code is self-explanatory and the comments describe its nature.

Complete the exitButton, save your project, and run it. Select a text file and display the contents in the TextBox.

You can view this solution under the Chapter 13 folder on the companion CD-ROM. The project is saved under its name, readAndWriteStream. Just copy the solution folder to your hard drive and double-click on the .sln file.

My.Computer.FileSystem Object

As stated before, My, the new namespace that is introduced with Framework 2.0, provides many features that can be used within your project. One of the new objects is My.Computer.FileSystem, which has many useful methods. It is recommended that you use features offered by this object if you want to manipulate text files within Visual Basic. What we discussed about IO.StreamReader and IO.StreamWriter is still valid and used for backward compatibility. Let's get familiar with some of the tools that are available within this object.

The ReadAllText method allows you to read the content of the text file. The ASCII or UTF-8 encoding can be specified within your codes. Here is an example:

```
fileSystemTextBox.Text = _
My.Computer.FileSystem.ReadAllText("readme.txt")
```

In the above statement, we are reading the content of the text file into a TextBox object. The TextBox's Multiline property is set to True.

The WriteAllText method is used to write the text to the specified file, which will be created if it cannot be found within the directory. You can set the Append feature to True to append the new text to the existing content:

```
My.Computer.FileSystem.WriteAllText _
    ("writeto.txt", fileSystemTextBox.Text, True)
```

In the above statement, we created the file named writeto and placed the content of the TextBox into it.

`My.Computer.FileSystem` provides many other features that are beyond the scope of this book. For more information please visit the following URL: *http://msdn2. microsoft.com/en-us/library/y32kbeb6.aspx*.

ON THE CD

We have created a simple project to show a few of these features. You can view this solution under the Chapter 13 folder on the companion CD-ROM. The project is saved under its name, `fileSystem`. Just copy the solution folder to your hard drive and double-click on the .sln file.

RELATIONAL DATABASES

Although a text file can have some kind of data structure, there is no relationship between the different fields of a record. However, today, the most popular database system is known as relational databases. Explaining and exploring the relational database system concept is beyond the scope of this book, but we will give you a brief introduction so you can understand it and use it in your projects. In the relational database system, the relational model is used to organize the database. We can briefly define the concept of database as follows:

■ A *database* is a collection of related *tables*.
■ A *table* is a group of related *records*.
■ A *record* consists of a group of related *fields*.
■ A *field* is a unit of *data*.

The appearance of a table is very similar to a spreadsheet, which is divided into rows and columns. However, tables and spreadsheets have different characteristics (see Figure 13.4).

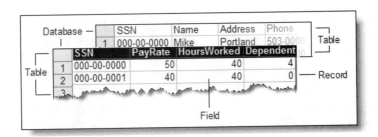

FIGURE 13.4 Relational database organization.

USING A DATABASE, SQL SERVER, AND ACCESS DATABASE

In most cases, the database is created outside the application program, using one of the popular software packages such as Microsoft Access™ or SQL Server™. It is also possible to create a database at runtime. Most databases come with a pool of samples that can be used as models. Both the SQL Server and Microsoft Access use samples known as Northwind. These premade samples are designed to provide different database models for new users. Most database packages come with a Wizard that helps you accomplish tasks.

Here is a URL that you can visit for more information: *http://msdn2.microsoft.com/en-us/library/5ey0sd99.aspx.*

ADO.NET 2.0

ADO (Active-X Data Objects) offers many classes to use to access and manipulate data. It allows you to create, distribute, share, and manipulate data. Two classes handle the data connection and data manipulation, which are separated from each other.

The new ADO.NET has many new features, including data tracing, database mirroring, and asynchronous processing. It can recognize many different data sources including Microsoft SQL Server and XML data sources. ADO.NET uses XML format to transmit datasets across a network. Because of this, the receiver should have XML capability to be able to process data. The receiving component does not have to have ADO.NET. This allows us to send datasets from one network to another without worrying about the structure of the receiving component.

Connection Objects: `BindingSource`

ADO provides different connection objects to be used for different data sources. For example, the connection object that is used to connect to SQL Server is different from the one that is used to connect to an Oracle database or XML data source.

By using the connection object, we find the data source and learn about its characteristics. In Visual Basic 2005, the connection object is called `BindingSource`. The `BindingSource` facilitates the communication between your program and the database. Once the wizard finds your database, it will copy it to your project folder if it is not already there. We will connect our application to the data source by using the Data Source Configuration Wizard. Once this task is complete, the `DataSet` will be generated.

`BindingSource.EndEdit` **Method**

When you have made changes to the data, including adding, modifying, or deleting, you need to call this method to apply the changes to the data source. The changes you have made remain pending until you execute this method. We call this method before we update the data source.

`DataSet` **Object**

Once the connection between your data source and `BindingSource` is established, the `DataSet` object will be generated. The `DataSet` is the representation of data source and relations that exists between tables. The `DataSet` will reside in the main memory of the computer as cache data and plays an important role in the architecture of ADO.NET.

The data will be populated into the `DataSet` and will be available for retrieval during the execution of your program. This memory-resident data can be changed and updated at any time. The `DataSet` is not connected to your database, and you will be dealing with the copy of it, which is loaded into the memory of the computer. The `DataSet` is created automatically once you use the `BindingSource` to make the connection with your data source.

`TableAdapter` **Object**

Once the `DataSet` is created, it becomes the job of the `TableAdapter` to become an interpreter between the `DataSet` and data source. The `TableAdaptor` provides many methods that can be used to make changes to the data source.

`Fill` **Method**

The `Fill` method is used to populate the `DataSet` with the selected table columns and rows from the data source. In other words, the `DataSet` can include a portion of the data source but not the entire data. Here is an example:

```
Me.StudentTableAdapter.Fill(Me.StudentDataSet.student)
```

`Update` **Method**

Once we manipulate the data that is included in our `DataSet`, we can use the `TableAdapter`'s `Update` method to change the content of our data source.

```
Me.StudentTableAdapter.Update(Me.StudentDataSet.student)
```

ClearBeforeFill Property

This method becomes handy when you want to make sure the latest data is displayed for the user or you want to append data to the table. By default this property is set to True and the table will be cleared before it is filled. However, you can set it to False to append new data to the existing one. Here is an example:

```
Me.StudentTableAdapter.ClearBeforeFill = False
```

Other methods can be used in your project. Review the MSDN library to explore additional methods available for TableAdapter and other referenced object. Here are more that you can look into:

- DataSet.HasChanges
- DataSet.AcceptChanges

BINDINGNAVIGATOR CONTROL

Most programmers make their own techniques to navigate through the displayed data. Although most of their techniques work, the users detect the lack of consistency among these techniques immediately.

Visual Basic 2005 introduces the BindingNavigator control, which provides a standard method to navigate through data. The BindingNavigator is a ToolStrip with data navigation controls on it. This ToolStrip has automated many features that used to be coded by programmers (see Figure 13.5).

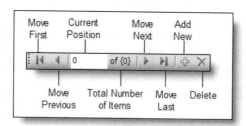

FIGURE 13.5 BindingNavigator's features.

DATAGRIDVIEW CONTROL

This is an excellent control for people who are used to viewing data in spreadsheet format. DataGridView can be used to display a small or large amount of the data. You can give the user the authority to read the data only or be able to edit it.

EXAMPLE 2

We are assuming that you have installed Visual Basic and SQL Server 2005 on your computer. Microsoft offers Visual Basic 2005 Express Edition bounded with Express MSDN and SQL Server 2005 Express edition at the following Web site: *http://msdn. microsoft.com/vstudio/express/vb/download/default.aspx.*

In this example, we will show you how to create the BindingSource, DataSet, and TableAdapter objects. We will add the DataGridView and BindingNavigator controls to our project. We will also add four TextBoxes to display individual fields within the database.

Start a new project and call it connectToData. Before we add any controls, let us create a connection to the database. As stated before, there are many sample databases that you could download from Microsoft and use for learning purposes. Here is a great link to the Microsoft Web site that you can use to download the latest versions of Northwind database samples: *http://www.microsoft.com/downloads/details.aspx?FamilyId=06616212-0356-46A0-8DA2-EEBC53A68034&displaylang= en%20.* The name of the installer file is SQL2000SampleDb.msi.

We have included a sample SQL data source in this project so you can use it as a testing tool for your projects. We have also included a Microsoft Access database for your practice as well. Lets us start now.

You have created a new project that has a blank form. We will create a Binding-Source object before we add any controls to our form. On the menu bar, click on the Data menu drop-down tab and select Add Data Source from the submenu (see Figure 13.6).

FIGURE 13.6   BindingNavigator's features.

This will start the Data Source Configuration Wizard. Select the Database icon and click. This task allows you to choose the data source type and tell the system where to find the data that your application will be using (see Figure 13.7). The next screen allows you to choose your data connection (see Figure 13.8).

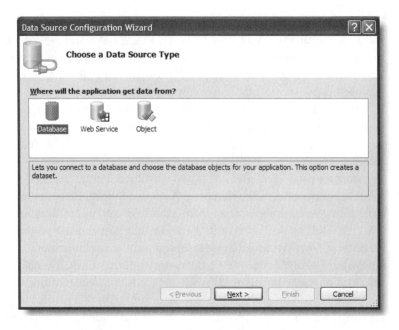

FIGURE 13.7 Data Source Configuration Wizard.

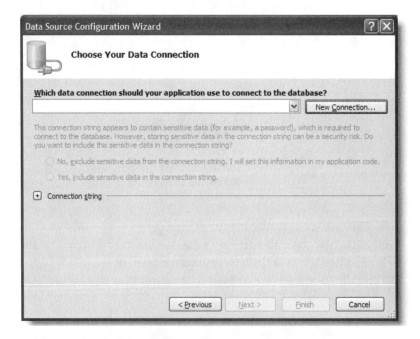

FIGURE 13.8 Choosing the data connection.

The next page is designed to let you add a connection by choosing the data source and database name (see Figure 13.9). Click on the Data Source Change button to change the default setting to the Microsoft SQL Server Database file (see Figure 13.10).

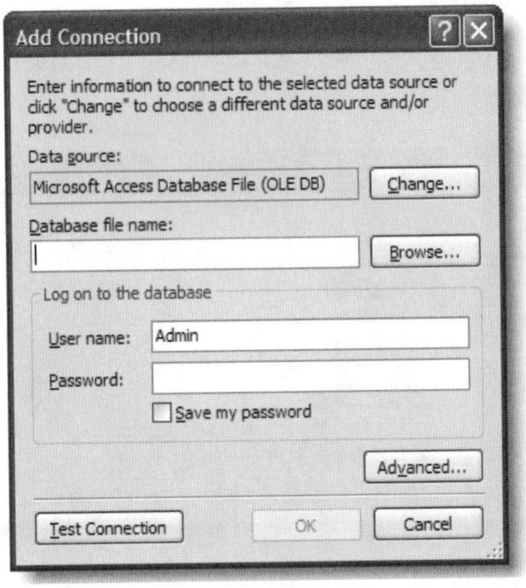

FIGURE 13.9   Adding the connection.

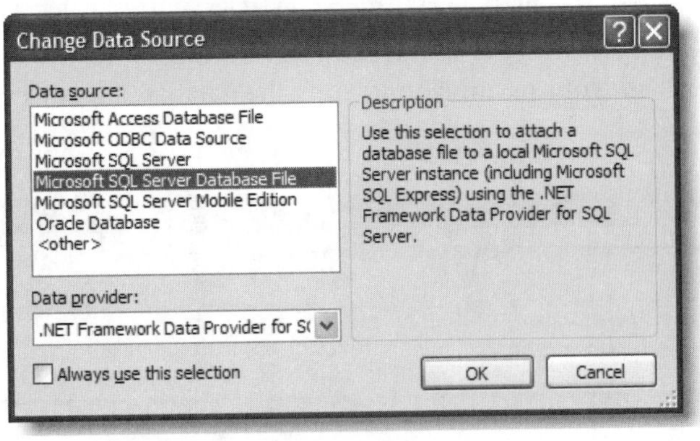

FIGURE 13.10   Changing the data source.

The SQL Sever 2005 has been used to develop the data source that you receive with this project. SQL (pronounced *sequel*) stands for *Structured Query Language*. This language is used to communicate with relational databases. The SQL Server, on the other hand, is a database management system that is designed to interact with re-lational databases. Your SQL database needs to communicate with the SQL Server.

Once you highlighted the Microsoft SQL Server Database file option, click on the *OK* button to get back to the previous screen. This time click on the Browse button to pick the database file name. This action takes you to the Select SQL Server Database File. You can either use the small file that we have selected for this project or use another SQL file. Our recommendation is to go with ours so you can compare the result. Once the database is selected, click on the Open button (see Figure 13.11).

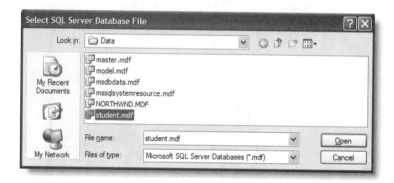

FIGURE 13.11   Select SQL Sever Database File page.

As soon as you click on Open, you will see the Data Source Configuration Wizard page that you saw before (Figure 13.8). The name of the database is placed in the Connection ComboBox. Click on the Next button to see the next screen. Visual Basic 2005 will ask your permission to copy the database file into your project (see Figure 13.12).

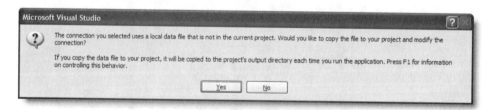

FIGURE 13.12   Copying the database into your project folder.

The database file will be copied into two different locations:

- Your project folder
- You debug folder that contains your executable file

When you access your database file and make changes to it, the result will be saved to the output file, which is located in Debug folder, within the Bin folder. The file that is located inside your project is not affected and will be used as an input file.

You have selected the database, and now it is your chance to select the tables and the fields within each table to be included in the DataSet. For now, pick the whole Student Table. (see Figure 13.13).

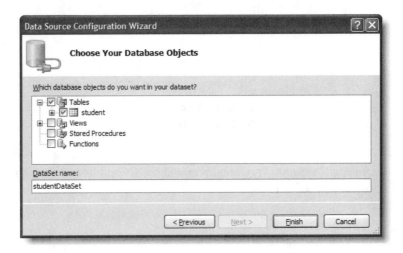

FIGURE 13.13 Choosing your database objects.

If you look inside your Solution Explorer, you will see two new files:

- Student.mdf database file
- StudentDataSet.xsd file

Now we need to add a few controls to our empty form. Drag a DataGridView control from your Toolbox and drop it on the form. This control is located under the Data group in your Toolbox. Now click on the Smart Tag, which is located on the top of the DataGridView, and choose the Student Table as the data source (see Figure 13.14).

Once the data source is identified, the column heading for your data source will appear on the DataGridView columns.

Next, we want to drag and drop a BindingNavigator onto your form. This is very similar to the ToolStrip you used before. Highlight the BindingNavigator and look for the BindingSource property in the Properties window. Use the drop-down menu and select the StudentBindingSource as the option.

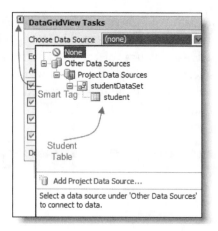

FIGURE 13.14 Choose the data source
for DataGridView.

In the Common Tray area, you will see several items (see Figure 13.15). Here are what you should see:

■ StudentDataSet
■ StudentBindingSource
■ StudentTableAdapter
■ StudentBindingNavigator

FIGURE 13.15 The binding components in the *Common Tray* area.

These components allow you to do additional tasks. For example, highlight the StudentBindingSource and click on its Smart Tag. You will see the following options:

■ Add Query
■ Preview Data

Click on the Preview Data option and click on Preview, which is located on the next page. You will see the data that your program is connected to. Similar options are available for the StudentTableAdapter component.

Now highlight the StudentDataSet and click on its Smart Tag, and from there, click on the Edit in DataSet Designer option. This will open the Student Table structure. You will see the fields for the student table. Right-click on the StudentTableAdapter and click on the Configure option (see Figure 13.16). This allows you to modify the fields, which needed to be included in the DataSet, and change other parameters within it (see Figure 13.17).

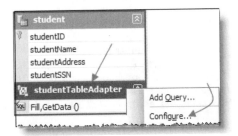

FIGURE 13.16 Configuring the StudentTableAdapter.

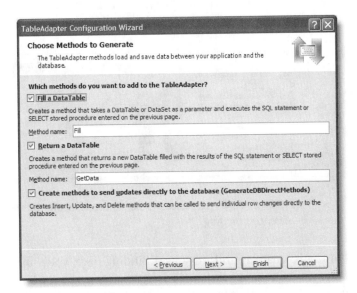

FIGURE 13.17 TableAdapter Configuration Wizard.

Configure them according to the screenshot. Click on the Finish button to complete this task or click on the Next button to see other options.

Let use go back to the Form. Add three more Buttons to the StudentBinding-Navigator that you added to the Form. These Buttons will do the following:

- Update the data source and DataSet
- Refresh the DataGridView
- Exit the program

Choose appropriate images for these three Buttons.

Now double-click the form and look under the Form_load subprocedure. You will notice that Visual Basic automatically has inserted the code for you:

```
Private Sub dataDisplayForm_Load _
(ByVal sender As System.Object, _
ByVal e As System.EventArgs) _
Handles MyBase.Load
    'TODO: This line of code loads data into the
    'StudentDataSet.student' table.
    Me.StudentTableAdapter.Fill(Me.StudentDataSet.student)

End Sub
```

Now add four Labels to your Form and bind them with individual fields of the table. To bind a Label to a specific field of your table, just highlight it and click on the plus sign next to DataBinding property in the Properties box. Click on the Advanced row and then click on the File Dialog button (see Figure 13.18).

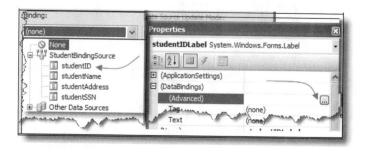

FIGURE 13.18 The Label Binding property and formatting and advanced binding.

In the Formatting and Advanced Binding page, you will see the Binding ComboBox. Open the ComboBox and expand the StudentBindingSource to see all fields within your table. Click on the StudentID field and bind it to the Label. Follow the same instructions for the other three Labels and bind them to the remaining fields. Save your project and run it. Figure 13.19 shows what you should see.

You can move from one row to another one by using the tools available in the BindingNavigator. The current record will also be displayed in the four Labels you added. You can add new records by clicking on the Add New button and remove records by clicking on the Delete button.

FIGURE 13.19 Example 2 screenshot

Double-click the updateDataButton, which is on the BindingNavigator and type the following:

```
Private Sub updateToolStripButton_Click _
(ByVal sender As System.Object, _
ByVal e As System.EventArgs) _
Handles updateToolStripButton.Click

    Try
        'applies the changes to the data source
        Me.StudentBindingSource.EndEdit()
        Me.StudentTableAdapter.Update(Me.StudentDataSet.student)
        MessageBox.Show _
        ("The data set and data source were updated", _
        "System Message", MessageBoxButtons.OK, _
        MessageBoxIcon.Information)
    Catch ex As Exception
        'in a case of problem, display this message
        MessageBox.Show _
        ("There was a problem updating the data source", _
        "System Message", MessageBoxButtons.OK, _
        MessageBoxIcon.Information)
    End Try

End Sub
```

As you can see in this code, the EndEdit method is used to apply the changes to the data source, and it is followed by the Update method.

When we change the data, we would like to refresh the DataGridView so we can see the new data. To accomplish this task, we will be using the Fill method.

Double-click on the refreshButton on the BindingNavigator and add the following code:

```
Private Sub refreshToolStripButton_Click _
(ByVal sender As System.Object, _
ByVal e As System.EventArgs) _
Handles refreshToolStripButton.Click
    'filling the table
            Me.StudentTableAdapter.Fill(Me.StudentDataSet.student)

End Sub
```

Complete the code for the Exit button and save and run the program. Click on the Add New button to see that a new row is added to the DataGridView for data entry. Clicking on the Delete button will remove a row from the DataGridView.

When you are done with your changes, click on the Update button to update your data source. After this action, you can click on the Refresh button to load the DataGridView with the updated data.

Once you leave the program and run it again, you will notice that the old data source without your changes is displayed in the DataGridView. You may wonder what happened to your changes. Your changes took place in a different data source. As you remember, during the connection and binding process, Visual Basic copied your data source into two different locations:

- The Project folder
- The Debug folder

The change occurred in the data source that is located in the Debug folder (output). You can run the EXE copy of your project, which is located in the Debug folder, to see your changes. You can also build your project, and an EXE copy of the file will be placed in the Release folder. However, the connection that you made at the design time refers to the original data source that is in the Project folder, not the output file that is in the Debug folder. There have been many discussions regarding the logic that is used to access these files. If you want to use different methods to copy your file and access it, please see the following URL: *http://blogs.msdn.com/ smartclientdata/archive/2005/08/26/456886.aspx.*

SERVER EXPLORER

The Server Explorer is a console used to manage your data within Visual Studio. You can view the connections to the databases and view the tables and fields through this powerful tool. You can also create databases and tables from within the Visual Studio

IDE. The Server Explorer appears below the Toolbox. If it not visible, click on the View menu item and select Server Explorer from the drop-down menu (see Figure 13.20).

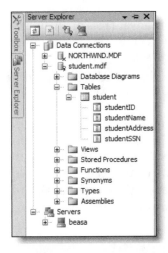

FIGURE 13.20   *Server Explorer.*

Here is an excellent sample provided by Microsoft. It is included within the MSDN help library: *http://msdn2.microsoft.com/en-us/library/518xbwd.aspx*. Please follow the instructions to download tyhe CreateDB.zip file and use it.

ON THE CD

You can view this solution under the Chapter 13 folder on the companion CD-ROM. The project is saved under its name, myDatabaseConncetion. Just copy the solution folder to your hard drive and double-click on the .sln file.

SUMMARY

In this chapter, the concepts of StreamRead and StreamWrite were explained You saw how text files can be read into a TextBox or saved as an output file. You learned how to create a text file and how to read the entire file or line by line. We also discussed relational databases and showed you how you can connect to them, create DataSets, and use update databases. We used the features of ADO.20 and all classes related to it.

Next

In Chapter 14 you will be introduced to the Web Forms and ASP pages. You will learn how to add Web controls to your pages and navigate through pages. You will become familiar with terms such as *Style Builder* and RequiredFieldValidator.

DISCUSSION QUESTIONS

1. What are the differences between text Files and relational databases? Please explain.
2. What are the advantages of relational databases over the text files?
3. Does ADO use the same connection methodology to connect to all databases? Justify your response.
4. Is there any differenced between SQL Sever databases and Microsoft Access?
5. What is the function of `DataGridView`? What is the role of `BindingNavigator`?

Exercise

Modify the `ImageListToolstrip` project you completed in Chapter 7 and add the following feature to it. The user can read text files into the text area and can write the content of the `TextBox` into an external file. Add another page to be able to manipulate relational databases. Figure 13.21 shows a suggested screen design.

FIGURE 13.21   Suggested screen design for the exercise.

Key Terms

- SQL Server
- ADO NET
- `BindingSource`
- `DataSet`
- `DataGridView`
- `TableAdapter`
- `BindingNavigater`

14   Web FORMS

In This Chapter

- Client/Server Terms
- ASP.NET 2.0
- How to Create a Web Form
- Publishing Your Web site

Up until now, you have been using Windows Forms for all of your projects. However, as you may know, you can create Web applications as well. Browsers can view the Web Forms that you design. Like databases, the concept of Web programming requires special attention. In this chapter we will cover the essential topics that can help you understand this concept.

CLIENT/SERVER TERMS

Every day, as part of your job or hobby, you surf the Internet to visit Web sites, use the links on your favorite pages, and download what you need for business or personal use. The pages that you download are located in special computers called *servers*. These computers are dedicated to provide Web services. Once you click on the link, a document, which is known as *Web page*, will be sent to your local computer for viewing. This local computer, which is known as a *client*, can view these pages by using special software called *browsers*. A Web page, which is written in HTML codes, can contain text materials and other instructions and will be interpreted by the browser. HTML stands for Hypertext Markup Language, which is the foundation for all Web pages you see on the Internet and intranets.

In addition to the remote servers, you could have your local host within your machine. The Visual Studio software helps you set up a local server.

ASP.NET 2.0

Although HTML provides the basic structure for static Web pages, it does not give programmers the tools they need to develop interactive programs. HTML is a markup language, not a programming language. To overcome the weakness of HTML, other programming languages such as Java (applets) and JavaScript have integrated themselves with HTML to provide better services to the demanding world. Microsoft developed ASP (Active Server Pages), which combines HTML tags with text, XML, and scripts. The servers process the scripts, which are the programming portion of these documents.

ASP.NET was the newest product of Microsoft that allowed users to use the visual editors to create Web pages within the IDE. ASP.NET 2.0 has made Web programming much easier than before. ASP.NET 2.0 created object-oriented Web pages that generate the HTML codes automatically. Each ASP document consists of Visual Basic instructions and HTML. Explaining all details about the Web server, type of Web sites, Internet Information Server(IIS), and other terms is beyond the scope of this book, but we will cover the basics in this chapter.

HOW TO CREATE A WEB FORM

Creating a Web Form in Visual Basic 2005 is not that much different from creating the Windows Form. Like the Windows Form, Visual Basic starts the Web development process by creating a default Web Form. The tools that you can use in Web Forms are different from those you used in the Windows Form.

New Toolbox

Once you start a Web project, you will notice new categories within your Toolbox. Here they are:

HTML controls: These controls are used for basic HTML operations. You cannot add Visual Basic codes to these controls. The client side will handle these controls.

Data Controls: These are the controls that are used in data handling such as connecting to the database and displaying data on the form.

Login Controls: These are designed to give you many options for username and password.

Validation Controls: These are used to validate the user's input including required field controls.

Navigation Controls: These controls include menus, site maps, and so on.

WebParts Controls: These allow users to change the components of the Web page.

Crystal Report Controls: These include tools for Crystal Report including Crystal Report Viewer.

Standards Controls: These controls are known as server side controls and give programmers many options to add codes to ASP.NET documents.

Style Builder

The *Style Builder* allows you to add the *Cascade Style Sheet* features to your controls. Eight tabs can be used to change the behavior of your controls. Many options are available to you. You can change the back color, text color, text size, and many other properties through the style builder.

Let us start a new Web project and then we will talk about other concepts.

EXAMPLE 1

Follow these instructions to create a simple Web page: Start your Visual Basic program, click on File, and choose the New Web Site option from the drop-down menu (see Figure 14.1). Choose ASP.NET Web site from this dialog box and then choose a location where you want to save this Web site. It could be anywhere on your hard drive or other media that you use (see Figure 14.2).

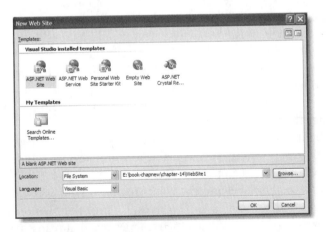

FIGURE 14.1   New Web Site dialog box.

Design and Source Tabs

A default blank Web page is opened for you. At the bottom of the page are the Design and Source tabs that allow you to toggle between the source editor and design

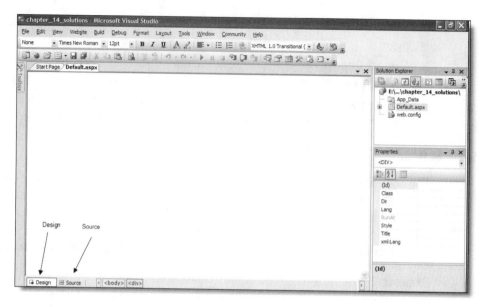

FIGURE 14.2 Default page.

editor. This is useful when you want to switch between the design and code editors. On the top of the page, type "This is My First Page."

Click on your Toolbox and expand the Standard category if it is not expanded. Using the tools in the Standard category, add a Label to your Form and while it is highlighted, look through the Properties window and change the ID property to nameLabel. Scroll down and change the Text property to Enter Your Name.

Add a TextBox to your form and change the ID property to nameTextBox. Scroll down and in the ToolTip property type "username=mike." This is a tip to the user to enter the correct username.

Right-click on the Label and choose Style from the drop-down list to be familiar with the options that are available to you. The Style Builder is available for other controls that we use in this page (see Figure 14.3).

Add another label and change its ID property to passwordLabel. Drag and drop a TextBox and name it passwordTextBox. Change the TextMode property of the passwordTextBox to Password. Add a ToolTip message that reads "password=vb2005."

Add two Buttons to your Form. One will have the caption Validate and the other one will read Clear. Change their ID properties according to the naming conventions.

Adding an Image

Add an Image control and name it passwordImage. Right-click on it and select Style from the drop-down list. Click on the Position tab and click on the Position Mode ComboBox. From the list of options, pick Offset From Normal Flow. This will allow

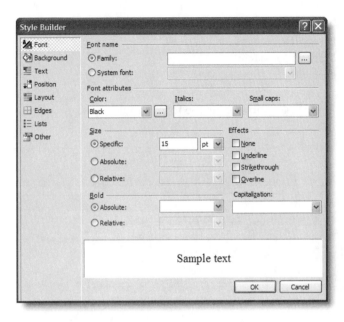

FIGURE 14.3 The *Style Builder*.

you to move the control to the desired position. We will not be adding an image at the design time, but if you want to do that, you could click on the ImageUrl property and choose the images you want to display in the Image control (see Figure 14.4). Instead of placing the image in the Image control at the design time, we will load the image at runtime. Highlight the Image control and set its Visible property to False.

FIGURE 14.4 *Select Image* dialog box.

RequiredFieldValidator

Now click on your Toolbox and expand the Validation category. Drag and drop the RequiredFieldValidator on your form. Highlight this control and change the following in its Properties window:

- `ControlToValidate:` `NameTextBox`
- `ErrorMessage:` `Name is required`
- `Display:` `Dynamic`
- `BorderStyle:` `Dotted`

Figure 14.5 shows how the form should look.

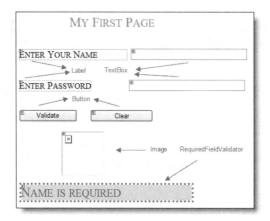

FIGURE 14.5 Example 1 screenshot.

Adding Codes

It is time to add codes to this program. Double-click the Validate button and add the following code:

```
Protected Sub validateButton_Click _
(ByVal sender As Object, _
ByVal e As System.EventArgs) _
Handles validateButton.Click
    'if the user name is mike and the password is vb2005
    'make the image box visible and
    ' display the book image in the image control
    If passwordTextBox.Text = "vb2005" _
    And NameTextBox.Text = "mike" Then
        passwordImage.Visible = True
        passwordImage.ImageUrl = "basic.jpg"
    Else
        'if not then change the back color of both controls to
        'yellow and display a message in the nametextbox
        NameTextBox.BackColor = Drawing.Color.Yellow
        passwordTextBox.BackColor = Drawing.Color.Yellow
        NameTextBox.Text = "Please Check name and password"

    End If
End Sub
```

The event subprocedure is identical to the one you used in the Windows Forms. The code is self-explanatory.

Now double-click the clearButton and add the following code:

```
Protected Sub clearButton_Click _
(ByVal sender As Object, _
ByVal e As System.EventArgs) _
Handles clearButton.Click
    'reset the controls
    NameTextBox.BackColor = Drawing.Color.White
    passwordTextBox.BackColor = Drawing.Color.White
    passwordTextBox.Text = Nothing
    NameTextBox.Text = Nothing
    passwordImage.ImageUrl = Nothing
    passwordImage.Visible = False
End Sub
```

This is very similar to what you did in Windows Forms.

Now save the program. As soon as you want to run the program, you will see the message shown in Figure 14.6. Select the Modify the Web.Config file to enable debugging. This will allow you to debug the Web page.

Your Web page is displayed in the default browser, not the Visual Basic environment. That is because of the ASP file extension that is set to be displayed in the browser (see Figure 14.7).

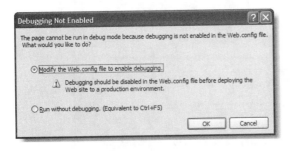

FIGURE 14.6 *Debugging Not Enabled* MessageBox.

FIGURE 14.7 Your first program in the Web browser.

If you look inside the folder that Visual Basic has created for you, you will notice several new files:

- *.aspx
- *.aspx.vb
- Web.config

The file with an extension of aspx is the ASP.NET file that will be displayed in the Web browser. The file with the extension of aspx.vb is the one that is generated by Visual Basic. The last one is the configuration file.

While the program is running, click on the Validate button while the TextBoxes are blank. The RequiredFieldValidator will pop up.

Adding More Pages

Like many other Web sites, you may need to include more pages. In order to do that, click on the Web site tab and select Add New Item from the list of options (see Figure 14.8). From the available pages, select Web Form. A new form will be added to the Solution Explorer.

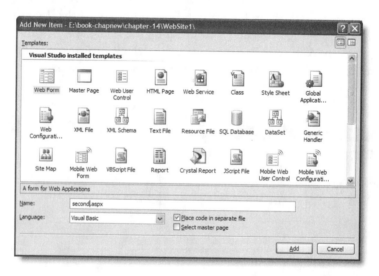

FIGURE 14.8 *Add New Item* dialog box.

HyperLink Control

The HyperLink control allows you to link the pages in your project together or connect you to the World Wide Web. The characteristics of this control are very similar to the LinkLabel control that we used in our Windows Forms. Add a HyperLink control to your first Form right under the RequiredFieldValidator. Right-click on it and select the *Style* option from the drop-down list. Select the Position tab, which is located within the Style Builder page. You will be doing this to all the controls you want to move.

While the HyperLink control is selected, change the ID name and type "Next Page" in its Text property. Find the NavigateUrl property and click on it. You should see the File Open button that will take you to the Select URL dialog box (see Figure 14.9).

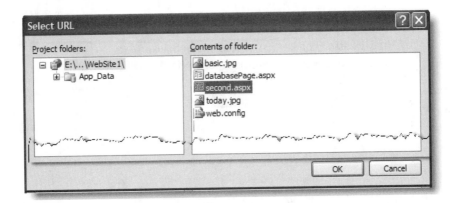

FIGURE 14.9   Select URL dialog box.

You should see the second page that you have added to your project. Select the second page and click OK. Now highlight the Solution Explorer and highlight your first page. Right-click on it and choose Set as Start Page from the drop-down list. This will set your first page as the startup page. You need to make this link invisible at the design time or within the Form load and make it visible under the Validate button. Now double-click on the name of your second page to work on it.

Calendar Control

The Calendar control is a very useful control that can minimize the user's errors. The Calendar control has its own Smart Tag and can be presented in different styles. Add the following to your second page:

- Four Labels
- One Calendar control
- One drop-down list
- Two HyperLink controls

We want the users to click on days they have worked each month to record them in the drop-down list. Once the user clicks on the dates in the drop-down list, the year will be extracted and displayed in the label.

One of the HyperLink controls is used to connect the second page to the third page, and the other one is used to send you to the publisher's Web site. The completed form should look like Figure 14.10.

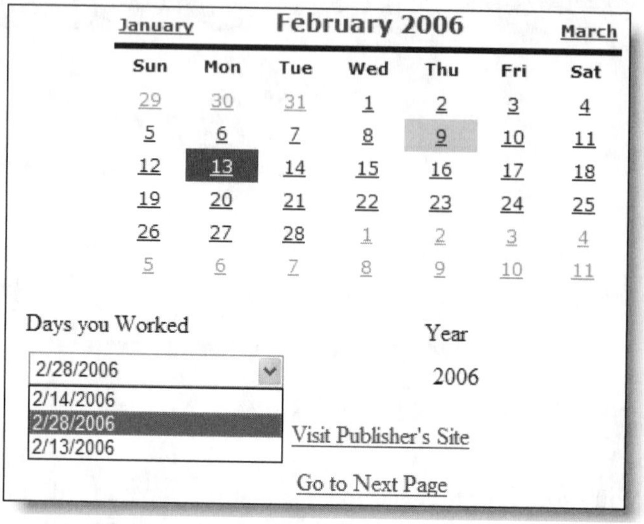

FIGURE 14.10   Second Form design.

You also need to find the Form's Title property and add a title to your page. This applies to all pages including page one. The title will appear on the tope of the Web page when it is displayed by the browser. Double-click the Calendar control and add the following statement under the SelectedChanged event subprocedure:

```
Protected Sub myCalendar_SelectionChanged _
(ByVal sender As Object, _
ByVal e As System.EventArgs) _
Handles myCalendar.SelectionChanged
    'add selected date to the combobox
    myDropDownList.Items.Add(myCalendar.SelectedDate)
End Sub
```

We display the selected day in the ComboBox.

```
Protected Sub _
myDropDownList_SelectedIndexChanged(ByVal sender As Object, _
ByVal e As System.EventArgs) Handles _
myDropDownList.SelectedIndexChanged
```

```
'show the year in the label
yearLabel.Text = _
Year(myDropDownList.SelectedItem.ToString)
End Sub
```

Please make sure that the `AutoPostBack` property of your `ComboBox` is set to `True`. Now add another `Form` to your project. Call this form `Database`. Highlight the Go to Next Page `HyperLink` control and connect it to your third page. Highlight the Visit Publisher's Site `HyperLink` control and type a URL in its `NavigateUrl` property (see Figure 14.11).

FIGURE 14.11 Adding URL to the `HyperLink` control.

Adding `DataSource` and `GridView` Tools

Now double-click on your third `Form` and add the following controls to it:

- One `Label`
- One `GridView` control
- One `HyperLink` control

Use the `GridView` control's Smart Tag to get into its Task Pane. Choose the Data Source drop-down menu and click on the New Data Source option (see Figure 14.12).

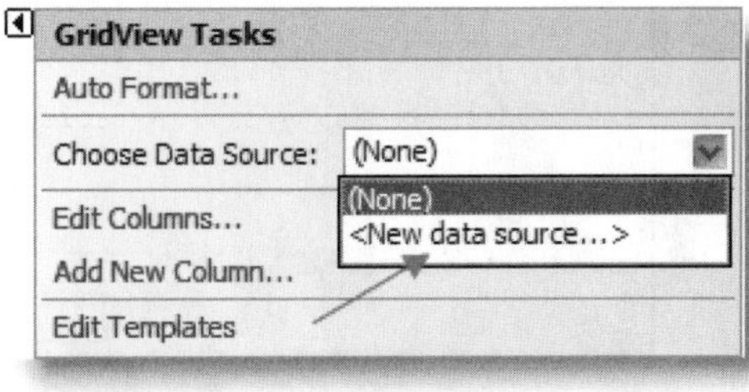

FIGURE 14.12 Adding a new data source.

To view and modify the Microsoft Access Database file, you may need the software on your machine. We are going to use a Microsoft Access Database. We have included a very small database inside the project folder.

Once you click on the New Data Source option, it will take you to the Data Source Configuration Wizard (see Figure 14.13). Select the Access Database icon and click on the Next button. In the following screen, click on Browse to get into the dialog box shown in Figure 14.14.

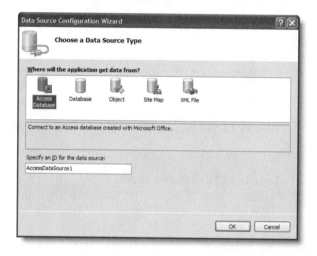

FIGURE 14.13 Data Source Configuration Wizard.

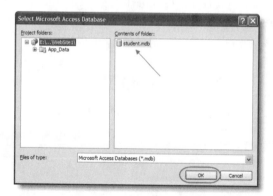

FIGURE 14.14 *Select Microsoft Access Database* dialog box.

Since we have already placed the database inside the project folder, it can recognize it. Select the database and click on the OK button. It will come back to the wizard screen that you saw before. This time, the name of the database is placed inside the Browse window. Click on Next to go to the next page. The next screen is called Configure Data Source, which allows you to pick specific columns of the table (see Figure 14.15). Once this done, your Grid should work (see Figure 14.16).

FIGURE 14.15 Configure data source.

Student Grade			
StudentClassID	**ClassID**	**StudentID**	**Grade**
1	100	10	A
2	200	20	C
3	300	30	B
Go to Page 1			

FIGURE 14.16 Form 3 screenshot.

Add another link under this page to take you to page one. You can add validation to make sure everything works. You can view this solution under the Chapter 14 folder on the companion CD-ROM. The project is saved under its name, Website1. Copy the solution folder to your hard drive and follow this instructions to run it:

1. Fire up your Visual Studio and click on File and Choose Open Web Site from the list of options.
2. In the Open Web Site dialog, point to the Website1 folder on your hard drive.
3. In the Solution Explorer, right click on FirstPage.aspx folder and choose the Set as Start Page option.
4. Hit F5 to run the project.
5. Enter "mike" as the name in the Enter Name TextBox
6. Enter vb2005 as a password in the Enter Password TextBox
7. Click on Validate and follow the instructions on the page.

PUBLISHING YOUR WEB SITE

Once you complete your project, go to the Build menu item and select Build Web Site. Once that is done, go to Build again and select Publish Web Site. There are few options available to you. You can publish it (see Figure 14.17). Once you click on the File dialog button, the screen shown in Figure 14.18 will show up.

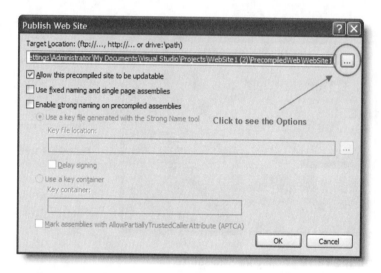

FIGURE 14.17 Publish the Web site.

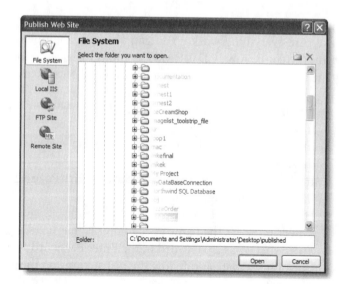

FIGURE 14.18 Options available for publishing your Web site.

SUMMARY

We introduced Web Form development and the new tools Microsoft has created. We discussed the concept of ASP.NET and showed you how to add images, Hyper-Links, and databases to your Web forms.

DISCUSSION QUESTIONS

1. Is there any difference between Web Forms and Window Forms? Please explain
2. What is the main function of ASP.NET? What does it do?
3. How many new tools can you name that you learned in this chapter?
4. What is the difference between HTML and ASP.NET?
5. What are the differences between HTML tools and standard tools?

Exercise

Add two more pages to your project, link them together, and add images at design time. Publish your work and try to access it from other computers.

Key Terms

- Client server environment
- ASP.NET
- *Style Builder*
- GridView
- DataSource

Appendix

A ASCII Character Codes

Code	Character
0	null
7	bell
8	backspace
9	Tab (horizontal)
10	LF (Line feed)
11	TAB (vertical)
12	FF (form feed)
13	Carriage Return
32	blank
33	!
34	"
35	#
36	$
37	
38	&
39	'(apostrophe)
40	(
41	)
42	*
43	+
44	, (comma)

→

Code	Character
45	-
46	. (Period)
47	/
48	0
49	1
50	2
51	3
52	4
53	5
54	6
55	7
56	8
57	9
58	:
59	;
60	<
61	=
62	>
63	?
64	@
65	A
66	B
67	C
68	D
69	E
70	F
71	G
72	H
73	I
74	J

→

Code	Character
75	K
76	L
77	M
78	N
79	O
80	P
81	Q
82	R
83	S
84	T
85	U
86	V
87	W
88	X
89	Y
90	Z
91	[
92	\
93	]
94	^
95	_
96	'
97	a
98	b
99	c
100	d
101	e
102	f
103	g
104	h

→

Code	Character
105	i
106	j
107	k
108	l
109	m
110	n
111	o
112	P
113	q
114	r
115	s
116	t
117	u
118	v
119	w
120	x
121	Y
122	z
123	{
124	|
125	}
126	~
127	Del

Appendix

B About the CD-ROM

The CD-ROM included with *Visual Basic 2005 by Practice* includes all of files necessary to complete the samples in the book. It also includes the images from the book in full color, and demos for you to use while working through the tutorials and exercises. The CD-ROM is autorun enabled and should display a menu once it is loaded. However, some systems are set to block the autorun feature. If the menu does not pop up automatically, use the explorer to find a file called index.htm, which is located within the CD-ROM's root directory. The index.htm is a menu that can be used to navigate through the significant files and folders within the CD-ROM. You can also use the Explorer to explore folders by yourself. The menu should also display the File and Folder tasks that can be used to copy the folders to your hard drive. If this feature is blocked by your system, then you can use the explorer to accomplish the same tasks.

FOLDERS

Images: All of the images from within the book in full color, which are set up by chapters.

Solutions: Most of the files necessary to complete the tutorials in the book including, backgrounds, textures, animations, data files, and images. These files are all in common formats that can be read by related applications, and they are set up in related folders. Except for a Microsoft Access file that is included in Chapter 14 and requires Microsoft Access software, you will see references to files that should be found within your system. Please refer to the chapter text for the specific instructions on how to use each sample program. You may need additional application programs such as Microsoft SQL Server 2005 and related packages to enhance your projects.

Multimedia: We have included a multimedia file which is located in the Chapter 2 folder. This is a video and audio file that can run independently.

Menu: Folder that provides supporting files for the Index.htm file.

Other Features

We have also included a file that contains all links we have referenced within the book. This file is named *links.htm* and is located within the root directory of the CD-ROM.

You should also see a ReadMe file within the root directory of the CD-ROM

Other files such as autorun.inf and shellrun.exe are used to run the menu automatically.

SYSTEM REQUIREMENTS

For general system requirements for Visual Studio 2005, please refer to Microsoft website at:

Here are the minimum requirements for using this CD-ROM:

- Windows 2000 with Service pack 4 or Windows XP Service pack 2. Windows XP professional with service pack 2 is recommended.
- Visual Basic 2005 (Visual Studio 2005 Professional is recommended)
- Microsoft Access software (recommended)
- Pentium with a minimum of 600 MHz processor (1 gig is recommended) with 192 MB RAM (256 or better recommended)
- CD-ROM drive
- Hard Drive with a minimum of 200 MB of free space to install the examples

INSTALLATION

To use this CD-ROM, you just need to make sure that your system matches at least the minimum system requirements. The image files are in .jpg, .gif and .tiff file formats and should be opened by common applications such as Microsoft's Paint program.

Index